SPECIAL EXITS

FANTAGRAPHICS BOOKS
7563 Lake City Way NE
Seattle, Washington 98115

Editor: Gary Groth
Book Design: Jacob Covey
Associate Publisher: Eric Reynolds
Publishers: Gary Groth & Kim Thompson

Distributed in the U.S. by W.W. Norton and Company,
Inc. (212-354-5000) | Distributed in Canada by the
Canadian Manda Group (416-516-0911) | Distributed
in the United Kingdom by Turnaround Distribution
(108-829-3009)

First Fantagraphics printing: September, 2010
ISBN: 978-1-60699-381-1 | Printed in China

SPECIAL EXITS

EXITS

{ A GRAPHIC MEMOIR }

JOYCE FARMER

FANTAGRAPHICS BOOKS

Cast of Characters

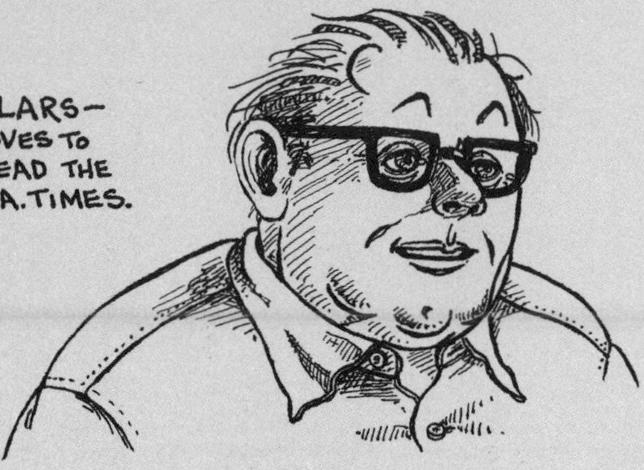

LARS—
LOVES TO
READ THE
L.A. TIMES.

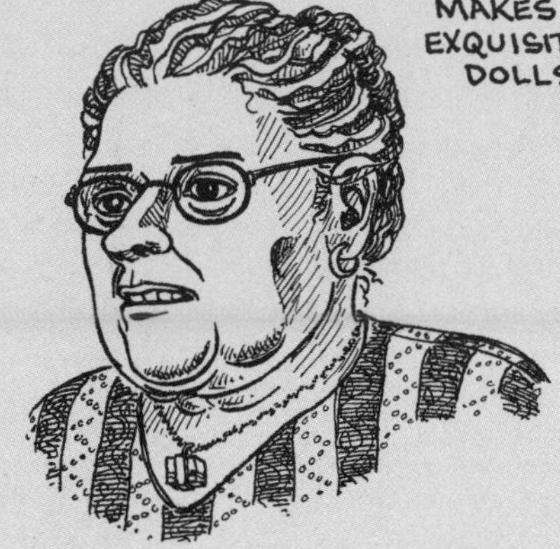

RACHEL—
MAKES
EXQUISITE
DOLLS.

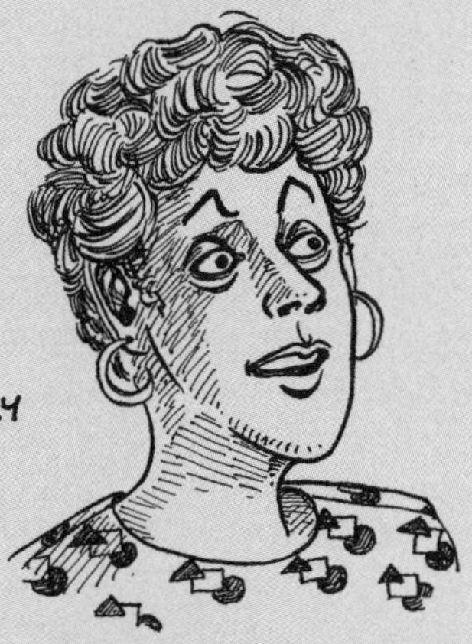

LAURA—
LARS' ONLY
CHILD.

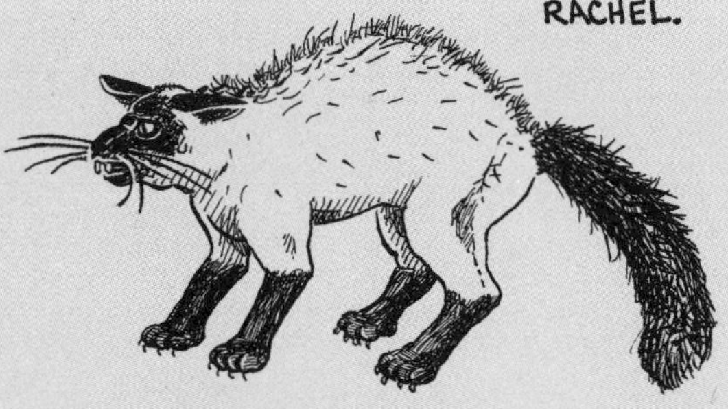

CHING—
ADORED BY
LARS AND
RACHEL.

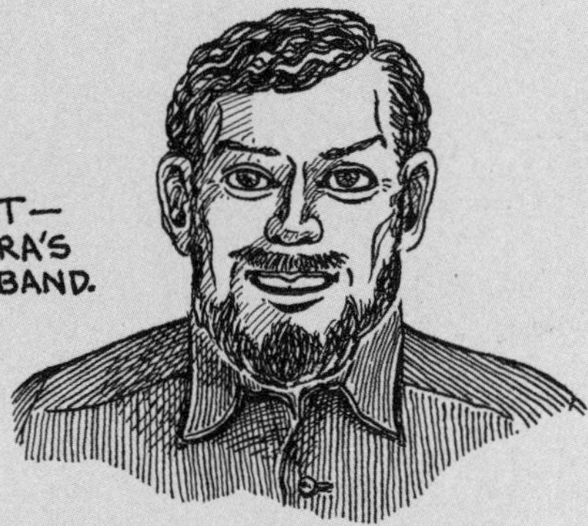

ART—
LAURA'S
HUSBAND.

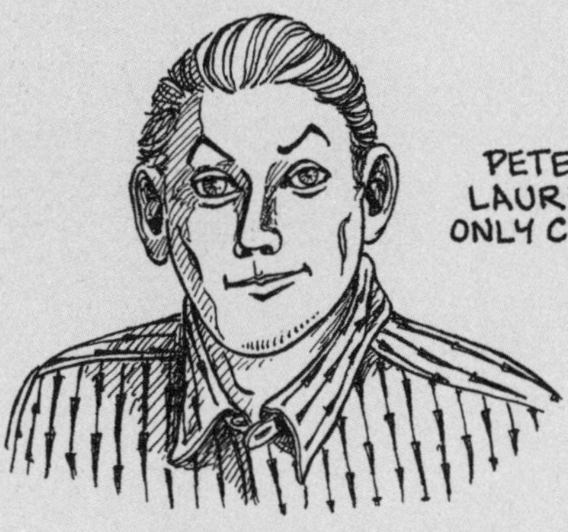

PETE—
LAURA'S
ONLY CHILD.

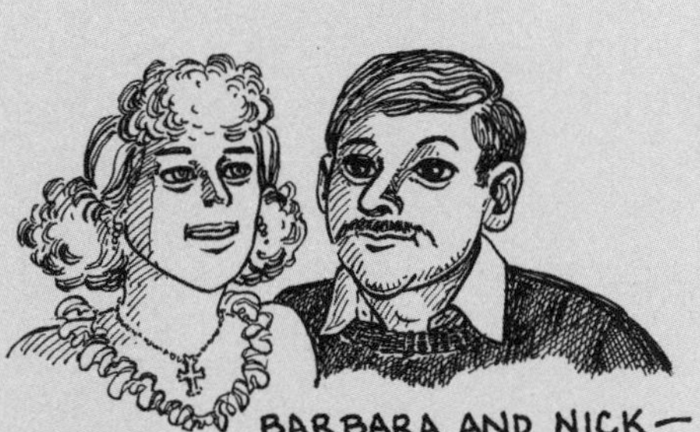

BARBARA AND NICK—
FAMILY FRIENDS.

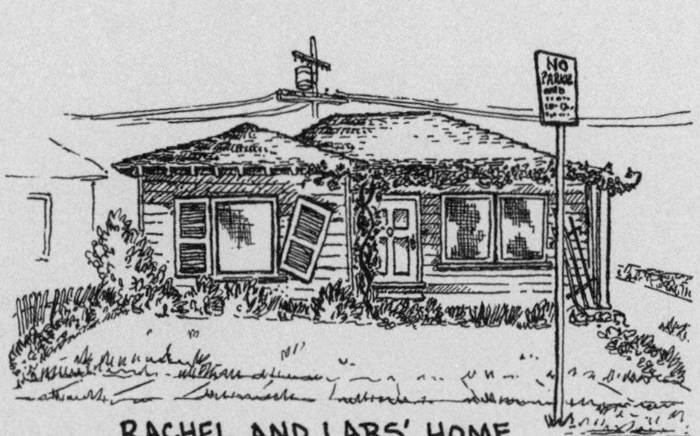

RACHEL AND LARS' HOME
IN SOUTH LOS ANGELES.

ACKNOWLEDGEMENTS

First, I must thank my parents, Roy and Esther Farmer, without whom there would be no book. Next, I thank my loving husband, Palma Goulet, who showed endless patience and indulgence for my creative process.

Karen Feinberg, text editor, kept the words flowing. Leonard Rifas, art editor, saved me from compositional errors. Elias Tabakeas convinced me to keep everything in perspective. All of them were involved from almost the start because a drawn book must be completely edited before it is inked. I appreciate all their suggestions even though I didn't always incorporate them.

Evanthia and Aristea Milingou, Barbara and Nick Kokkinis, and Dora Kyriopoulou provided delightful studio spaces over the years in my beloved Greece, where I created many of the pages.

Susan Hartley, OD, and Baruch Kupperman, MD, eye specialists, have kept my vision problems in the background for ten years, for which I thank them both profusely.

And not least, my support system of friends and colleagues has given spot-on feedback of the manuscript and/or atta-girls. I sincerely thank them all: Julie Bini, Lyn Chevli, Dorothea Clymer, Adrienne Cohen, Robert Crumb, Mary Fleener, Roberta Gregory, Sam Gross, Gary Groth, Allan Hansen, Trina Robbins, Frank J. Rose, Mary R. Stack, Bruce Taylor, Charles Tureaud, M.C. Tureaud, Paul Van Der Linden, and Elizabeth Wales.

1

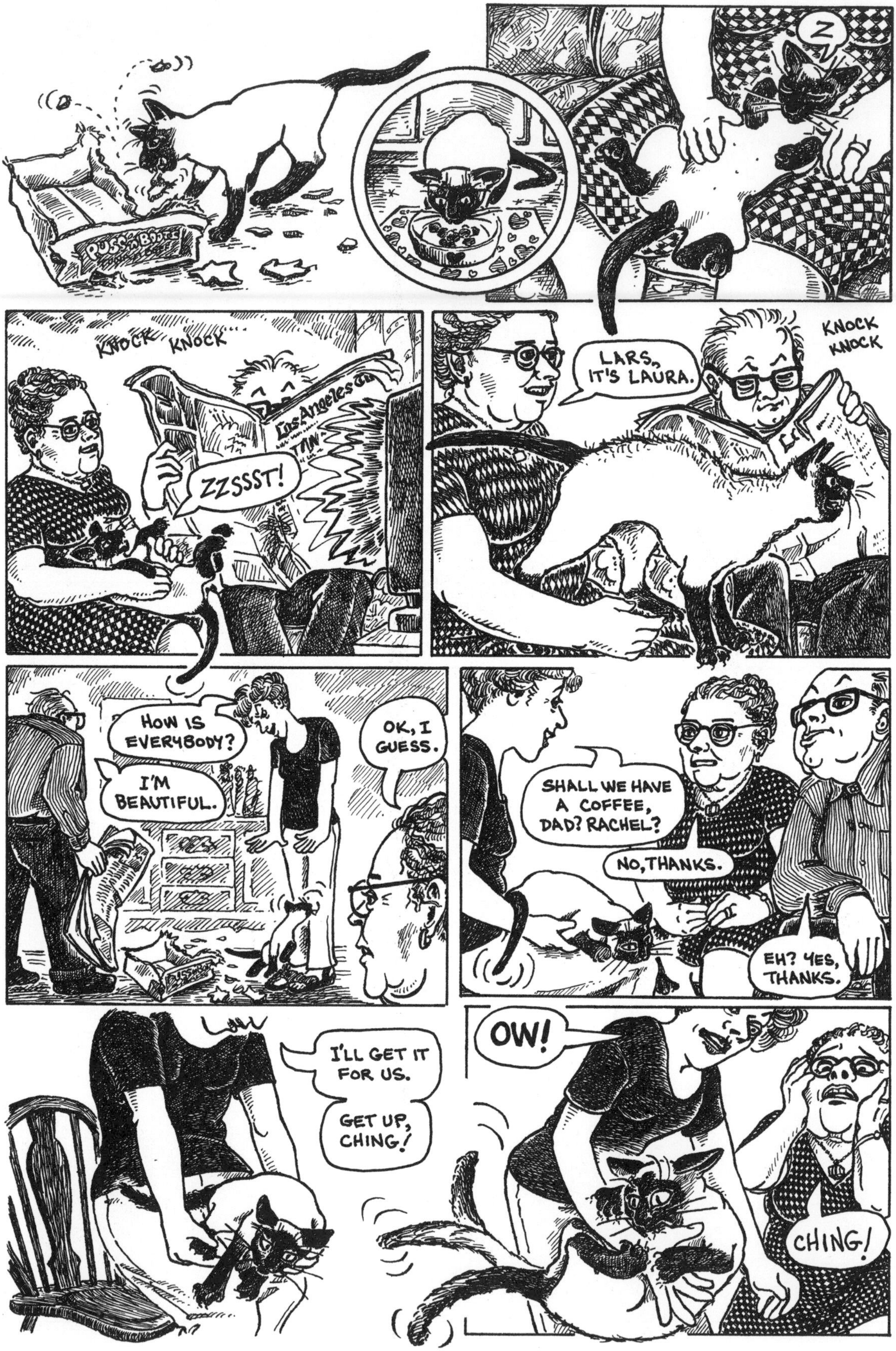
PUSS 'N BOOTS
KNOCK KNOCK
ZZSSST!
Los Angeles Times
LARS, IT'S LAURA.
KNOCK KNOCK
HOW IS EVERYBODY?
I'M BEAUTIFUL.
OK, I GUESS.
SHALL WE HAVE A COFFEE, DAD? RACHEL?
NO, THANKS.
EH? YES, THANKS.
I'LL GET IT FOR US.
GET UP, CHING!
OW!
CHING!

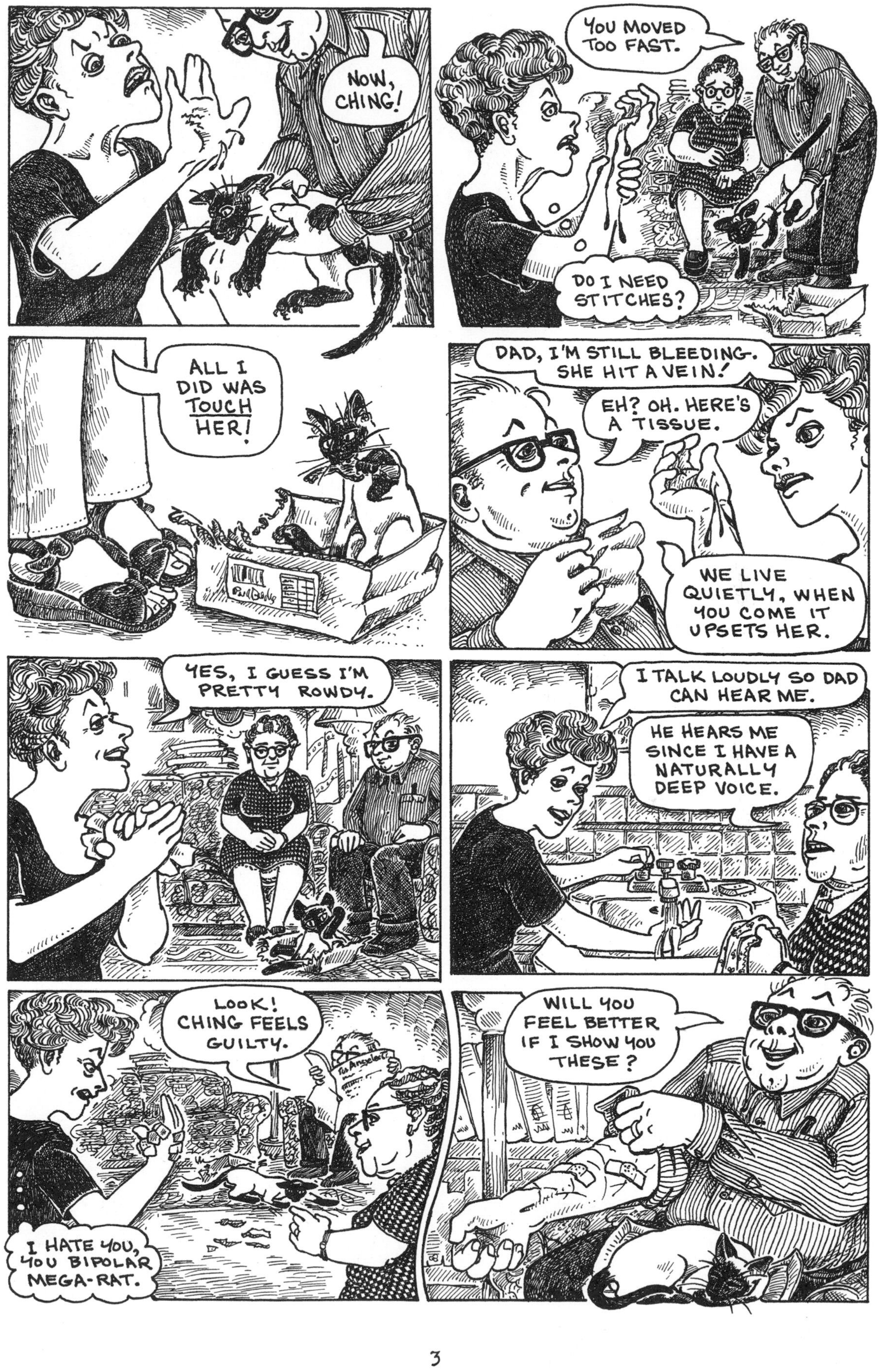
NOW, CHING!
YOU MOVED TOO FAST.
DO I NEED STITCHES?
ALL I DID WAS TOUCH HER!
DAD, I'M STILL BLEEDING. SHE HIT A VEIN!
EH? OH. HERE'S A TISSUE.
WE LIVE QUIETLY, WHEN YOU COME IT UPSETS HER.
YES, I GUESS I'M PRETTY ROWDY.
I TALK LOUDLY SO DAD CAN HEAR ME.
HE HEARS ME SINCE I HAVE A NATURALLY DEEP VOICE.
LOOK! CHING FEELS GUILTY.
I HATE YOU, YOU BIPOLAR MEGA-RAT.
WILL YOU FEEL BETTER IF I SHOW YOU THESE?

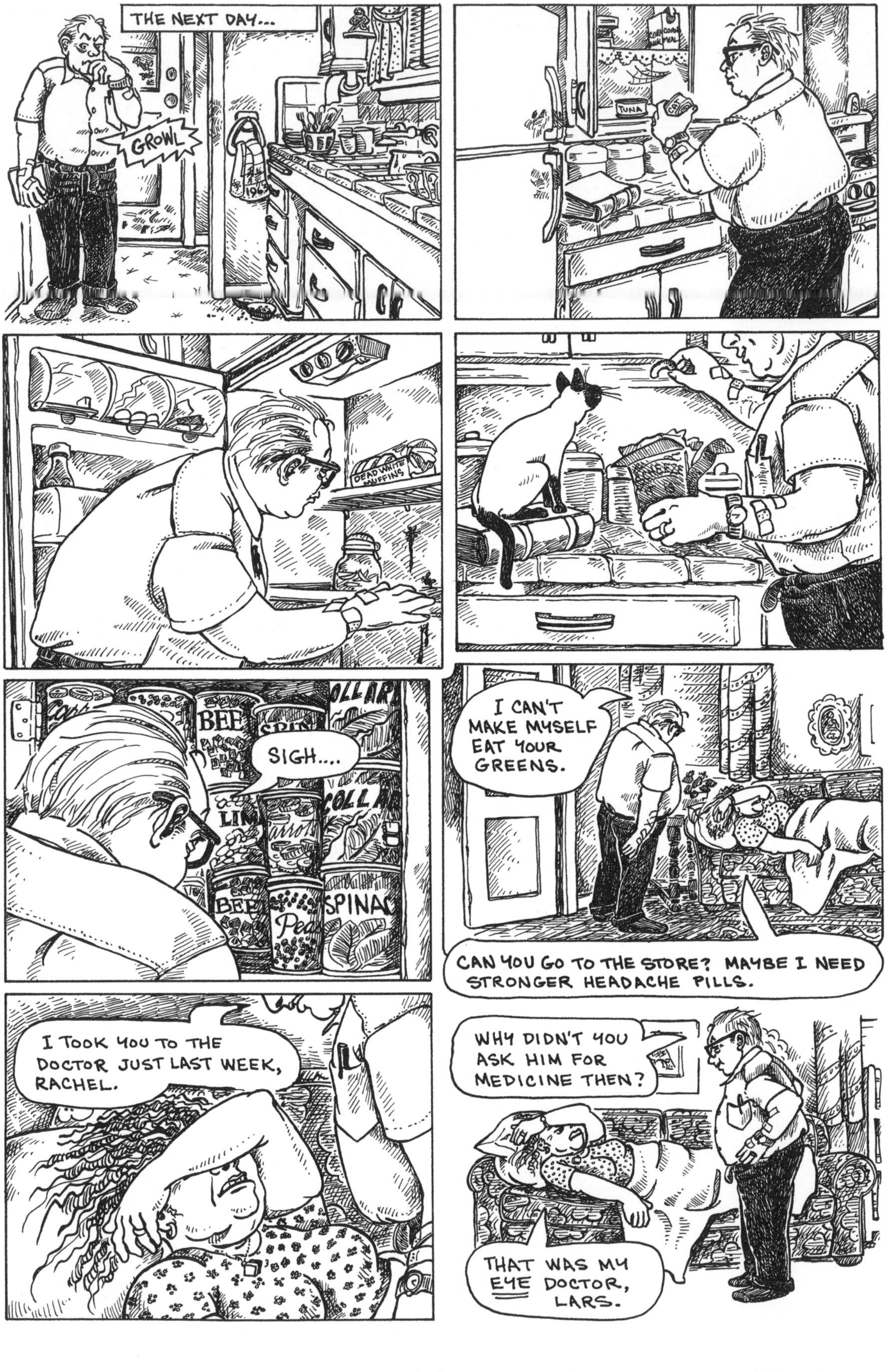
THE NEXT DAY...
GROWL
CORN MEAL
TUNA
DEAD WHITE MUFFINS
SIGH....
I CAN'T MAKE MYSELF EAT YOUR GREENS.
CAN YOU GO TO THE STORE? MAYBE I NEED STRONGER HEADACHE PILLS.
I TOOK YOU TO THE DOCTOR JUST LAST WEEK, RACHEL.
WHY DIDN'T YOU ASK HIM FOR MEDICINE THEN?
THAT WAS MY EYE DOCTOR, LARS.

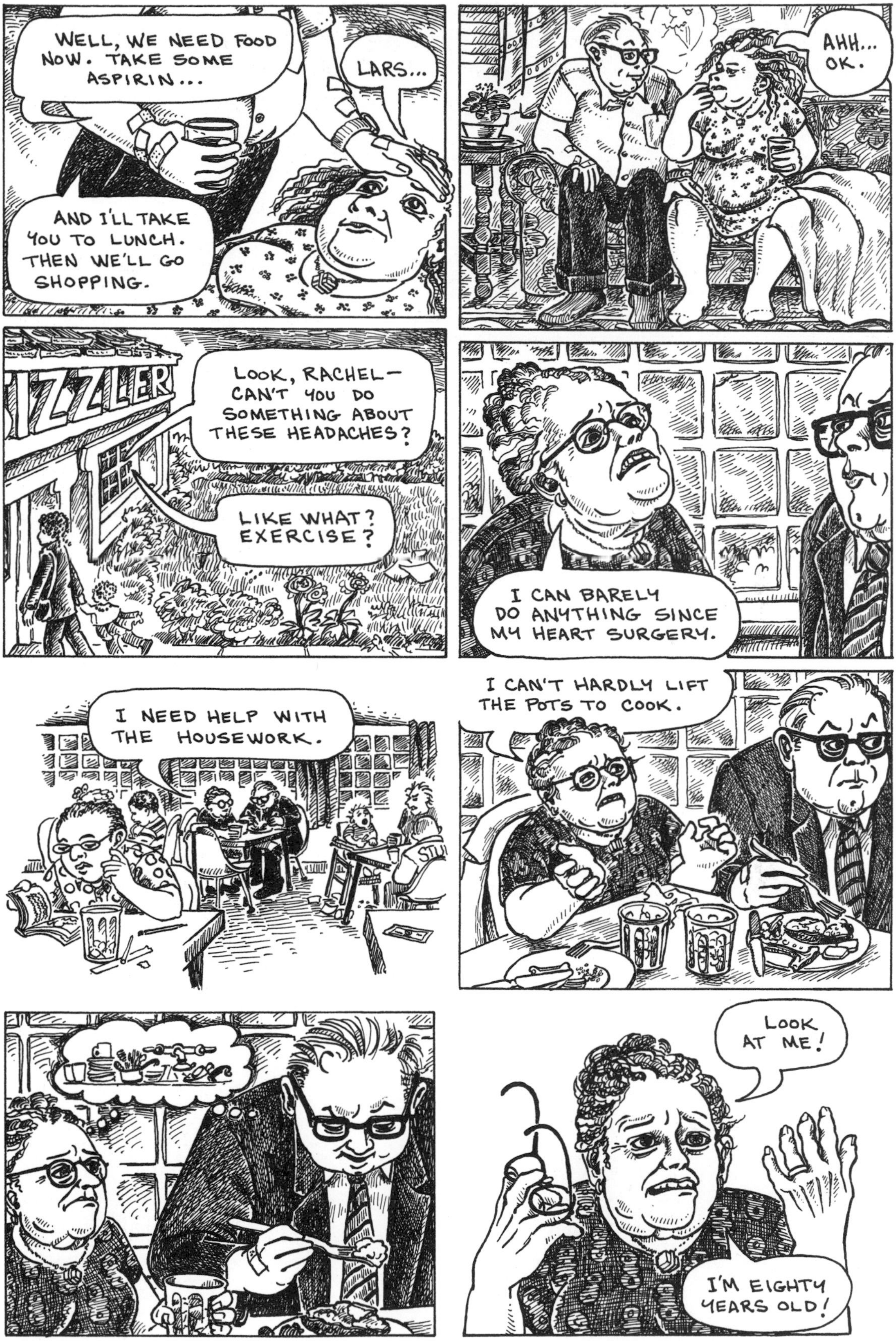
WELL, WE NEED FOOD NOW. TAKE SOME ASPIRIN...
LARS...
AND I'LL TAKE YOU TO LUNCH. THEN WE'LL GO SHOPPING.
AHH... OK.
IZZLER
LOOK, RACHEL- CAN'T YOU DO SOMETHING ABOUT THESE HEADACHES?
LIKE WHAT? EXERCISE?
I CAN BARELY DO ANYTHING SINCE MY HEART SURGERY.
I NEED HELP WITH THE HOUSEWORK.
I CAN'T HARDLY LIFT THE POTS TO COOK.
LOOK AT ME!
I'M EIGHTY YEARS OLD!

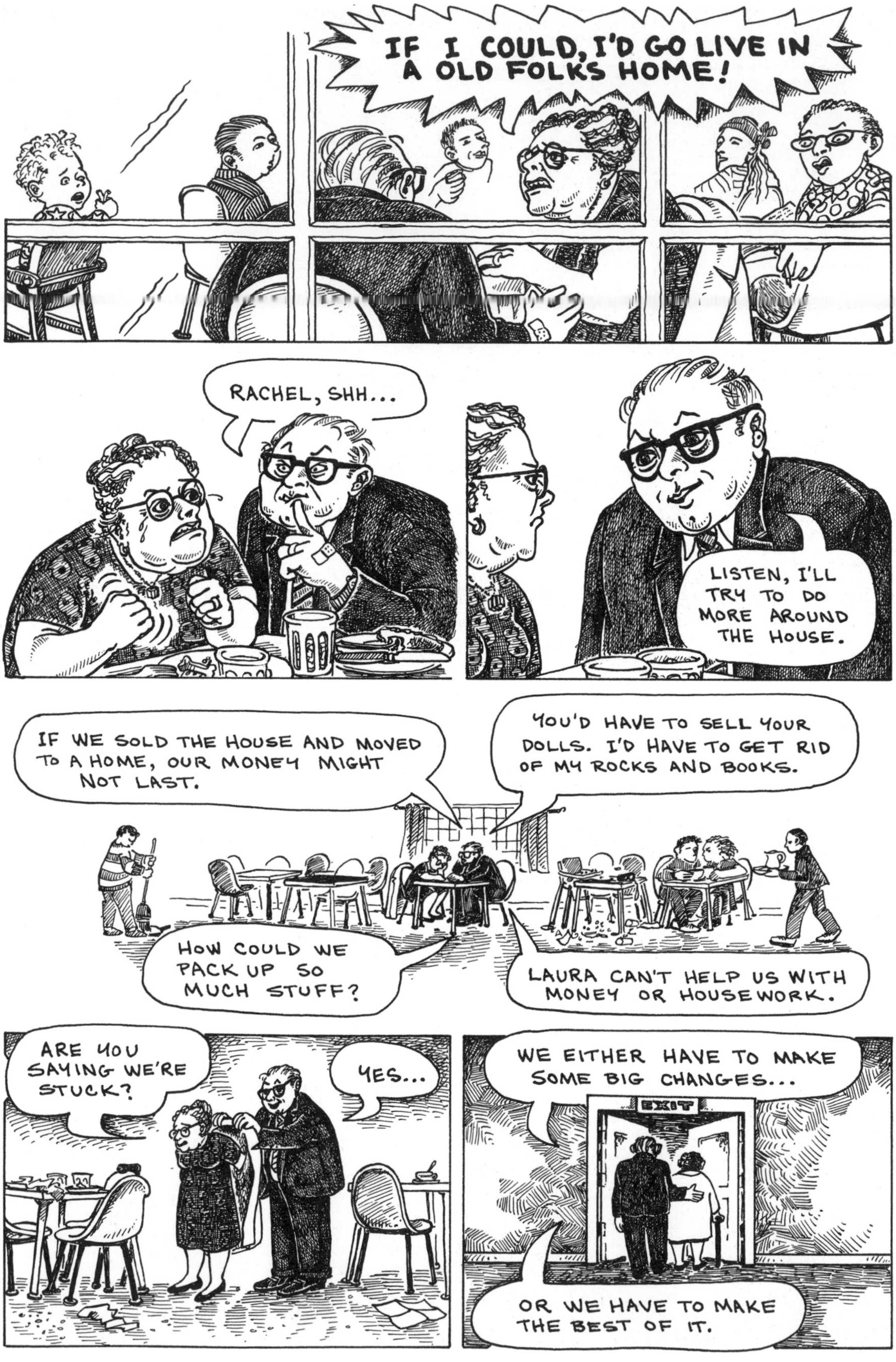
IF I COULD, I'D GO LIVE IN A OLD FOLKS HOME!
RACHEL, SHH...
LISTEN, I'LL TRY TO DO MORE AROUND THE HOUSE.
IF WE SOLD THE HOUSE AND MOVED TO A HOME, OUR MONEY MIGHT NOT LAST.
YOU'D HAVE TO SELL YOUR DOLLS. I'D HAVE TO GET RID OF MY ROCKS AND BOOKS.
HOW COULD WE PACK UP SO MUCH STUFF?
LAURA CAN'T HELP US WITH MONEY OR HOUSEWORK.
ARE YOU SAYING WE'RE STUCK?
YES...
WE EITHER HAVE TO MAKE SOME BIG CHANGES...
EXIT
OR WE HAVE TO MAKE THE BEST OF IT.

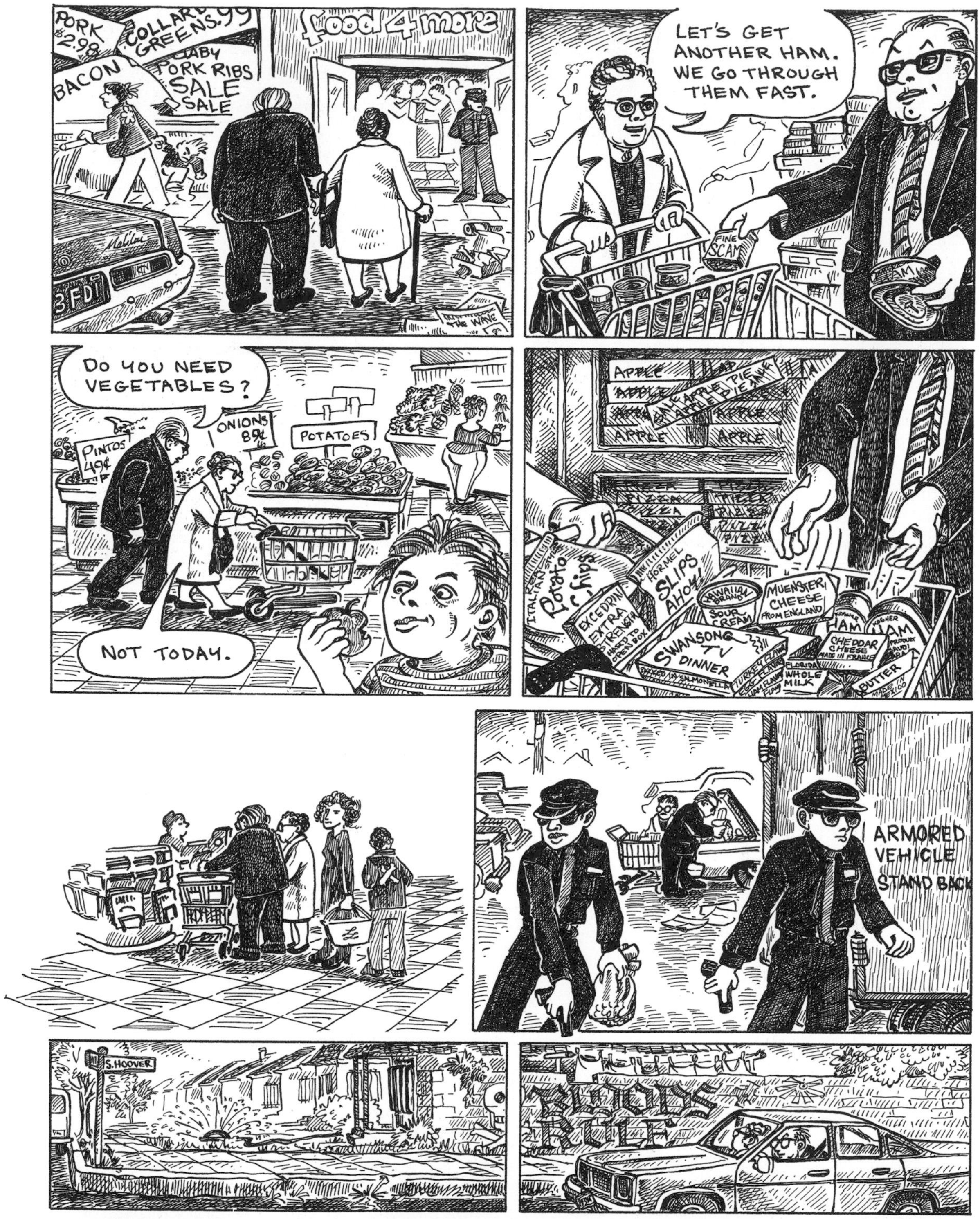
PORK $2.98
COLLARD GREENS .99
BABY PORK RIBS SALE SALE
BACON
food 4 more
THE WAVE
LET'S GET ANOTHER HAM. WE GO THROUGH THEM FAST.
FINE SCAM
DO YOU NEED VEGETABLES?
PINTOS 49¢
ONIONS 89¢
POTATOES
NOT TODAY.
APPLE
SLIPS AHOY
MUENSTER CHEESE FROM ENGLAND
SOUR CREAM
EXCEDRIN EXTRA STRENGTH HARD TO OPEN BOX
SWANSONG TV DINNER
CHEDDAR CHEESE MADE IN FRANCE
WHOLE MILK
BUTTER
ARMORED VEHICLE STAND BACK
S.HOOVER

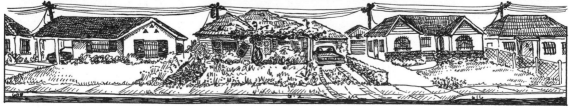

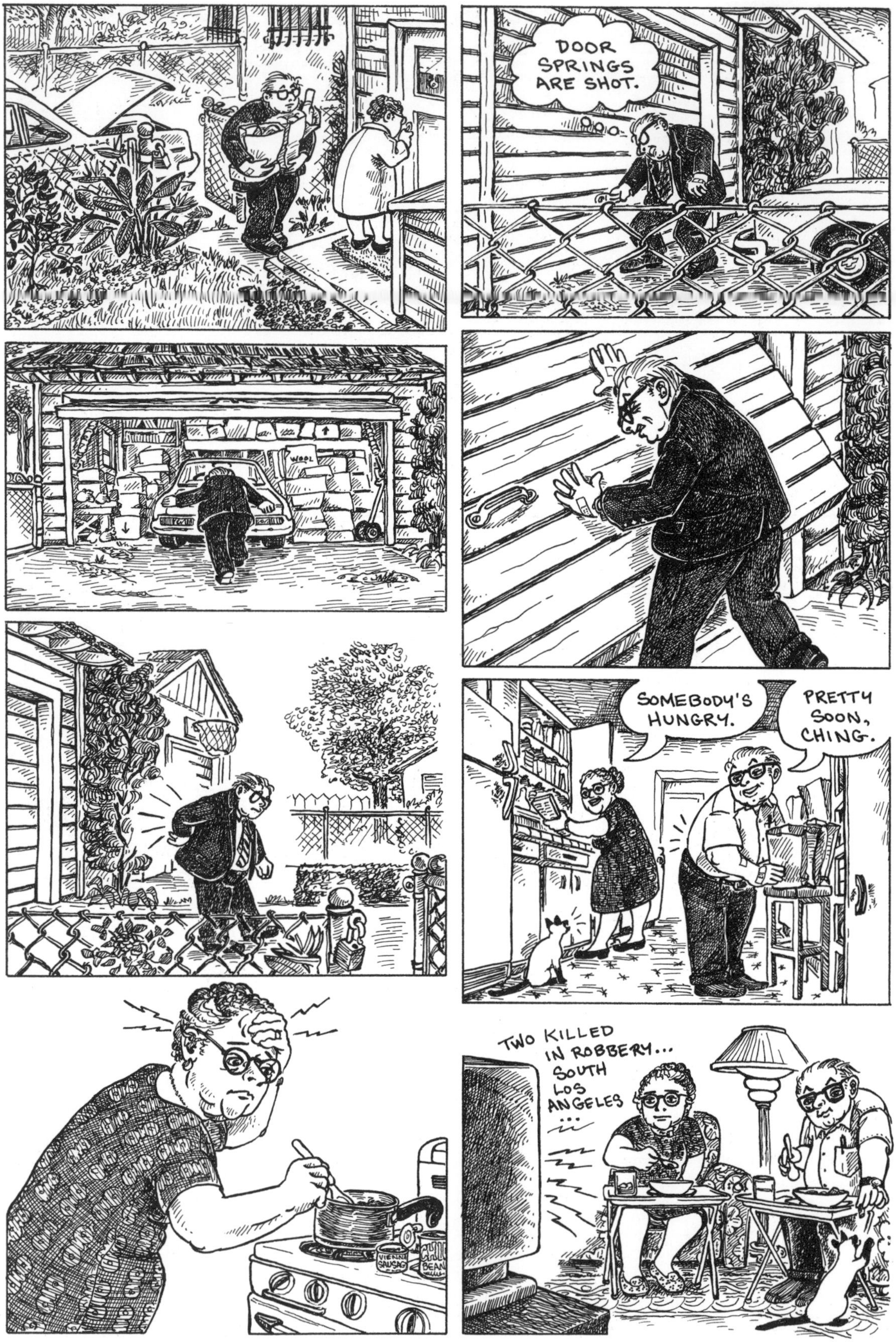
DOOR SPRINGS ARE SHOT.
WOOL
SOMEBODY'S HUNGRY.
PRETTY SOON, CHING.
TWO KILLED IN ROBBERY... SOUTH LOS ANGELES ...

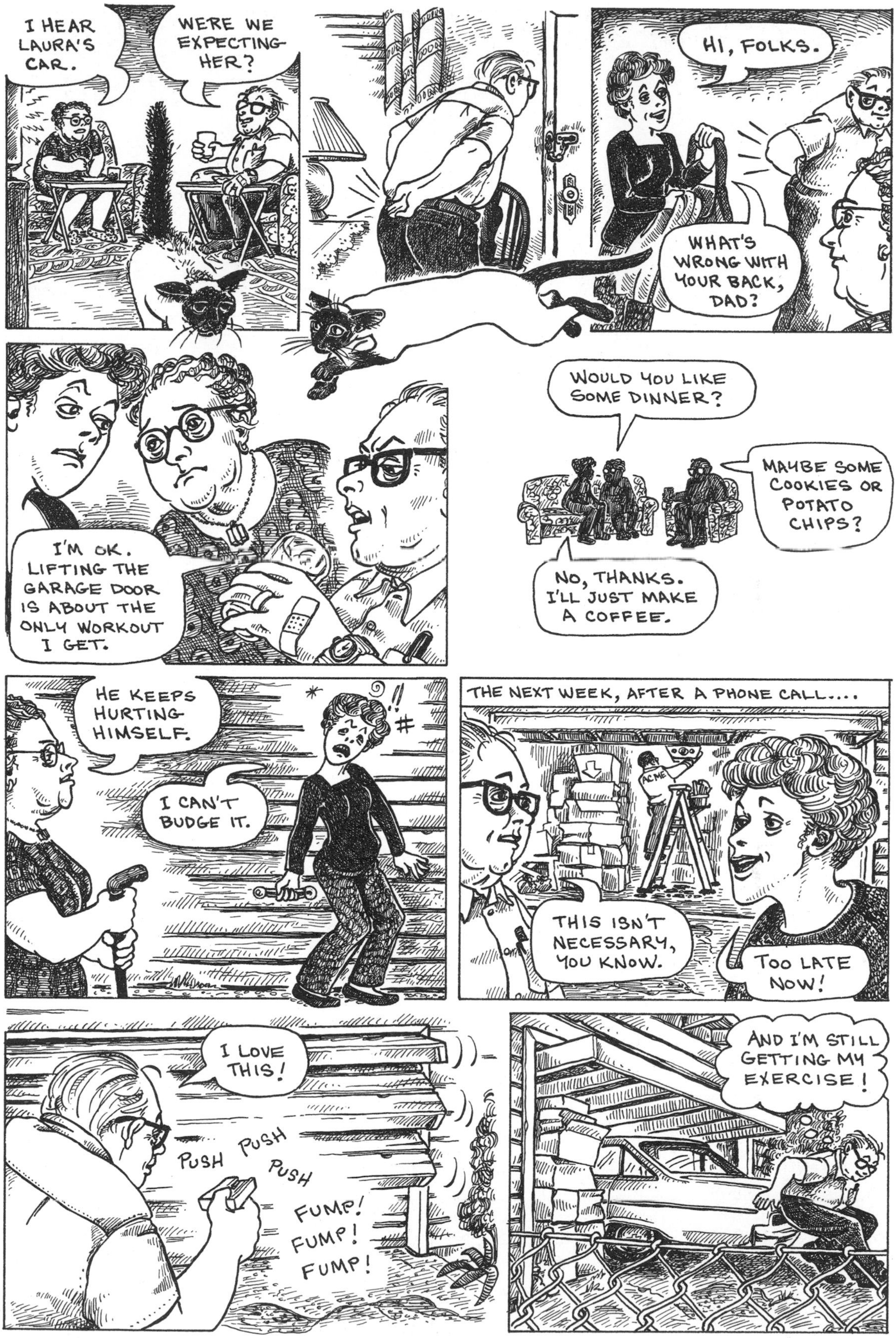

I HEAR LAURA'S CAR.
WERE WE EXPECTING HER?
HI, FOLKS.
WHAT'S WRONG WITH YOUR BACK, DAD?
I'M OK. LIFTING THE GARAGE DOOR IS ABOUT THE ONLY WORKOUT I GET.
WOULD YOU LIKE SOME DINNER?
MAYBE SOME COOKIES OR POTATO CHIPS?
NO, THANKS. I'LL JUST MAKE A COFFEE.
HE KEEPS HURTING HIMSELF.
I CAN'T BUDGE IT.
THE NEXT WEEK, AFTER A PHONE CALL....
ACME
THIS ISN'T NECESSARY, YOU KNOW.
TOO LATE NOW!
I LOVE THIS!
PUSH PUSH PUSH
FUMP! FUMP! FUMP!
AND I'M STILL GETTING MY EXERCISE!

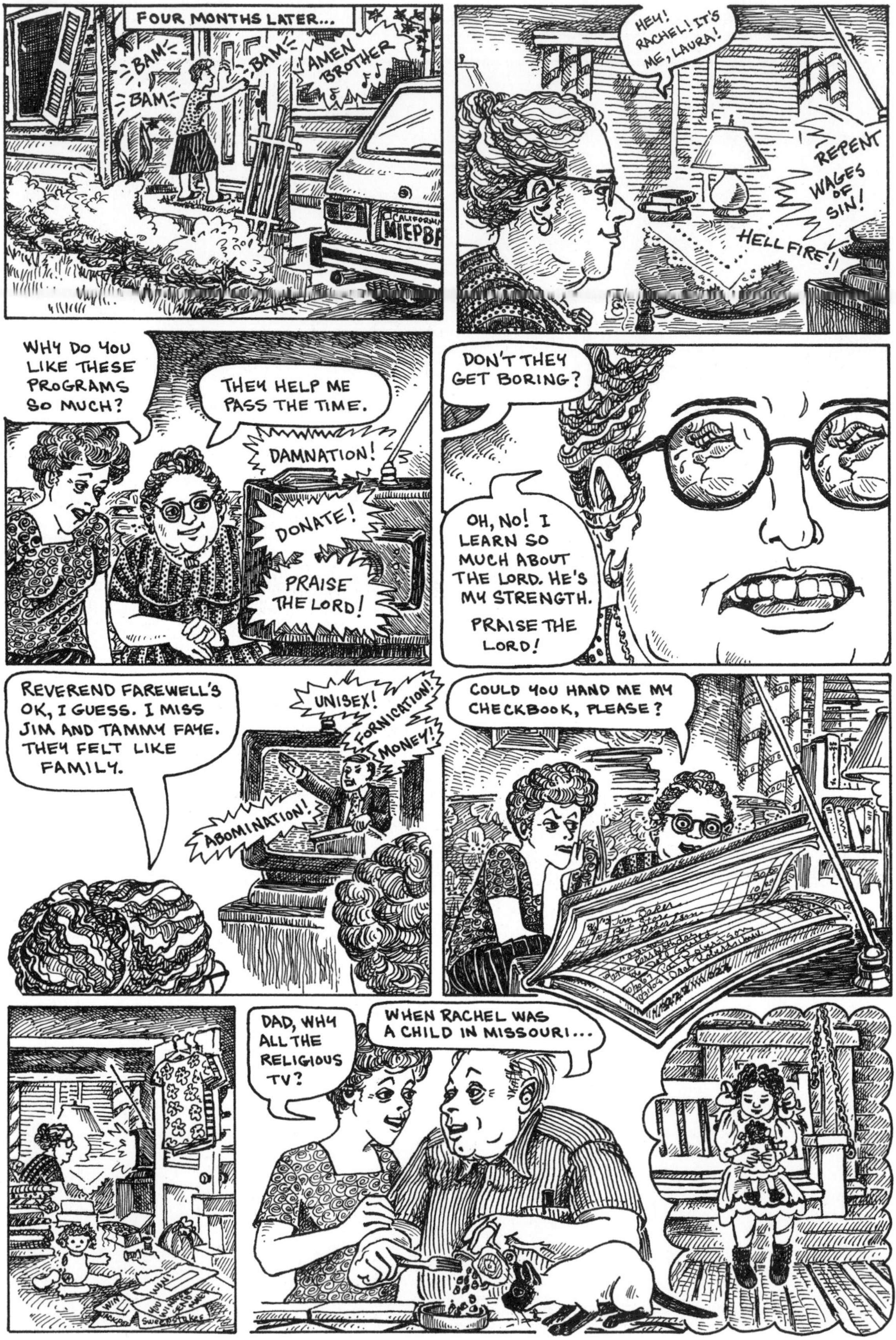
FOUR MONTHS LATER...
BAM
BAM
BAM
AMEN BROTHER
HEY! RACHEL! IT'S ME, LAURA!
REPENT
WAGES OF SIN!
HELL FIRE!
WHY DO YOU LIKE THESE PROGRAMS SO MUCH?
THEY HELP ME PASS THE TIME.
DAMNATION!
DONATE!
PRAISE THE LORD!
DON'T THEY GET BORING?
OH, NO! I LEARN SO MUCH ABOUT THE LORD. HE'S MY STRENGTH.
PRAISE THE LORD!
REVEREND FAREWELL'S OK, I GUESS. I MISS JIM AND TAMMY FAYE. THEY FELT LIKE FAMILY.
UNISEX!
FORNICATION!
MONEY!
ABOMINATION!
COULD YOU HAND ME MY CHECKBOOK, PLEASE?
DAD, WHY ALL THE RELIGIOUS TV?
WHEN RACHEL WAS A CHILD IN MISSOURI...

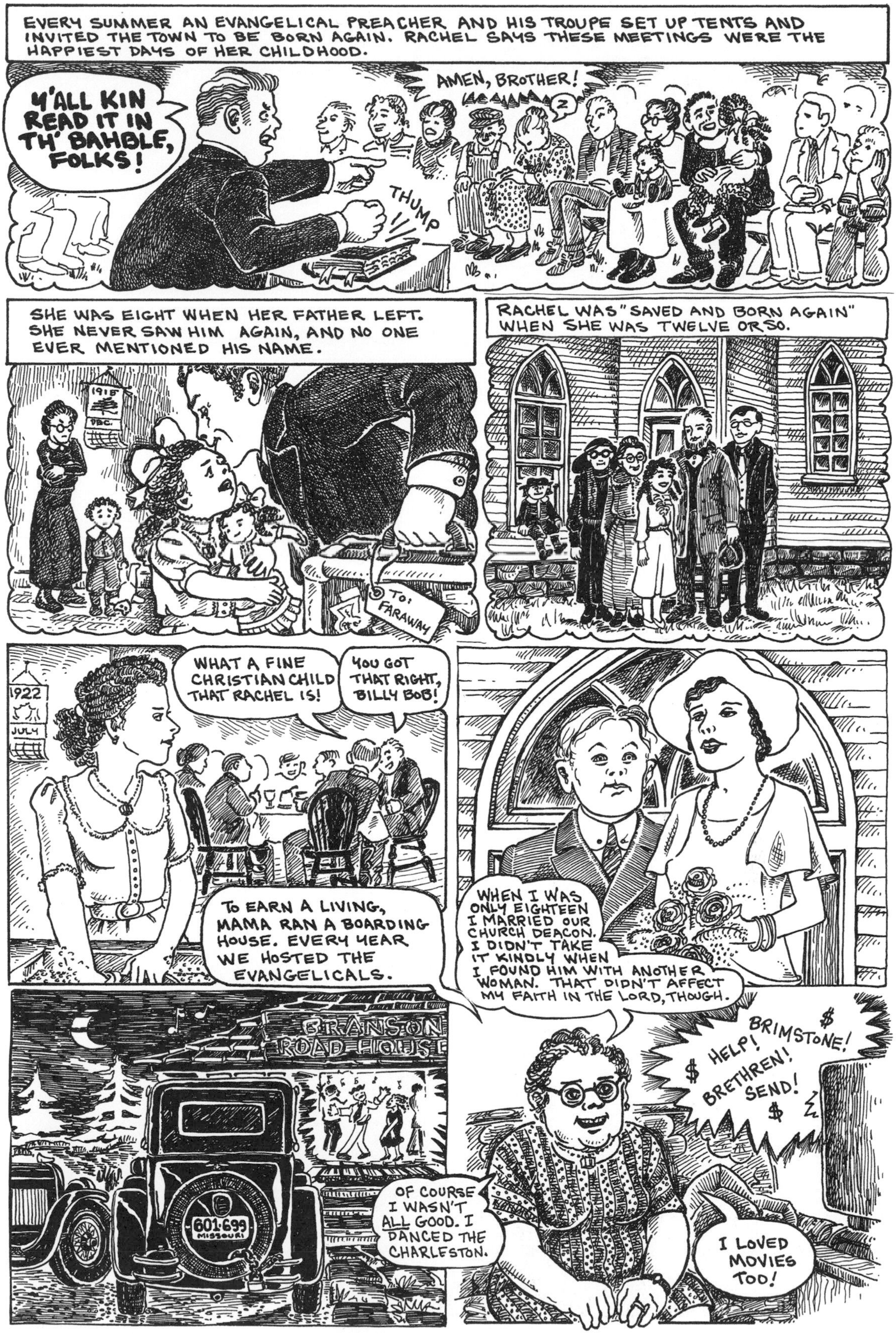

EVERY SUMMER AN EVANGELICAL PREACHER AND HIS TROUPE SET UP TENTS AND INVITED THE TOWN TO BE BORN AGAIN. RACHEL SAYS THESE MEETINGS WERE THE HAPPIEST DAYS OF HER CHILDHOOD.
Y'ALL KIN READ IT IN TH' BAHBLE, FOLKS!
AMEN, BROTHER!
THUMP
SHE WAS EIGHT WHEN HER FATHER LEFT. SHE NEVER SAW HIM AGAIN, AND NO ONE EVER MENTIONED HIS NAME.
1915 DEC.
TO: FARAWAY
RACHEL WAS "SAVED AND BORN AGAIN" WHEN SHE WAS TWELVE OR SO.
1922 JULY
WHAT A FINE CHRISTIAN CHILD THAT RACHEL IS!
YOU GOT THAT RIGHT, BILLY BOB!
TO EARN A LIVING, MAMA RAN A BOARDING HOUSE. EVERY YEAR WE HOSTED THE EVANGELICALS.
WHEN I WAS ONLY EIGHTEEN I MARRIED OUR CHURCH DEACON. I DIDN'T TAKE IT KINDLY WHEN I FOUND HIM WITH ANOTHER WOMAN. THAT DIDN'T AFFECT MY FAITH IN THE LORD, THOUGH.
BRANSON ROAD HOUSE
601·699 MISSOURI
$ HELP! BRIMSTONE! BRETHREN! SEND! $ $
OF COURSE I WASN'T ALL GOOD. I DANCED THE CHARLESTON.
I LOVED MOVIES TOO!

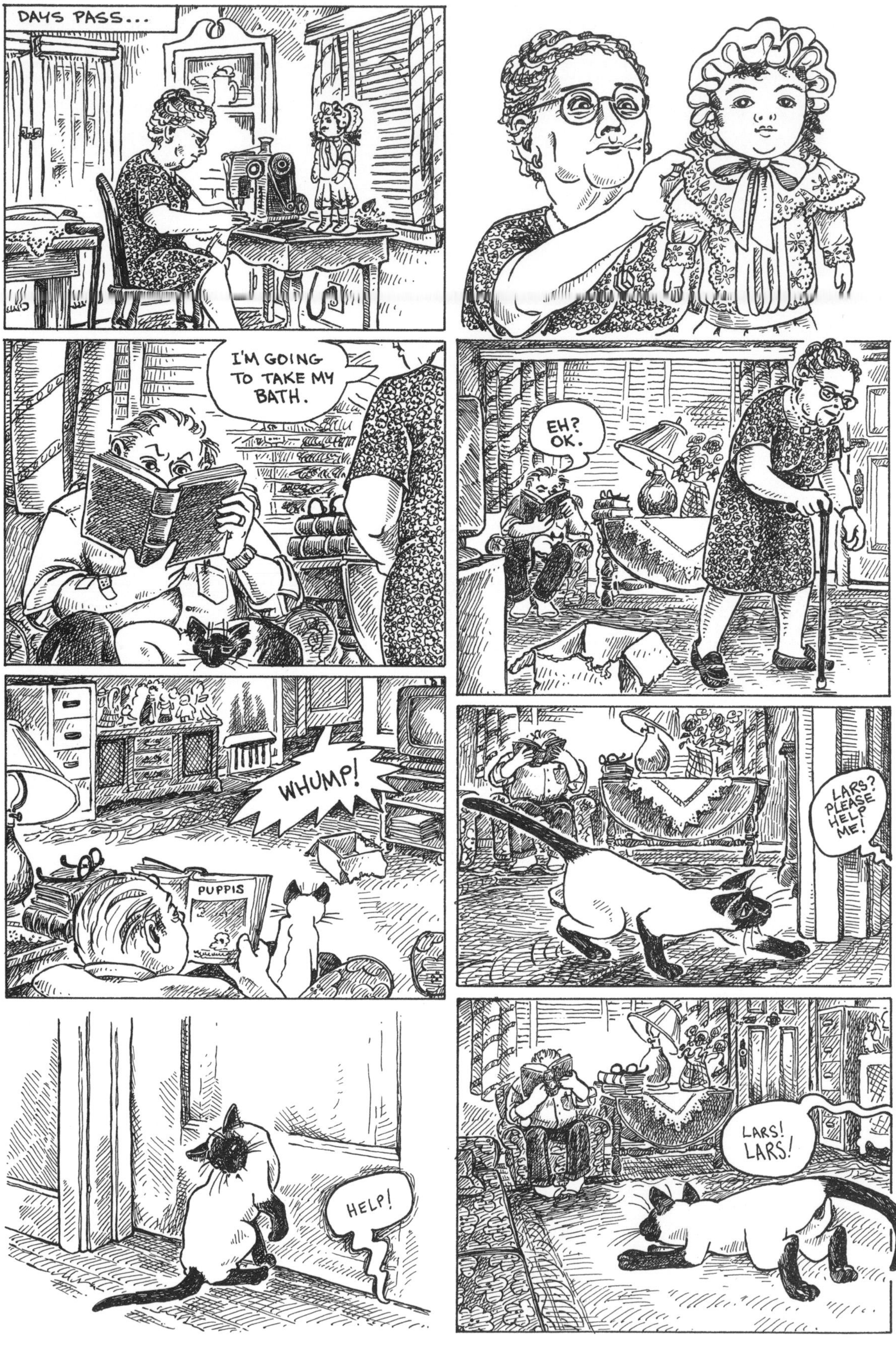
DAYS PASS...
I'M GOING TO TAKE MY BATH.
EH? OK.
WHUMP!
PUPPIS
LARS? PLEASE HELP ME!
HELP!
LARS! LARS!

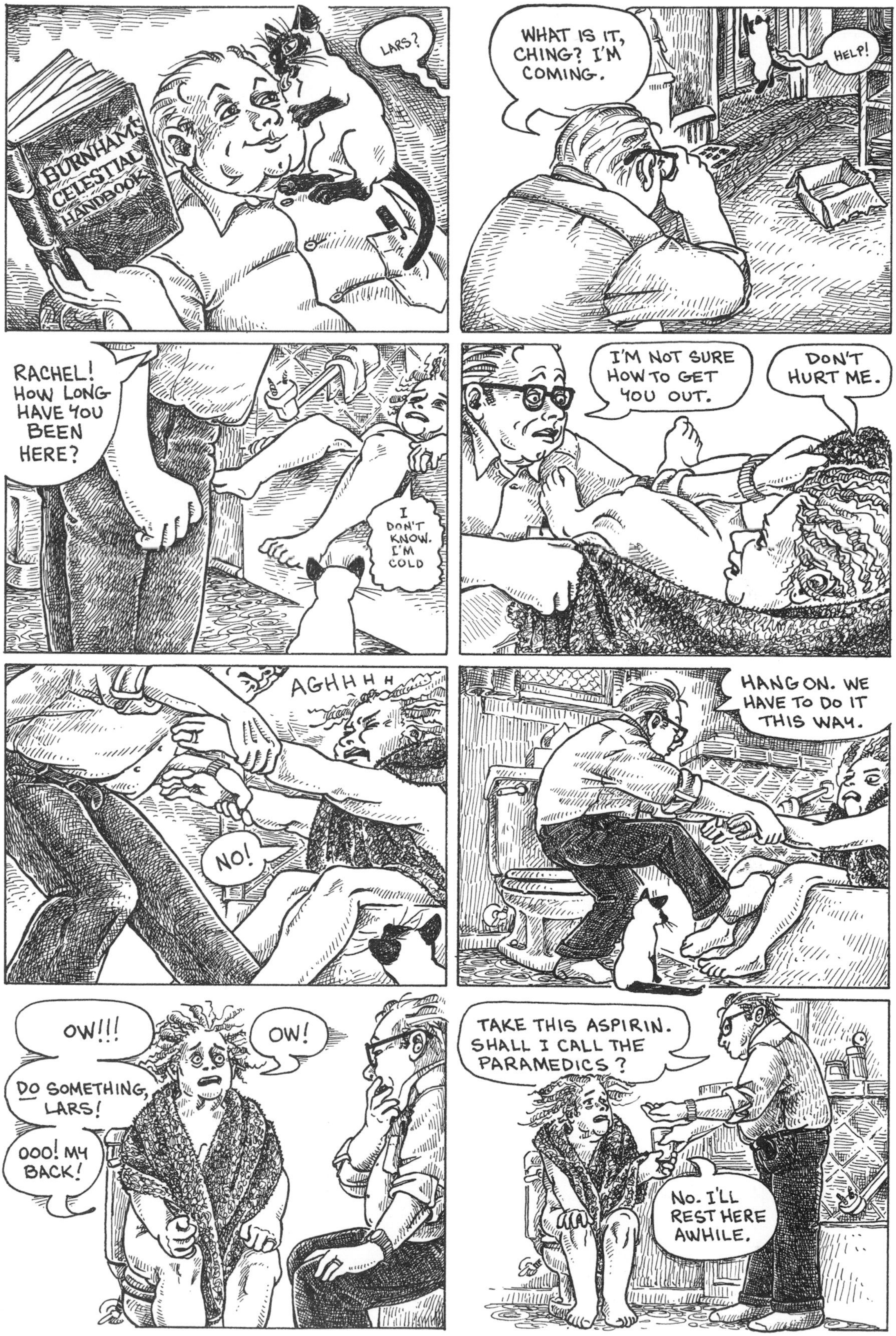
BURNHAM'S CELESTIAL HANDBOOK
LARS?
WHAT IS IT, CHING? I'M COMING.
HELP!
RACHEL! HOW LONG HAVE YOU BEEN HERE?
I DON'T KNOW. I'M COLD
I'M NOT SURE HOW TO GET YOU OUT.
DON'T HURT ME.
AGHHHH
NO!
HANG ON. WE HAVE TO DO IT THIS WAY.
OW!!!
OW!
DO SOMETHING, LARS!
OOO! MY BACK!
TAKE THIS ASPIRIN. SHALL I CALL THE PARAMEDICS?
NO. I'LL REST HERE AWHILE.

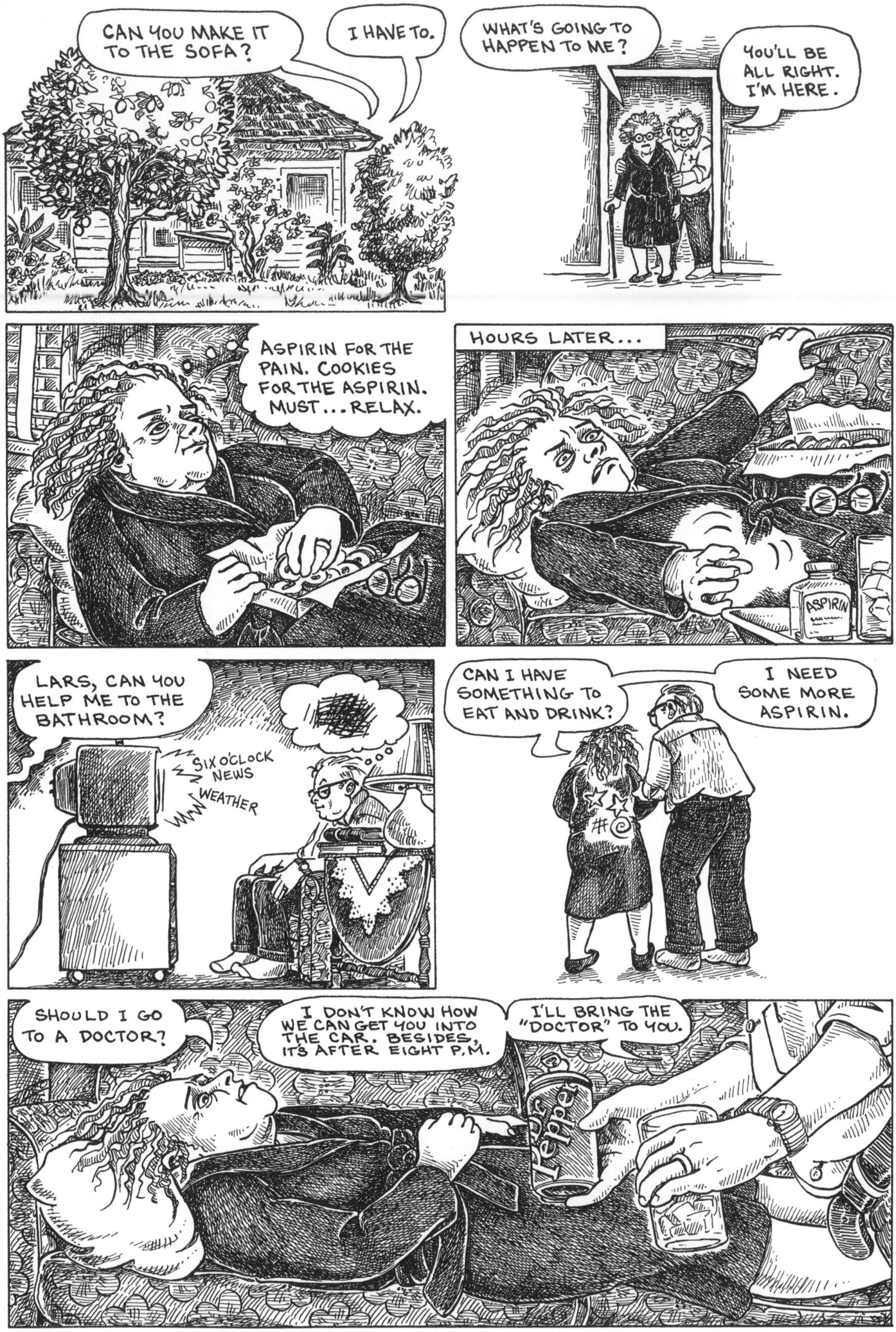
CAN YOU MAKE IT TO THE SOFA?
I HAVE TO.
WHAT'S GOING TO HAPPEN TO ME?
YOU'LL BE ALL RIGHT. I'M HERE.
ASPIRIN FOR THE PAIN. COOKIES FOR THE ASPIRIN. MUST... RELAX.
HOURS LATER...
ASPIRIN
LARS, CAN YOU HELP ME TO THE BATHROOM?
SIX O'CLOCK NEWS
WEATHER
CAN I HAVE SOMETHING TO EAT AND DRINK?
I NEED SOME MORE ASPIRIN.
SHOULD I GO TO A DOCTOR?
I DON'T KNOW HOW WE CAN GET YOU INTO THE CAR. BESIDES, IT'S AFTER EIGHT P.M.
I'LL BRING THE "DOCTOR" TO YOU.
Pepper

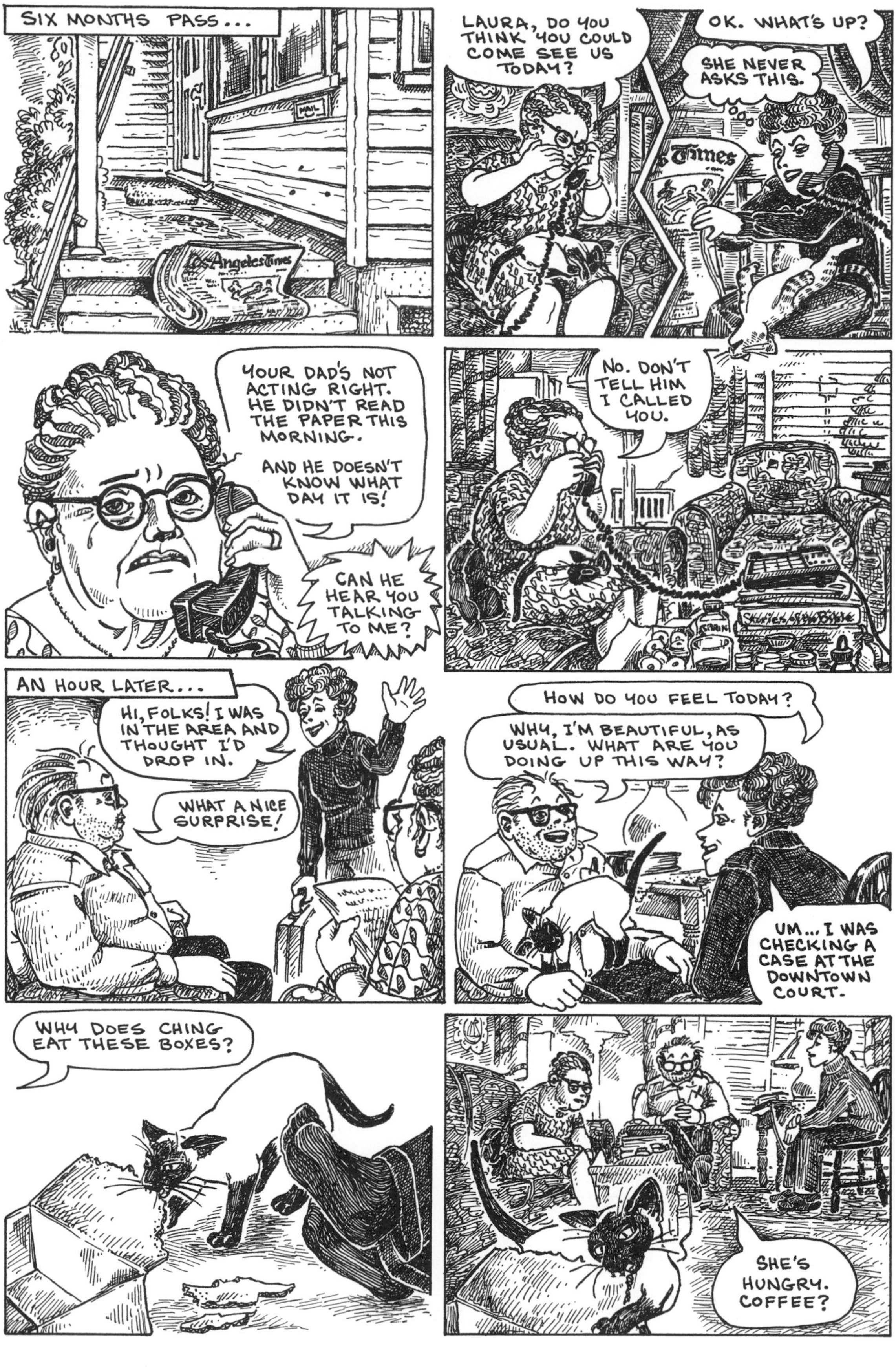
SIX MONTHS PASS...
LAURA, DO YOU THINK YOU COULD COME SEE US TODAY?
OK. WHAT'S UP?
SHE NEVER ASKS THIS.
YOUR DAD'S NOT ACTING RIGHT. HE DIDN'T READ THE PAPER THIS MORNING.
AND HE DOESN'T KNOW WHAT DAY IT IS!
CAN HE HEAR YOU TALKING TO ME?
NO. DON'T TELL HIM I CALLED YOU.
AN HOUR LATER...
HI, FOLKS! I WAS IN THE AREA AND THOUGHT I'D DROP IN.
WHAT A NICE SURPRISE!
HOW DO YOU FEEL TODAY?
WHY, I'M BEAUTIFUL, AS USUAL. WHAT ARE YOU DOING UP THIS WAY?
UM... I WAS CHECKING A CASE AT THE DOWNTOWN COURT.
WHY DOES CHING EAT THESE BOXES?
SHE'S HUNGRY. COFFEE?

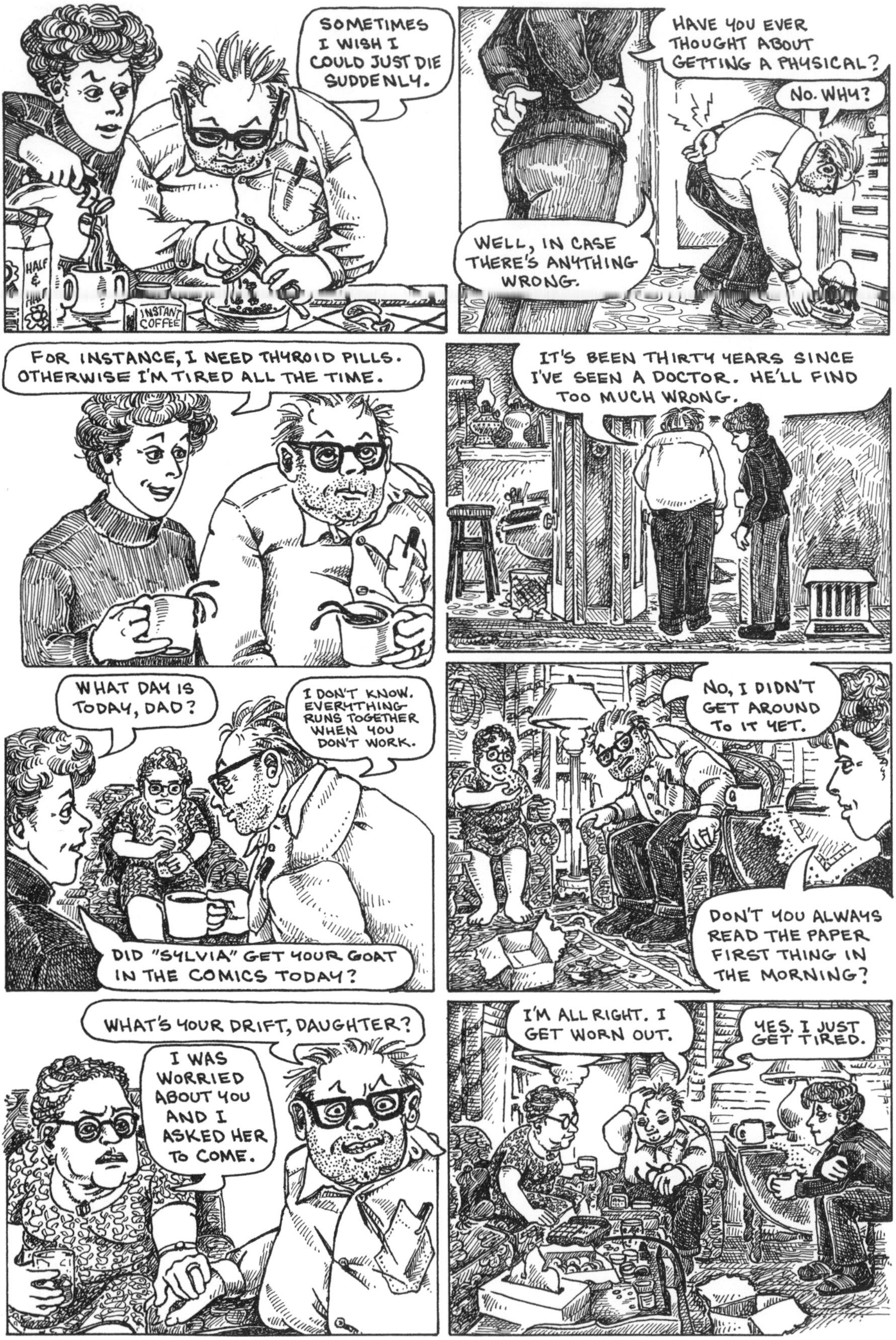
SOMETIMES I WISH I COULD JUST DIE SUDDENLY.
INSTANT COFFEE
HAVE YOU EVER THOUGHT ABOUT GETTING A PHYSICAL?
NO. WHY?
WELL, IN CASE THERE'S ANYTHING WRONG.
FOR INSTANCE, I NEED THYROID PILLS. OTHERWISE I'M TIRED ALL THE TIME.
IT'S BEEN THIRTY YEARS SINCE I'VE SEEN A DOCTOR. HE'LL FIND TOO MUCH WRONG.
WHAT DAY IS TODAY, DAD?
I DON'T KNOW. EVERYTHING RUNS TOGETHER WHEN YOU DON'T WORK.
DID "SYLVIA" GET YOUR GOAT IN THE COMICS TODAY?
NO, I DIDN'T GET AROUND TO IT YET.
DON'T YOU ALWAYS READ THE PAPER FIRST THING IN THE MORNING?
WHAT'S YOUR DRIFT, DAUGHTER?
I WAS WORRIED ABOUT YOU AND I ASKED HER TO COME.
I'M ALL RIGHT. I GET WORN OUT.
YES. I JUST GET TIRED.

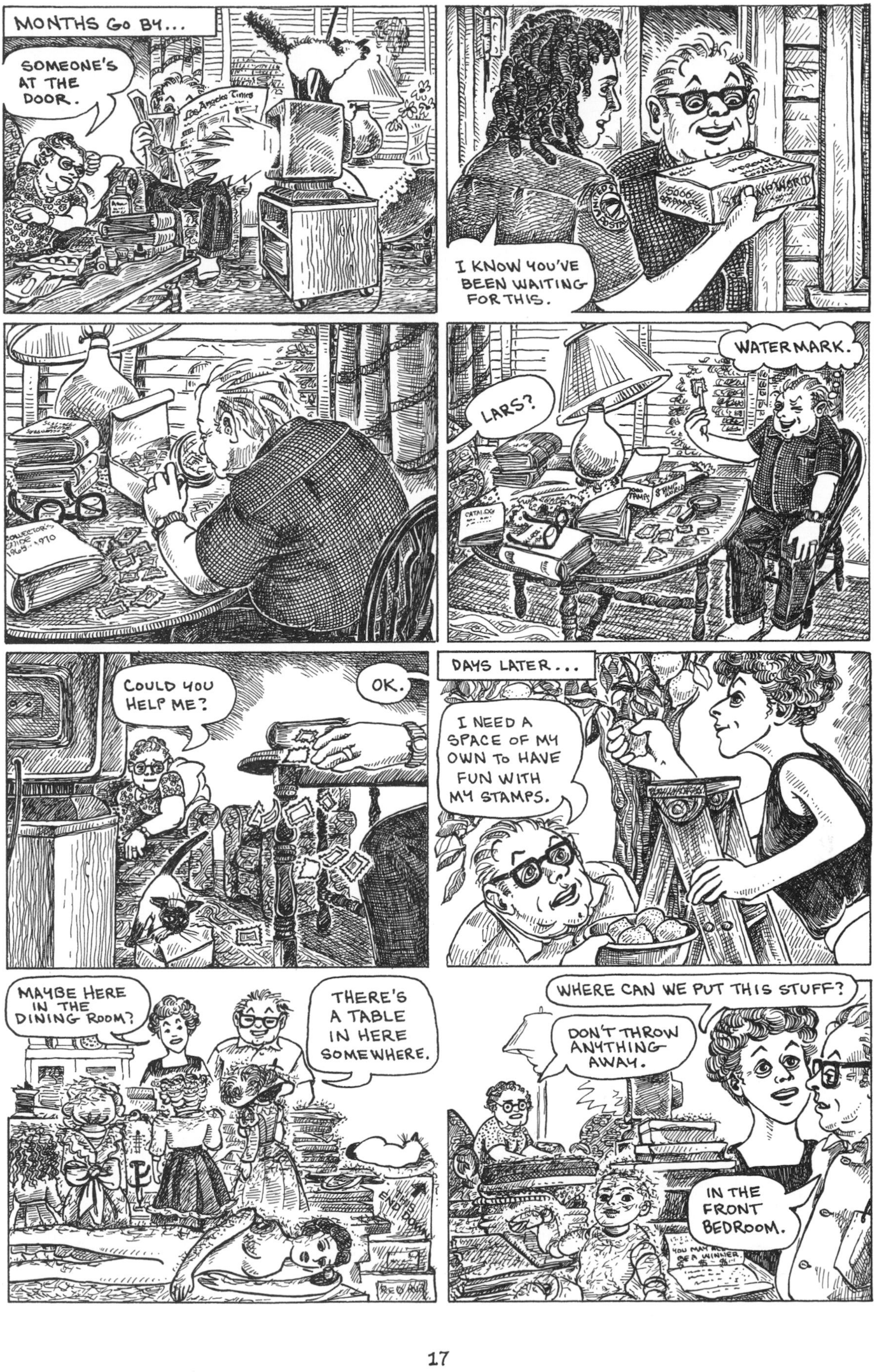
MONTHS GO BY...
SOMEONE'S AT THE DOOR.
I KNOW YOU'VE BEEN WAITING FOR THIS.
COLLECTOR'S GUIDE 1969-1970
LARS?
WATERMARK.
COULD YOU HELP ME?
OK.
DAYS LATER...
I NEED A SPACE OF MY OWN TO HAVE FUN WITH MY STAMPS.
MAYBE HERE IN THE DINING ROOM?
THERE'S A TABLE IN HERE SOMEWHERE.
WHERE CAN WE PUT THIS STUFF?
DON'T THROW ANYTHING AWAY.
IN THE FRONT BEDROOM.

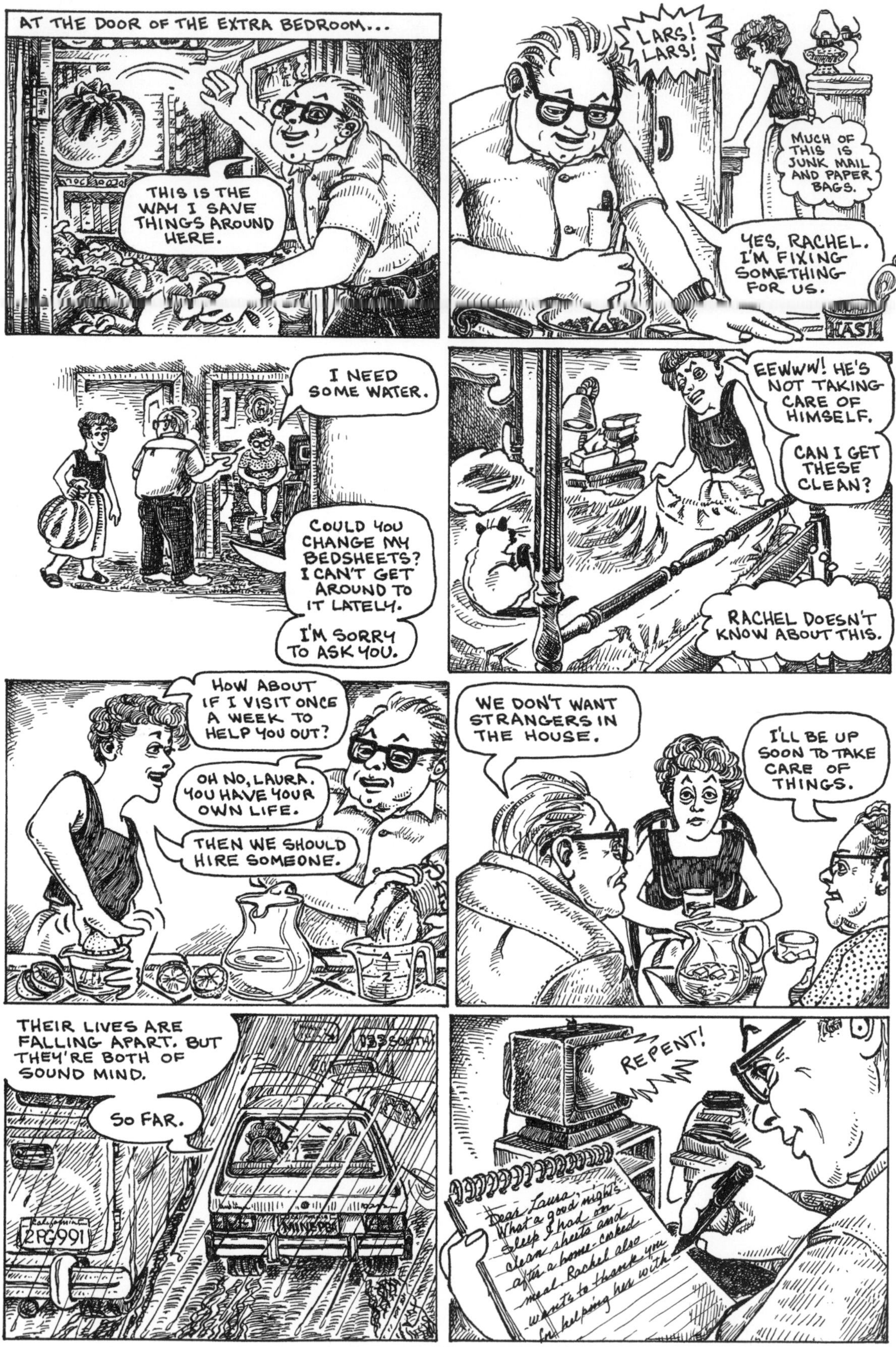
AT THE DOOR OF THE EXTRA BEDROOM...
THIS IS THE WAY I SAVE THINGS AROUND HERE.
LARS! LARS!
MUCH OF THIS IS JUNK MAIL AND PAPER BAGS.
YES, RACHEL. I'M FIXING SOMETHING FOR US.
HASH
I NEED SOME WATER.
COULD YOU CHANGE MY BEDSHEETS? I CAN'T GET AROUND TO IT LATELY.
I'M SORRY TO ASK YOU.
EEWWW! HE'S NOT TAKING CARE OF HIMSELF.
CAN I GET THESE CLEAN?
RACHEL DOESN'T KNOW ABOUT THIS.
HOW ABOUT IF I VISIT ONCE A WEEK TO HELP YOU OUT?
OH NO, LAURA. YOU HAVE YOUR OWN LIFE.
THEN WE SHOULD HIRE SOMEONE.
WE DON'T WANT STRANGERS IN THE HOUSE.
I'LL BE UP SOON TO TAKE CARE OF THINGS.
THEIR LIVES ARE FALLING APART. BUT THEY'RE BOTH OF SOUND MIND.
So FAR.
2PG991
REPENT!
Dear Laura,
What a good night's sleep I had on clean sheets and after a home-cooked meal. Rachel also wants to thank you for helping her with

MONTHS LATER LAURA CLEARS THE TABLE.

THERE MUST BE HUNDREDS OF THESE BITS OF CLOTH.

WHAT ARE YOU DOING IN THERE?

REARRANGING THINGS.

DAD NEEDS SOME TABLESPACE, RACHEL, FOR PAPERWORK.

I SEE. BUT DON'T THROW OUT ANYTHING.

IN TIME....

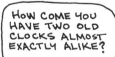
HOW COME YOU HAVE TWO OLD CLOCKS ALMOST EXACTLY ALIKE?

THEY'RE ABOUT THE SAME AGE. THIS BELONGED TO MY DANISH GRANDPARENTS.

YOU PULL A LEVER IF YOU WANT TO HEAR IT CHIME.

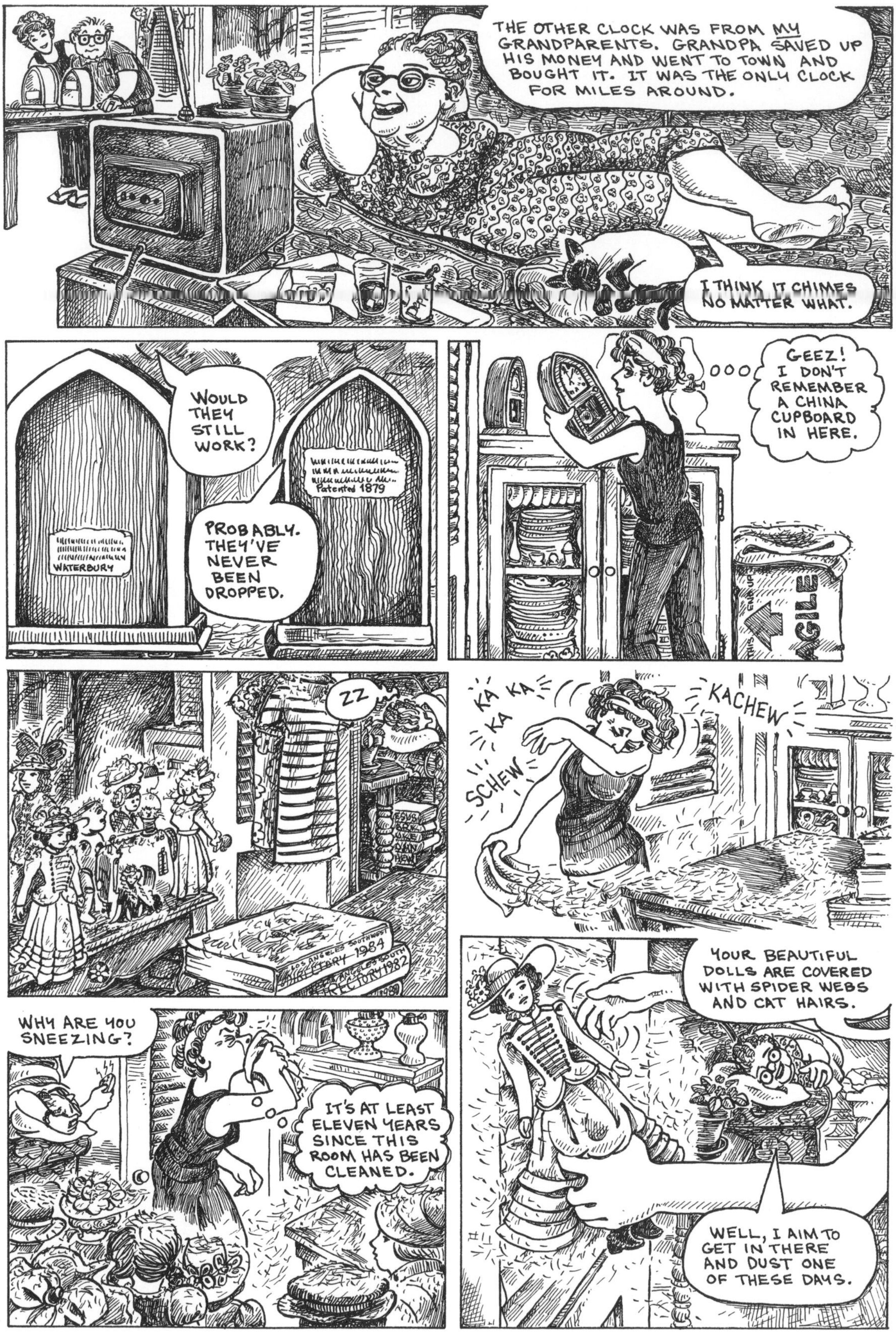
THE OTHER CLOCK WAS FROM MY GRANDPARENTS. GRANDPA SAVED UP HIS MONEY AND WENT TO TOWN AND BOUGHT IT. IT WAS THE ONLY CLOCK FOR MILES AROUND.
I THINK IT CHIMES NO MATTER WHAT.
WOULD THEY STILL WORK?
PROBABLY. THEY'VE NEVER BEEN DROPPED.
Patented 1879
WATERBURY
GEEZ! I DON'T REMEMBER A CHINA CUPBOARD IN HERE.
FRAGILE
ZZ
LOS ANGELES SOUTHWEST DIRECTORY 1984
LOS ANGELES SOUTH DIRECTORY 1982
KA KA KA
SCHEW
KACHEW
YOUR BEAUTIFUL DOLLS ARE COVERED WITH SPIDER WEBS AND CAT HAIRS.
WELL, I AIM TO GET IN THERE AND DUST ONE OF THESE DAYS.
WHY ARE YOU SNEEZING?
IT'S AT LEAST ELEVEN YEARS SINCE THIS ROOM HAS BEEN CLEANED.

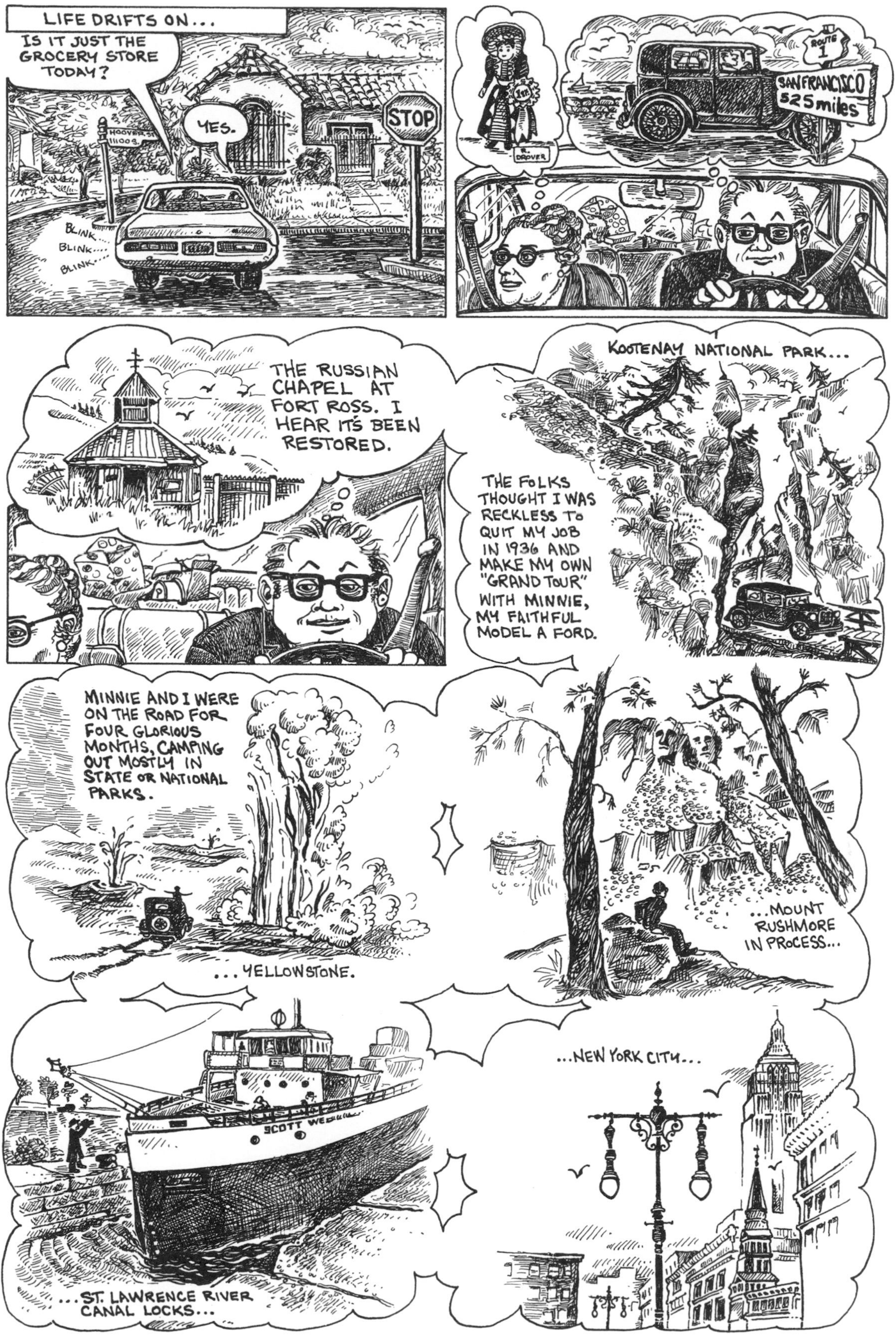

LIFE DRIFTS ON...
IS IT JUST THE GROCERY STORE TODAY?
YES.
STOP
BLINK... BLINK... BLINK...
SAN FRANCISCO 525 miles
ROUTE 1
THE RUSSIAN CHAPEL AT FORT ROSS. I HEAR IT'S BEEN RESTORED.
KOOTENAY NATIONAL PARK...
THE FOLKS THOUGHT I WAS RECKLESS TO QUIT MY JOB IN 1936 AND MAKE MY OWN "GRAND TOUR" WITH MINNIE, MY FAITHFUL MODEL A FORD.
MINNIE AND I WERE ON THE ROAD FOR FOUR GLORIOUS MONTHS, CAMPING OUT MOSTLY IN STATE OR NATIONAL PARKS.
...YELLOWSTONE.
...MOUNT RUSHMORE IN PROCESS...
SCOTT WE...
...ST. LAWRENCE RIVER CANAL LOCKS...
...NEW YORK CITY...

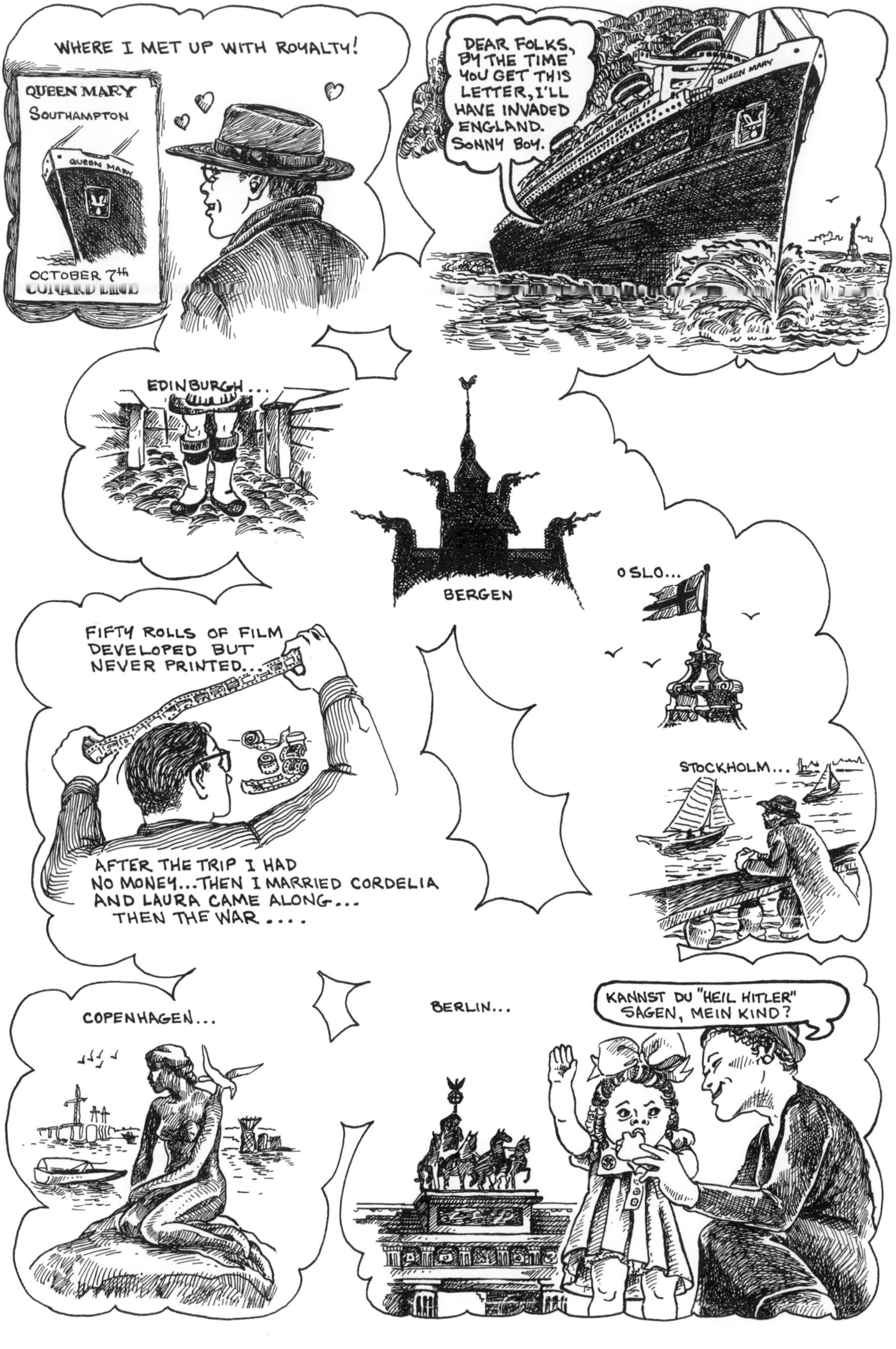

WHERE I MET UP WITH ROYALTY!
QUEEN MARY
SOUTHAMPTON
QUEEN MARY
OCTOBER 7th
DEAR FOLKS, BY THE TIME YOU GET THIS LETTER, I'LL HAVE INVADED ENGLAND. SONNY BOY.
QUEEN MARY
EDINBURGH...
BERGEN
OSLO...
FIFTY ROLLS OF FILM DEVELOPED BUT NEVER PRINTED...
AFTER THE TRIP I HAD NO MONEY...THEN I MARRIED CORDELIA AND LAURA CAME ALONG... THEN THE WAR....
STOCKHOLM...
COPENHAGEN...
BERLIN...
KANNST DU "HEIL HITLER" SAGEN, MEIN KIND?

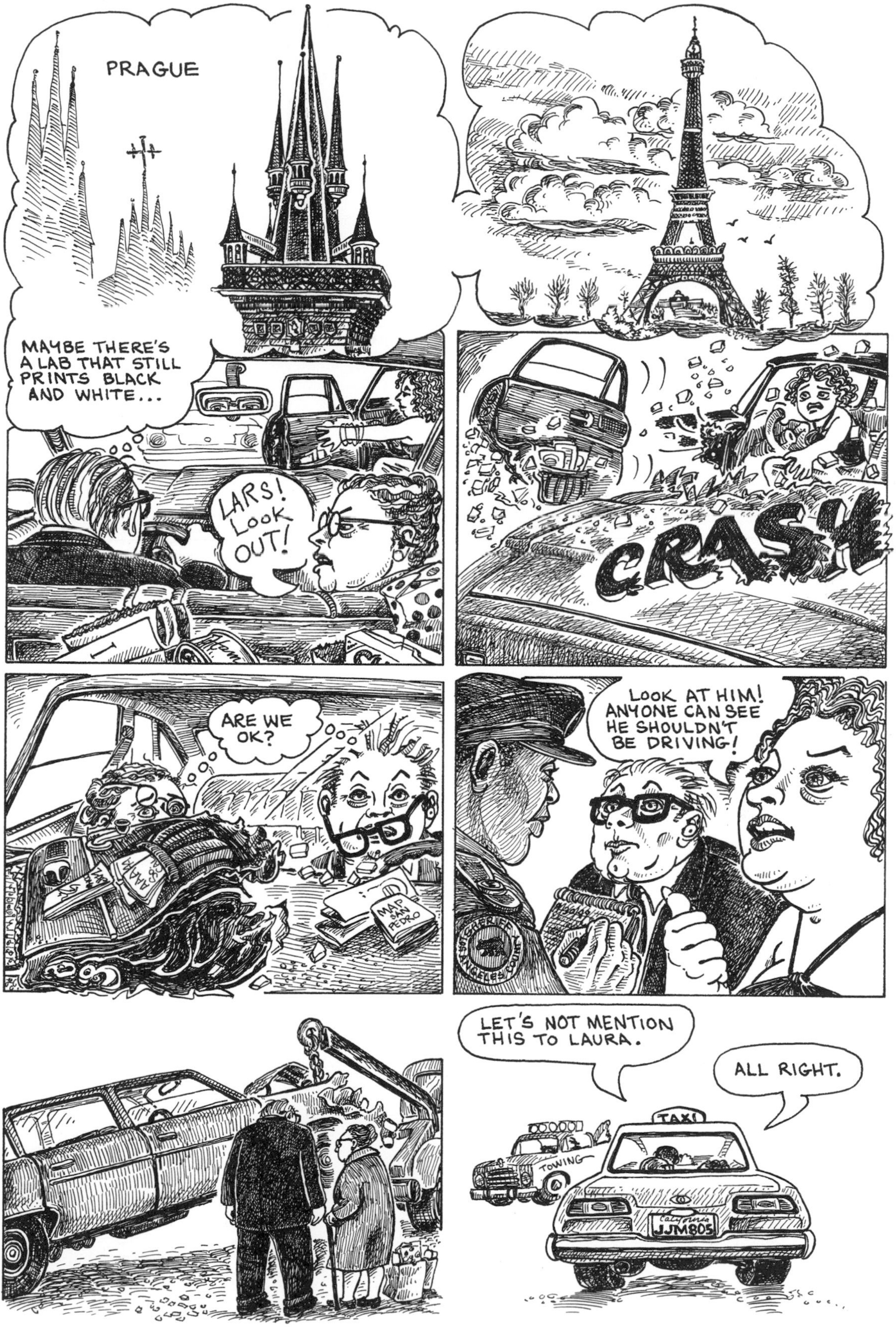
PRAGUE
MAYBE THERE'S A LAB THAT STILL PRINTS BLACK AND WHITE...
LARS! LOOK OUT!
CRASH
ARE WE OK?
MAP SAN PEDRO
LOOK AT HIM! ANYONE CAN SEE HE SHOULDN'T BE DRIVING!
LET'S NOT MENTION THIS TO LAURA.
ALL RIGHT.
TAXI
TOWING
JJM805

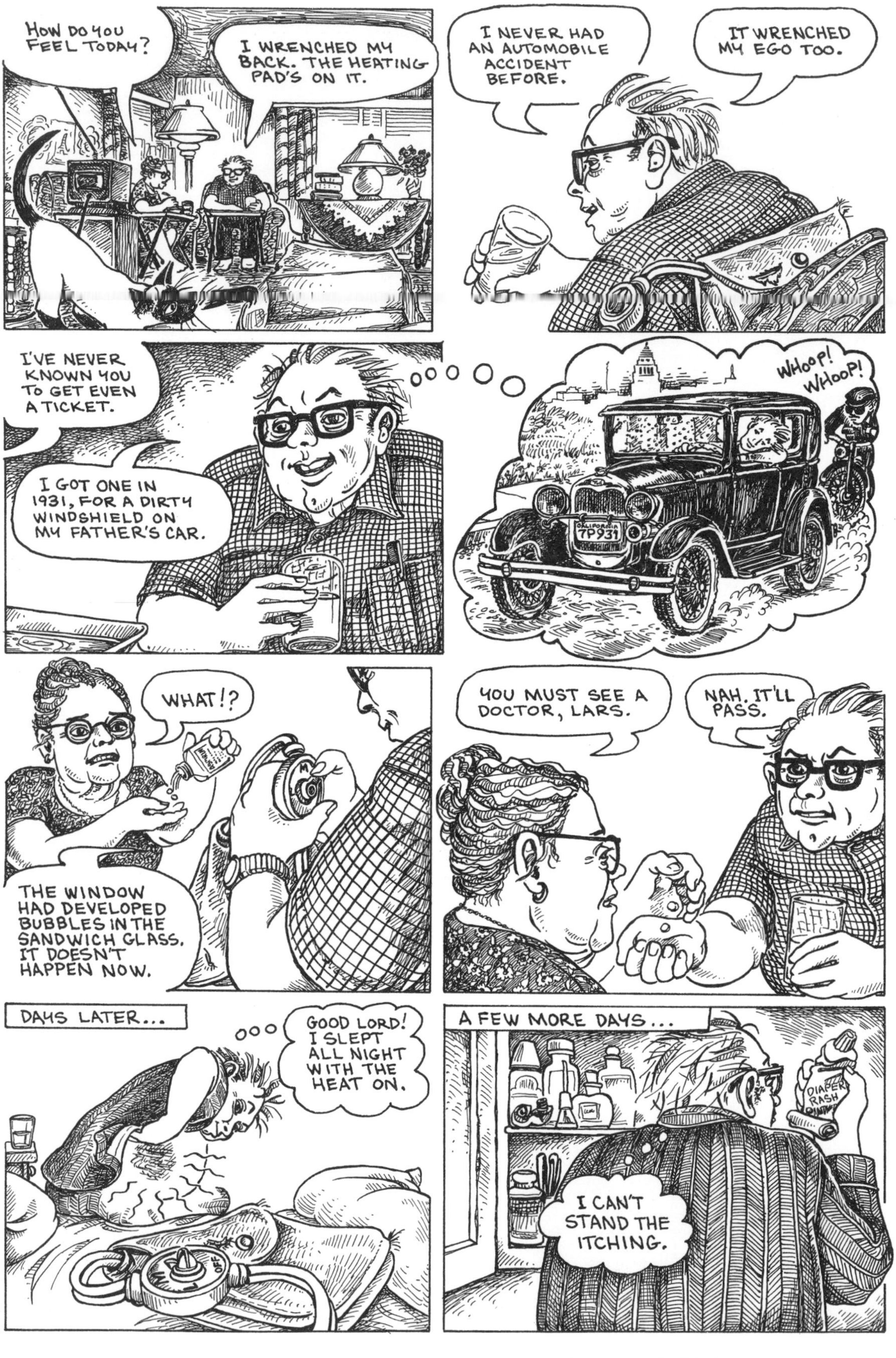
HOW DO YOU FEEL TODAY?
I WRENCHED MY BACK. THE HEATING PAD'S ON IT.
I NEVER HAD AN AUTOMOBILE ACCIDENT BEFORE.
IT WRENCHED MY EGO TOO.
I'VE NEVER KNOWN YOU TO GET EVEN A TICKET.
I GOT ONE IN 1931, FOR A DIRTY WINDSHIELD ON MY FATHER'S CAR.
WHOOP! WHOOP!
CALIFORNIA 7P931
WHAT!?
THE WINDOW HAD DEVELOPED BUBBLES IN THE SANDWICH GLASS. IT DOESN'T HAPPEN NOW.
YOU MUST SEE A DOCTOR, LARS.
NAH. IT'LL PASS.
DAYS LATER...
GOOD LORD! I SLEPT ALL NIGHT WITH THE HEAT ON.
A FEW MORE DAYS...
DIAPER RASH
I CAN'T STAND THE ITCHING.

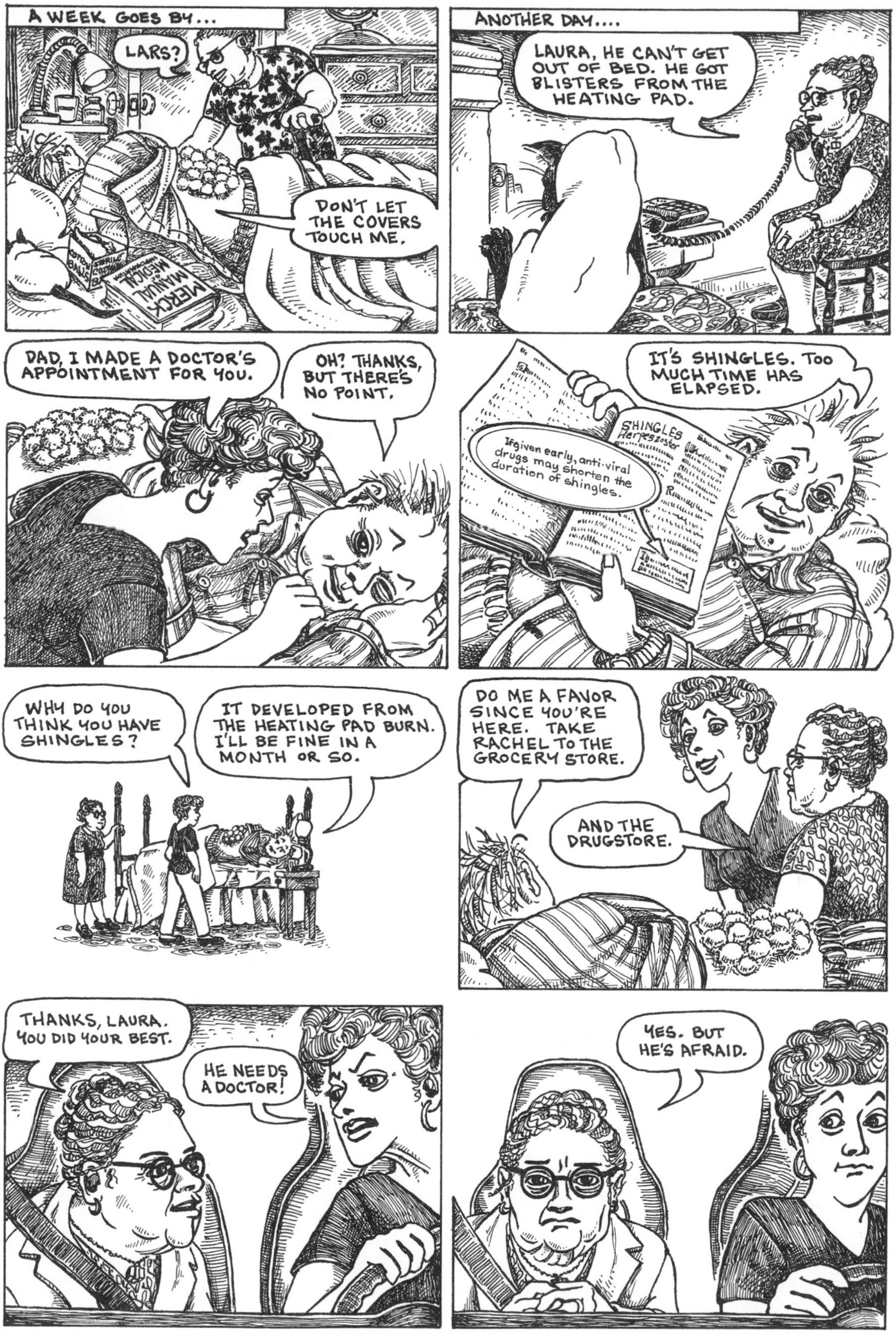
A WEEK GOES BY...
LARS?
DON'T LET THE COVERS TOUCH ME.
MERCK MANUAL MEDICAL
ANOTHER DAY....
LAURA, HE CAN'T GET OUT OF BED. HE GOT BLISTERS FROM THE HEATING PAD.
DAD, I MADE A DOCTOR'S APPOINTMENT FOR YOU.
OH? THANKS, BUT THERE'S NO POINT.
IT'S SHINGLES. TOO MUCH TIME HAS ELAPSED.
SHINGLES Herpes zoster
If given early, anti-viral drugs may shorten the duration of shingles.
WHY DO YOU THINK YOU HAVE SHINGLES?
IT DEVELOPED FROM THE HEATING PAD BURN. I'LL BE FINE IN A MONTH OR SO.
DO ME A FAVOR SINCE YOU'RE HERE. TAKE RACHEL TO THE GROCERY STORE.
AND THE DRUGSTORE.
THANKS, LAURA. YOU DID YOUR BEST.
HE NEEDS A DOCTOR!
YES. BUT HE'S AFRAID.

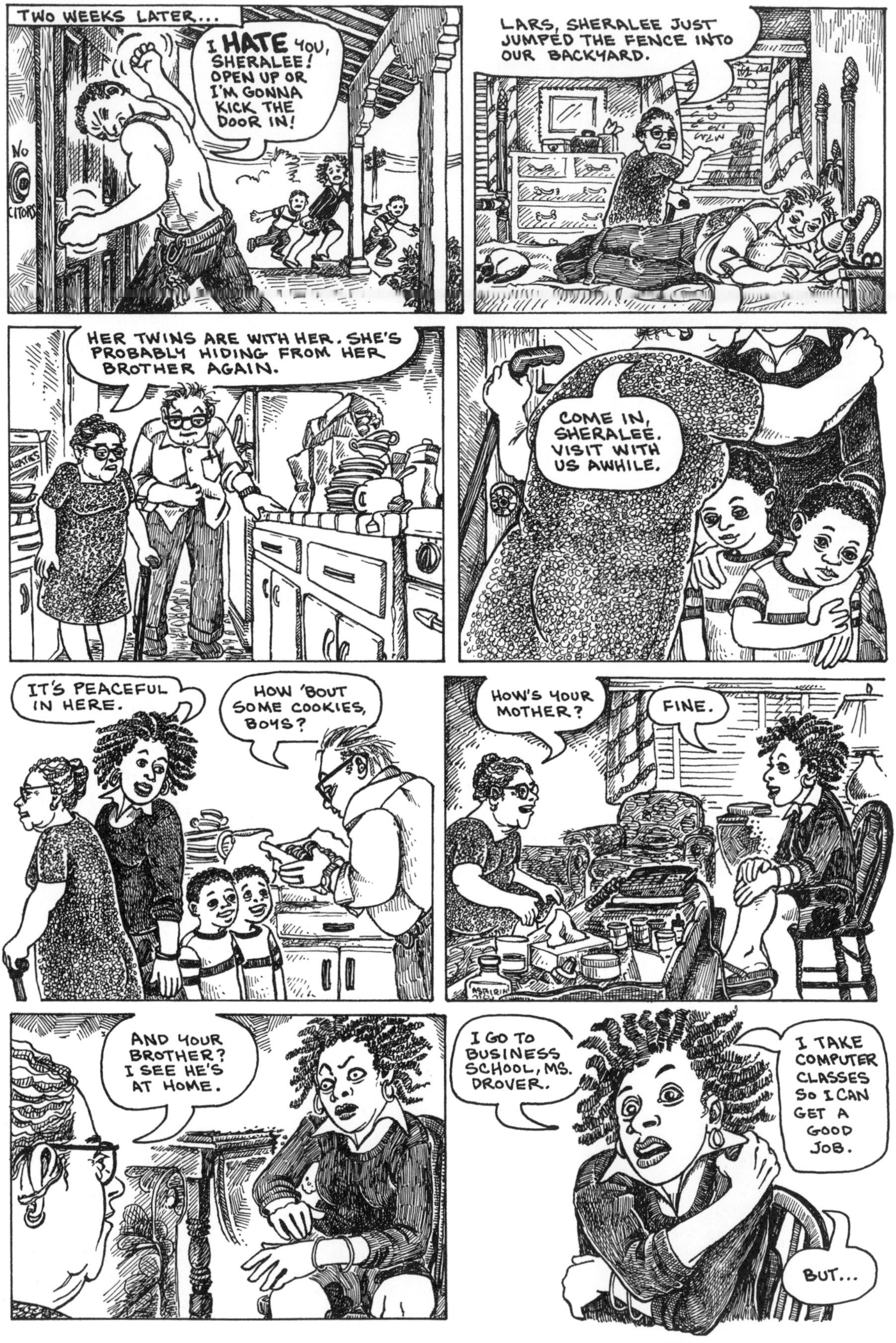
TWO WEEKS LATER...
I HATE YOU, SHERALEE! OPEN UP OR I'M GONNA KICK THE DOOR IN!
LARS, SHERALEE JUST JUMPED THE FENCE INTO OUR BACKYARD.
HER TWINS ARE WITH HER. SHE'S PROBABLY HIDING FROM HER BROTHER AGAIN.
COME IN, SHERALEE. VISIT WITH US AWHILE.
IT'S PEACEFUL IN HERE.
HOW 'BOUT SOME COOKIES, BOYS?
HOW'S YOUR MOTHER?
FINE.
AND YOUR BROTHER? I SEE HE'S AT HOME.
I GO TO BUSINESS SCHOOL, MS. DROVER.
I TAKE COMPUTER CLASSES SO I CAN GET A GOOD JOB.
BUT...

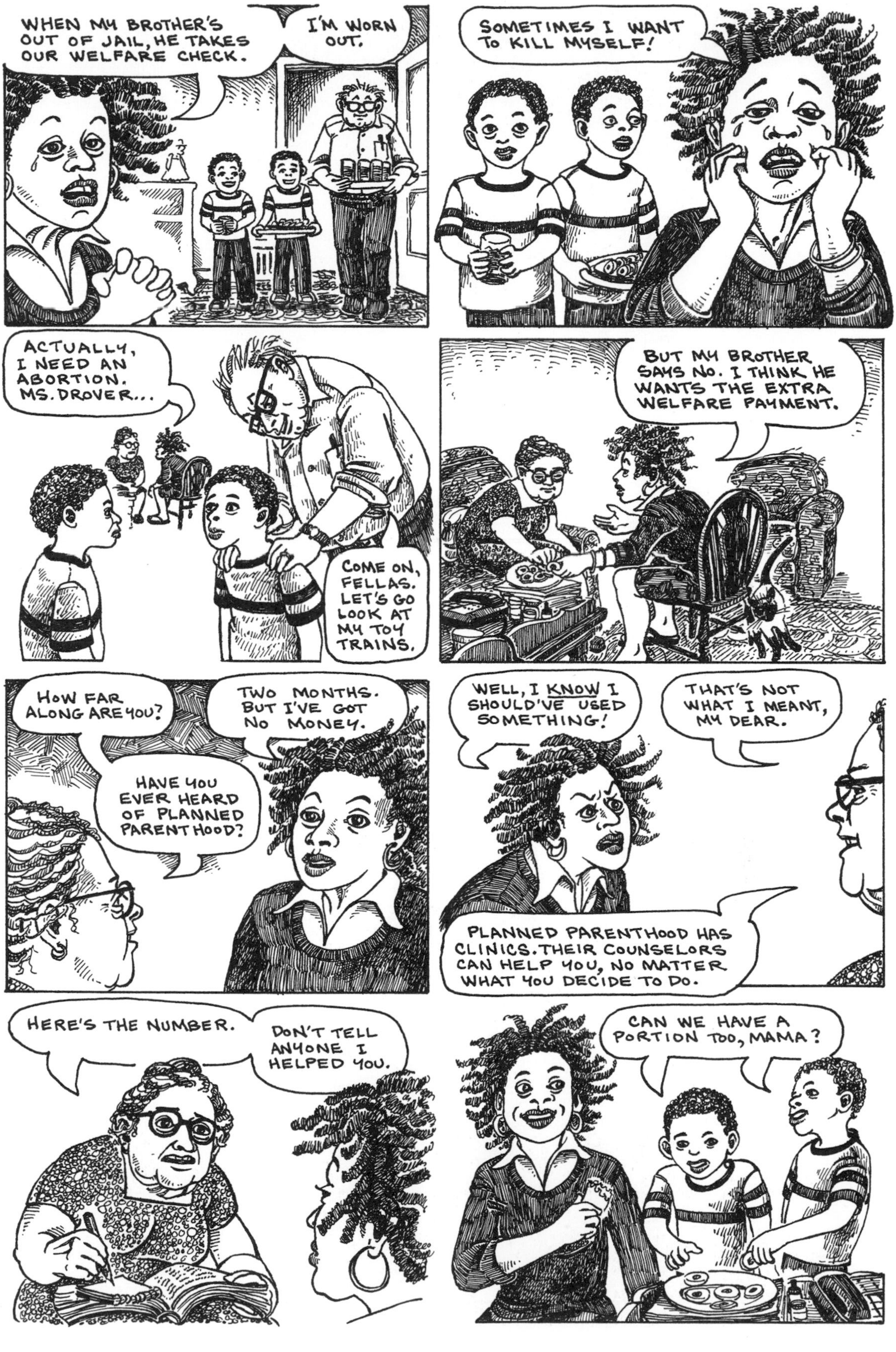
WHEN MY BROTHER'S OUT OF JAIL, HE TAKES OUR WELFARE CHECK.
I'M WORN OUT.
SOMETIMES I WANT TO KILL MYSELF!
ACTUALLY, I NEED AN ABORTION. MS. DROVER...
COME ON, FELLAS. LET'S GO LOOK AT MY TOY TRAINS.
BUT MY BROTHER SAYS NO. I THINK HE WANTS THE EXTRA WELFARE PAYMENT.
HOW FAR ALONG ARE YOU?
TWO MONTHS. BUT I'VE GOT NO MONEY.
HAVE YOU EVER HEARD OF PLANNED PARENTHOOD?
WELL, I KNOW I SHOULD'VE USED SOMETHING!
THAT'S NOT WHAT I MEANT, MY DEAR.
PLANNED PARENTHOOD HAS CLINICS. THEIR COUNSELORS CAN HELP YOU, NO MATTER WHAT YOU DECIDE TO DO.
HERE'S THE NUMBER.
DON'T TELL ANYONE I HELPED YOU.
CAN WE HAVE A PORTION TOO, MAMA?

2

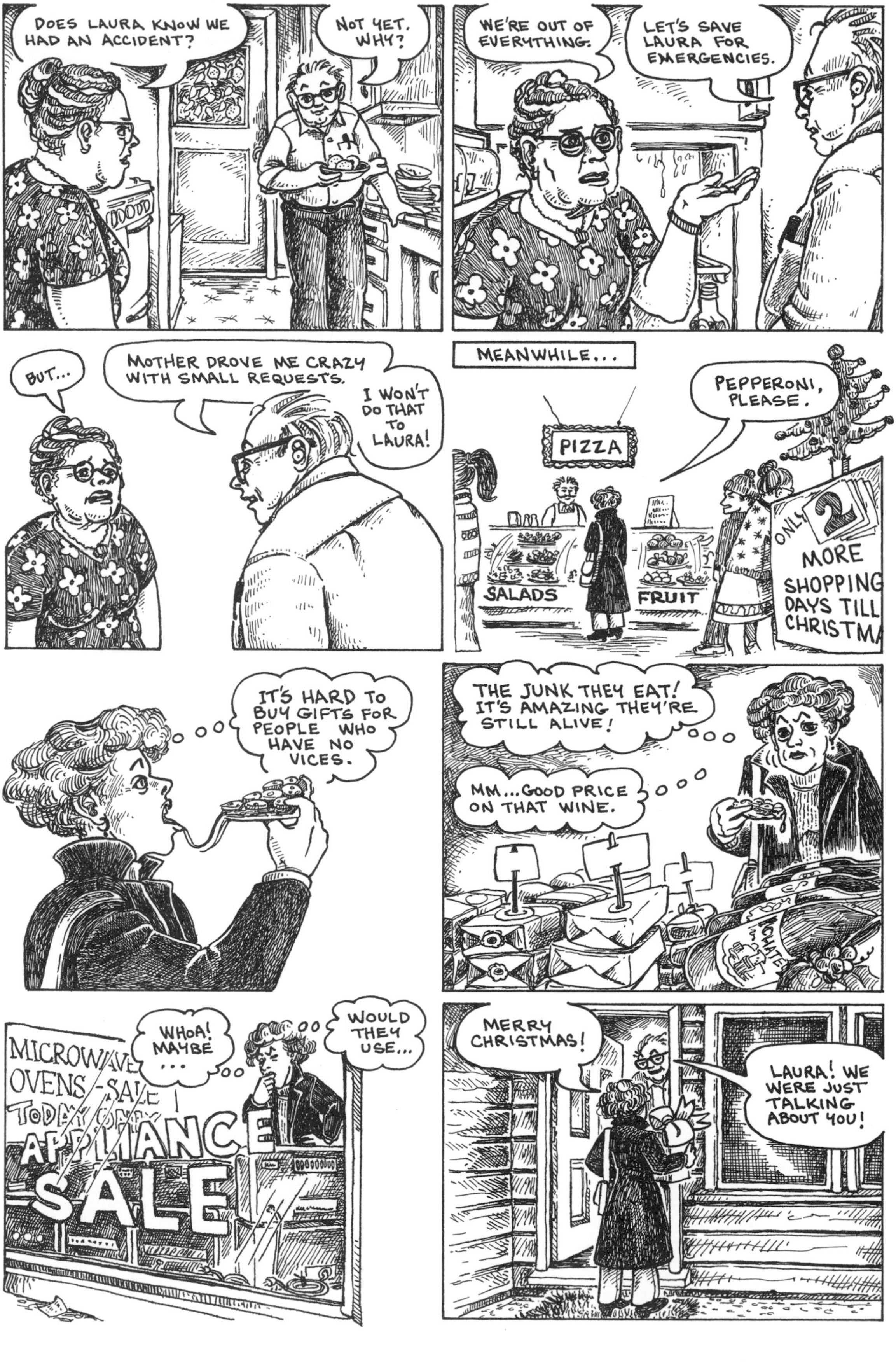
DOES LAURA KNOW WE HAD AN ACCIDENT?
NOT YET. WHY?
WE'RE OUT OF EVERYTHING.
LET'S SAVE LAURA FOR EMERGENCIES.
BUT...
MOTHER DROVE ME CRAZY WITH SMALL REQUESTS.
I WON'T DO THAT TO LAURA!
MEANWHILE...
PIZZA
PEPPERONI, PLEASE.
SALADS
FRUIT
ONLY 2 MORE SHOPPING DAYS TILL CHRISTMA
IT'S HARD TO BUY GIFTS FOR PEOPLE WHO HAVE NO VICES.
THE JUNK THEY EAT! IT'S AMAZING THEY'RE STILL ALIVE!
MM...GOOD PRICE ON THAT WINE.
MICROWAVE OVENS-SALE
APPLIANCE SALE
WHOA! MAYBE ...
WOULD THEY USE...
MERRY CHRISTMAS!
LAURA! WE WERE JUST TALKING ABOUT YOU!

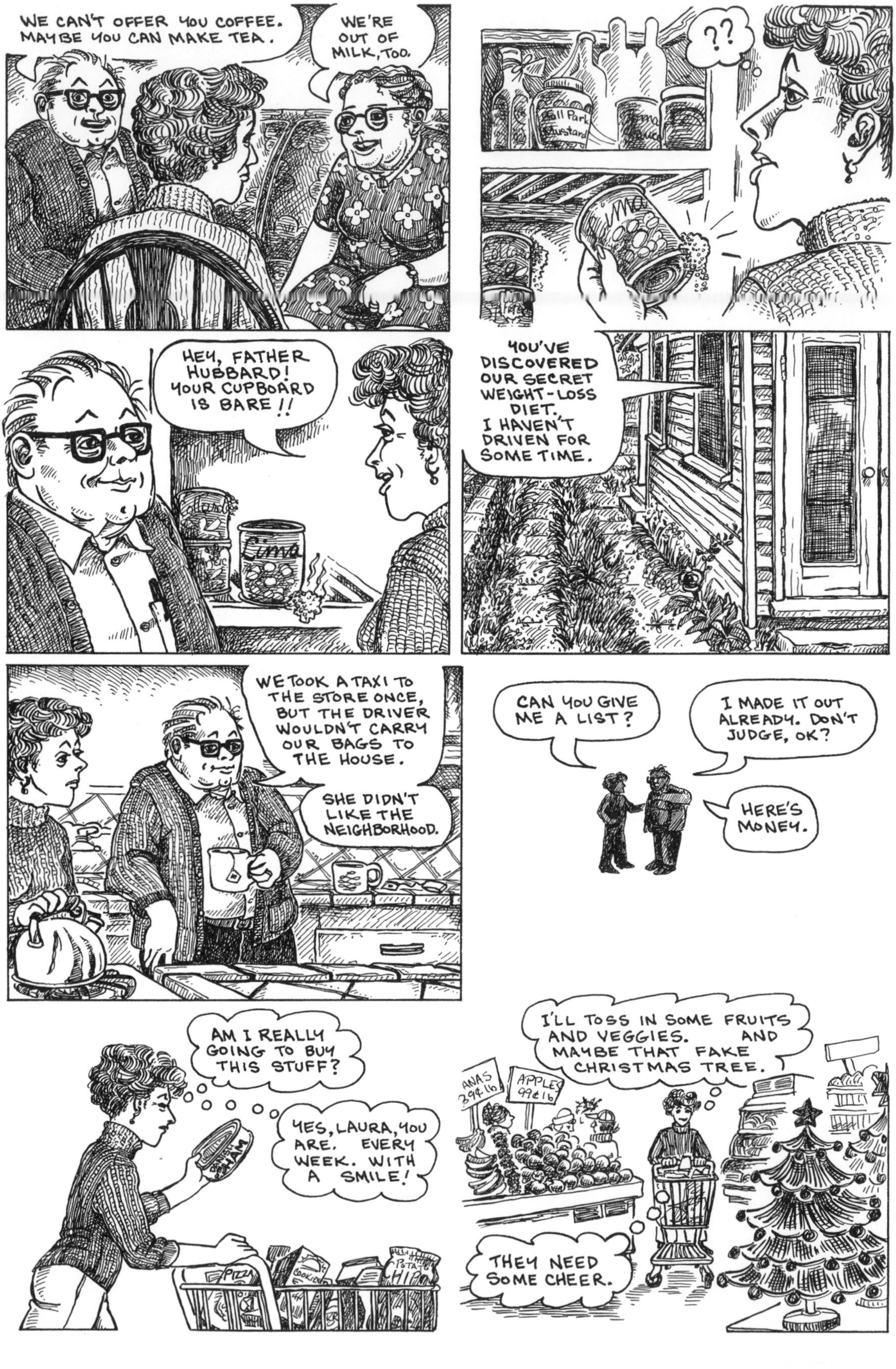
WE CAN'T OFFER YOU COFFEE. MAYBE YOU CAN MAKE TEA.
WE'RE OUT OF MILK, TOO.
??
Ball Park Mustard
HEY, FATHER HUBBARD! YOUR CUPBOARD IS BARE!!
Lima
YOU'VE DISCOVERED OUR SECRET WEIGHT-LOSS DIET. I HAVEN'T DRIVEN FOR SOME TIME.
WE TOOK A TAXI TO THE STORE ONCE, BUT THE DRIVER WOULDN'T CARRY OUR BAGS TO THE HOUSE.
SHE DIDN'T LIKE THE NEIGHBORHOOD.
CAN YOU GIVE ME A LIST?
I MADE IT OUT ALREADY. DON'T JUDGE, OK?
HERE'S MONEY.
AM I REALLY GOING TO BUY THIS STUFF?
YES, LAURA, YOU ARE. EVERY WEEK. WITH A SMILE!
PIZZA
COOKIES
I'LL TOSS IN SOME FRUITS AND VEGGIES. AND MAYBE THAT FAKE CHRISTMAS TREE.
APPLES 99¢ lb
THEY NEED SOME CHEER.

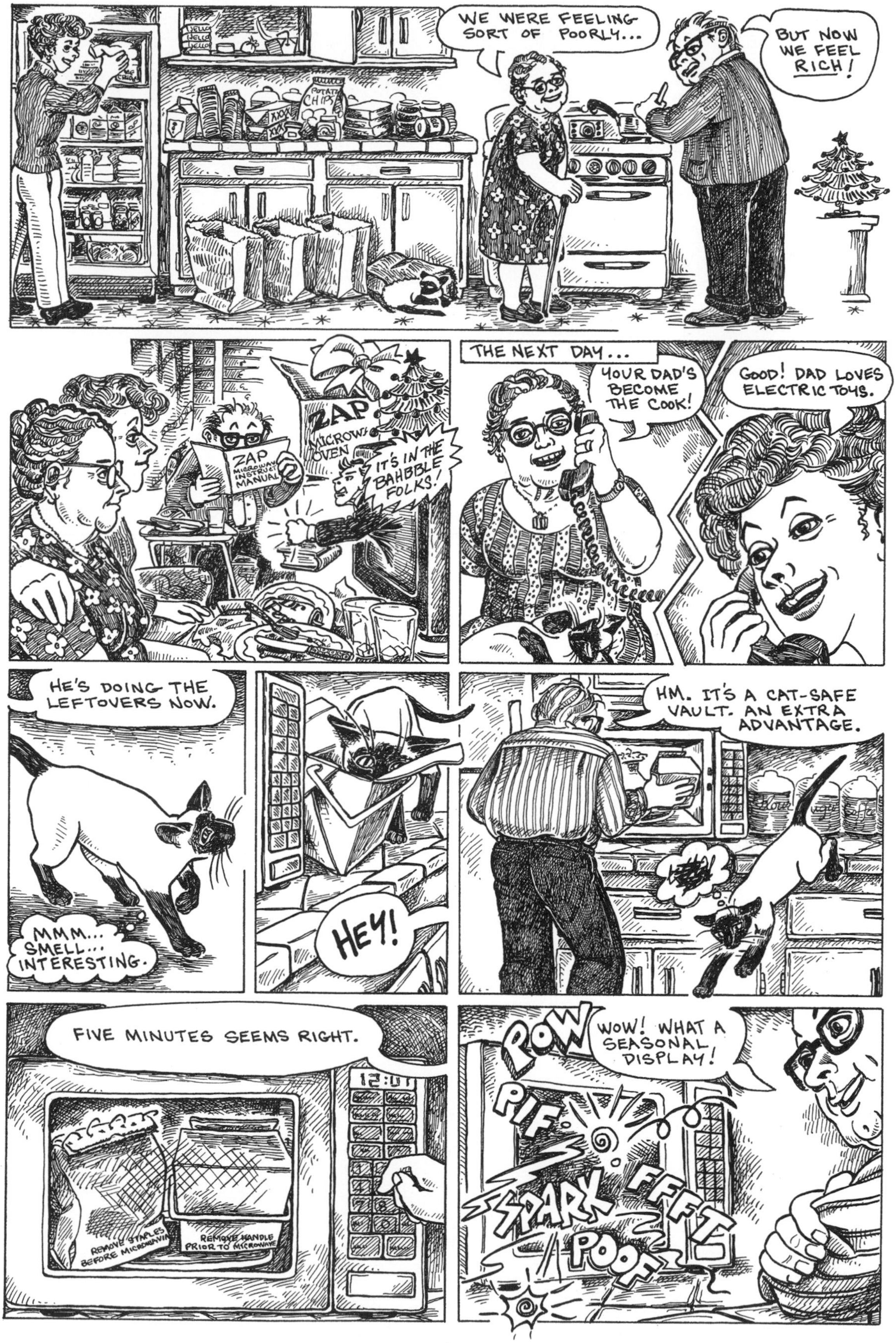
WE WERE FEELING SORT OF POORLY...
BUT NOW WE FEEL RICH!
POTATO CHIPS
ZAP MICROWAVE OVEN
ZAP MICROWAVE INSTRUCTION MANUAL
IT'S IN THE BAHBBLE FOLKS!
THE NEXT DAY...
YOUR DAD'S BECOME THE COOK!
GOOD! DAD LOVES ELECTRIC TOYS.
HE'S DOING THE LEFTOVERS NOW.
MMM... SMELL... INTERESTING.
HEY!
HM. IT'S A CAT-SAFE VAULT. AN EXTRA ADVANTAGE.
FIVE MINUTES SEEMS RIGHT.
12:01
REMOVE STAPLES BEFORE MICROWAVING
REMOVE HANDLE PRIOR TO MICROWAVE
POW
WOW! WHAT A SEASONAL DISPLAY!
PIF
SPARK
FFFT
POOF

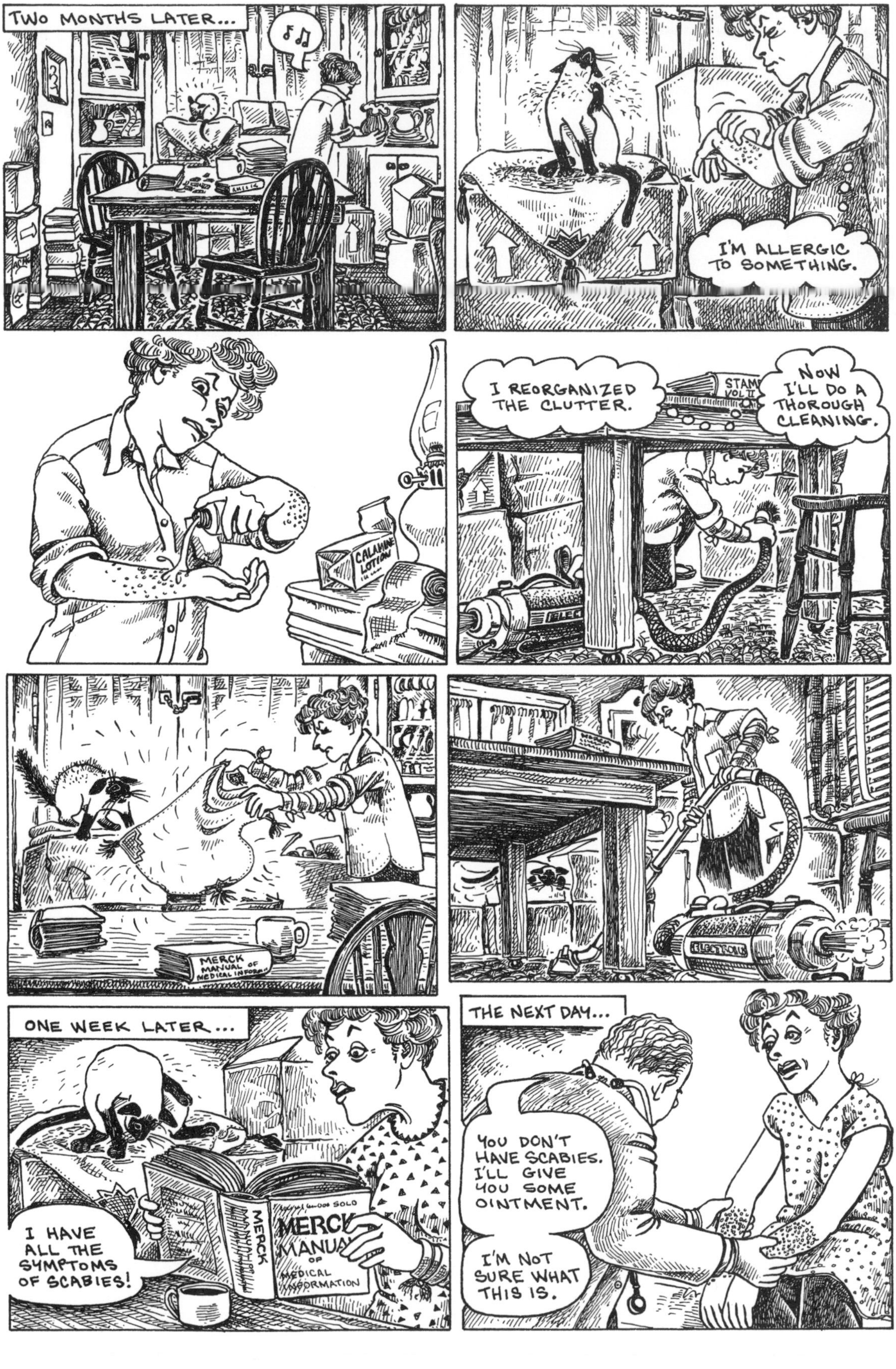
TWO MONTHS LATER...
I'M ALLERGIC TO SOMETHING.
CALAMINE LOTION
I REORGANIZED THE CLUTTER.
NOW I'LL DO A THOROUGH CLEANING.
STAMP VOL II
MERCK MANUAL OF MEDICAL INFORM...
ELECTROLUX
ONE WEEK LATER...
I HAVE ALL THE SYMPTOMS OF SCABIES!
MERCK MANUAL OF MEDICAL INFORMATION
THE NEXT DAY...
YOU DON'T HAVE SCABIES. I'LL GIVE YOU SOME OINTMENT.
I'M NOT SURE WHAT THIS IS.

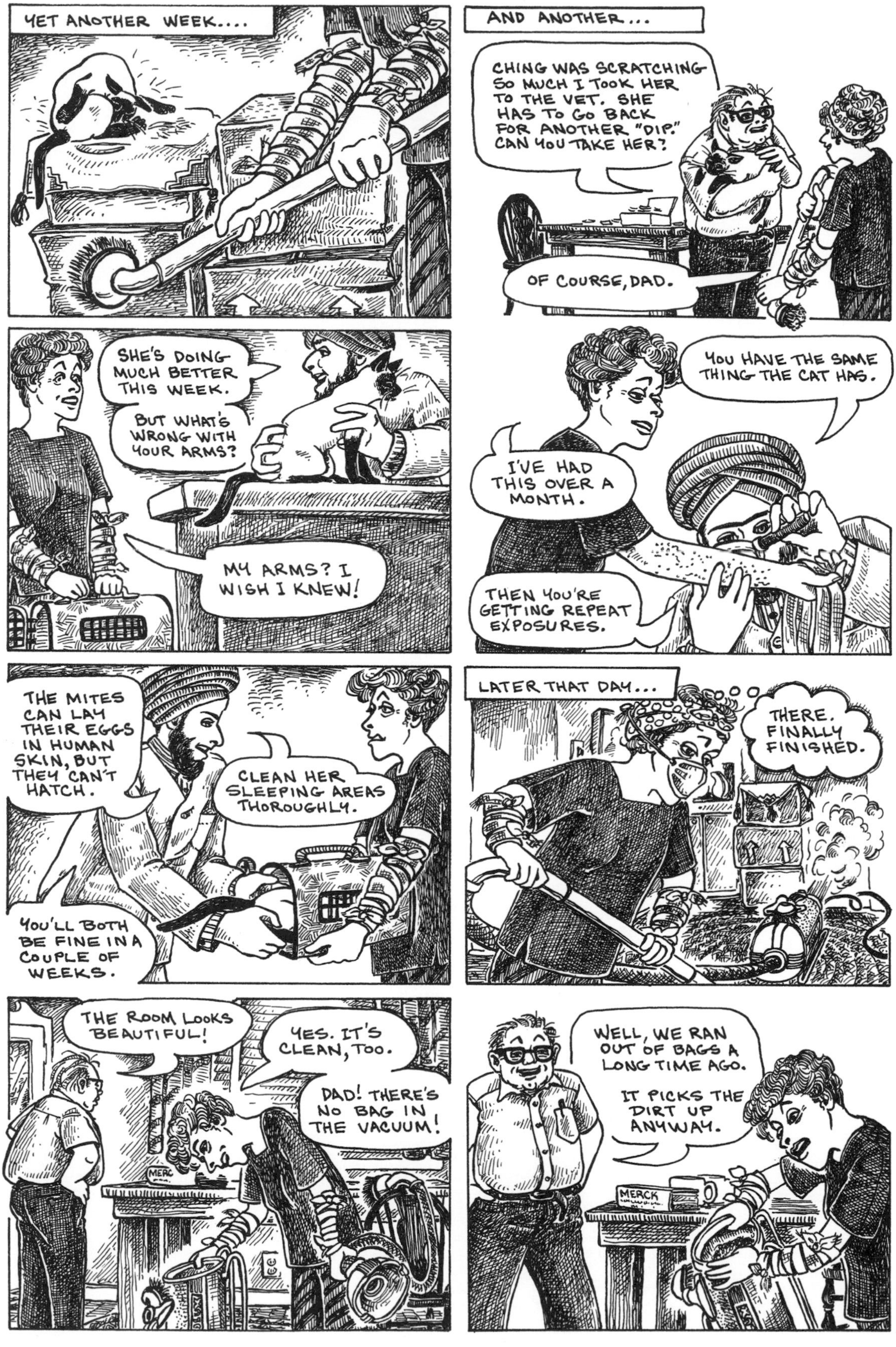

YET ANOTHER WEEK....
AND ANOTHER...
CHING WAS SCRATCHING SO MUCH I TOOK HER TO THE VET. SHE HAS TO GO BACK FOR ANOTHER "DIP." CAN YOU TAKE HER?
OF COURSE, DAD.
SHE'S DOING MUCH BETTER THIS WEEK.
BUT WHAT'S WRONG WITH YOUR ARMS?
MY ARMS? I WISH I KNEW!
YOU HAVE THE SAME THING THE CAT HAS.
I'VE HAD THIS OVER A MONTH.
THEN YOU'RE GETTING REPEAT EXPOSURES.
THE MITES CAN LAY THEIR EGGS IN HUMAN SKIN, BUT THEY CAN'T HATCH.
CLEAN HER SLEEPING AREAS THOROUGHLY.
YOU'LL BOTH BE FINE IN A COUPLE OF WEEKS.
LATER THAT DAY...
THERE. FINALLY FINISHED.
THE ROOM LOOKS BEAUTIFUL!
YES. IT'S CLEAN, TOO.
DAD! THERE'S NO BAG IN THE VACUUM!
MERC
WELL, WE RAN OUT OF BAGS A LONG TIME AGO.
IT PICKS THE DIRT UP ANYWAY.
MERCK

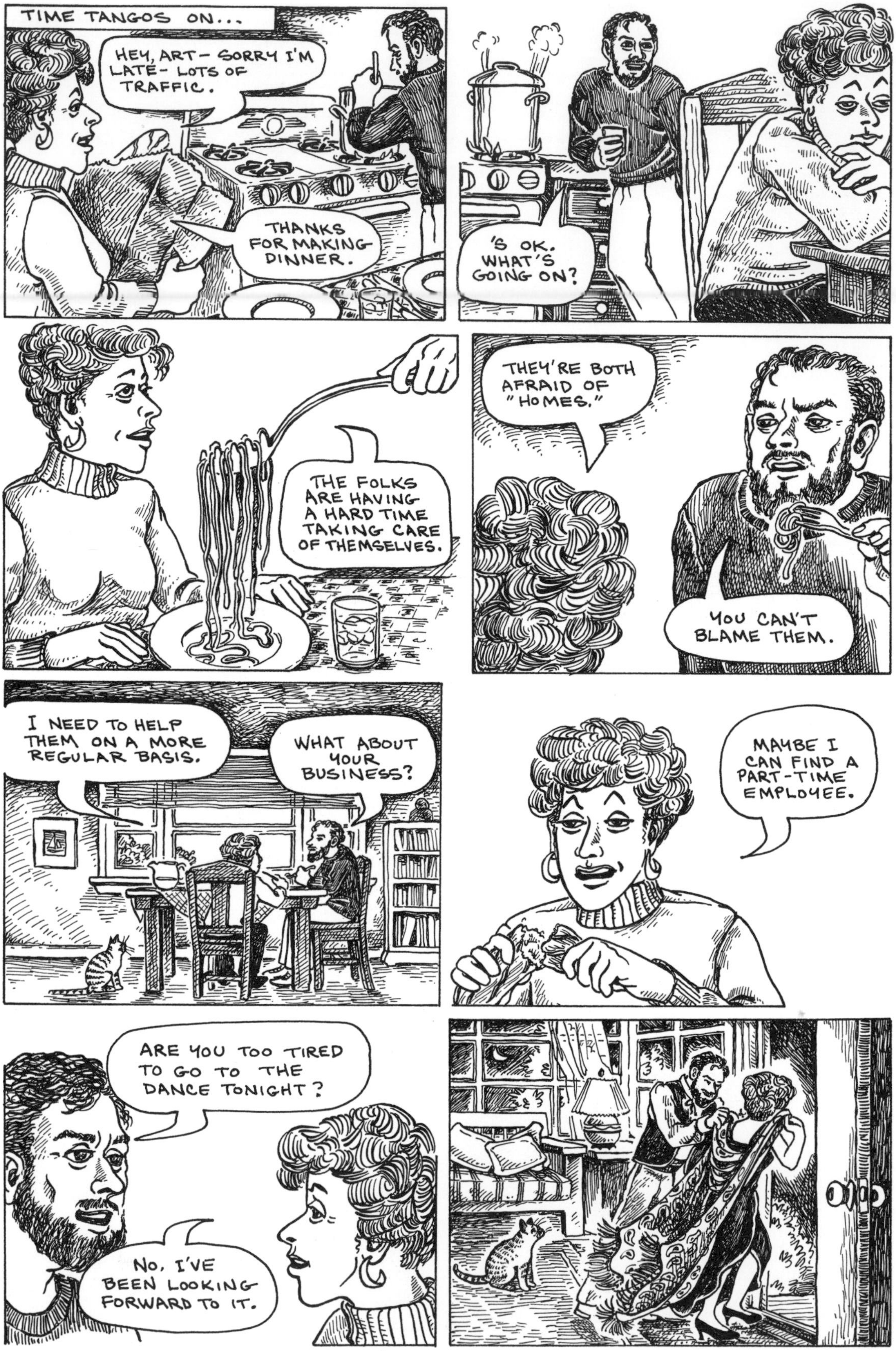
TIME TANGOS ON...
HEY, ART- SORRY I'M LATE- LOTS OF TRAFFIC.
THANKS FOR MAKING DINNER.
'S OK. WHAT'S GOING ON?
THE FOLKS ARE HAVING A HARD TIME TAKING CARE OF THEMSELVES.
THEY'RE BOTH AFRAID OF "HOMES."
YOU CAN'T BLAME THEM.
I NEED TO HELP THEM ON A MORE REGULAR BASIS.
WHAT ABOUT YOUR BUSINESS?
MAYBE I CAN FIND A PART-TIME EMPLOYEE.
ARE YOU TOO TIRED TO GO TO THE DANCE TONIGHT?
NO, I'VE BEEN LOOKING FORWARD TO IT.

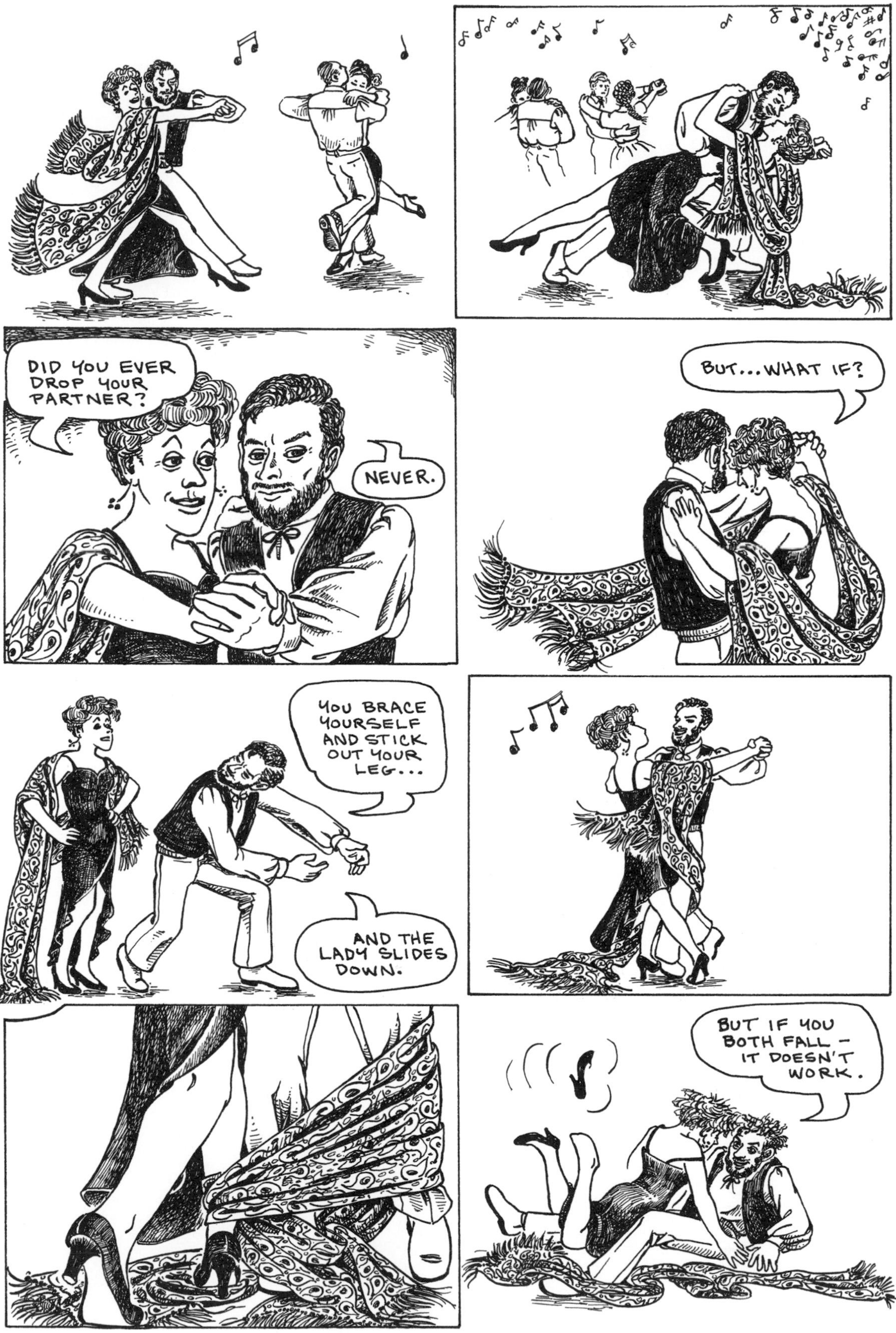
DID YOU EVER DROP YOUR PARTNER?
NEVER.
BUT... WHAT IF?
YOU BRACE YOURSELF AND STICK OUT YOUR LEG...
AND THE LADY SLIDES DOWN.
BUT IF YOU BOTH FALL – IT DOESN'T WORK.

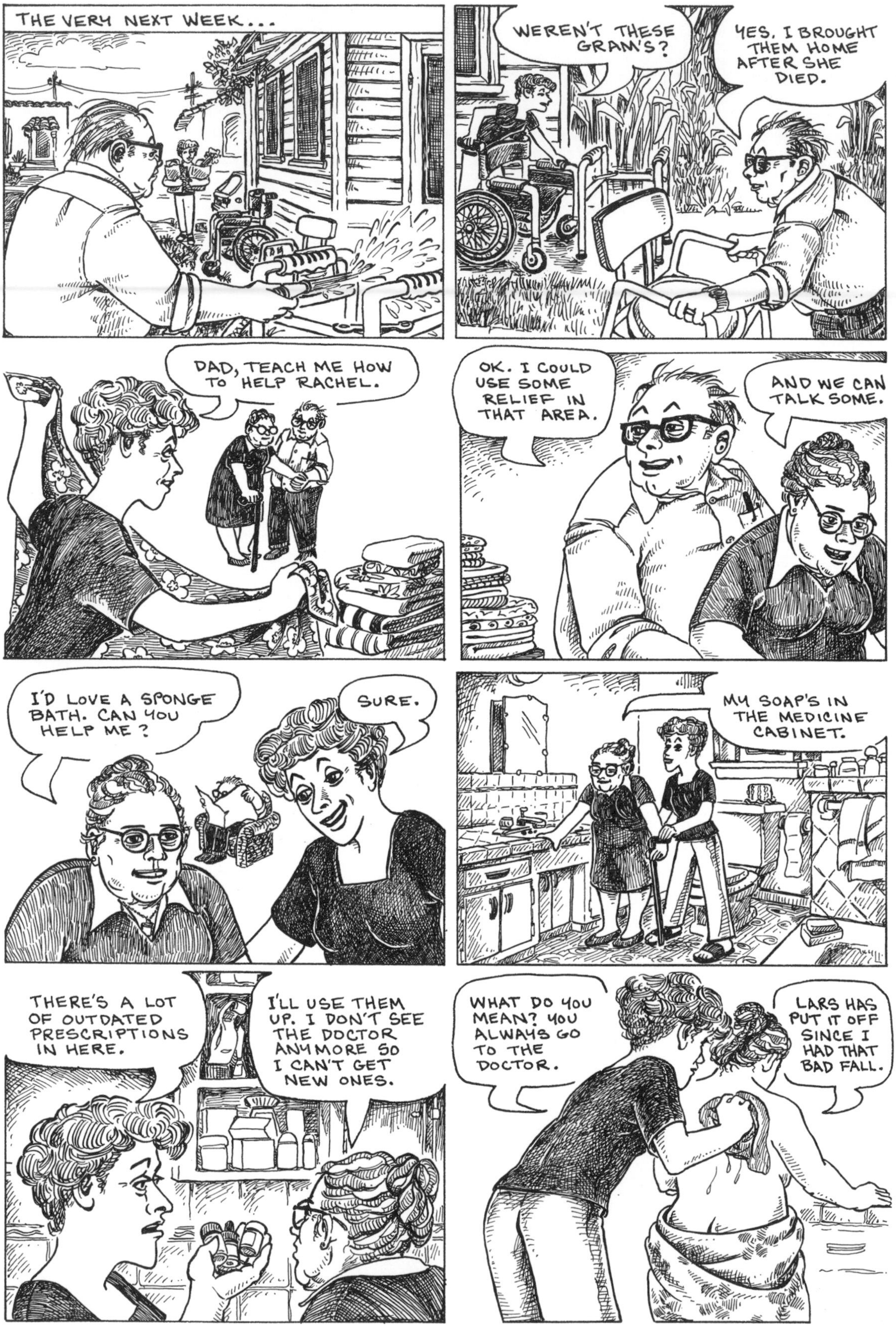
THE VERY NEXT WEEK...
WEREN'T THESE GRAM'S?
YES. I BROUGHT THEM HOME AFTER SHE DIED.
DAD, TEACH ME HOW TO HELP RACHEL.
OK. I COULD USE SOME RELIEF IN THAT AREA.
AND WE CAN TALK SOME.
I'D LOVE A SPONGE BATH. CAN YOU HELP ME?
SURE.
MY SOAP'S IN THE MEDICINE CABINET.
THERE'S A LOT OF OUTDATED PRESCRIPTIONS IN HERE.
I'LL USE THEM UP. I DON'T SEE THE DOCTOR ANYMORE SO I CAN'T GET NEW ONES.
WHAT DO YOU MEAN? YOU ALWAYS GO TO THE DOCTOR.
LARS HAS PUT IT OFF SINCE I HAD THAT BAD FALL.

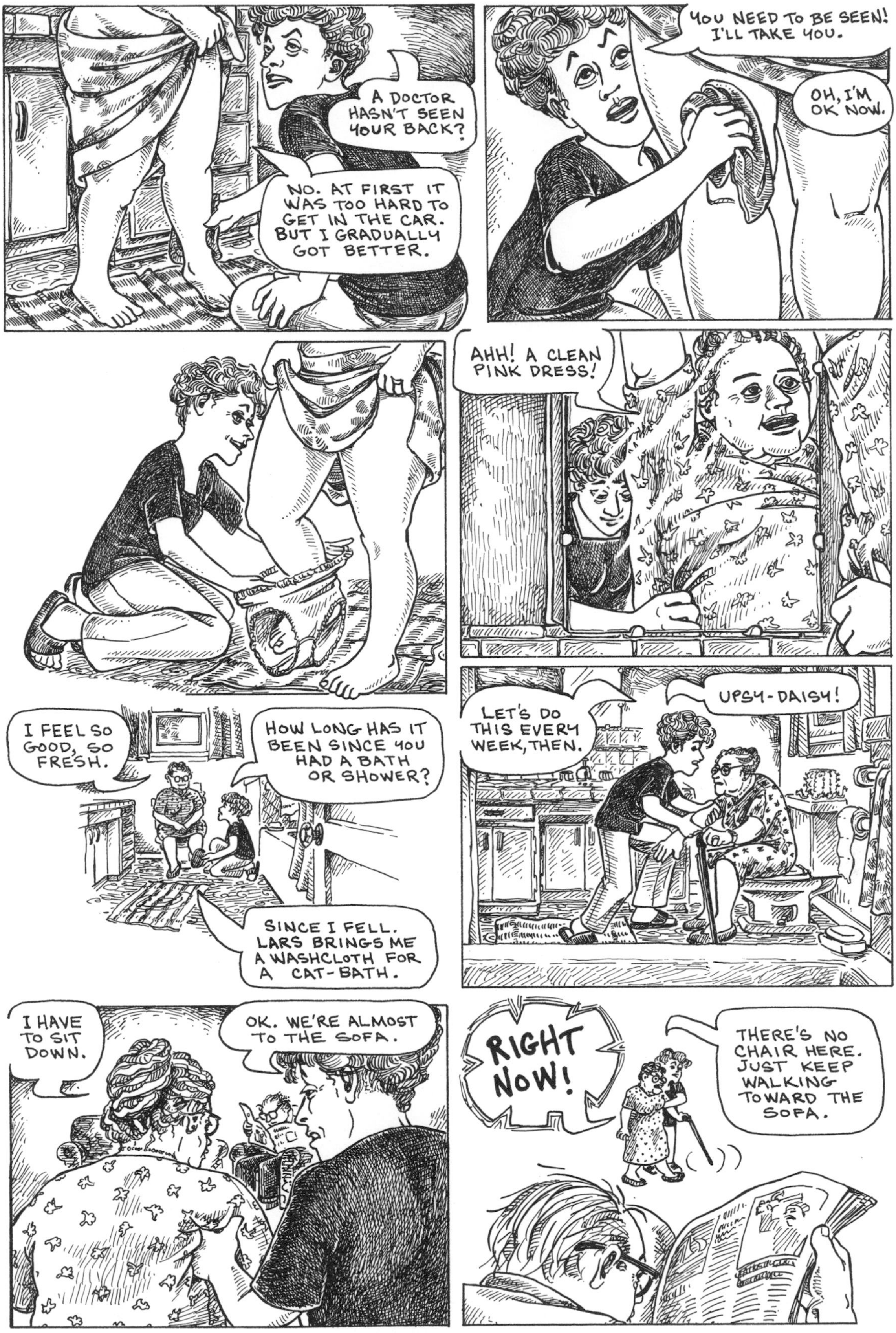
A DOCTOR HASN'T SEEN YOUR BACK?
NO. AT FIRST IT WAS TOO HARD TO GET IN THE CAR. BUT I GRADUALLY GOT BETTER.
YOU NEED TO BE SEEN! I'LL TAKE YOU.
OH, I'M OK NOW.
AHH! A CLEAN PINK DRESS!
I FEEL SO GOOD, SO FRESH.
HOW LONG HAS IT BEEN SINCE YOU HAD A BATH OR SHOWER?
SINCE I FELL. LARS BRINGS ME A WASHCLOTH FOR A CAT-BATH.
LET'S DO THIS EVERY WEEK, THEN.
UPSY-DAISY!
I HAVE TO SIT DOWN.
OK. WE'RE ALMOST TO THE SOFA.
RIGHT NOW!
THERE'S NO CHAIR HERE. JUST KEEP WALKING TOWARD THE SOFA.

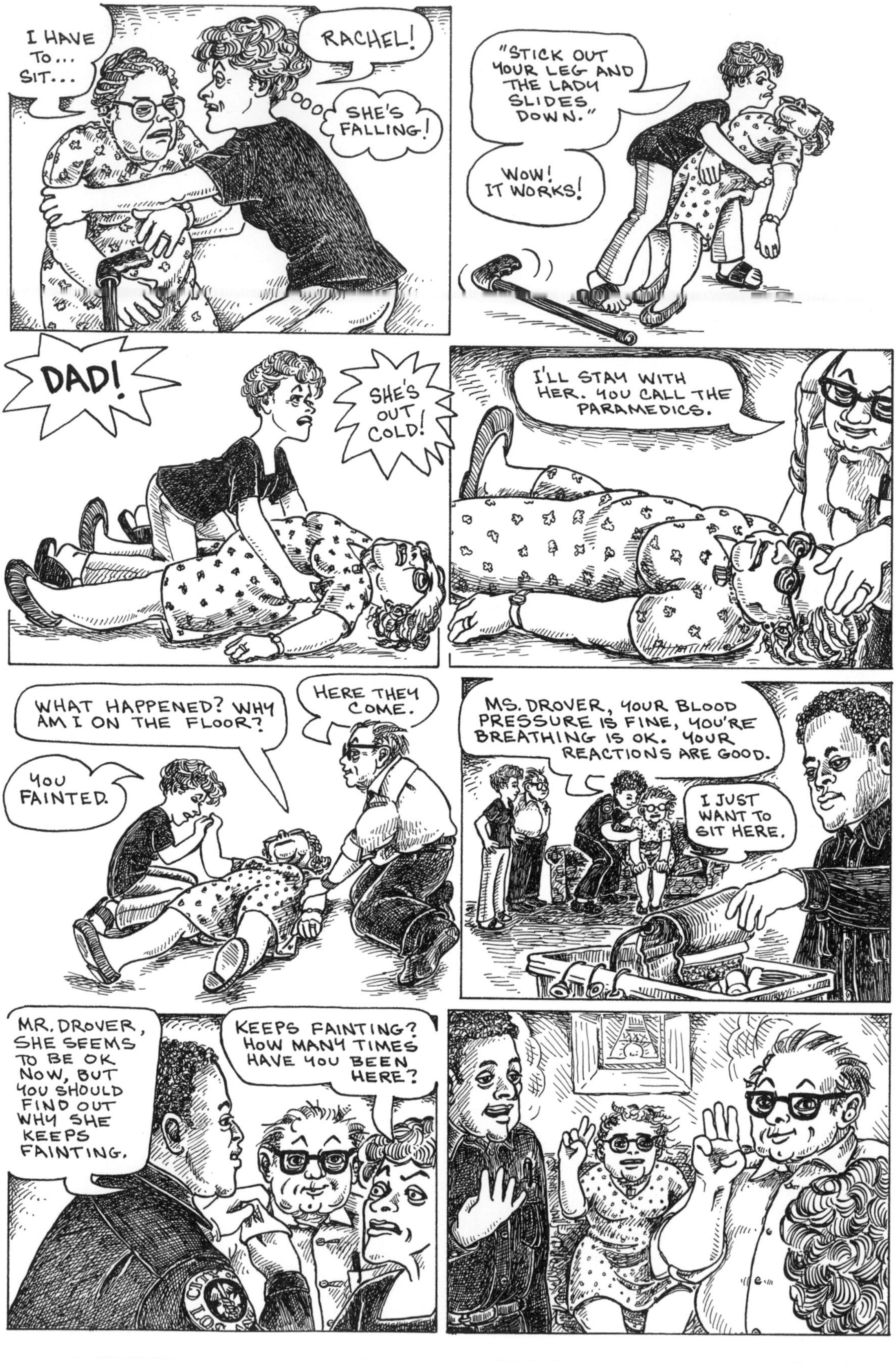
I HAVE TO... SIT...
RACHEL!
OOO SHE'S FALLING!
"STICK OUT YOUR LEG AND THE LADY SLIDES DOWN."
WOW! IT WORKS!
DAD!
SHE'S OUT COLD!
I'LL STAY WITH HER. YOU CALL THE PARAMEDICS.
WHAT HAPPENED? WHY AM I ON THE FLOOR?
YOU FAINTED.
HERE THEY COME.
MS. DROVER, YOUR BLOOD PRESSURE IS FINE, YOU'RE BREATHING IS OK. YOUR REACTIONS ARE GOOD.
I JUST WANT TO SIT HERE.
MR. DROVER, SHE SEEMS TO BE OK NOW, BUT YOU SHOULD FIND OUT WHY SHE KEEPS FAINTING.
KEEPS FAINTING? HOW MANY TIMES HAVE YOU BEEN HERE?

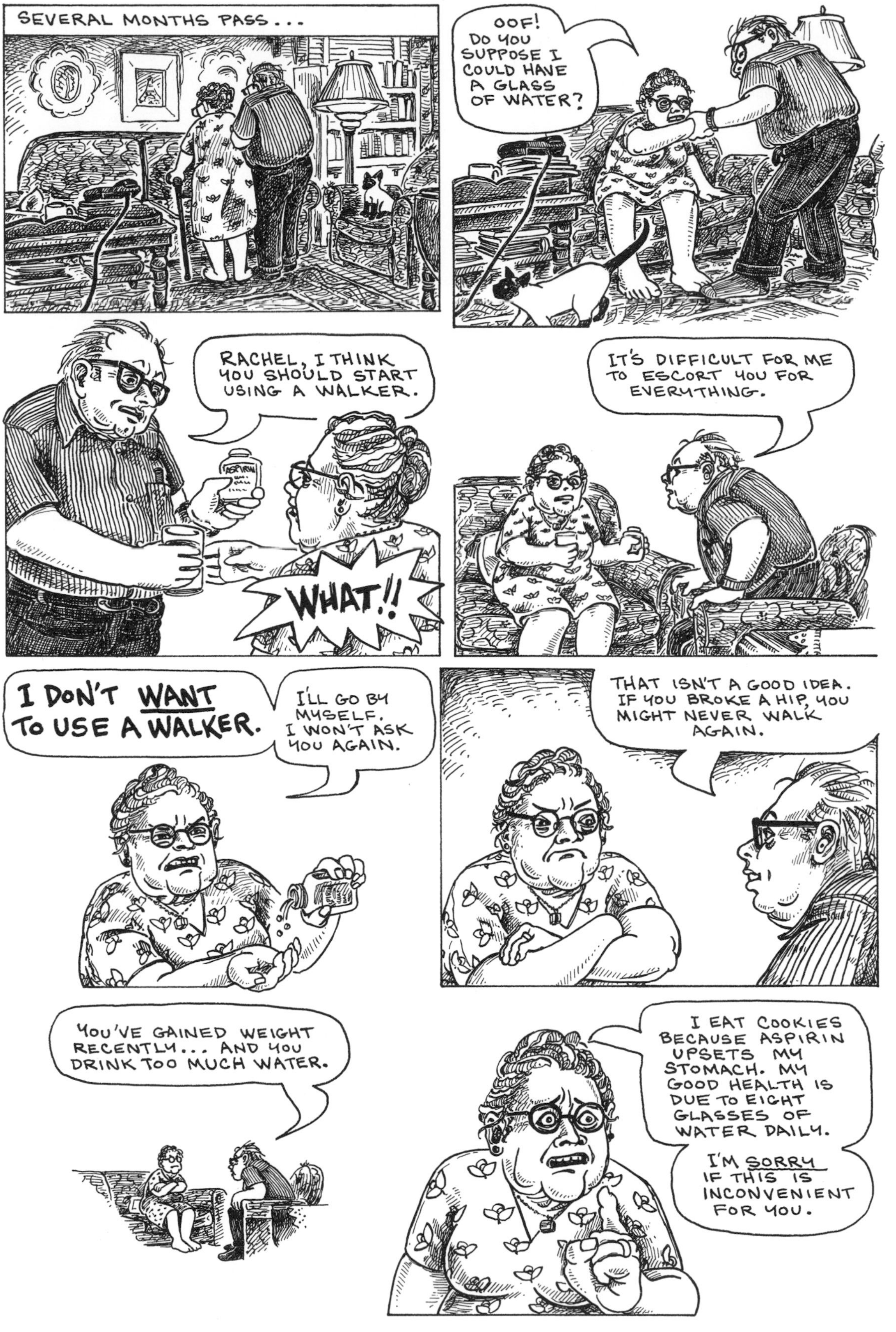
SEVERAL MONTHS PASS...
OOF! DO YOU SUPPOSE I COULD HAVE A GLASS OF WATER?
RACHEL, I THINK YOU SHOULD START USING A WALKER.
WHAT!!
IT'S DIFFICULT FOR ME TO ESCORT YOU FOR EVERYTHING.
I DON'T WANT TO USE A WALKER.
I'LL GO BY MYSELF. I WON'T ASK YOU AGAIN.
THAT ISN'T A GOOD IDEA. IF YOU BROKE A HIP, YOU MIGHT NEVER WALK AGAIN.
YOU'VE GAINED WEIGHT RECENTLY... AND YOU DRINK TOO MUCH WATER.
I EAT COOKIES BECAUSE ASPIRIN UPSETS MY STOMACH. MY GOOD HEALTH IS DUE TO EIGHT GLASSES OF WATER DAILY.
I'M SORRY IF THIS IS INCONVENIENT FOR YOU.

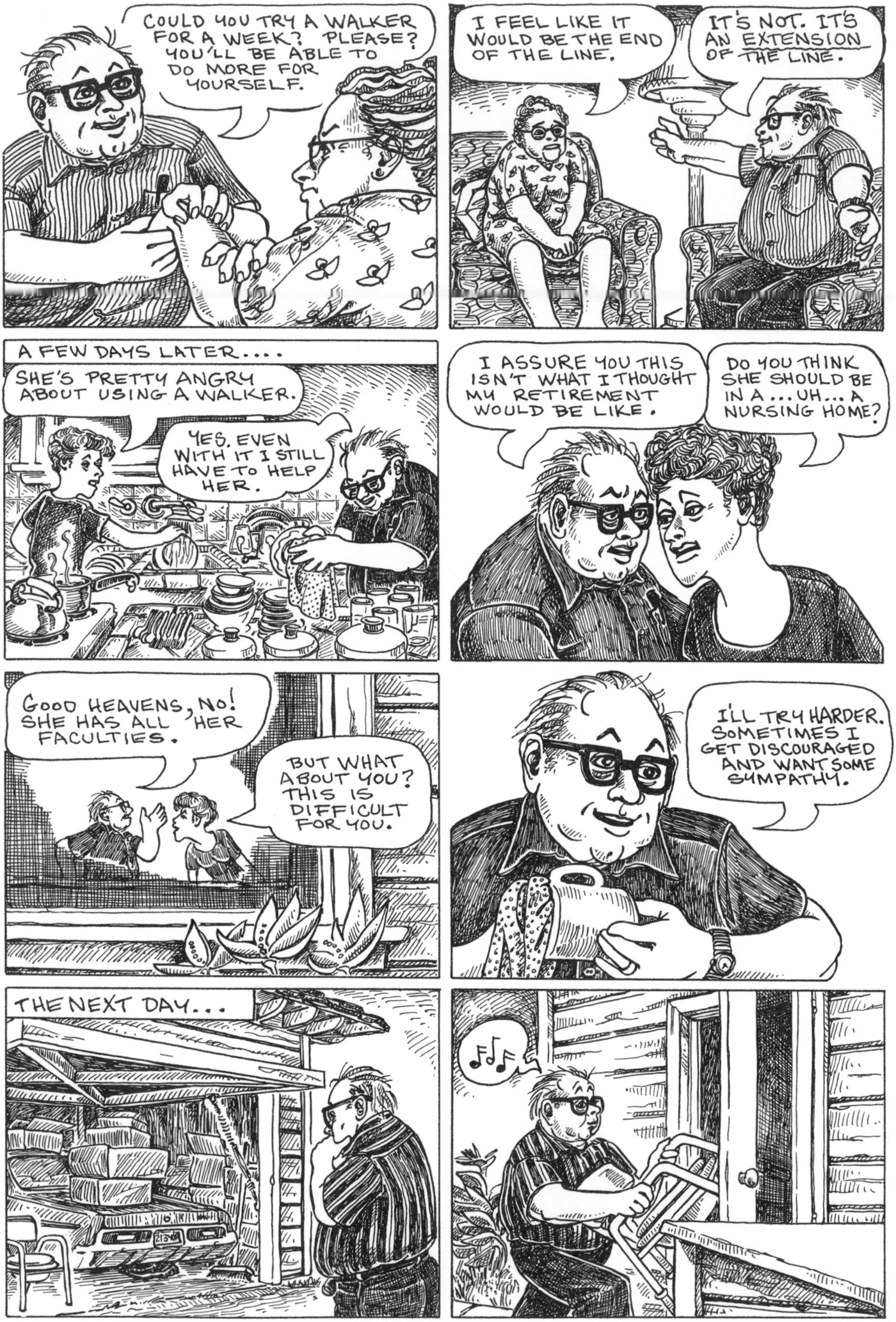
COULD YOU TRY A WALKER FOR A WEEK? PLEASE? YOU'LL BE ABLE TO DO MORE FOR YOURSELF.
I FEEL LIKE IT WOULD BE THE END OF THE LINE.
IT'S NOT. IT'S AN EXTENSION OF THE LINE.
A FEW DAYS LATER....
SHE'S PRETTY ANGRY ABOUT USING A WALKER.
YES. EVEN WITH IT I STILL HAVE TO HELP HER.
I ASSURE YOU THIS ISN'T WHAT I THOUGHT MY RETIREMENT WOULD BE LIKE.
DO YOU THINK SHE SHOULD BE IN A...UH...A NURSING HOME?
GOOD HEAVENS, NO! SHE HAS ALL HER FACULTIES.
BUT WHAT ABOUT YOU? THIS IS DIFFICULT FOR YOU.
I'LL TRY HARDER. SOMETIMES I GET DISCOURAGED AND WANT SOME SYMPATHY.
THE NEXT DAY...

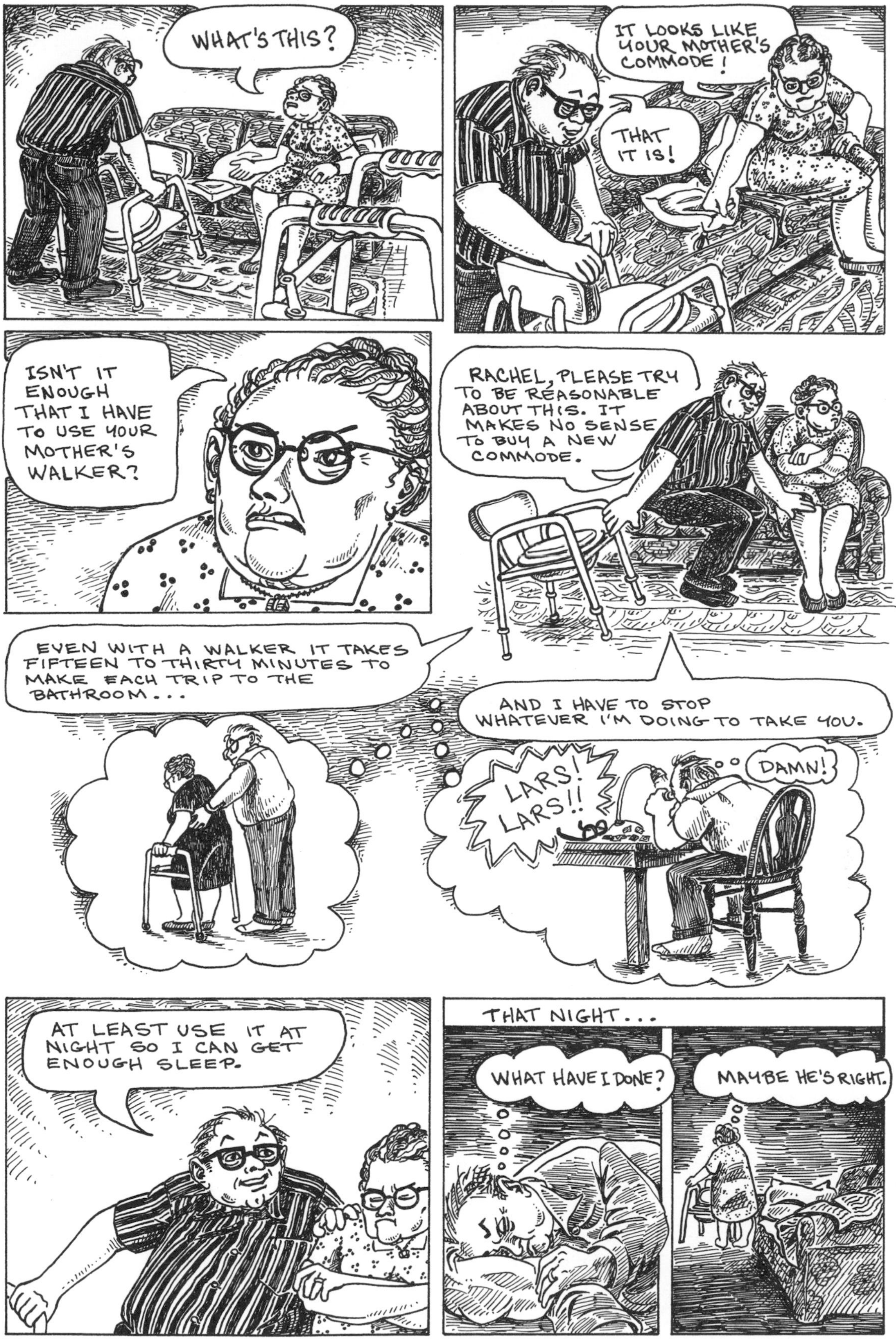

WHAT'S THIS?
IT LOOKS LIKE YOUR MOTHER'S COMMODE!
THAT IT IS!
ISN'T IT ENOUGH THAT I HAVE TO USE YOUR MOTHER'S WALKER?
RACHEL, PLEASE TRY TO BE REASONABLE ABOUT THIS. IT MAKES NO SENSE TO BUY A NEW COMMODE.
EVEN WITH A WALKER IT TAKES FIFTEEN TO THIRTY MINUTES TO MAKE EACH TRIP TO THE BATHROOM...
AND I HAVE TO STOP WHATEVER I'M DOING TO TAKE YOU.
LARS! LARS!!
DAMN!
AT LEAST USE IT AT NIGHT SO I CAN GET ENOUGH SLEEP.
THAT NIGHT...
WHAT HAVE I DONE?
MAYBE HE'S RIGHT.

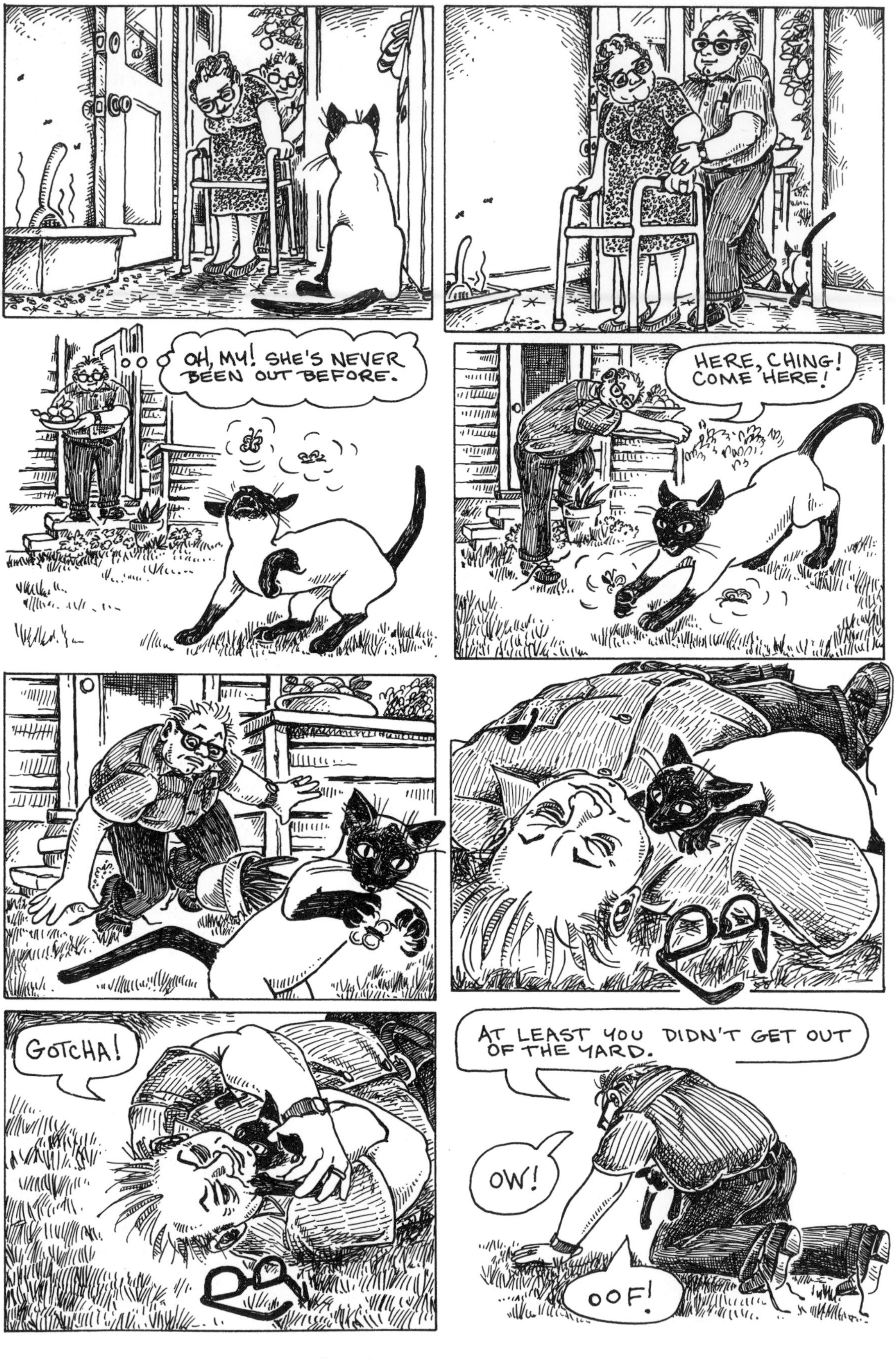
OH, MY! SHE'S NEVER BEEN OUT BEFORE.
HERE, CHING! COME HERE!
GOTCHA!
AT LEAST YOU DIDN'T GET OUT OF THE YARD.
OW!
OOF!

3

A FEW MONTHS LATER...

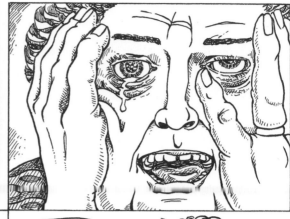

LARS!

HURRY, LARS!

BRING A BOWL! I'M SICK!

I HAVE A TERRIBLE HEADACHE AND MY EYE IS THROBBING.

CALM DOWN. THESE BAD HEADACHES NEVER LAST LONG. ASPIRIN? TUMS?

YES.

OH!

WHAT DID I DO?

YOU MISSED THE TABLE, THAT'S ALL.

WOULD YOU LIKE AN ICE BAG?

44

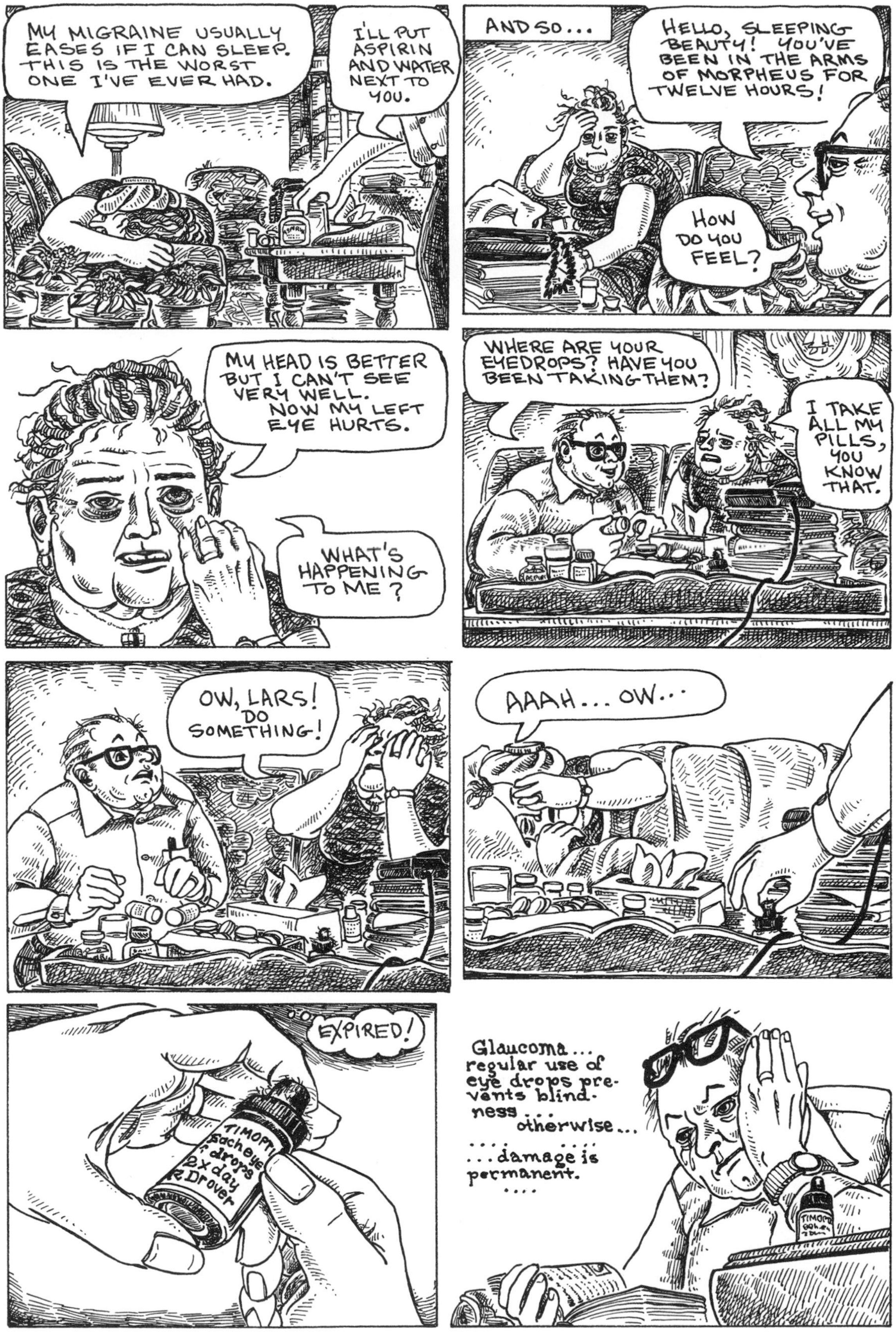
MY MIGRAINE USUALLY EASES IF I CAN SLEEP. THIS IS THE WORST ONE I'VE EVER HAD.
I'LL PUT ASPIRIN AND WATER NEXT TO YOU.
AND SO...
HELLO, SLEEPING BEAUTY! YOU'VE BEEN IN THE ARMS OF MORPHEUS FOR TWELVE HOURS!
HOW DO YOU FEEL?
MY HEAD IS BETTER BUT I CAN'T SEE VERY WELL. NOW MY LEFT EYE HURTS.
WHAT'S HAPPENING TO ME?
WHERE ARE YOUR EYEDROPS? HAVE YOU BEEN TAKING THEM?
I TAKE ALL MY PILLS, YOU KNOW THAT.
OW, LARS! DO SOMETHING!
AAAH... OW...
EXPIRED!
TIMOPTI
Each eye
drops
2x day
R.Drover
Glaucoma... regular use of eye drops prevents blindness... otherwise...
....damage is permanent.
....

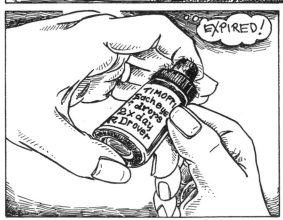

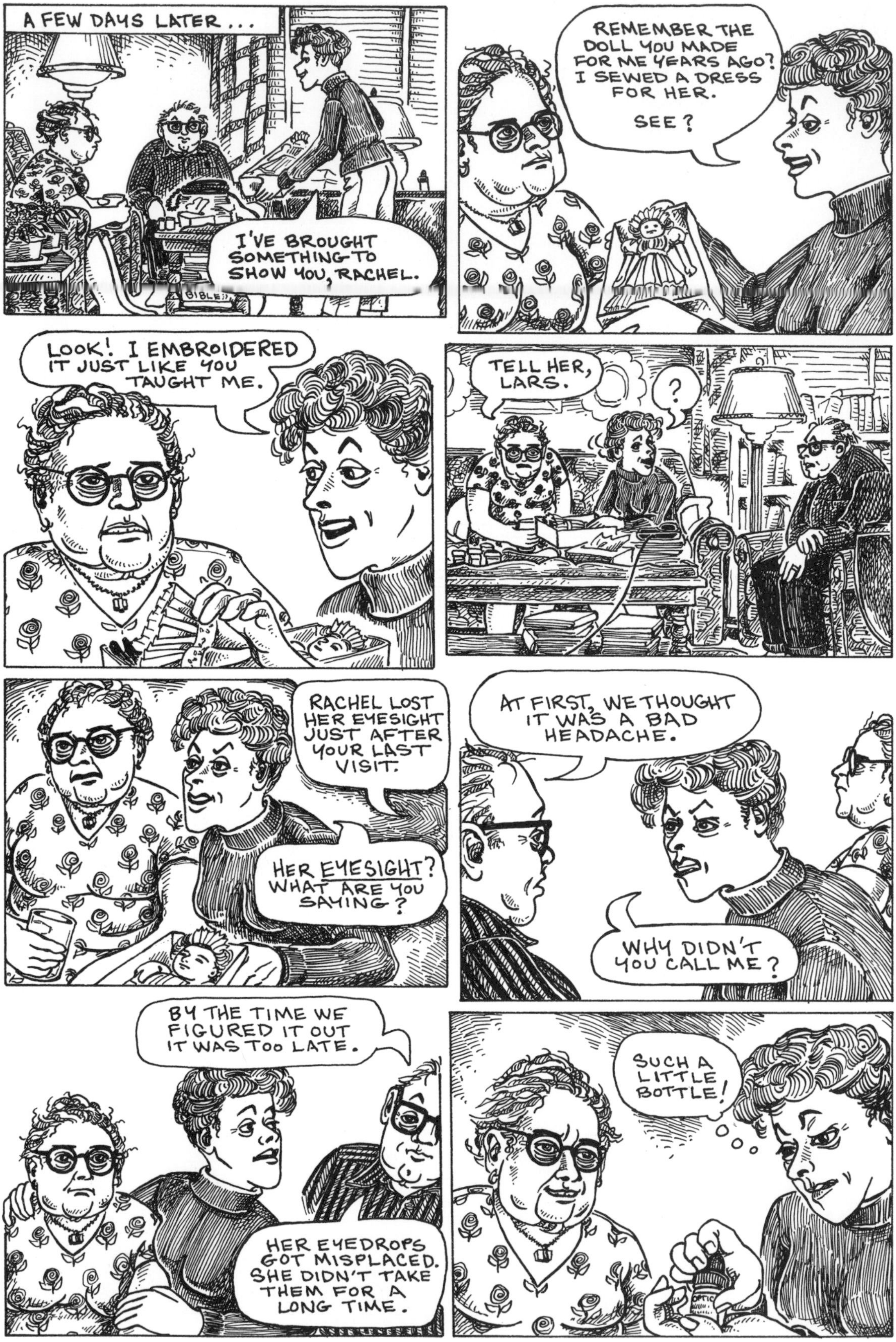
A FEW DAYS LATER...
I'VE BROUGHT SOMETHING TO SHOW YOU, RACHEL.
BIBLE
REMEMBER THE DOLL YOU MADE FOR ME YEARS AGO? I SEWED A DRESS FOR HER.
SEE?
LOOK! I EMBROIDERED IT JUST LIKE YOU TAUGHT ME.
TELL HER, LARS.
?
RACHEL LOST HER EYESIGHT JUST AFTER YOUR LAST VISIT.
HER EYESIGHT? WHAT ARE YOU SAYING?
AT FIRST, WE THOUGHT IT WAS A BAD HEADACHE.
WHY DIDN'T YOU CALL ME?
BY THE TIME WE FIGURED IT OUT IT WAS TOO LATE.
HER EYEDROPS GOT MISPLACED. SHE DIDN'T TAKE THEM FOR A LONG TIME.
SUCH A LITTLE BOTTLE!

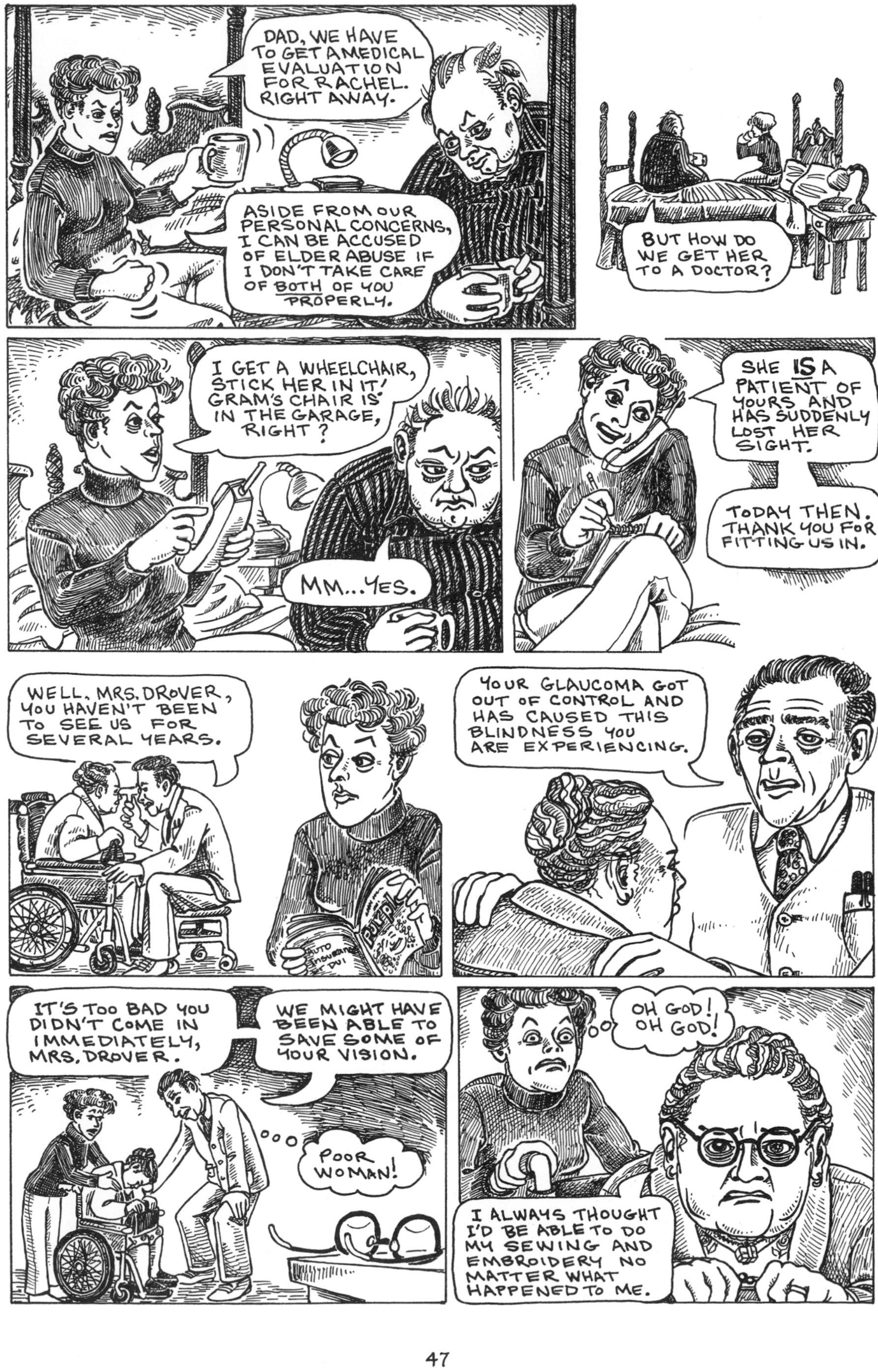
DAD, WE HAVE TO GET A MEDICAL EVALUATION FOR RACHEL. RIGHT AWAY.
ASIDE FROM OUR PERSONAL CONCERNS, I CAN BE ACCUSED OF ELDER ABUSE IF I DON'T TAKE CARE OF BOTH OF YOU PROPERLY.
BUT HOW DO WE GET HER TO A DOCTOR?
I GET A WHEELCHAIR, STICK HER IN IT! GRAM'S CHAIR IS IN THE GARAGE, RIGHT?
MM...YES.
SHE IS A PATIENT OF YOURS AND HAS SUDDENLY LOST HER SIGHT.
TODAY THEN. THANK YOU FOR FITTING US IN.
WELL, MRS. DROVER, YOU HAVEN'T BEEN TO SEE US FOR SEVERAL YEARS.
YOUR GLAUCOMA GOT OUT OF CONTROL AND HAS CAUSED THIS BLINDNESS YOU ARE EXPERIENCING.
IT'S TOO BAD YOU DIDN'T COME IN IMMEDIATELY, MRS. DROVER.
WE MIGHT HAVE BEEN ABLE TO SAVE SOME OF YOUR VISION.
POOR WOMAN!
OH GOD! OH GOD!
I ALWAYS THOUGHT I'D BE ABLE TO DO MY SEWING AND EMBROIDERY NO MATTER WHAT HAPPENED TO ME.

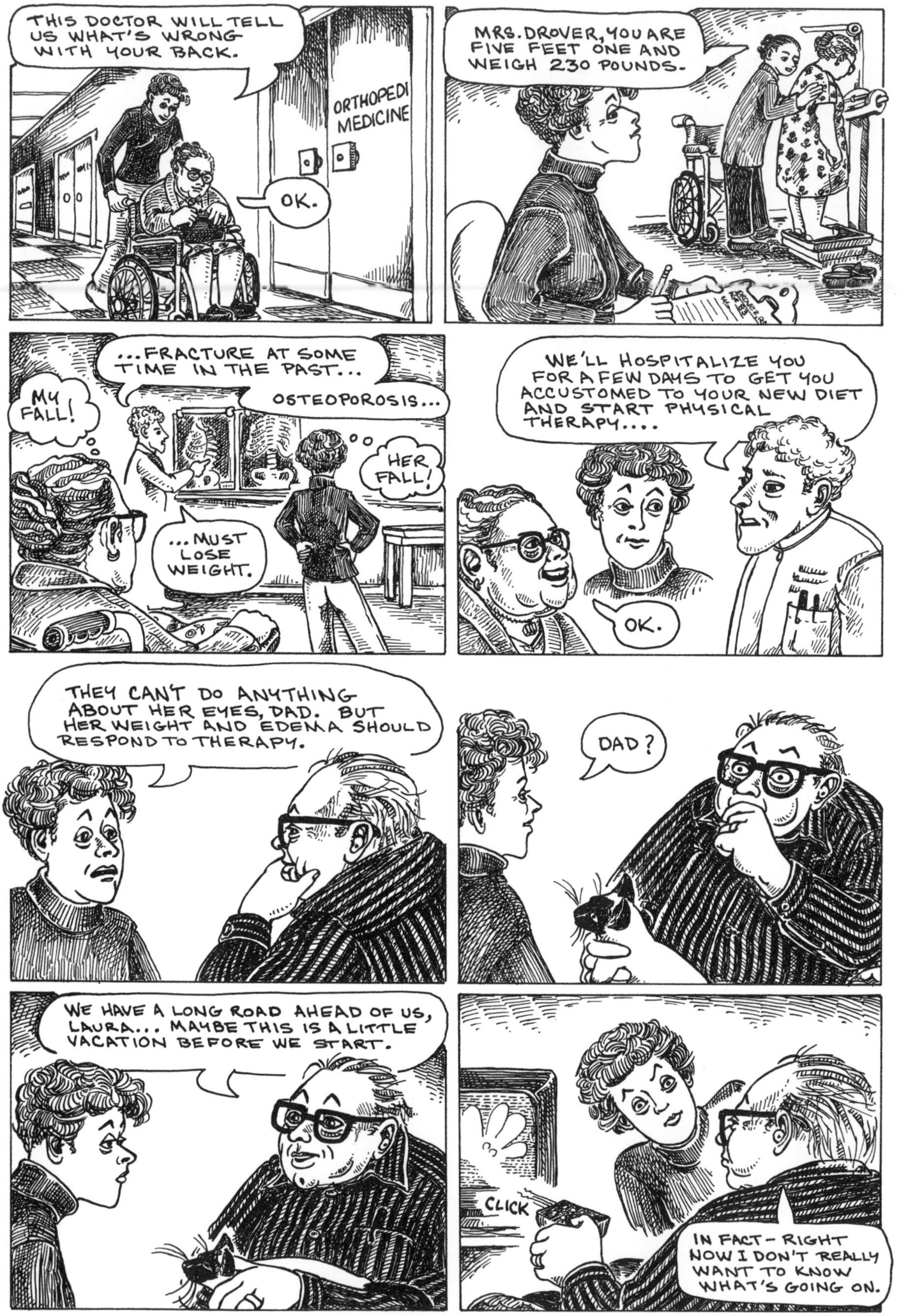
THIS DOCTOR WILL TELL US WHAT'S WRONG WITH YOUR BACK.
ORTHOPEDI MEDICINE
OK.
MRS. DROVER, YOU ARE FIVE FEET ONE AND WEIGH 230 POUNDS.
...FRACTURE AT SOME TIME IN THE PAST...
MY FALL!
OSTEOPOROSIS...
HER FALL!
...MUST LOSE WEIGHT.
WE'LL HOSPITALIZE YOU FOR A FEW DAYS TO GET YOU ACCUSTOMED TO YOUR NEW DIET AND START PHYSICAL THERAPY....
OK.
THEY CAN'T DO ANYTHING ABOUT HER EYES, DAD. BUT HER WEIGHT AND EDEMA SHOULD RESPOND TO THERAPY.
DAD?
WE HAVE A LONG ROAD AHEAD OF US, LAURA... MAYBE THIS IS A LITTLE VACATION BEFORE WE START.
CLICK
IN FACT - RIGHT NOW I DON'T REALLY WANT TO KNOW WHAT'S GOING ON.

4

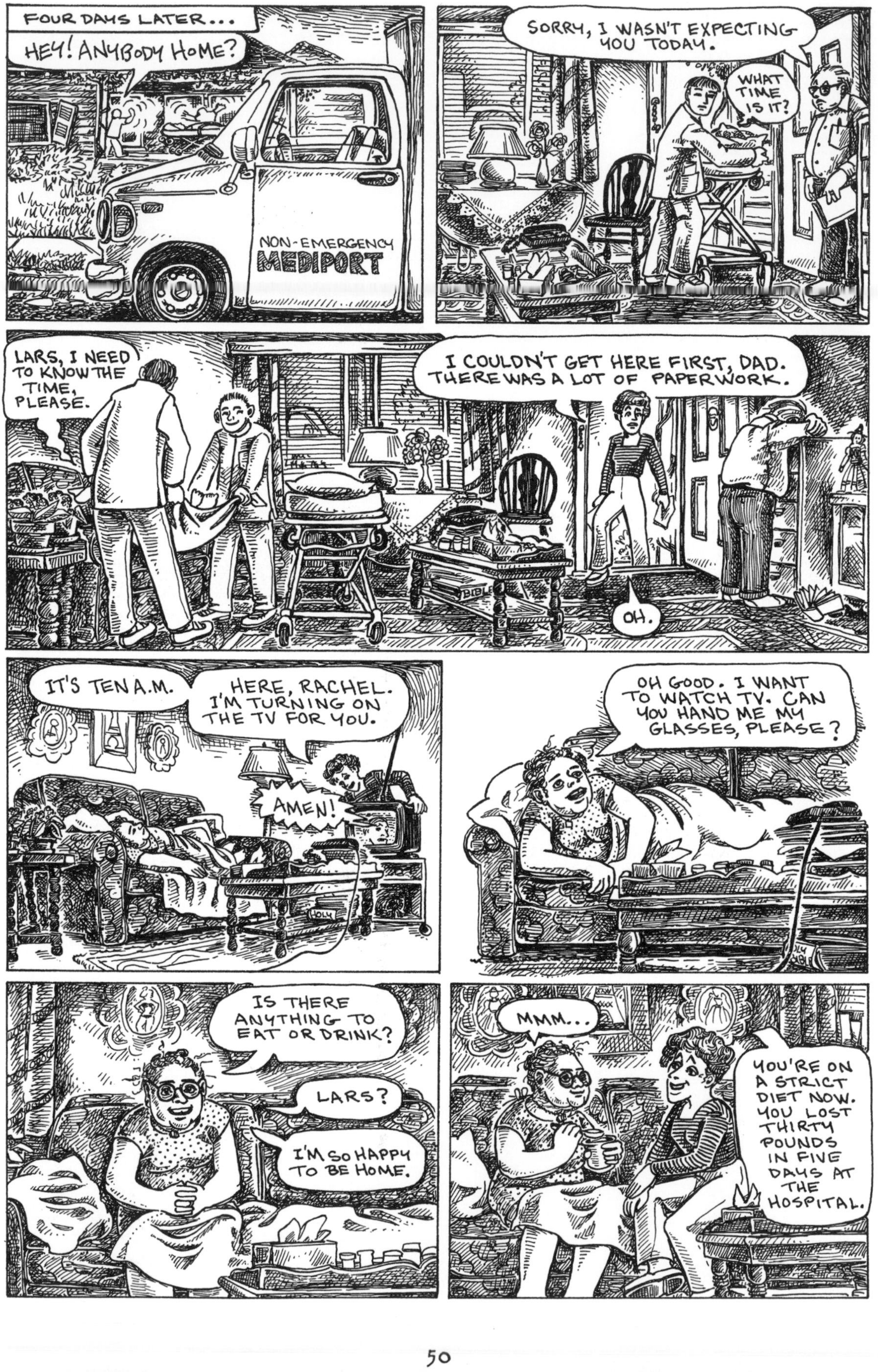
FOUR DAYS LATER...
HEY! ANYBODY HOME?
NON-EMERGENCY
MEDIPORT
SORRY, I WASN'T EXPECTING YOU TODAY.
WHAT TIME IS IT?
LARS, I NEED TO KNOW THE TIME, PLEASE.
I COULDN'T GET HERE FIRST, DAD. THERE WAS A LOT OF PAPERWORK.
OH.
BIBLE
IT'S TEN A.M.
HERE, RACHEL. I'M TURNING ON THE TV FOR YOU.
AMEN!
HOLY
OH GOOD. I WANT TO WATCH TV. CAN YOU HAND ME MY GLASSES, PLEASE?
IS THERE ANYTHING TO EAT OR DRINK?
LARS?
I'M SO HAPPY TO BE HOME.
MMM...
YOU'RE ON A STRICT DIET NOW. YOU LOST THIRTY POUNDS IN FIVE DAYS AT THE HOSPITAL.

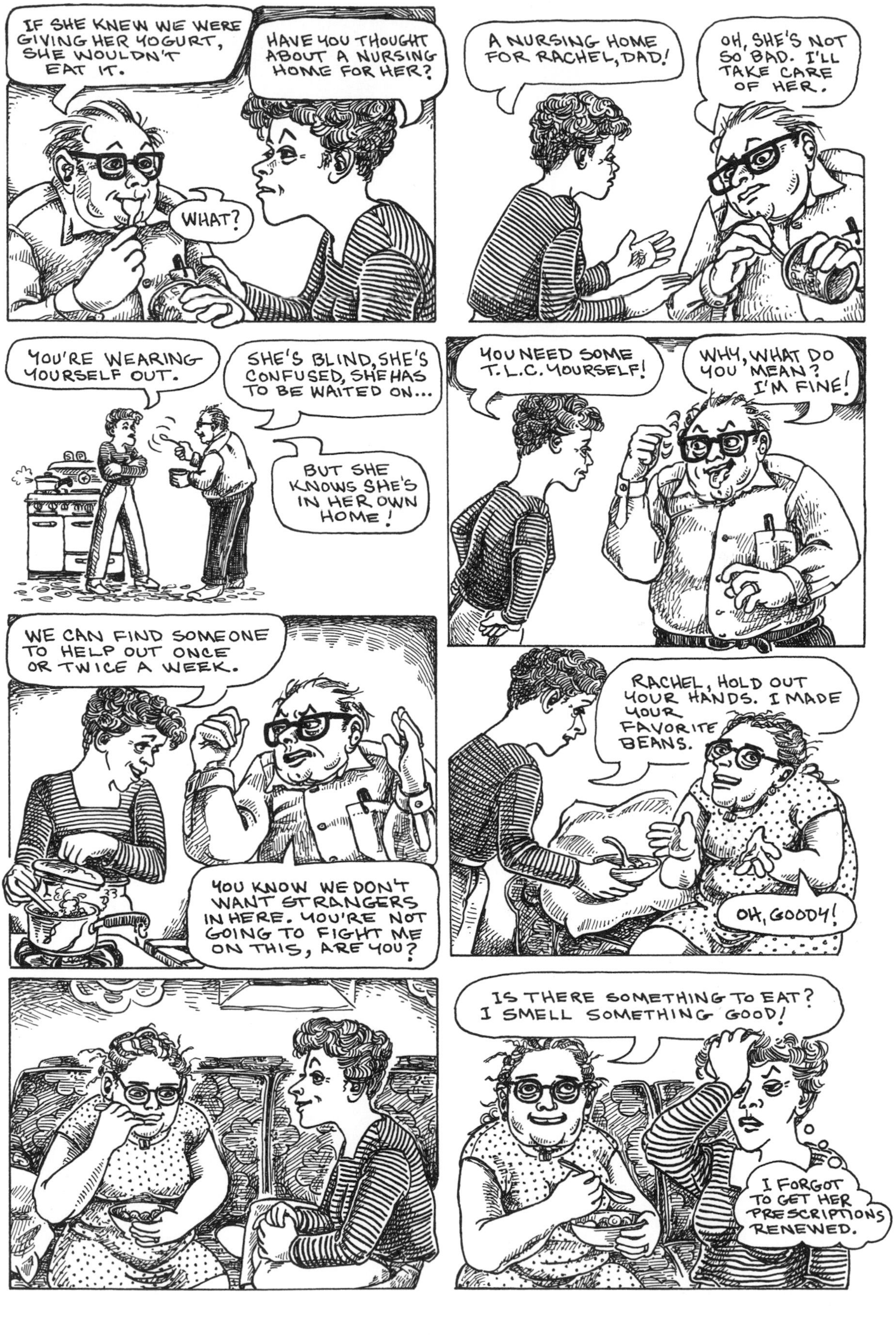
IF SHE KNEW WE WERE GIVING HER YOGURT, SHE WOULDN'T EAT IT.
HAVE YOU THOUGHT ABOUT A NURSING HOME FOR HER?
WHAT?
A NURSING HOME FOR RACHEL, DAD!
OH, SHE'S NOT SO BAD. I'LL TAKE CARE OF HER.
YOU'RE WEARING YOURSELF OUT.
SHE'S BLIND, SHE'S CONFUSED, SHE HAS TO BE WAITED ON...
BUT SHE KNOWS SHE'S IN HER OWN HOME!
YOU NEED SOME T.L.C. YOURSELF!
WHY, WHAT DO YOU MEAN? I'M FINE!
WE CAN FIND SOMEONE TO HELP OUT ONCE OR TWICE A WEEK.
YOU KNOW WE DON'T WANT STRANGERS IN HERE. YOU'RE NOT GOING TO FIGHT ME ON THIS, ARE YOU?
RACHEL, HOLD OUT YOUR HANDS. I MADE YOUR FAVORITE BEANS.
OH, GOODY!
IS THERE SOMETHING TO EAT? I SMELL SOMETHING GOOD!
I FORGOT TO GET HER PRESCRIPTIONS RENEWED.

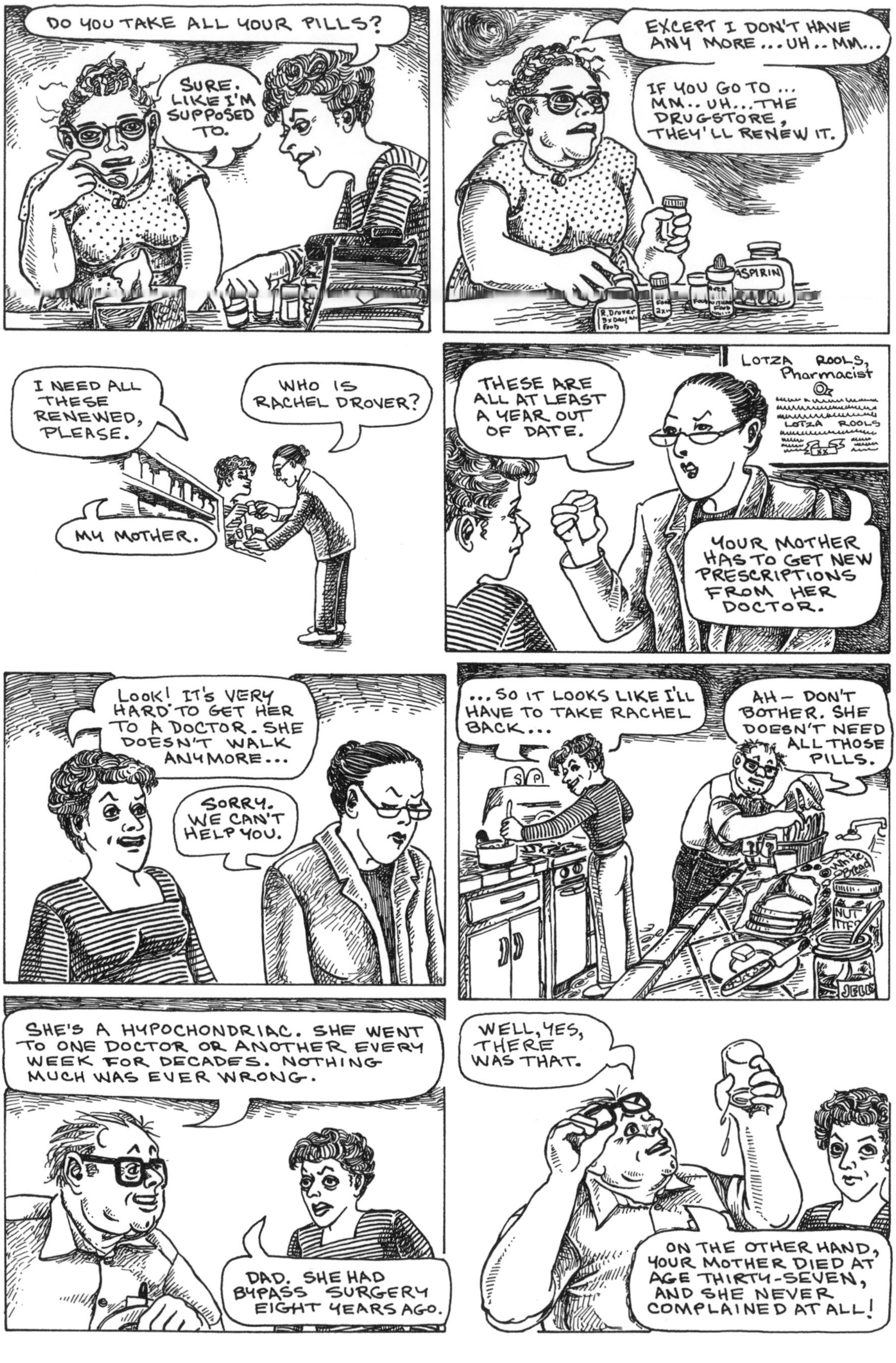
DO YOU TAKE ALL YOUR PILLS?
SURE. LIKE I'M SUPPOSED TO.
EXCEPT I DON'T HAVE ANY MORE... UH.. MM...
IF YOU GO TO ... MM.. UH... THE DRUGSTORE, THEY'LL RENEW IT.
ASPIRIN
R. Drover
I NEED ALL THESE RENEWED, PLEASE.
WHO IS RACHEL DROVER?
MY MOTHER.
LOTZA ROOLS, Pharmacist
LOTZA ROOLS
THESE ARE ALL AT LEAST A YEAR OUT OF DATE.
YOUR MOTHER HAS TO GET NEW PRESCRIPTIONS FROM HER DOCTOR.
LOOK! IT'S VERY HARD TO GET HER TO A DOCTOR. SHE DOESN'T WALK ANYMORE...
SORRY. WE CAN'T HELP YOU.
...SO IT LOOKS LIKE I'LL HAVE TO TAKE RACHEL BACK...
AH- DON'T BOTHER. SHE DOESN'T NEED ALL THOSE PILLS.
S P
White Bread
NUT
JELL
SHE'S A HYPOCHONDRIAC. SHE WENT TO ONE DOCTOR OR ANOTHER EVERY WEEK FOR DECADES. NOTHING MUCH WAS EVER WRONG.
DAD. SHE HAD BYPASS SURGERY EIGHT YEARS AGO.
WELL, YES, THERE WAS THAT.
ON THE OTHER HAND, YOUR MOTHER DIED AT AGE THIRTY-SEVEN, AND SHE NEVER COMPLAINED AT ALL!

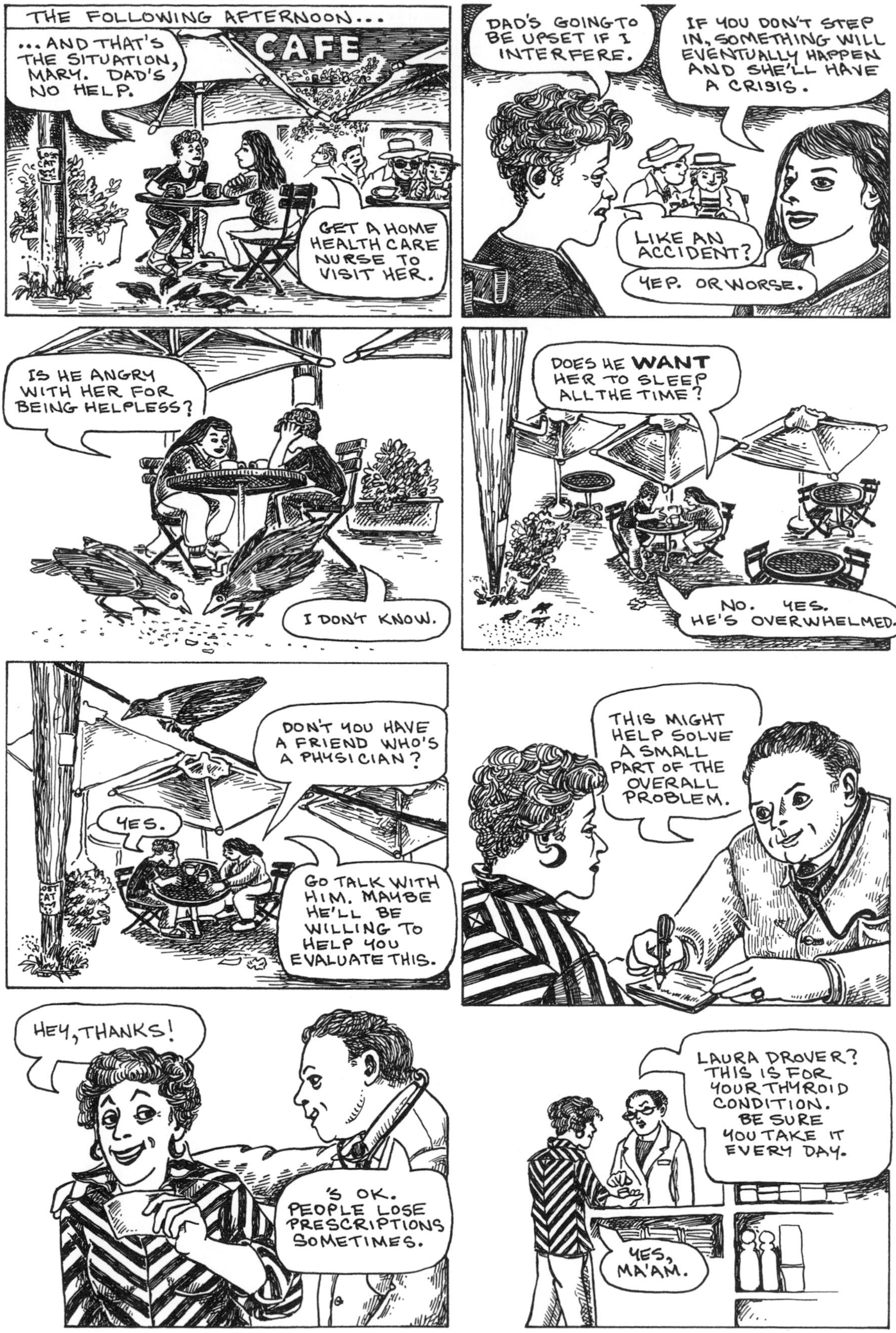
THE FOLLOWING AFTERNOON...
...AND THAT'S THE SITUATION, MARY. DAD'S NO HELP.
CAFE
GET A HOME HEALTH CARE NURSE TO VISIT HER.
DAD'S GOING TO BE UPSET IF I INTERFERE.
IF YOU DON'T STEP IN, SOMETHING WILL EVENTUALLY HAPPEN AND SHE'LL HAVE A CRISIS.
LIKE AN ACCIDENT?
YEP. OR WORSE.
IS HE ANGRY WITH HER FOR BEING HELPLESS?
I DON'T KNOW.
DOES HE WANT HER TO SLEEP ALL THE TIME?
NO. YES. HE'S OVERWHELMED.
DON'T YOU HAVE A FRIEND WHO'S A PHYSICIAN?
YES.
GO TALK WITH HIM. MAYBE HE'LL BE WILLING TO HELP YOU EVALUATE THIS.
THIS MIGHT HELP SOLVE A SMALL PART OF THE OVERALL PROBLEM.
HEY, THANKS!
'S OK. PEOPLE LOSE PRESCRIPTIONS SOMETIMES.
LAURA DROVER? THIS IS FOR YOUR THYROID CONDITION. BE SURE YOU TAKE IT EVERY DAY.
YES, MA'AM.

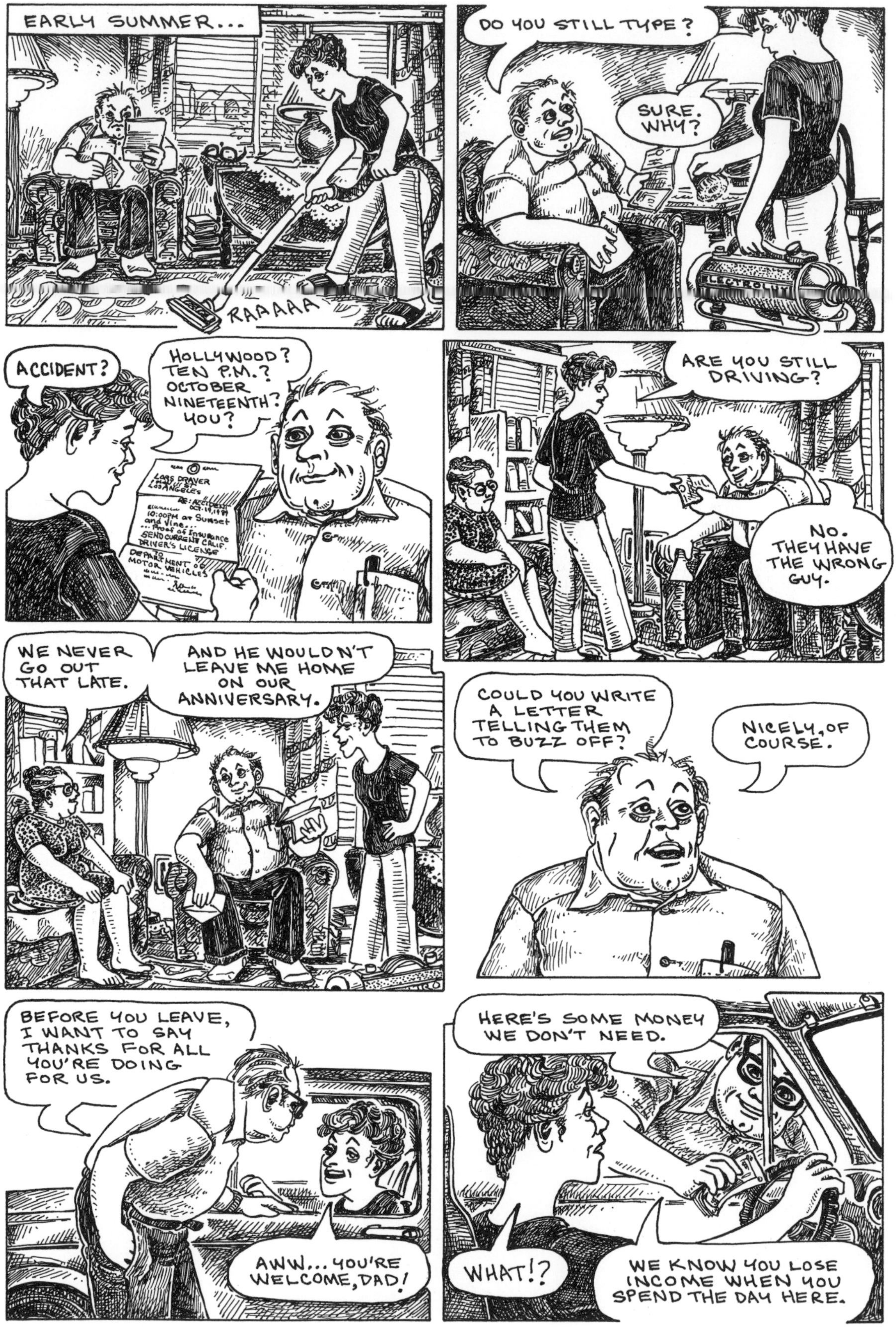
EARLY SUMMER...
RAAAAA
DO YOU STILL TYPE?
SURE. WHY?
ACCIDENT?
HOLLYWOOD? TEN P.M.? OCTOBER NINETEENTH? YOU?
ARE YOU STILL DRIVING?
NO. THEY HAVE THE WRONG GUY.
WE NEVER GO OUT THAT LATE.
AND HE WOULDN'T LEAVE ME HOME ON OUR ANNIVERSARY.
COULD YOU WRITE A LETTER TELLING THEM TO BUZZ OFF?
NICELY, OF COURSE.
BEFORE YOU LEAVE, I WANT TO SAY THANKS FOR ALL YOU'RE DOING FOR US.
AWW... YOU'RE WELCOME, DAD!
HERE'S SOME MONEY WE DON'T NEED.
WHAT!?
WE KNOW YOU LOSE INCOME WHEN YOU SPEND THE DAY HERE.

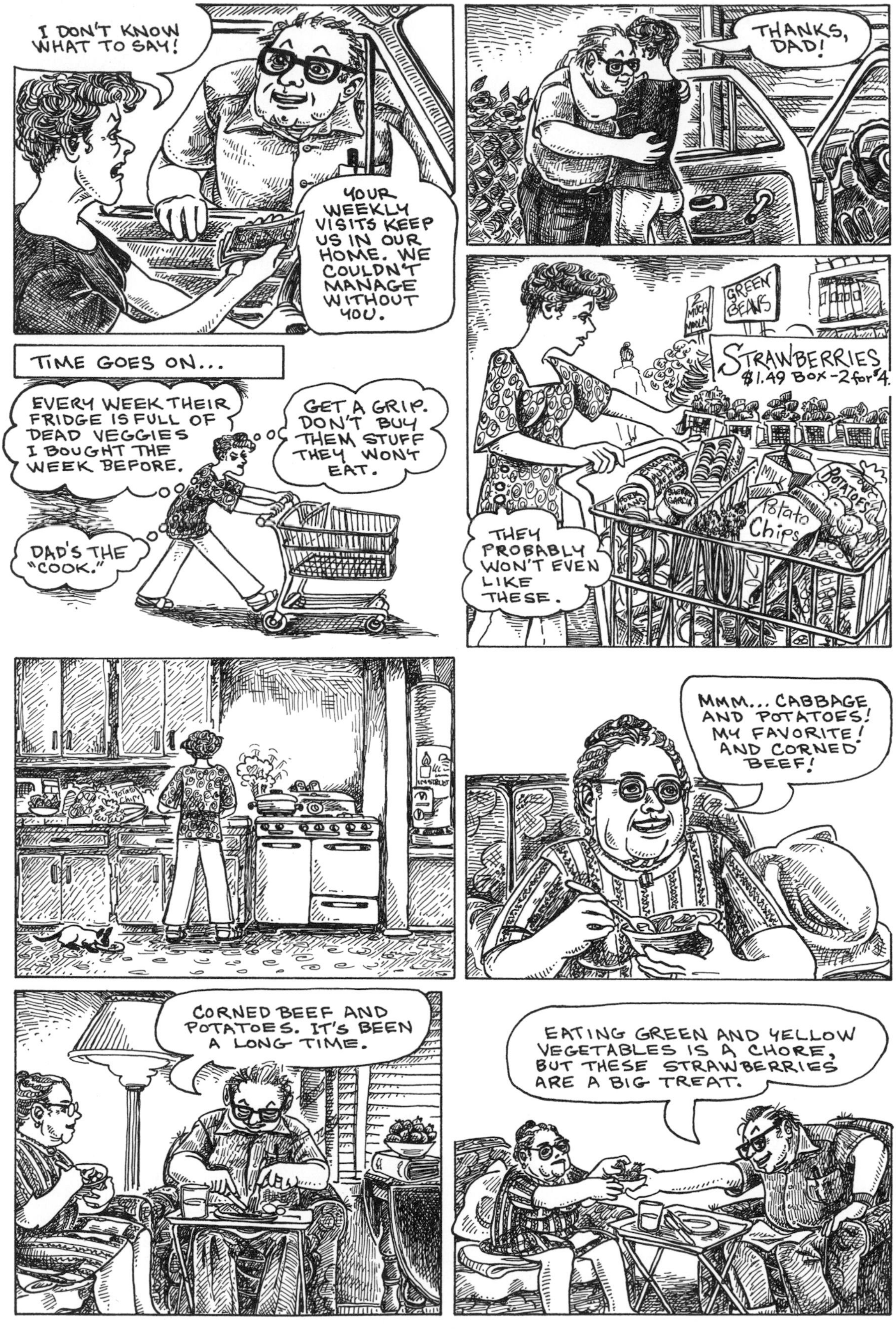
I DON'T KNOW WHAT TO SAY!
YOUR WEEKLY VISITS KEEP US IN OUR HOME. WE COULDN'T MANAGE WITHOUT YOU.
THANKS, DAD!
TIME GOES ON...
EVERY WEEK THEIR FRIDGE IS FULL OF DEAD VEGGIES I BOUGHT THE WEEK BEFORE.
GET A GRIP. DON'T BUY THEM STUFF THEY WON'T EAT.
DAD'S THE "COOK."
2 MUCH MOOLA
GREEN BEANS
STRAWBERRIES $1.49 Box - 2 for $4.
MILK
POTATOES
Potato Chips
THEY PROBABLY WON'T EVEN LIKE THESE.
MMM... CABBAGE AND POTATOES! MY FAVORITE! AND CORNED BEEF!
CORNED BEEF AND POTATOES. IT'S BEEN A LONG TIME.
EATING GREEN AND YELLOW VEGETABLES IS A CHORE, BUT THESE STRAWBERRIES ARE A BIG TREAT.

A MONTH LATER...

RACHEL STILL SEEMS TO BE SLEEPING A LOT. MAYBE THE THYROID PILLS AREN'T WORKING.

I GAVE THEM TO HER FOR A WEEK BUT I DIDN'T SEE ANY IMPROVEMENT, SO I STOPPED.

SHE NEEDS THEM FOR AT LEAST A MONTH TO SHOW A DIFFERENCE.

OUR PRESCRIPTIONS HAPPEN TO BE THE SAME. I **HAVE** TO HAVE MINE, OTHERWISE I'M NOT MENTALLY ALERT.

WELLLL, OK. IF YOU'RE SURE.

AND THIS MULTIVITAMIN. EVERY DAY!

YOU SHOULD TAKE THEM TOO, YOU KNOW.

AH, I GET WHAT I NEED FROM MY FOOD. I'M OK.

TWO DAYS LATER...

HERE, RACHEL. IT'S TIME TO TURN BACK THE CLOCK.

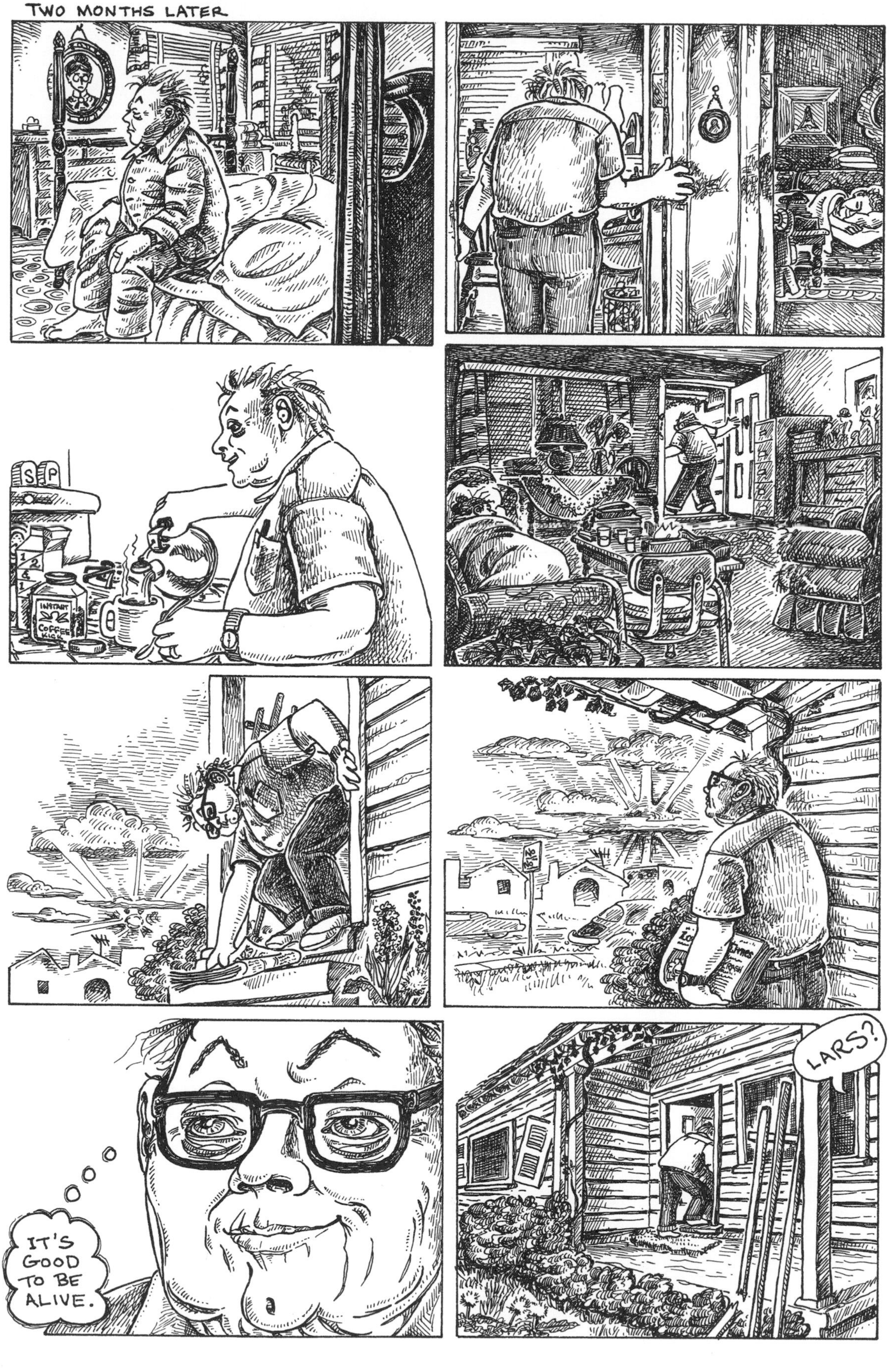
TWO MONTHS LATER
IT'S GOOD TO BE ALIVE.
LARS?

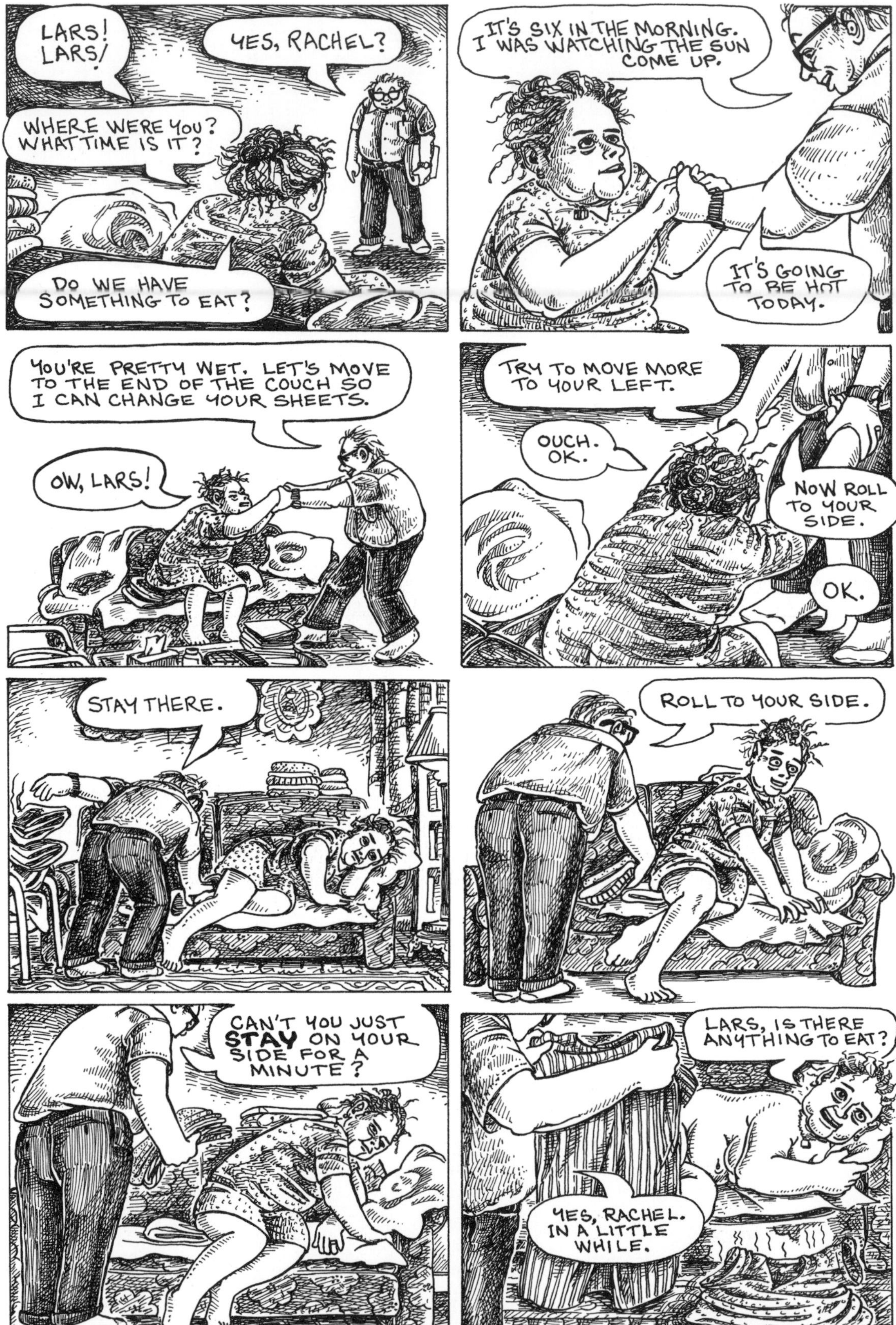
LARS! LARS!
YES, RACHEL?
WHERE WERE YOU? WHAT TIME IS IT?
DO WE HAVE SOMETHING TO EAT?
IT'S SIX IN THE MORNING. I WAS WATCHING THE SUN COME UP.
IT'S GOING TO BE HOT TODAY.
YOU'RE PRETTY WET. LET'S MOVE TO THE END OF THE COUCH SO I CAN CHANGE YOUR SHEETS.
OW, LARS!
TRY TO MOVE MORE TO YOUR LEFT.
OUCH. OK.
NOW ROLL TO YOUR SIDE.
OK.
STAY THERE.
ROLL TO YOUR SIDE.
CAN'T YOU JUST STAY ON YOUR SIDE FOR A MINUTE?
LARS, IS THERE ANYTHING TO EAT?
YES, RACHEL. IN A LITTLE WHILE.

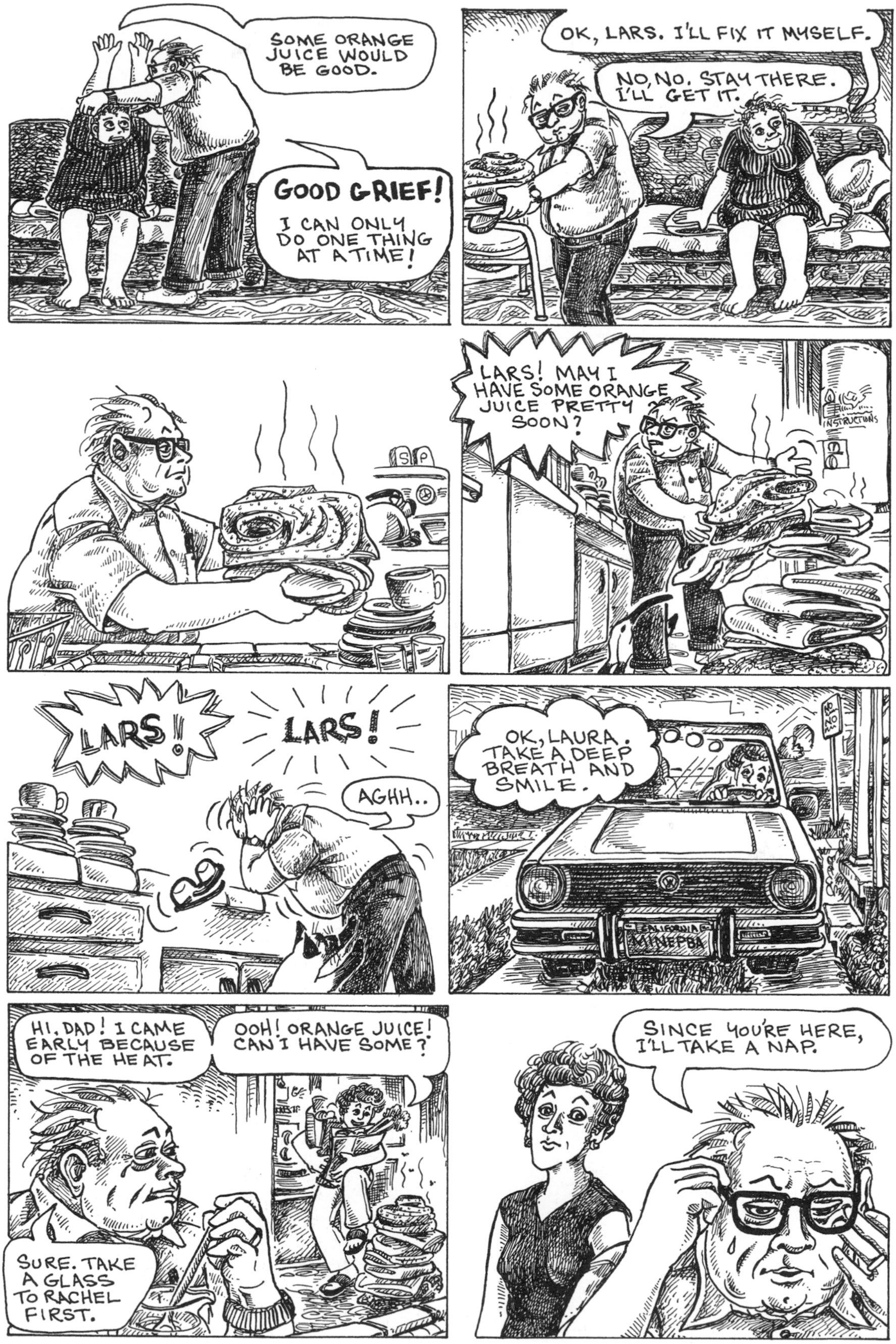
SOME ORANGE JUICE WOULD BE GOOD.
GOOD GRIEF! I CAN ONLY DO ONE THING AT A TIME!
OK, LARS. I'LL FIX IT MYSELF.
NO, NO. STAY THERE. I'LL GET IT.
LARS! MAY I HAVE SOME ORANGE JUICE PRETTY SOON?
INSTRUCTIONS
LARS!
LARS!
AGHH..
OK, LAURA. TAKE A DEEP BREATH AND SMILE.
CALIFORNIA
MINEPBA
HI, DAD! I CAME EARLY BECAUSE OF THE HEAT.
OOH! ORANGE JUICE! CAN I HAVE SOME?
SURE. TAKE A GLASS TO RACHEL FIRST.
SINCE YOU'RE HERE, I'LL TAKE A NAP.

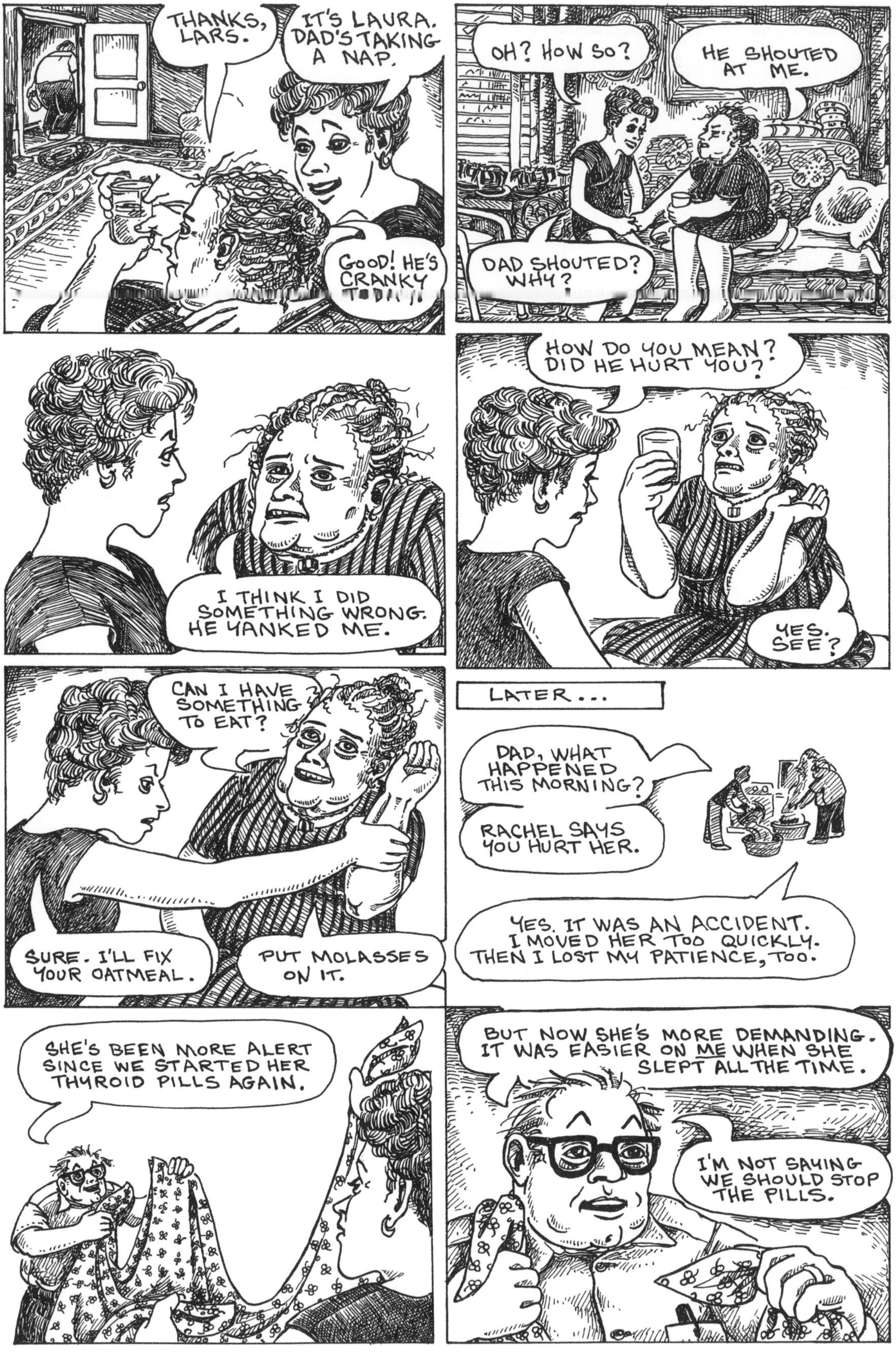

THANKS, LARS.
IT'S LAURA. DAD'S TAKING A NAP.
GOOD! HE'S CRANKY TODAY.
OH? HOW SO?
HE SHOUTED AT ME.
DAD SHOUTED? WHY?
I THINK I DID SOMETHING WRONG. HE YANKED ME.
HOW DO YOU MEAN? DID HE HURT YOU?
YES. SEE?
CAN I HAVE SOMETHING TO EAT?
SURE. I'LL FIX YOUR OATMEAL.
PUT MOLASSES ON IT.
LATER...
DAD, WHAT HAPPENED THIS MORNING?
RACHEL SAYS YOU HURT HER.
YES. IT WAS AN ACCIDENT. I MOVED HER TOO QUICKLY. THEN I LOST MY PATIENCE, TOO.
SHE'S BEEN MORE ALERT SINCE WE STARTED HER THYROID PILLS AGAIN.
BUT NOW SHE'S MORE DEMANDING. IT WAS EASIER ON ME WHEN SHE SLEPT ALL THE TIME.
I'M NOT SAYING WE SHOULD STOP THE PILLS.

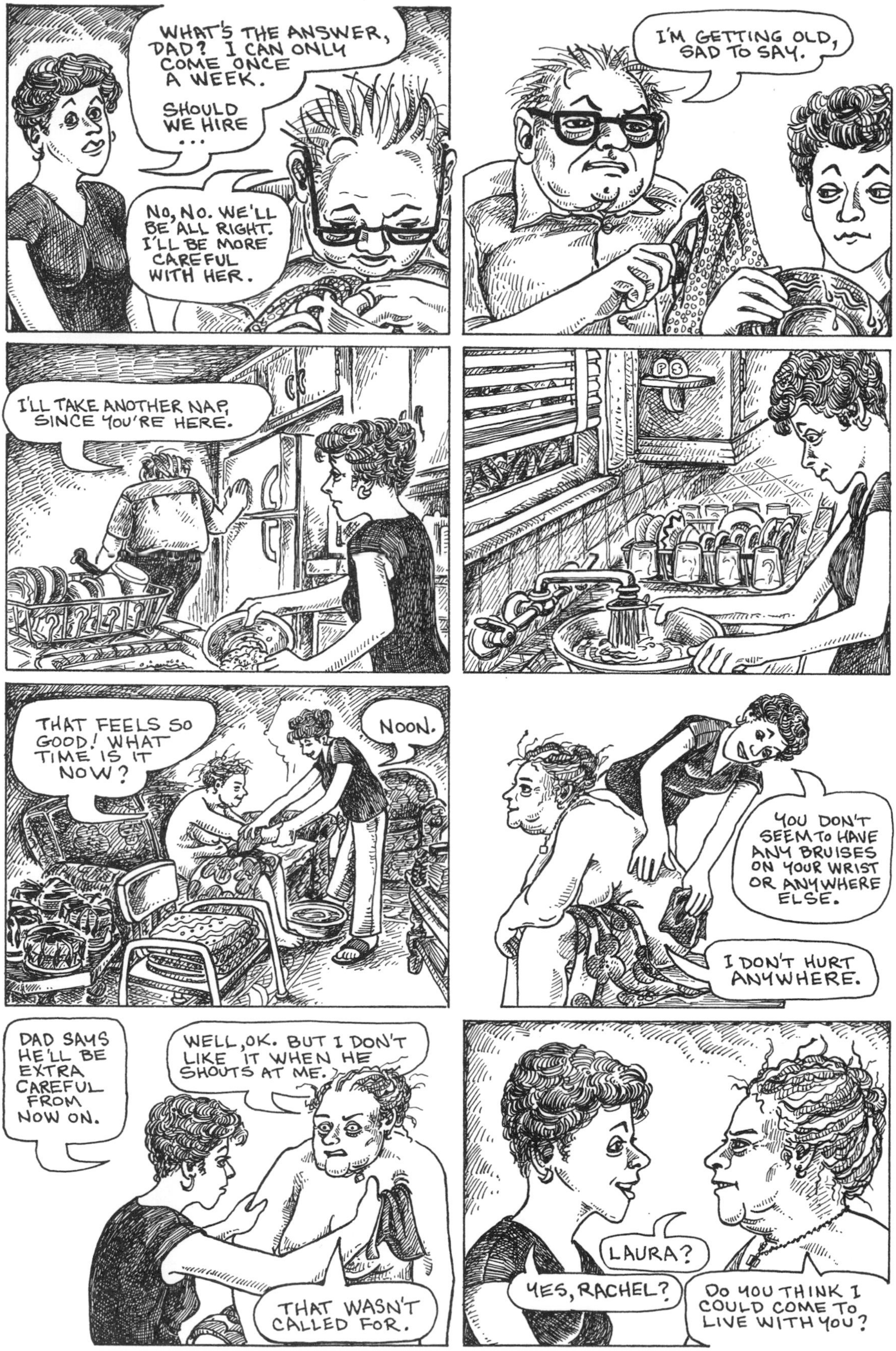
WHAT'S THE ANSWER, DAD? I CAN ONLY COME ONCE A WEEK.
SHOULD WE HIRE ...
No, No. WE'LL BE ALL RIGHT. I'LL BE MORE CAREFUL WITH HER.
I'M GETTING OLD, SAD TO SAY.
I'LL TAKE ANOTHER NAP, SINCE YOU'RE HERE.
THAT FEELS SO GOOD! WHAT TIME IS IT NOW?
NOON.
YOU DON'T SEEM TO HAVE ANY BRUISES ON YOUR WRIST OR ANYWHERE ELSE.
I DON'T HURT ANYWHERE.
DAD SAYS HE'LL BE EXTRA CAREFUL FROM NOW ON.
WELL, OK. BUT I DON'T LIKE IT WHEN HE SHOUTS AT ME.
THAT WASN'T CALLED FOR.
LAURA?
YES, RACHEL?
Do YOU THINK I COULD COME TO LIVE WITH YOU?

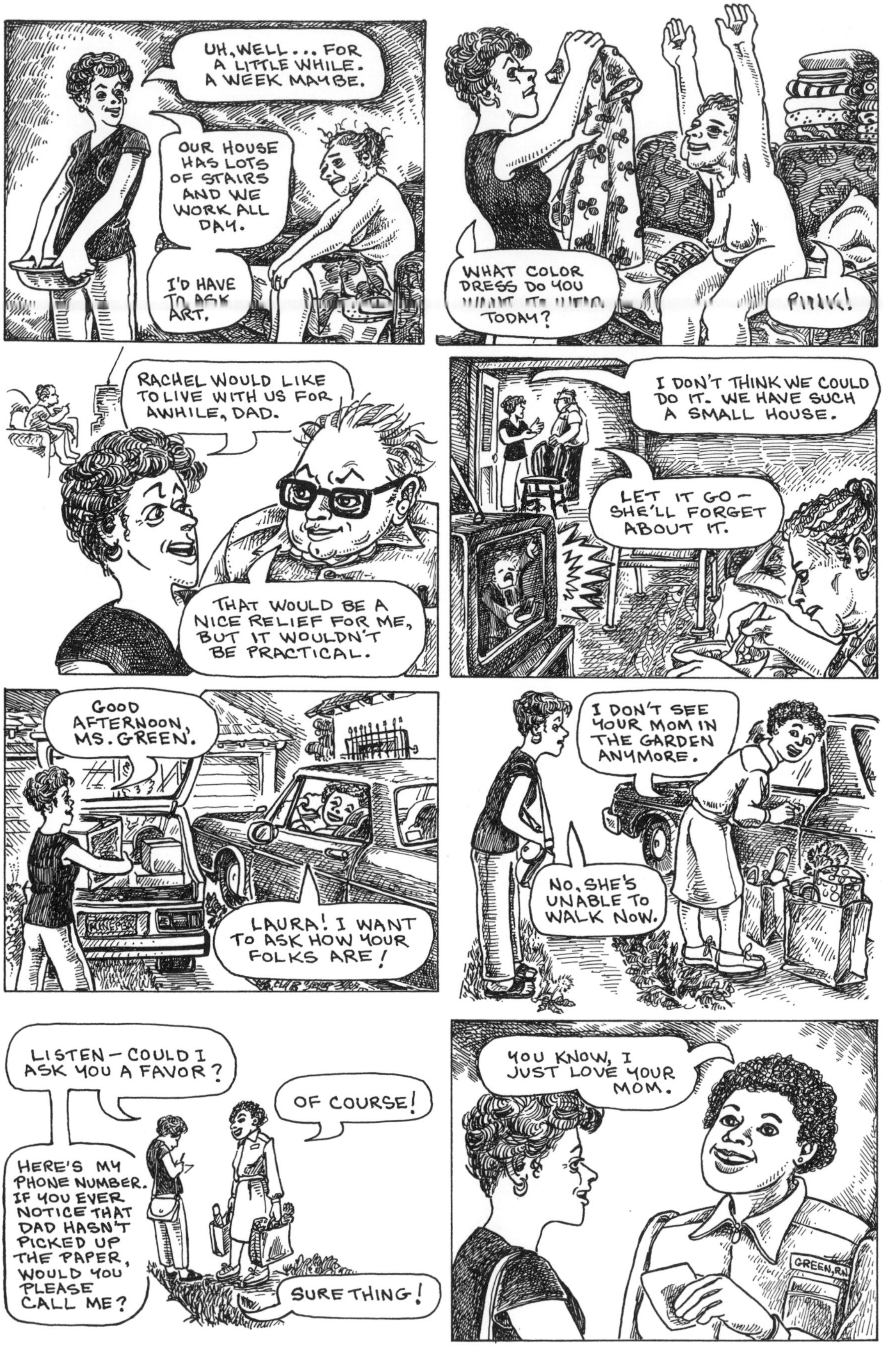
UH, WELL... FOR A LITTLE WHILE. A WEEK MAYBE.
OUR HOUSE HAS LOTS OF STAIRS AND WE WORK ALL DAY.
I'D HAVE TO ASK ART.
WHAT COLOR DRESS DO YOU
TODAY?
PINK!
RACHEL WOULD LIKE TO LIVE WITH US FOR AWHILE, DAD.
THAT WOULD BE A NICE RELIEF FOR ME, BUT IT WOULDN'T BE PRACTICAL.
I DON'T THINK WE COULD DO IT. WE HAVE SUCH A SMALL HOUSE.
LET IT GO— SHE'LL FORGET ABOUT IT.
GOOD AFTERNOON, MS. GREEN.
LAURA! I WANT TO ASK HOW YOUR FOLKS ARE!
I DON'T SEE YOUR MOM IN THE GARDEN ANYMORE.
NO, SHE'S UNABLE TO WALK NOW.
LISTEN—COULD I ASK YOU A FAVOR?
OF COURSE!
HERE'S MY PHONE NUMBER. IF YOU EVER NOTICE THAT DAD HASN'T PICKED UP THE PAPER, WOULD YOU PLEASE CALL ME?
SURE THING!
YOU KNOW, I JUST LOVE YOUR MOM.
GREEN, RN

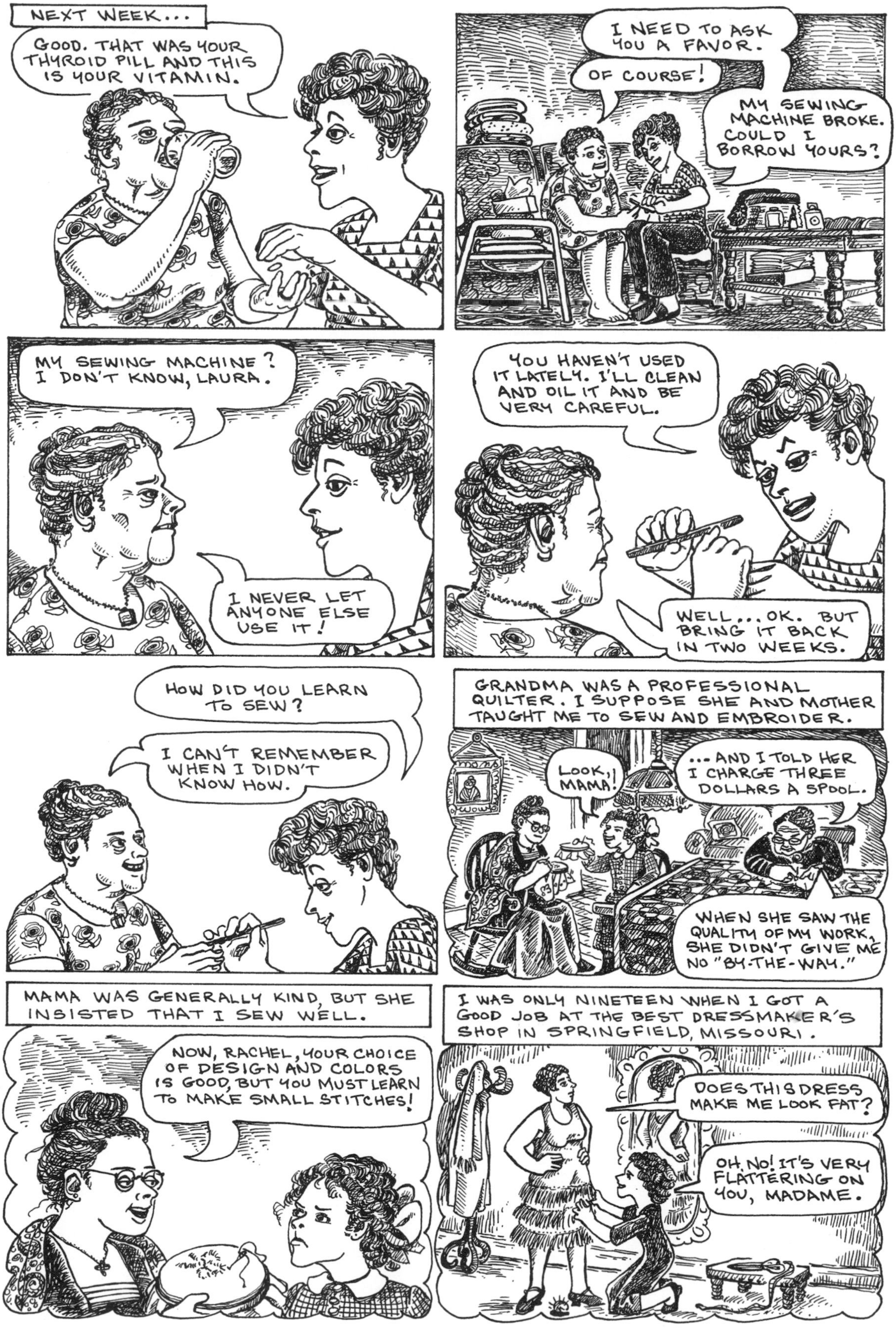

NEXT WEEK...
GOOD. THAT WAS YOUR THYROID PILL AND THIS IS YOUR VITAMIN.
I NEED TO ASK YOU A FAVOR.
OF COURSE!
MY SEWING MACHINE BROKE. COULD I BORROW YOURS?
MY SEWING MACHINE? I DON'T KNOW, LAURA.
I NEVER LET ANYONE ELSE USE IT!
YOU HAVEN'T USED IT LATELY. I'LL CLEAN AND OIL IT AND BE VERY CAREFUL.
WELL... OK. BUT BRING IT BACK IN TWO WEEKS.
HOW DID YOU LEARN TO SEW?
I CAN'T REMEMBER WHEN I DIDN'T KNOW HOW.
GRANDMA WAS A PROFESSIONAL QUILTER. I SUPPOSE SHE AND MOTHER TAUGHT ME TO SEW AND EMBROIDER.
LOOK, MAMA!
...AND I TOLD HER I CHARGE THREE DOLLARS A SPOOL.
WHEN SHE SAW THE QUALITY OF MY WORK, SHE DIDN'T GIVE ME NO "BY-THE-WAY."
MAMA WAS GENERALLY KIND, BUT SHE INSISTED THAT I SEW WELL.
NOW, RACHEL, YOUR CHOICE OF DESIGN AND COLORS IS GOOD, BUT YOU MUST LEARN TO MAKE SMALL STITCHES!
I WAS ONLY NINETEEN WHEN I GOT A GOOD JOB AT THE BEST DRESSMAKER'S SHOP IN SPRINGFIELD, MISSOURI.
DOES THIS DRESS MAKE ME LOOK FAT?
OH, NO! IT'S VERY FLATTERING ON YOU, MADAME.

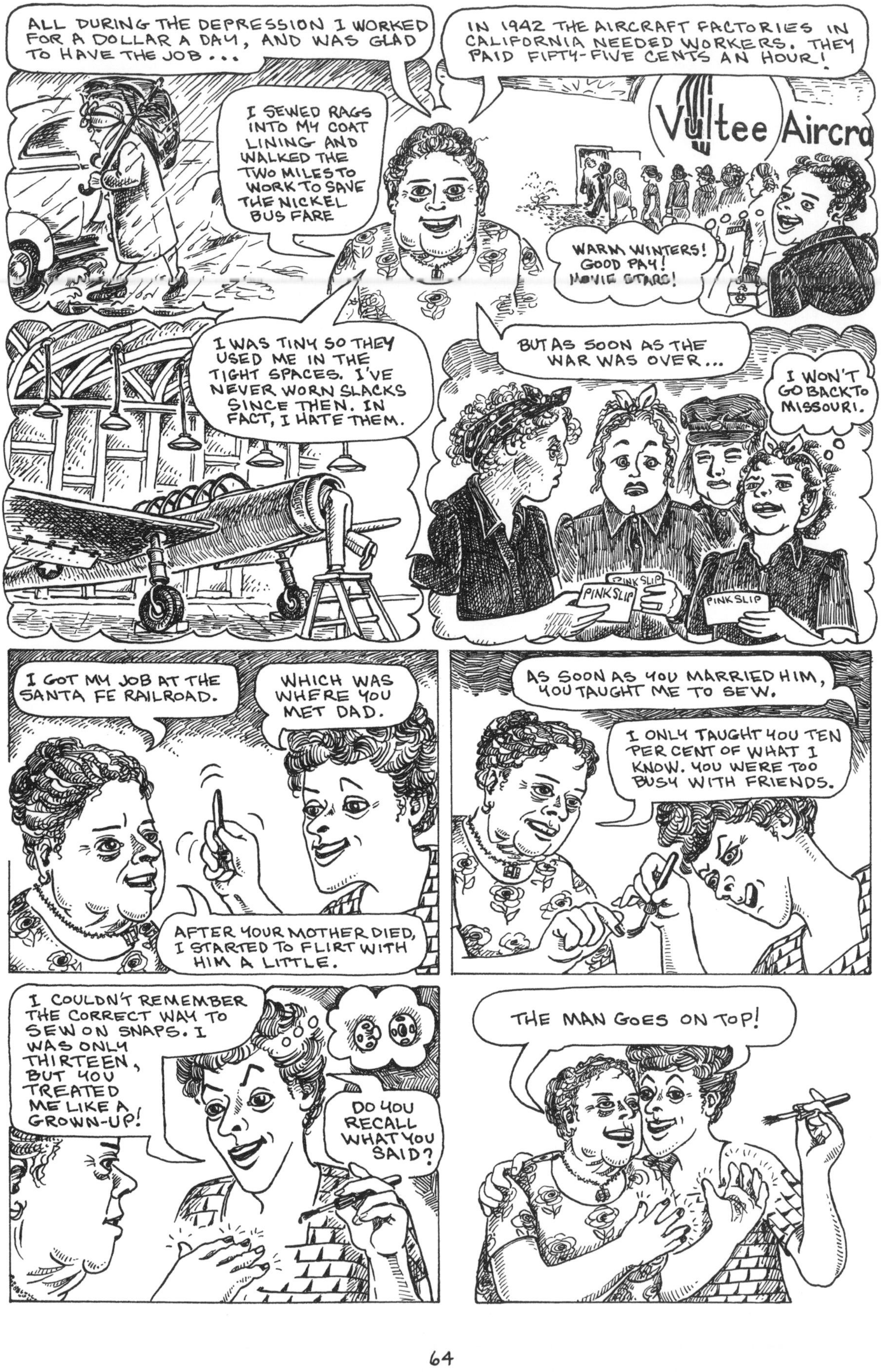

ALL DURING THE DEPRESSION I WORKED FOR A DOLLAR A DAY, AND WAS GLAD TO HAVE THE JOB...
I SEWED RAGS INTO MY COAT LINING AND WALKED THE TWO MILES TO WORK TO SAVE THE NICKEL BUS FARE
IN 1942 THE AIRCRAFT FACTORIES IN CALIFORNIA NEEDED WORKERS. THEY PAID FIFTY-FIVE CENTS AN HOUR!
Vultee Aircra
WARM WINTERS! GOOD PAY! MOVIE STARS!
I WAS TINY SO THEY USED ME IN THE TIGHT SPACES. I'VE NEVER WORN SLACKS SINCE THEN. IN FACT, I HATE THEM.
BUT AS SOON AS THE WAR WAS OVER...
I WON'T GO BACK TO MISSOURI.
PINK SLIP
PINK SLIP
PINK SLIP
I GOT MY JOB AT THE SANTA FE RAILROAD.
WHICH WAS WHERE YOU MET DAD.
AFTER YOUR MOTHER DIED, I STARTED TO FLIRT WITH HIM A LITTLE.
AS SOON AS YOU MARRIED HIM, YOU TAUGHT ME TO SEW.
I ONLY TAUGHT YOU TEN PER CENT OF WHAT I KNOW. YOU WERE TOO BUSY WITH FRIENDS.
I COULDN'T REMEMBER THE CORRECT WAY TO SEW ON SNAPS. I WAS ONLY THIRTEEN, BUT YOU TREATED ME LIKE A GROWN-UP!
DO YOU RECALL WHAT YOU SAID?
THE MAN GOES ON TOP!

5

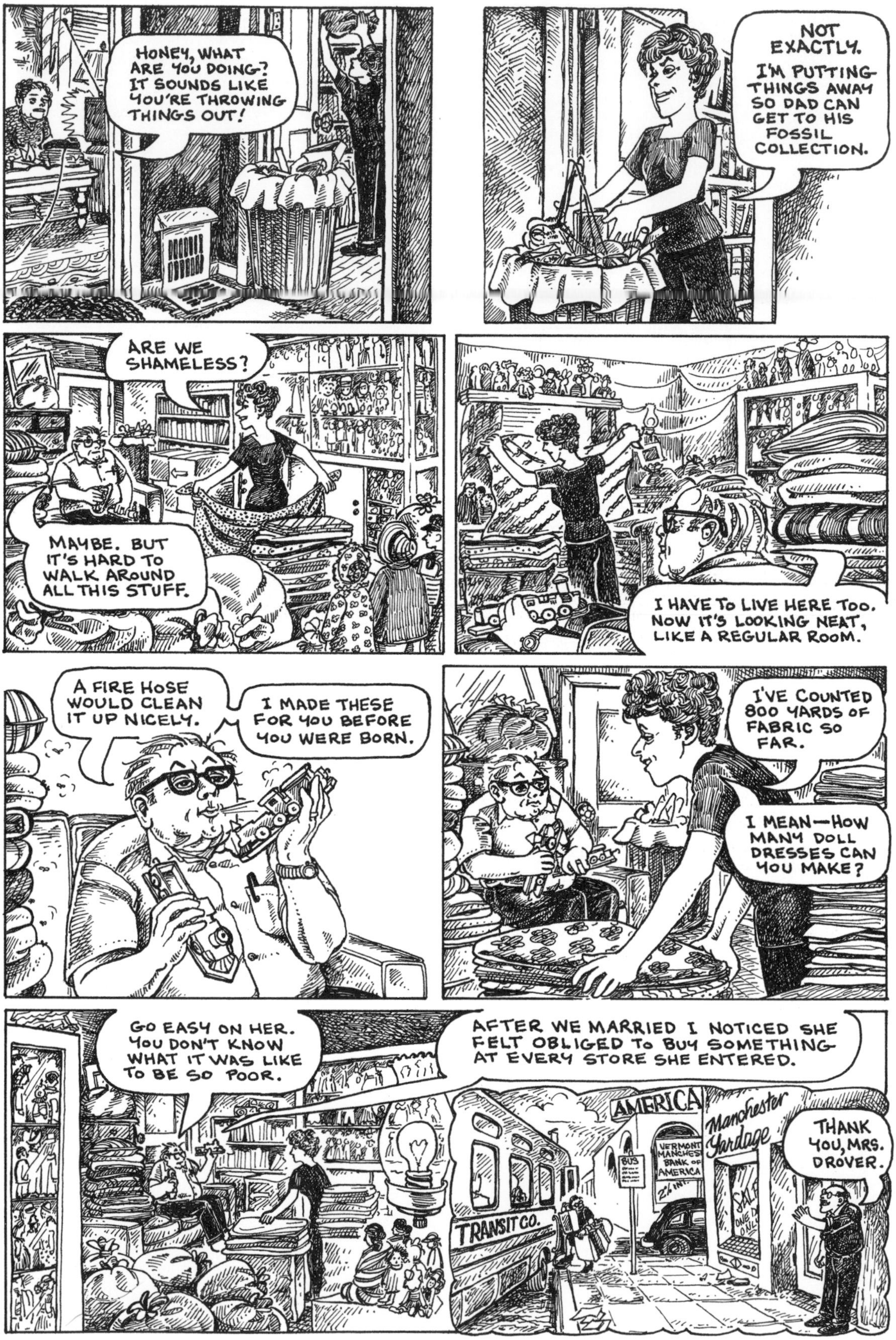
HONEY, WHAT ARE YOU DOING? IT SOUNDS LIKE YOU'RE THROWING THINGS OUT!
NOT EXACTLY.
I'M PUTTING THINGS AWAY SO DAD CAN GET TO HIS FOSSIL COLLECTION.
ARE WE SHAMELESS?
MAYBE. BUT IT'S HARD TO WALK AROUND ALL THIS STUFF.
I HAVE TO LIVE HERE TOO. NOW IT'S LOOKING NEAT, LIKE A REGULAR ROOM.
A FIRE HOSE WOULD CLEAN IT UP NICELY.
I MADE THESE FOR YOU BEFORE YOU WERE BORN.
I'VE COUNTED 800 YARDS OF FABRIC SO FAR.
I MEAN—HOW MANY DOLL DRESSES CAN YOU MAKE?
GO EASY ON HER. YOU DON'T KNOW WHAT IT WAS LIKE TO BE SO POOR.
AFTER WE MARRIED I NOTICED SHE FELT OBLIGED TO BUY SOMETHING AT EVERY STORE SHE ENTERED.
AMERICA
Manchester Yardage
VERMONT MANCHEST BANK OF AMERICA
TRANSIT CO.
THANK YOU, MRS. DROVER.

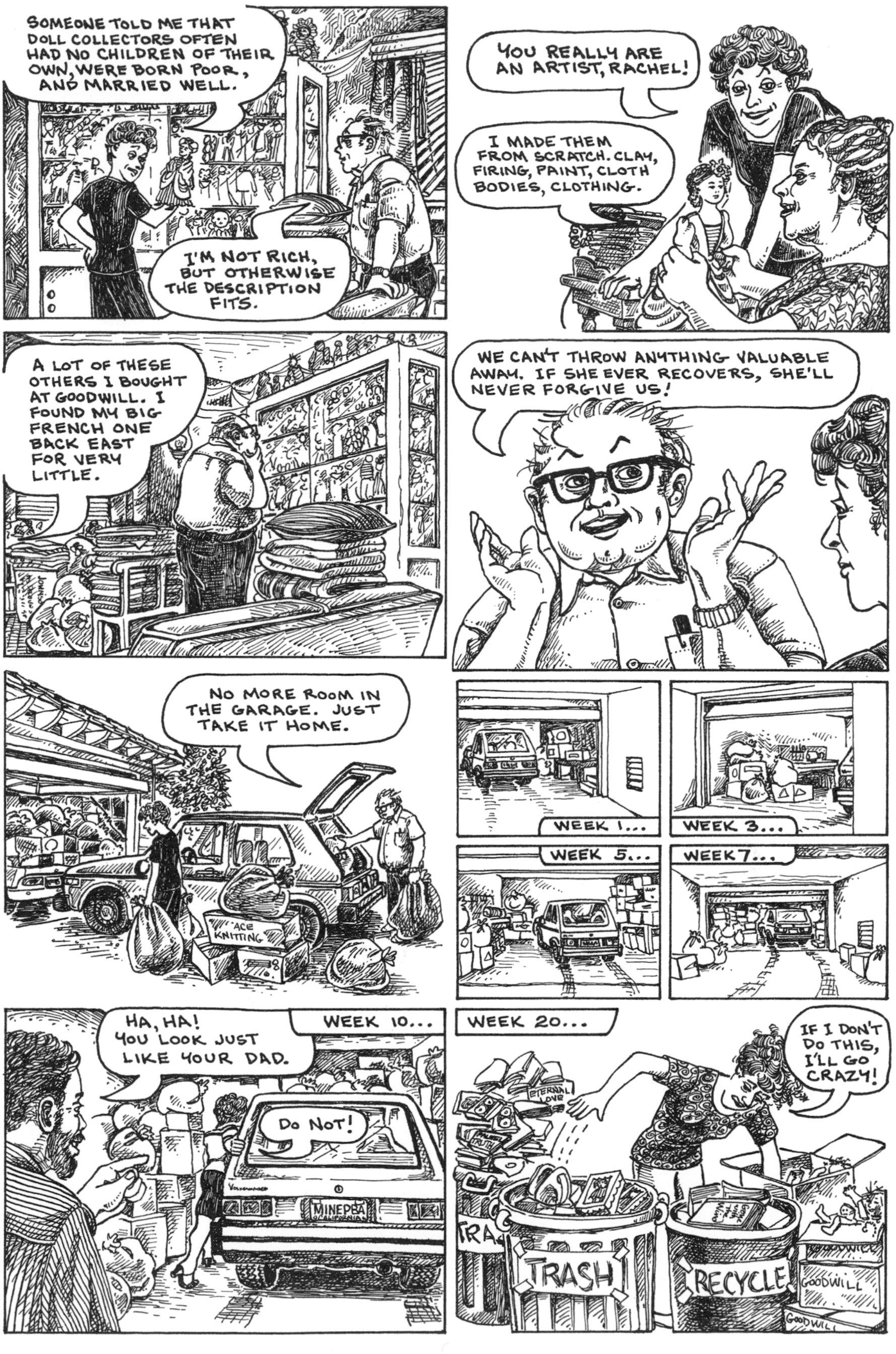
SOMEONE TOLD ME THAT DOLL COLLECTORS OFTEN HAD NO CHILDREN OF THEIR OWN, WERE BORN POOR, AND MARRIED WELL.
I'M NOT RICH, BUT OTHERWISE THE DESCRIPTION FITS.
YOU REALLY ARE AN ARTIST, RACHEL!
I MADE THEM FROM SCRATCH. CLAY, FIRING, PAINT, CLOTH BODIES, CLOTHING.
A LOT OF THESE OTHERS I BOUGHT AT GOODWILL. I FOUND MY BIG FRENCH ONE BACK EAST FOR VERY LITTLE.
WE CAN'T THROW ANYTHING VALUABLE AWAY. IF SHE EVER RECOVERS, SHE'LL NEVER FORGIVE US!
NO MORE ROOM IN THE GARAGE. JUST TAKE IT HOME.
ACE KNITTING
WEEK 1...
WEEK 3...
WEEK 5...
WEEK 7...
WEEK 10...
HA, HA! YOU LOOK JUST LIKE YOUR DAD.
DO NOT!
MINEPBA
WEEK 20...
IF I DON'T DO THIS, I'LL GO CRAZY!
ETERNAL LOVE
TRASH
RECYCLE
GOODWILL
GOODWILL

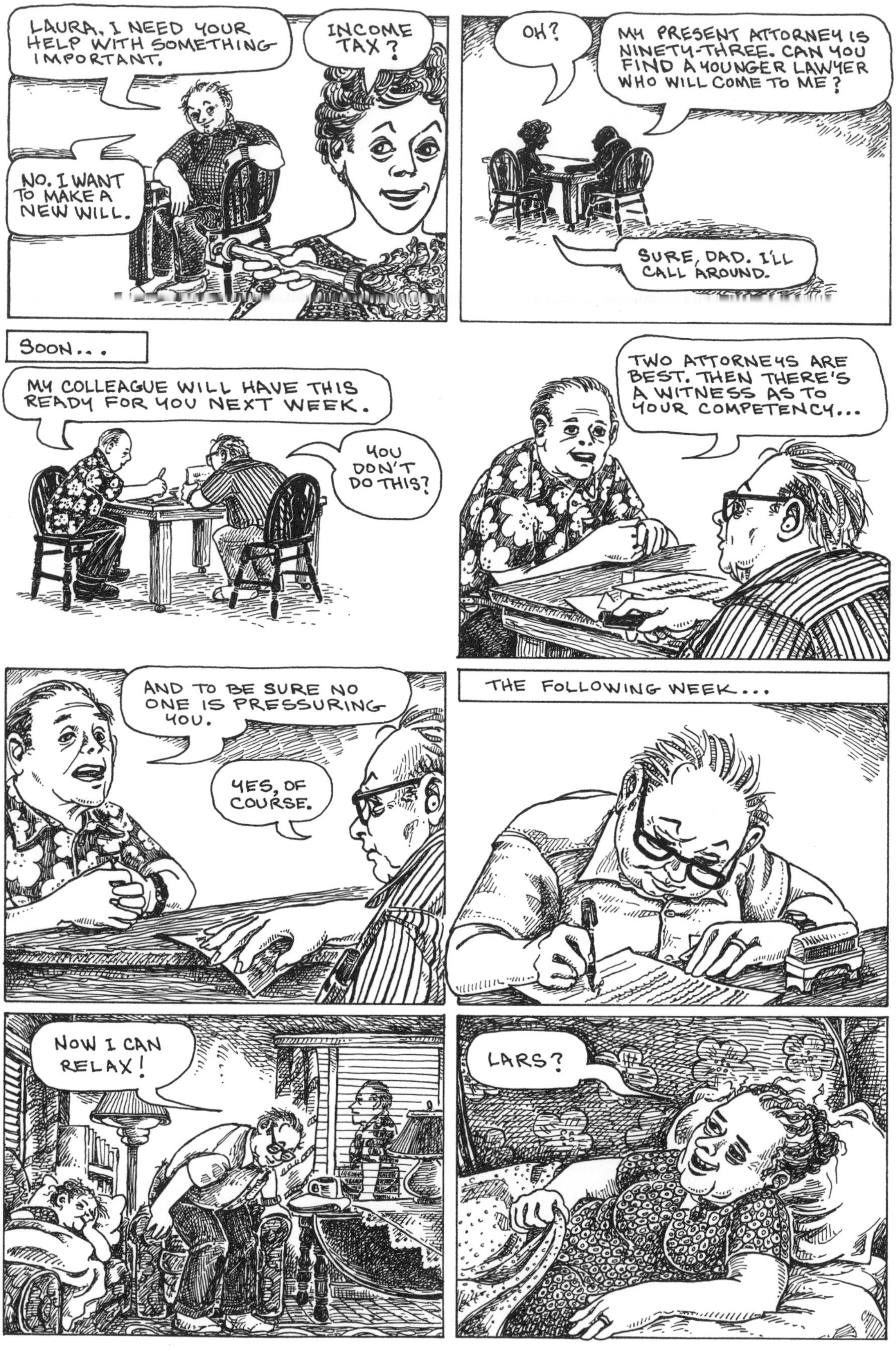

LAURA, I NEED YOUR HELP WITH SOMETHING IMPORTANT.
INCOME TAX?
NO. I WANT TO MAKE A NEW WILL.
OH?
MY PRESENT ATTORNEY IS NINETY-THREE. CAN YOU FIND A YOUNGER LAWYER WHO WILL COME TO ME?
SURE, DAD. I'LL CALL AROUND.
SOON...
MY COLLEAGUE WILL HAVE THIS READY FOR YOU NEXT WEEK.
YOU DON'T DO THIS?
TWO ATTORNEYS ARE BEST. THEN THERE'S A WITNESS AS TO YOUR COMPETENCY...
AND TO BE SURE NO ONE IS PRESSURING YOU.
YES, OF COURSE.
THE FOLLOWING WEEK...
NOW I CAN RELAX!
LARS?

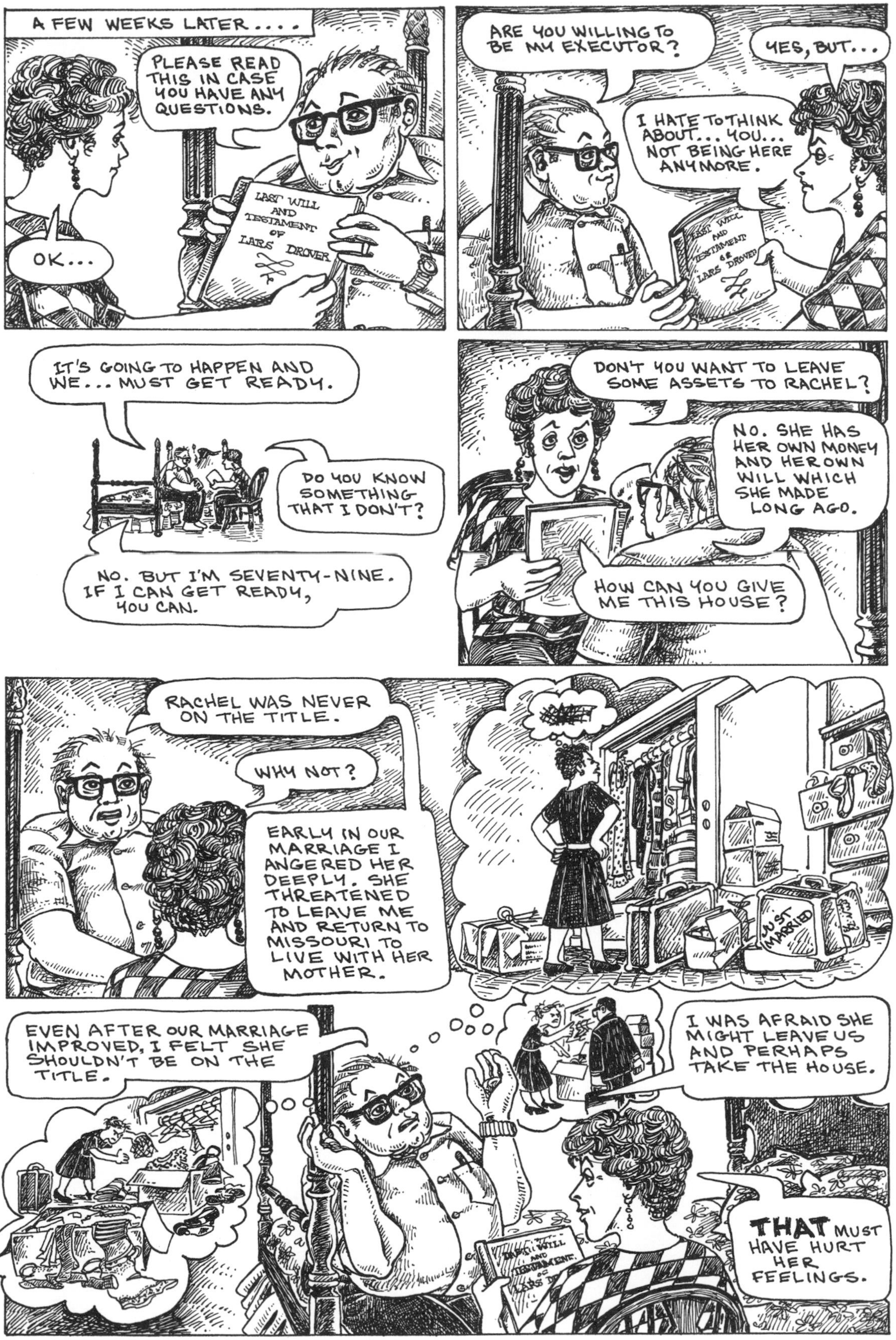
A FEW WEEKS LATER....
PLEASE READ THIS IN CASE YOU HAVE ANY QUESTIONS.
LAST WILL AND TESTAMENT OF LARS DROVER
OK...
ARE YOU WILLING TO BE MY EXECUTOR?
YES, BUT...
I HATE TO THINK ABOUT... YOU... NOT BEING HERE ANYMORE.
IT'S GOING TO HAPPEN AND WE... MUST GET READY.
DO YOU KNOW SOMETHING THAT I DON'T?
NO. BUT I'M SEVENTY-NINE. IF I CAN GET READY, YOU CAN.
DON'T YOU WANT TO LEAVE SOME ASSETS TO RACHEL?
NO. SHE HAS HER OWN MONEY AND HER OWN WILL WHICH SHE MADE LONG AGO.
HOW CAN YOU GIVE ME THIS HOUSE?
RACHEL WAS NEVER ON THE TITLE.
WHY NOT?
EARLY IN OUR MARRIAGE I ANGERED HER DEEPLY. SHE THREATENED TO LEAVE ME AND RETURN TO MISSOURI TO LIVE WITH HER MOTHER.
JUST MARRIED
EVEN AFTER OUR MARRIAGE IMPROVED, I FELT SHE SHOULDN'T BE ON THE TITLE.
I WAS AFRAID SHE MIGHT LEAVE US AND PERHAPS TAKE THE HOUSE.
THAT MUST HAVE HURT HER FEELINGS.

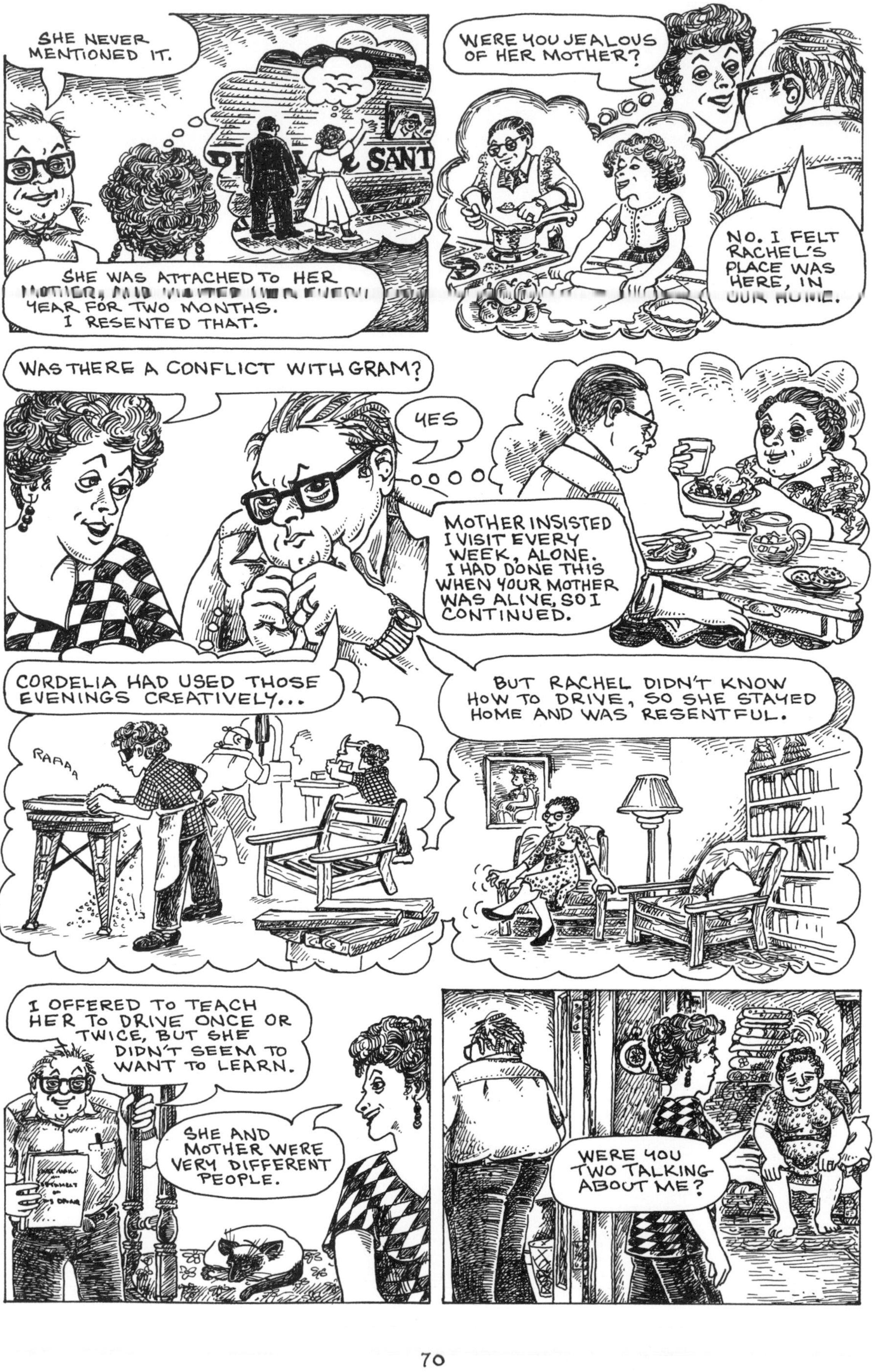

SHE NEVER MENTIONED IT.
SHE WAS ATTACHED TO HER MOTHER, AND VISITED HER EVERY YEAR FOR TWO MONTHS. I RESENTED THAT.
WERE YOU JEALOUS OF HER MOTHER?
NO. I FELT RACHEL'S PLACE WAS HERE, IN OUR HOME.
WAS THERE A CONFLICT WITH GRAM?
YES
MOTHER INSISTED I VISIT EVERY WEEK, ALONE. I HAD DONE THIS WHEN YOUR MOTHER WAS ALIVE, SO I CONTINUED.
CORDELIA HAD USED THOSE EVENINGS CREATIVELY...
RAAAA
BUT RACHEL DIDN'T KNOW HOW TO DRIVE, SO SHE STAYED HOME AND WAS RESENTFUL.
I OFFERED TO TEACH HER TO DRIVE ONCE OR TWICE, BUT SHE DIDN'T SEEM TO WANT TO LEARN.
SHE AND MOTHER WERE VERY DIFFERENT PEOPLE.
WERE YOU TWO TALKING ABOUT ME?

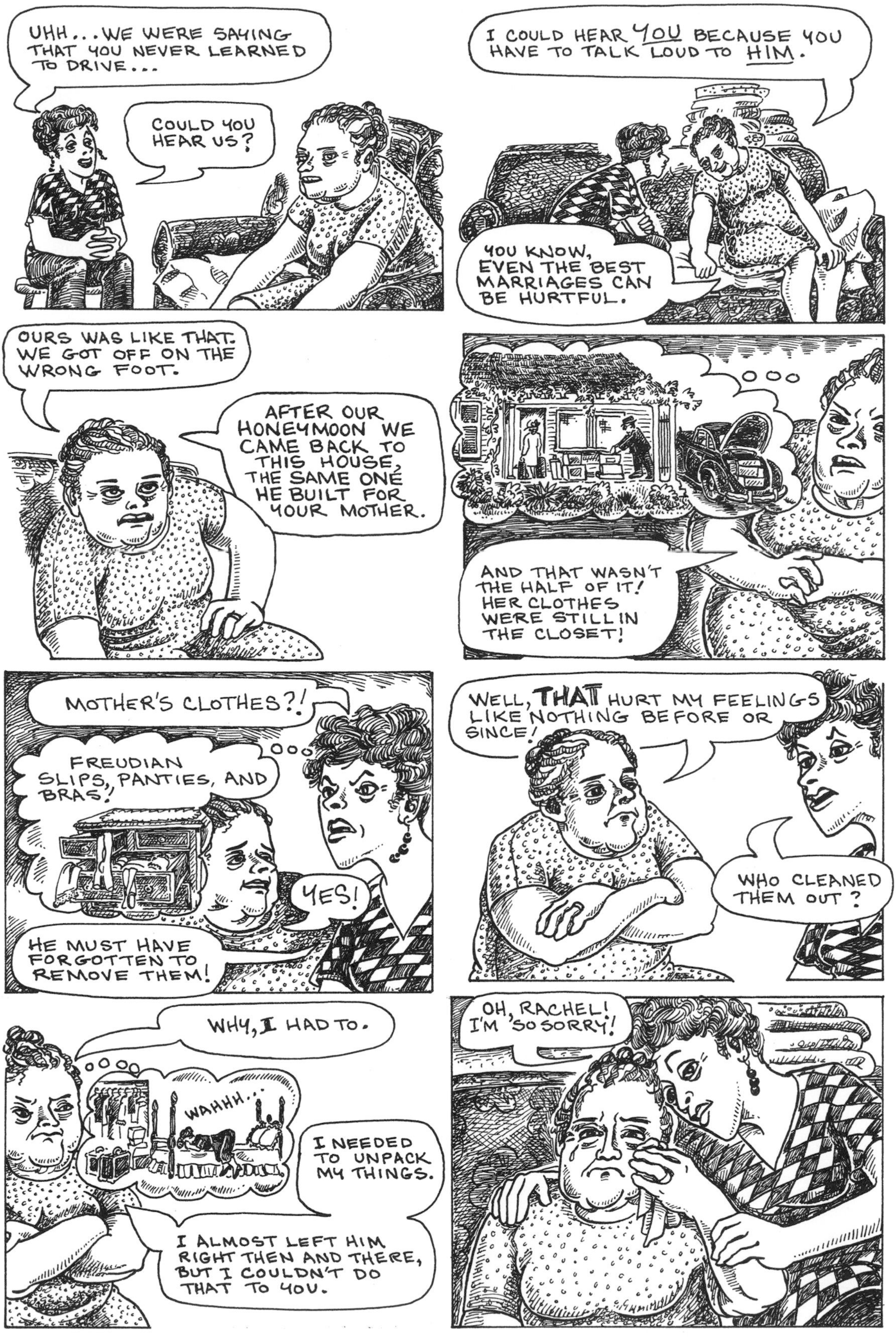
UHH...WE WERE SAYING THAT YOU NEVER LEARNED TO DRIVE...
COULD YOU HEAR US?
I COULD HEAR YOU BECAUSE YOU HAVE TO TALK LOUD TO HIM.
YOU KNOW, EVEN THE BEST MARRIAGES CAN BE HURTFUL.
OURS WAS LIKE THAT. WE GOT OFF ON THE WRONG FOOT.
AFTER OUR HONEYMOON WE CAME BACK TO THIS HOUSE, THE SAME ONE HE BUILT FOR YOUR MOTHER.
AND THAT WASN'T THE HALF OF IT! HER CLOTHES WERE STILL IN THE CLOSET!
MOTHER'S CLOTHES?!
FREUDIAN SLIPS, PANTIES, AND BRAS.
YES!
HE MUST HAVE FORGOTTEN TO REMOVE THEM!
WELL, THAT HURT MY FEELINGS LIKE NOTHING BEFORE OR SINCE!
WHO CLEANED THEM OUT?
WHY, I HAD TO.
WAHHH...
I NEEDED TO UNPACK MY THINGS.
I ALMOST LEFT HIM RIGHT THEN AND THERE, BUT I COULDN'T DO THAT TO YOU.
OH, RACHEL! I'M SO SORRY!

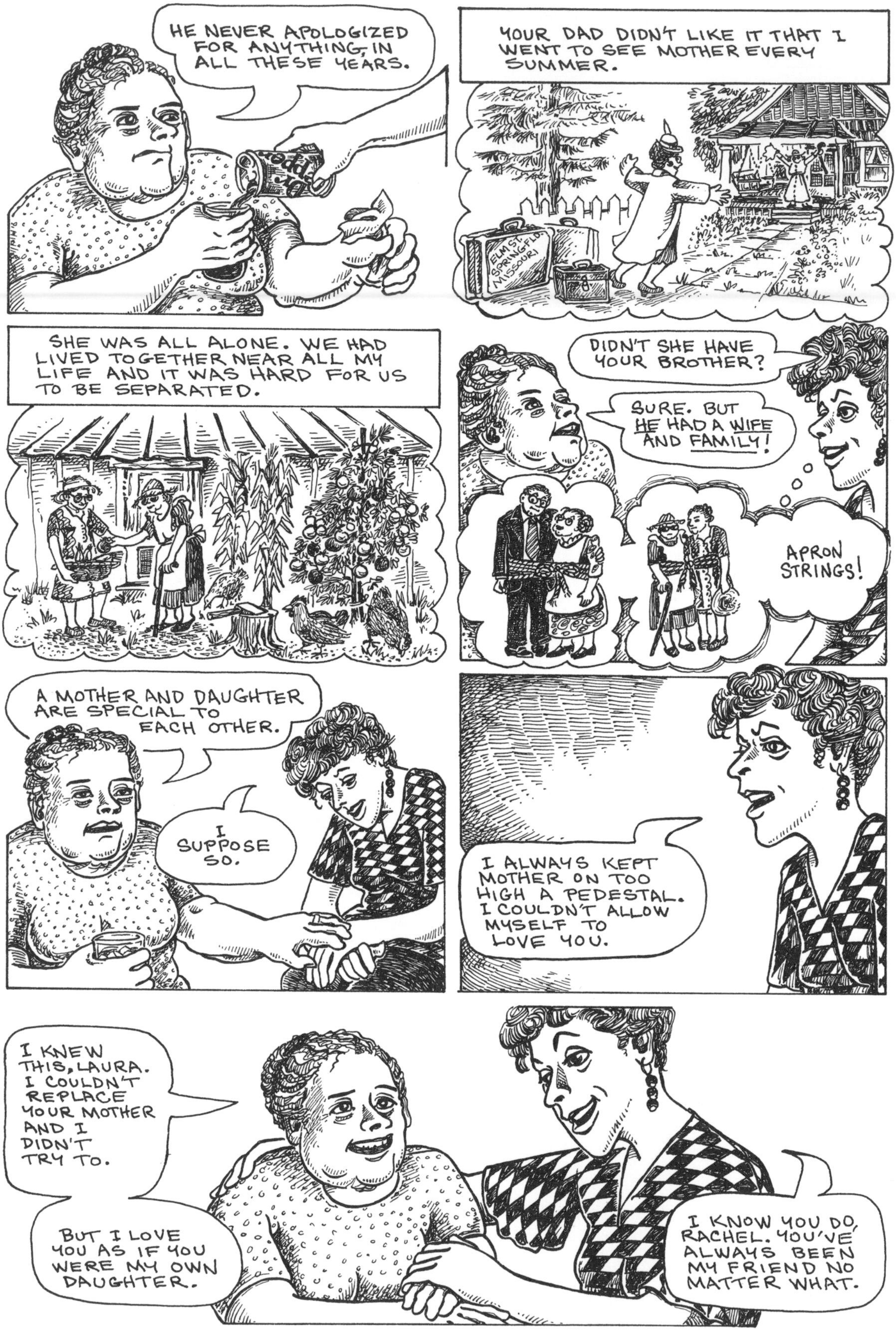
HE NEVER APOLOGIZED FOR ANYTHING, IN ALL THESE YEARS.
YOUR DAD DIDN'T LIKE IT THAT I WENT TO SEE MOTHER EVERY SUMMER.
ELM ST. SPRINGFLD. MISSOURI
SHE WAS ALL ALONE. WE HAD LIVED TOGETHER NEAR ALL MY LIFE AND IT WAS HARD FOR US TO BE SEPARATED.
DIDN'T SHE HAVE YOUR BROTHER?
SURE. BUT HE HAD A WIFE AND FAMILY!
APRON STRINGS!
A MOTHER AND DAUGHTER ARE SPECIAL TO EACH OTHER.
I SUPPOSE SO.
I ALWAYS KEPT MOTHER ON TOO HIGH A PEDESTAL. I COULDN'T ALLOW MYSELF TO LOVE YOU.
I KNEW THIS, LAURA. I COULDN'T REPLACE YOUR MOTHER AND I DIDN'T TRY TO.
BUT I LOVE YOU AS IF YOU WERE MY OWN DAUGHTER.
I KNOW YOU DO, RACHEL. YOU'VE ALWAYS BEEN MY FRIEND NO MATTER WHAT.

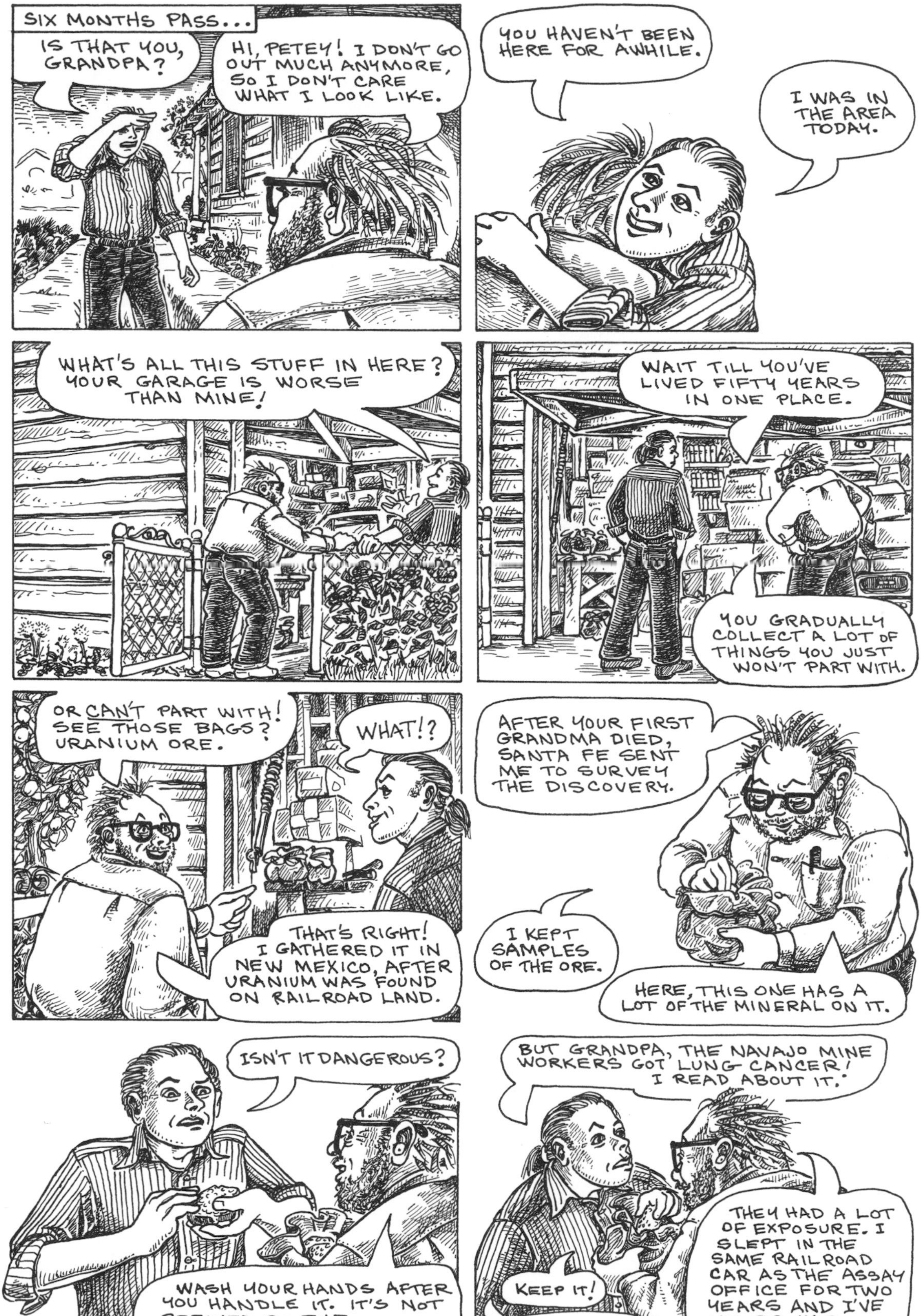
SIX MONTHS PASS...
IS THAT YOU, GRANDPA?
HI, PETEY! I DON'T GO OUT MUCH ANYMORE, SO I DON'T CARE WHAT I LOOK LIKE.
YOU HAVEN'T BEEN HERE FOR AWHILE.
I WAS IN THE AREA TODAY.
WHAT'S ALL THIS STUFF IN HERE? YOUR GARAGE IS WORSE THAN MINE!
WAIT TILL YOU'VE LIVED FIFTY YEARS IN ONE PLACE.
YOU GRADUALLY COLLECT A LOT OF THINGS YOU JUST WON'T PART WITH.
OR CAN'T PART WITH! SEE THOSE BAGS? URANIUM ORE.
WHAT!?
THAT'S RIGHT! I GATHERED IT IN NEW MEXICO, AFTER URANIUM WAS FOUND ON RAILROAD LAND.
AFTER YOUR FIRST GRANDMA DIED, SANTA FE SENT ME TO SURVEY THE DISCOVERY.
I KEPT SAMPLES OF THE ORE.
HERE, THIS ONE HAS A LOT OF THE MINERAL ON IT.
ISN'T IT DANGEROUS?
WASH YOUR HANDS AFTER YOU HANDLE IT. IT'S NOT REFINED SO THE RADIOACTIVITY IS LOW.
BUT GRANDPA, THE NAVAJO MINE WORKERS GOT LUNG CANCER! I READ ABOUT IT.
KEEP IT!
UH, NO THANKS.
THEY HAD A LOT OF EXPOSURE. I SLEPT IN THE SAME RAILROAD CAR AS THE ASSAY OFFICE FOR TWO YEARS AND I'VE NEVER HAD ANY PROBLEM.

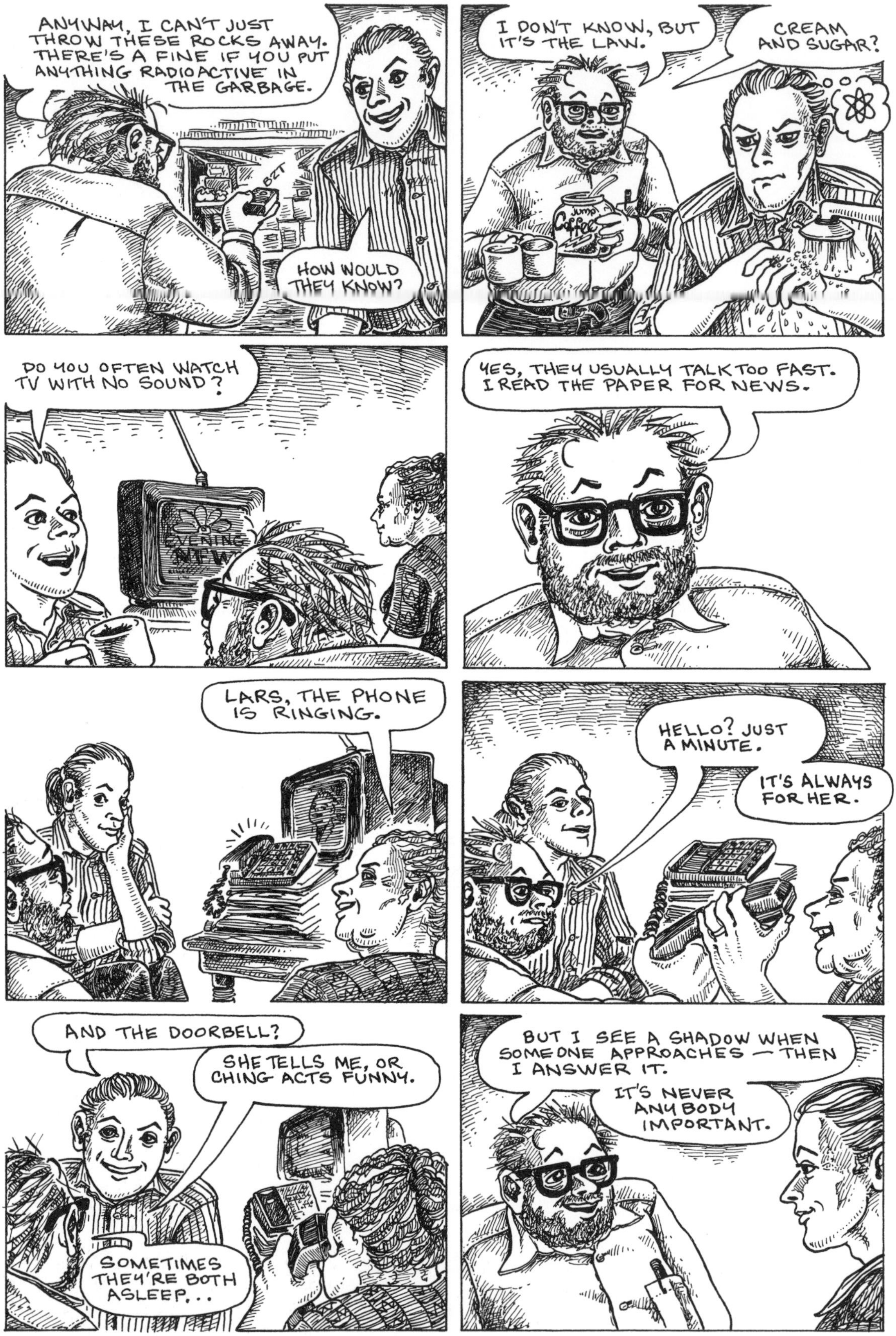
ANYWAY, I CAN'T JUST THROW THESE ROCKS AWAY. THERE'S A FINE IF YOU PUT ANYTHING RADIOACTIVE IN THE GARBAGE.
BZT
HOW WOULD THEY KNOW?
I DON'T KNOW, BUT IT'S THE LAW.
CREAM AND SUGAR?
DO YOU OFTEN WATCH TV WITH NO SOUND?
EVENING NEWS
YES, THEY USUALLY TALK TOO FAST. I READ THE PAPER FOR NEWS.
LARS, THE PHONE IS RINGING.
HELLO? JUST A MINUTE.
IT'S ALWAYS FOR HER.
AND THE DOORBELL?
SHE TELLS ME, OR CHING ACTS FUNNY.
SOMETIMES THEY'RE BOTH ASLEEP...
BUT I SEE A SHADOW WHEN SOMEONE APPROACHES — THEN I ANSWER IT.
IT'S NEVER ANYBODY IMPORTANT.

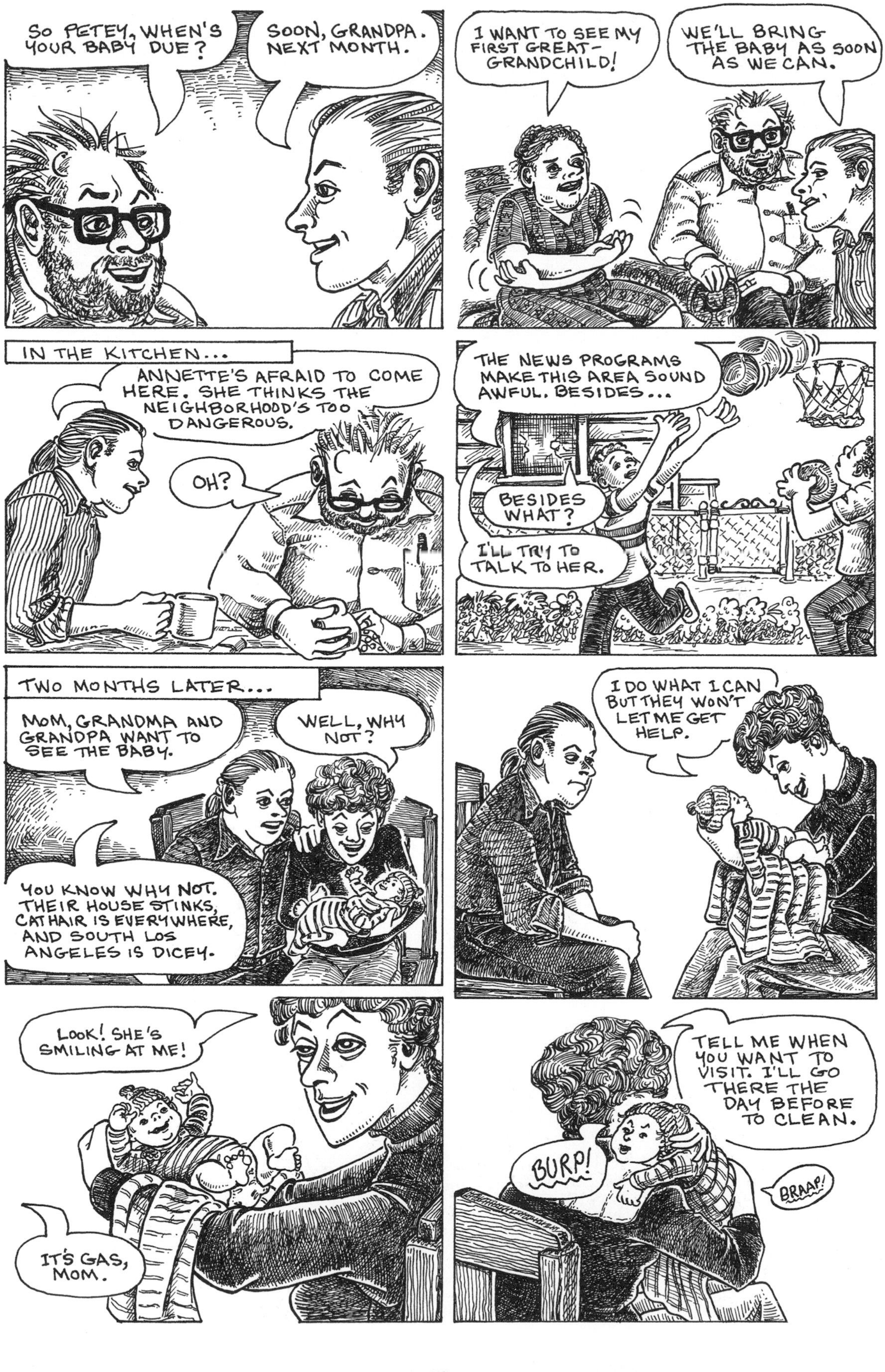
So PETEY, WHEN'S YOUR BABY DUE?
SOON, GRANDPA. NEXT MONTH.
I WANT TO SEE MY FIRST GREAT-GRANDCHILD!
WE'LL BRING THE BABY AS SOON AS WE CAN.
IN THE KITCHEN...
ANNETTE'S AFRAID TO COME HERE. SHE THINKS THE NEIGHBORHOOD'S TOO DANGEROUS.
OH?
THE NEWS PROGRAMS MAKE THIS AREA SOUND AWFUL. BESIDES...
BESIDES WHAT?
I'LL TRY TO TALK TO HER.
TWO MONTHS LATER...
MOM, GRANDMA AND GRANDPA WANT TO SEE THE BABY.
WELL, WHY NOT?
YOU KNOW WHY NOT. THEIR HOUSE STINKS, CAT HAIR IS EVERYWHERE, AND SOUTH LOS ANGELES IS DICEY.
I DO WHAT I CAN BUT THEY WON'T LET ME GET HELP.
LOOK! SHE'S SMILING AT ME!
IT'S GAS, MOM.
TELL ME WHEN YOU WANT TO VISIT. I'LL GO THERE THE DAY BEFORE TO CLEAN.
BURP!
BRAAP!

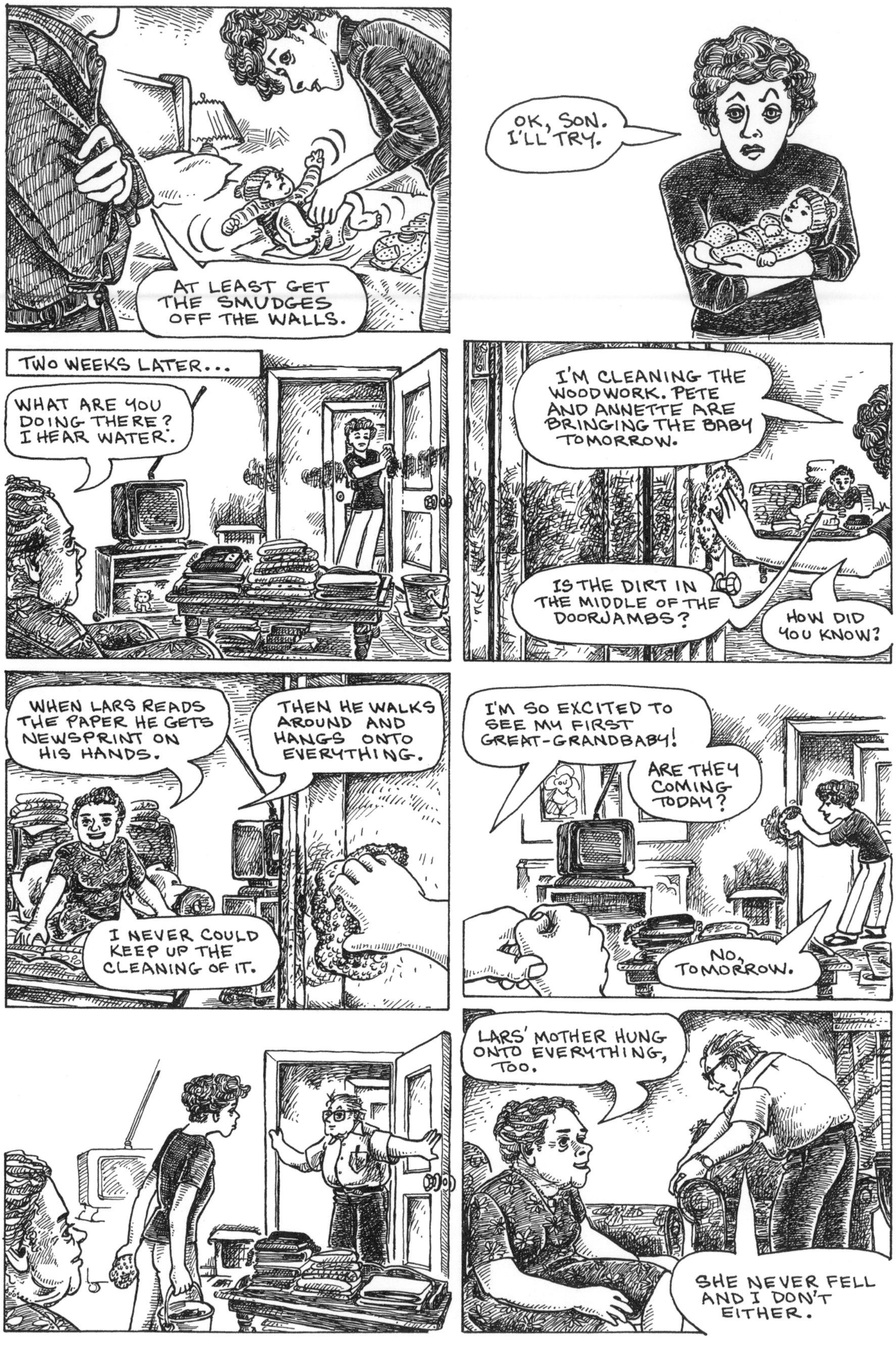
AT LEAST GET THE SMUDGES OFF THE WALLS.
OK, SON. I'LL TRY.
TWO WEEKS LATER...
WHAT ARE YOU DOING THERE? I HEAR WATER.
I'M CLEANING THE WOODWORK. PETE AND ANNETTE ARE BRINGING THE BABY TOMORROW.
IS THE DIRT IN THE MIDDLE OF THE DOORJAMBS?
HOW DID YOU KNOW?
WHEN LARS READS THE PAPER HE GETS NEWSPRINT ON HIS HANDS.
THEN HE WALKS AROUND AND HANGS ONTO EVERYTHING.
I NEVER COULD KEEP UP THE CLEANING OF IT.
I'M SO EXCITED TO SEE MY FIRST GREAT-GRANDBABY!
ARE THEY COMING TODAY?
NO, TOMORROW.
LARS' MOTHER HUNG ONTO EVERYTHING, TOO.
SHE NEVER FELL AND I DON'T EITHER.

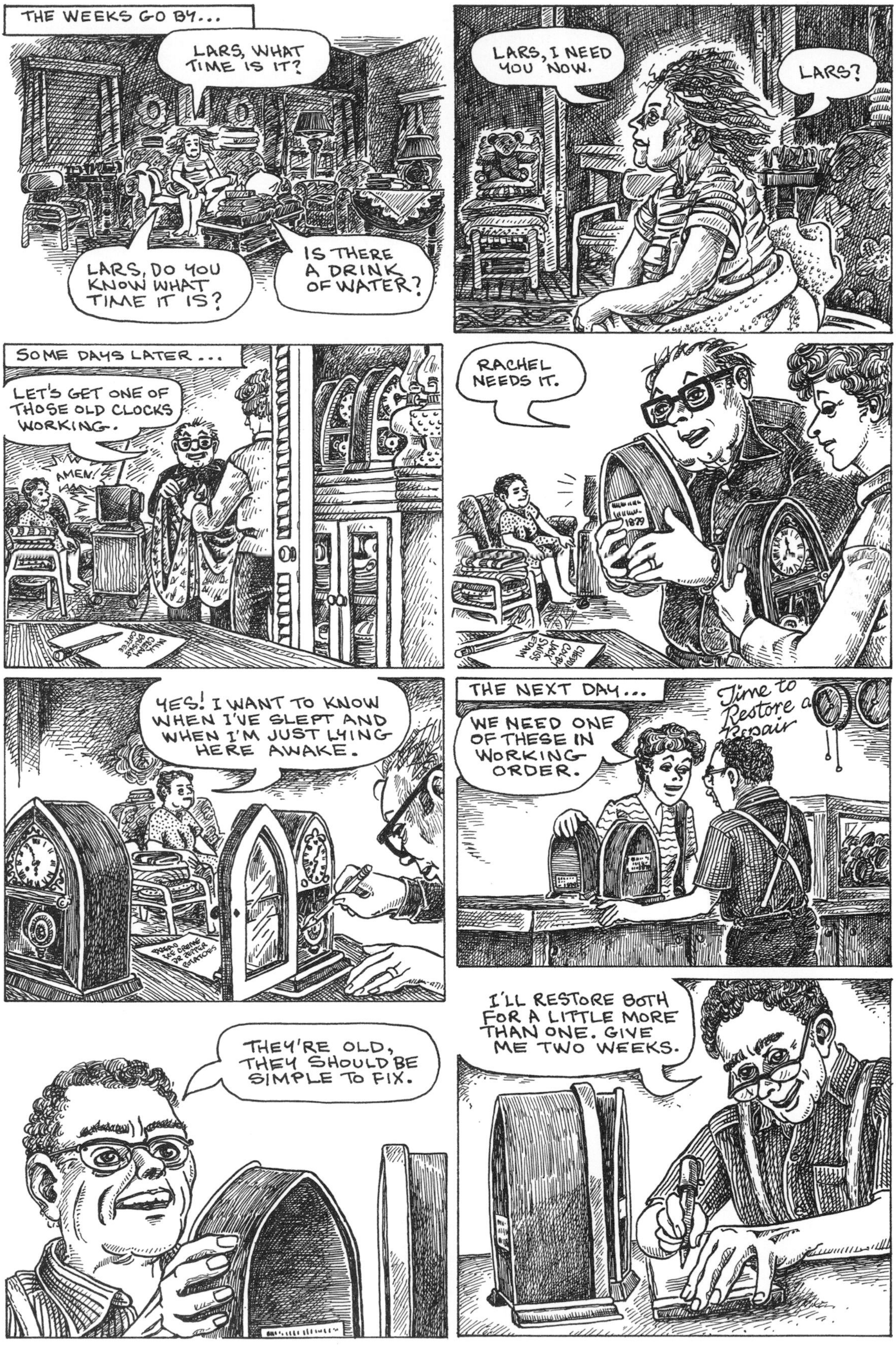
THE WEEKS GO BY...
LARS, WHAT TIME IS IT?
LARS, DO YOU KNOW WHAT TIME IT IS?
IS THERE A DRINK OF WATER?
LARS, I NEED YOU NOW.
LARS?
SOME DAYS LATER...
LET'S GET ONE OF THOSE OLD CLOCKS WORKING.
AMEN!
RACHEL NEEDS IT.
YES! I WANT TO KNOW WHEN I'VE SLEPT AND WHEN I'M JUST LYING HERE AWAKE.
THE NEXT DAY...
WE NEED ONE OF THESE IN WORKING ORDER.
THEY'RE OLD, THEY SHOULD BE SIMPLE TO FIX.
I'LL RESTORE BOTH FOR A LITTLE MORE THAN ONE. GIVE ME TWO WEEKS.

6

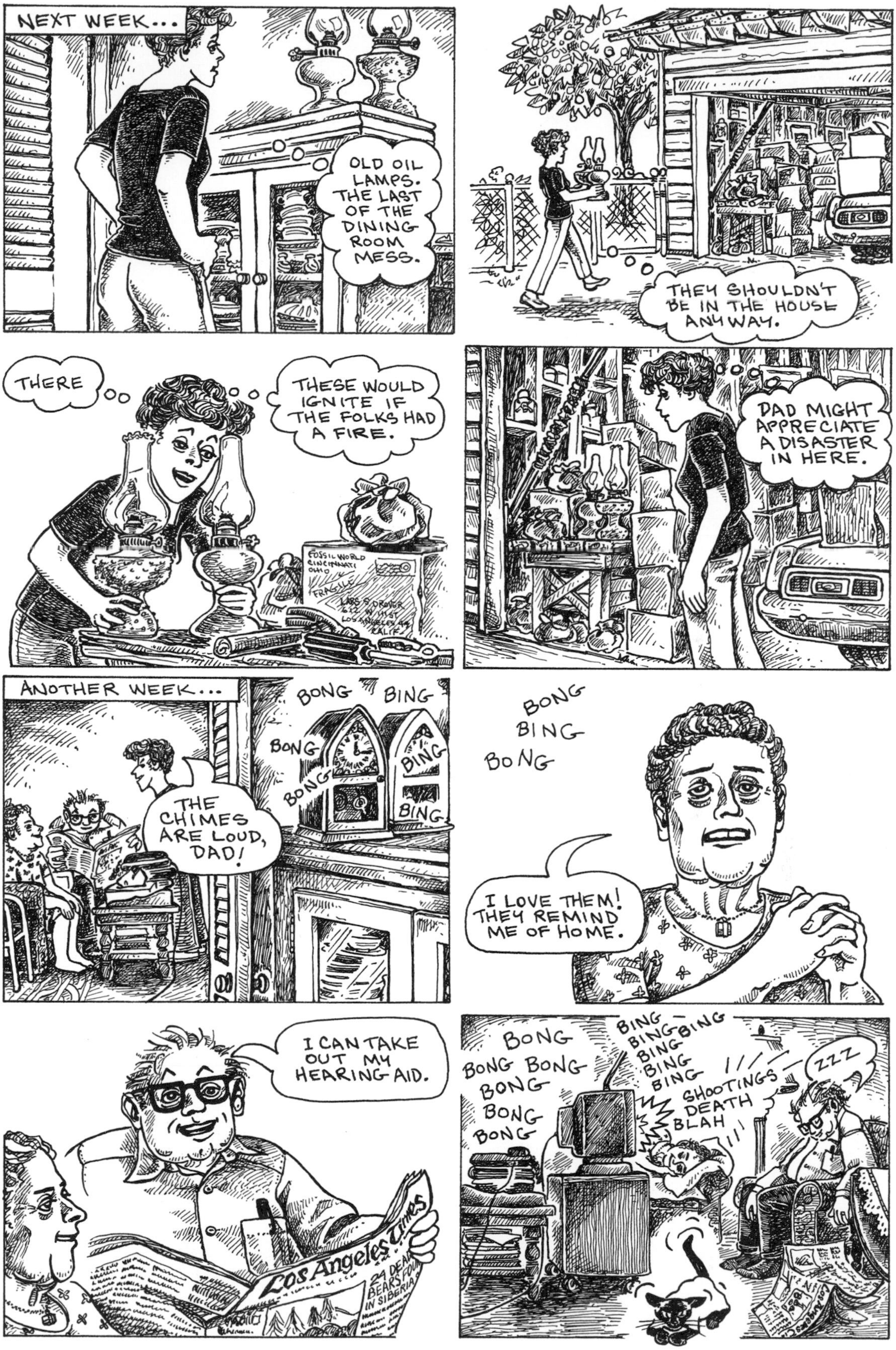
NEXT WEEK...
OLD OIL LAMPS. THE LAST OF THE DINING ROOM MESS.
THEY SHOULDN'T BE IN THE HOUSE ANYWAY.
THERE
THESE WOULD IGNITE IF THE FOLKS HAD A FIRE.
DAD MIGHT APPRECIATE A DISASTER IN HERE.
ANOTHER WEEK...
BONG BING BONG BONG BING BING
THE CHIMES ARE LOUD, DAD!
BONG BING BONG
I LOVE THEM! THEY REMIND ME OF HOME.
I CAN TAKE OUT MY HEARING AID.
Los Angeles Times
BONG BONG BONG BONG BONG BONG
BING BING BING BING BING BING
SHOOTINGS DEATH BLAH
ZZZ

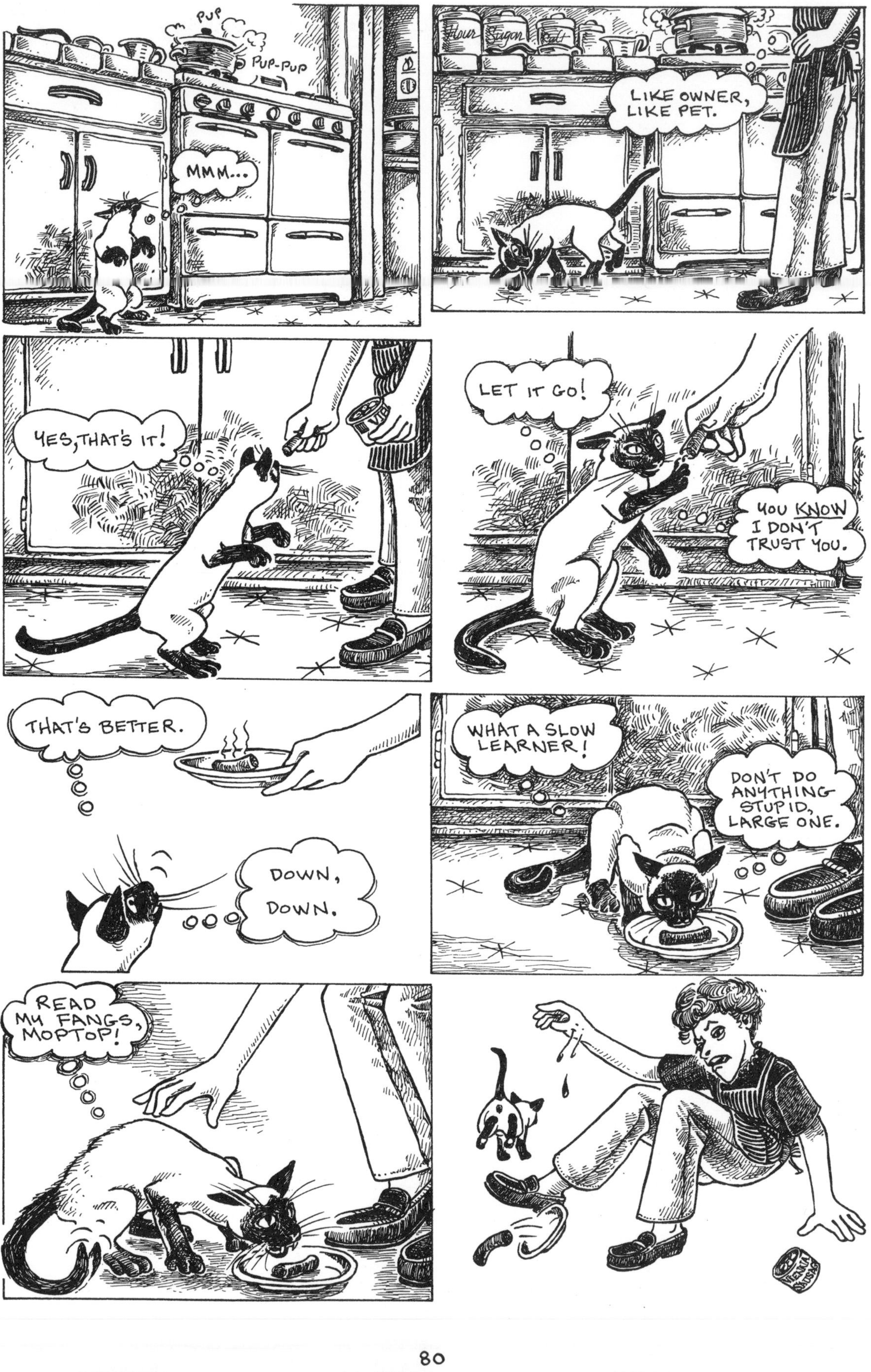
PUP
PUP-PUP
MMM...
LIKE OWNER, LIKE PET.
YES, THAT'S IT!
LET IT GO!
YOU KNOW I DON'T TRUST YOU.
THAT'S BETTER.
DOWN, DOWN.
WHAT A SLOW LEARNER!
DON'T DO ANYTHING STUPID, LARGE ONE.
READ MY FANGS, MOPTOP!

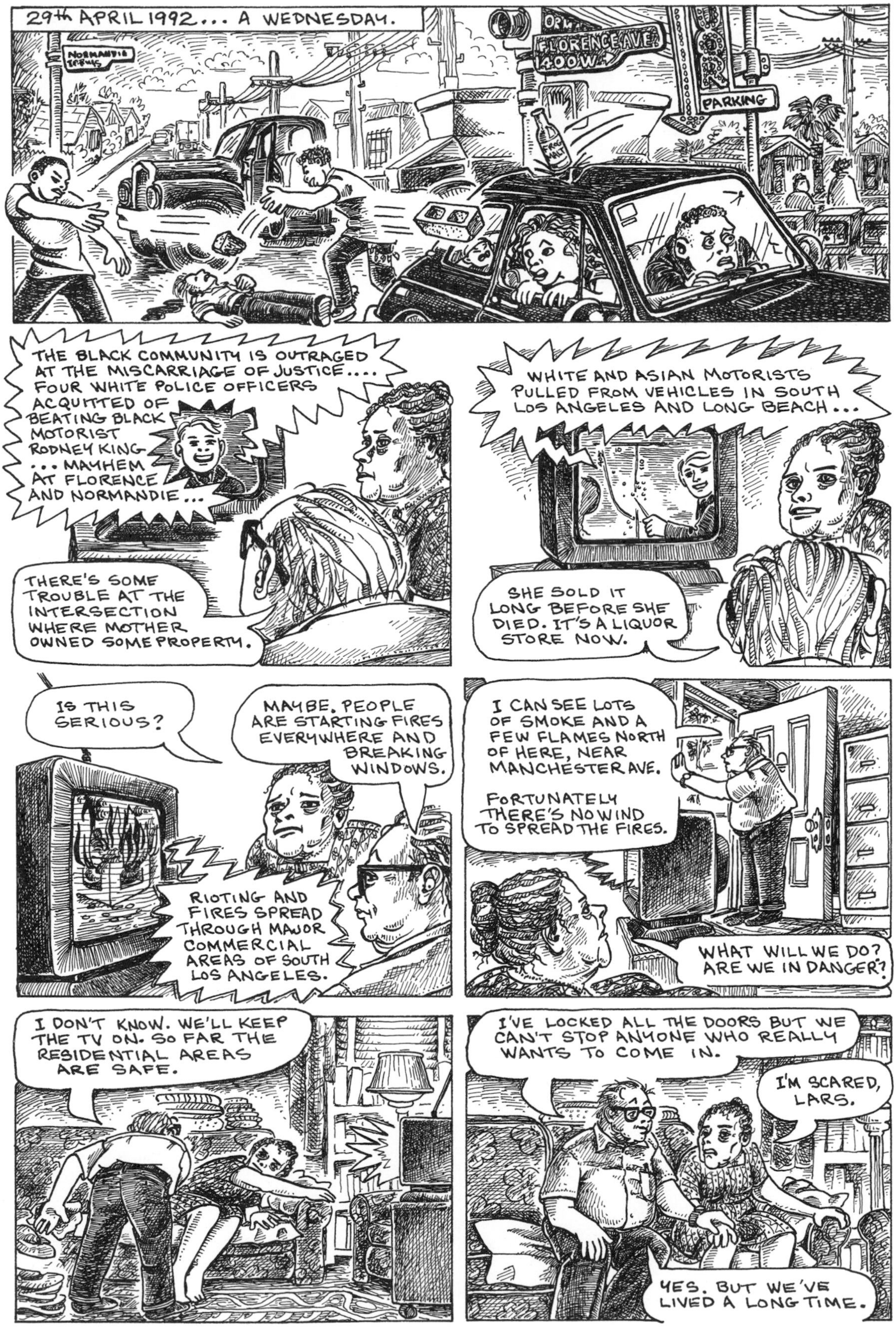
29th APRIL 1992... A WEDNESDAY.
FLORENCE AVE 1400 W
PARKING
THE BLACK COMMUNITY IS OUTRAGED AT THE MISCARRIAGE OF JUSTICE.... FOUR WHITE POLICE OFFICERS ACQUITTED OF BEATING BLACK MOTORIST RODNEY KING ...MAYHEM AT FLORENCE AND NORMANDIE...
THERE'S SOME TROUBLE AT THE INTERSECTION WHERE MOTHER OWNED SOME PROPERTY.
WHITE AND ASIAN MOTORISTS PULLED FROM VEHICLES IN SOUTH LOS ANGELES AND LONG BEACH...
SHE SOLD IT LONG BEFORE SHE DIED. IT'S A LIQUOR STORE NOW.
IS THIS SERIOUS?
MAYBE. PEOPLE ARE STARTING FIRES EVERYWHERE AND BREAKING WINDOWS.
RIOTING AND FIRES SPREAD THROUGH MAJOR COMMERCIAL AREAS OF SOUTH LOS ANGELES.
I CAN SEE LOTS OF SMOKE AND A FEW FLAMES NORTH OF HERE, NEAR MANCHESTER AVE.
FORTUNATELY THERE'S NO WIND TO SPREAD THE FIRES.
WHAT WILL WE DO? ARE WE IN DANGER?
I DON'T KNOW. WE'LL KEEP THE TV ON. SO FAR THE RESIDENTIAL AREAS ARE SAFE.
I'VE LOCKED ALL THE DOORS BUT WE CAN'T STOP ANYONE WHO REALLY WANTS TO COME IN.
I'M SCARED, LARS.
YES. BUT WE'VE LIVED A LONG TIME.

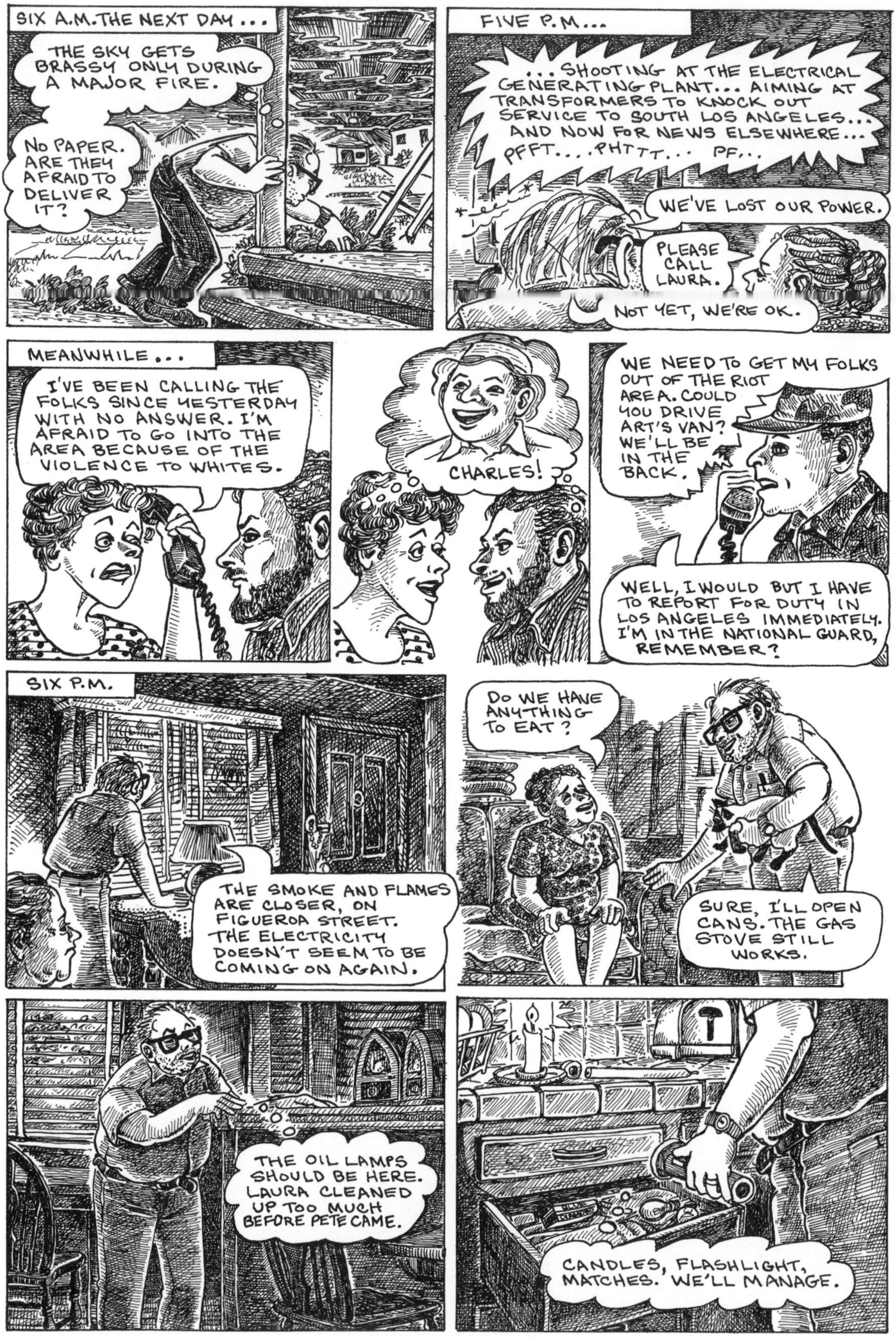
SIX A.M. THE NEXT DAY...
THE SKY GETS BRASSY ONLY DURING A MAJOR FIRE.
NO PAPER. ARE THEY AFRAID TO DELIVER IT?
FIVE P.M...
...SHOOTING AT THE ELECTRICAL GENERATING PLANT... AIMING AT TRANSFORMERS TO KNOCK OUT SERVICE TO SOUTH LOS ANGELES... AND NOW FOR NEWS ELSEWHERE... PFFT....PHTTTT... PF,..
WE'VE LOST OUR POWER.
PLEASE CALL LAURA.
NOT YET, WE'RE OK.
MEANWHILE...
I'VE BEEN CALLING THE FOLKS SINCE YESTERDAY WITH NO ANSWER. I'M AFRAID TO GO INTO THE AREA BECAUSE OF THE VIOLENCE TO WHITES.
CHARLES!
WE NEED TO GET MY FOLKS OUT OF THE RIOT AREA. COULD YOU DRIVE ART'S VAN? WE'LL BE IN THE BACK.
WELL, I WOULD BUT I HAVE TO REPORT FOR DUTY IN LOS ANGELES IMMEDIATELY. I'M IN THE NATIONAL GUARD, REMEMBER?
SIX P.M.
THE SMOKE AND FLAMES ARE CLOSER, ON FIGUEROA STREET. THE ELECTRICITY DOESN'T SEEM TO BE COMING ON AGAIN.
DO WE HAVE ANYTHING TO EAT?
SURE, I'LL OPEN CANS. THE GAS STOVE STILL WORKS.
THE OIL LAMPS SHOULD BE HERE. LAURA CLEANED UP TOO MUCH BEFORE PETE CAME.
CANDLES, FLASHLIGHT, MATCHES. WE'LL MANAGE.

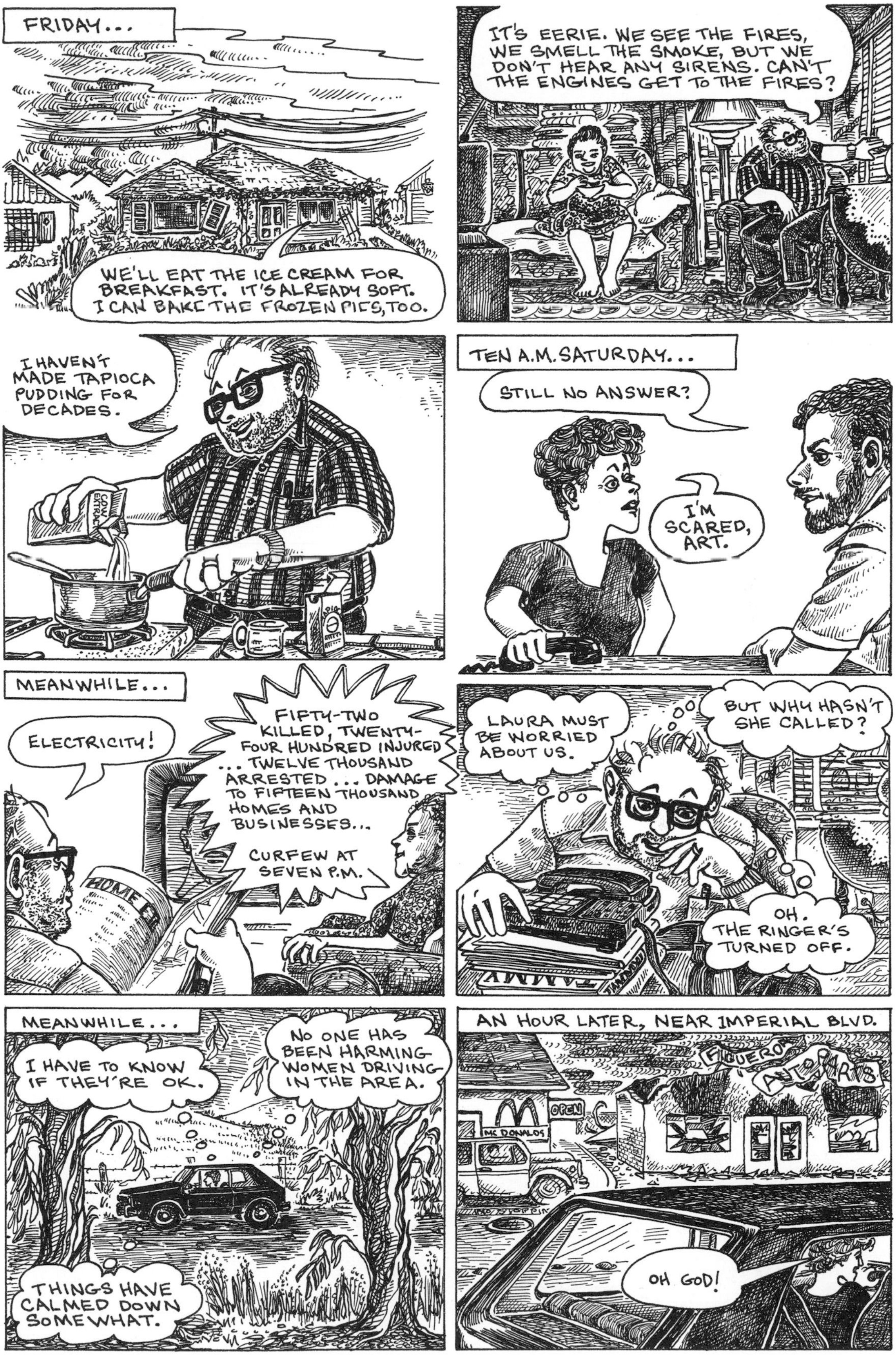
FRIDAY...
WE'LL EAT THE ICE CREAM FOR BREAKFAST. IT'S ALREADY SOFT. I CAN BAKE THE FROZEN PIES, TOO.
IT'S EERIE. WE SEE THE FIRES, WE SMELL THE SMOKE, BUT WE DON'T HEAR ANY SIRENS. CAN'T THE ENGINES GET TO THE FIRES?
I HAVEN'T MADE TAPIOCA PUDDING FOR DECADES.
TEN A.M. SATURDAY...
STILL NO ANSWER?
I'M SCARED, ART.
MEANWHILE...
ELECTRICITY!
FIFTY-TWO KILLED, TWENTY-FOUR HUNDRED INJURED ... TWELVE THOUSAND ARRESTED ... DAMAGE TO FIFTEEN THOUSAND HOMES AND BUSINESSES...
CURFEW AT SEVEN P.M.
LAURA MUST BE WORRIED ABOUT US.
BUT WHY HASN'T SHE CALLED?
OH. THE RINGER'S TURNED OFF.
MEANWHILE...
I HAVE TO KNOW IF THEY'RE OK.
NO ONE HAS BEEN HARMING WOMEN DRIVING IN THE AREA.
THINGS HAVE CALMED DOWN SOMEWHAT.
AN HOUR LATER, NEAR IMPERIAL BLVD.
OPEN
MC DONALDS
OH GOD!

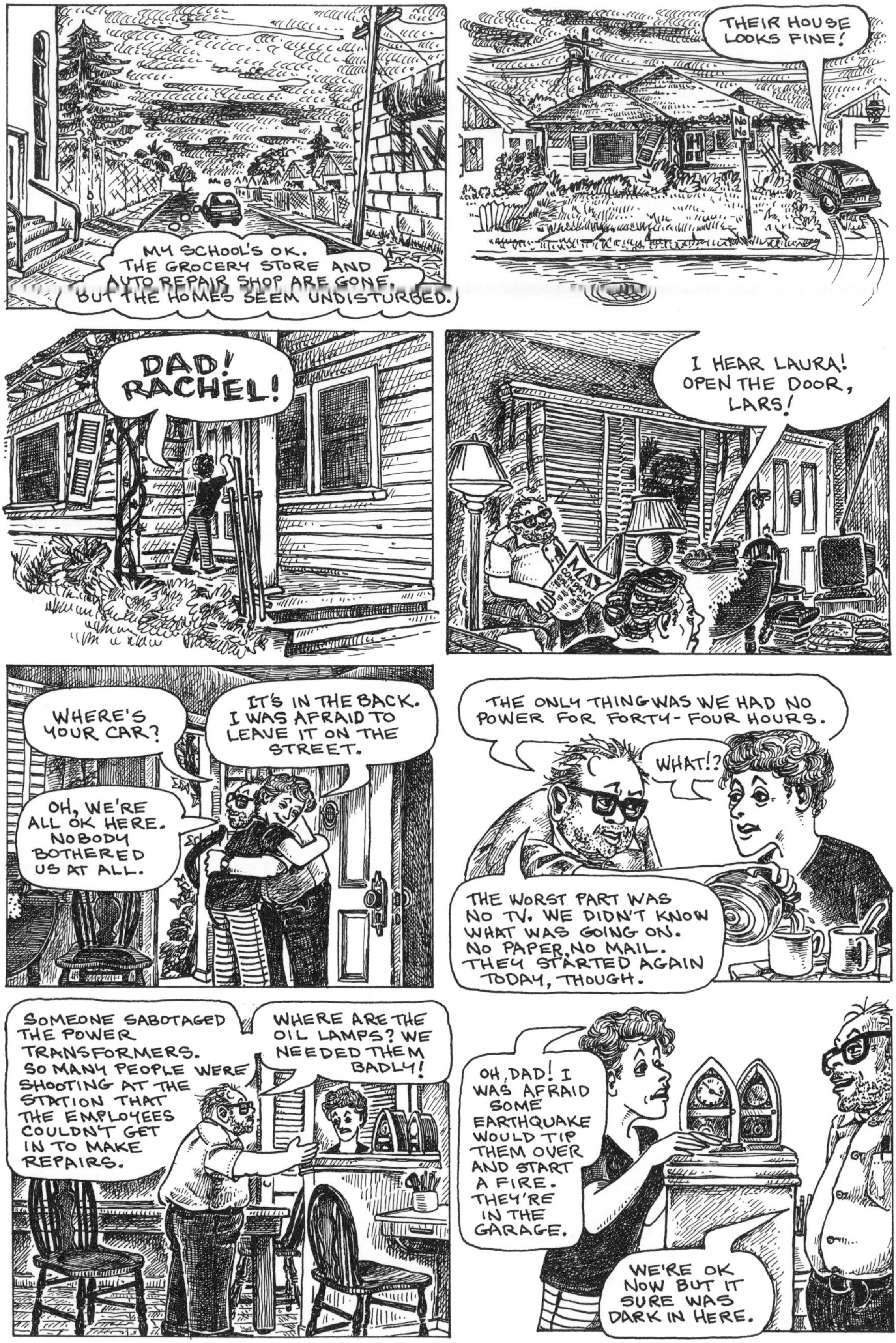
MY SCHOOL'S OK. THE GROCERY STORE AND AUTO REPAIR SHOP ARE GONE, BUT THE HOMES SEEM UNDISTURBED.
THEIR HOUSE LOOKS FINE!
NO
DAD! RACHEL!
I HEAR LAURA! OPEN THE DOOR, LARS!
MAY COMPANY
WHERE'S YOUR CAR?
IT'S IN THE BACK. I WAS AFRAID TO LEAVE IT ON THE STREET.
OH, WE'RE ALL OK HERE. NOBODY BOTHERED US AT ALL.
THE ONLY THING WAS WE HAD NO POWER FOR FORTY-FOUR HOURS.
WHAT!?
THE WORST PART WAS NO TV. WE DIDN'T KNOW WHAT WAS GOING ON. NO PAPER, NO MAIL. THEY STARTED AGAIN TODAY, THOUGH.
SOMEONE SABOTAGED THE POWER TRANSFORMERS. SO MANY PEOPLE WERE SHOOTING AT THE STATION THAT THE EMPLOYEES COULDN'T GET IN TO MAKE REPAIRS.
WHERE ARE THE OIL LAMPS? WE NEEDED THEM BADLY!
OH, DAD! I WAS AFRAID SOME EARTHQUAKE WOULD TIP THEM OVER AND START A FIRE. THEY'RE IN THE GARAGE.
WE'RE OK NOW BUT IT SURE WAS DARK IN HERE.

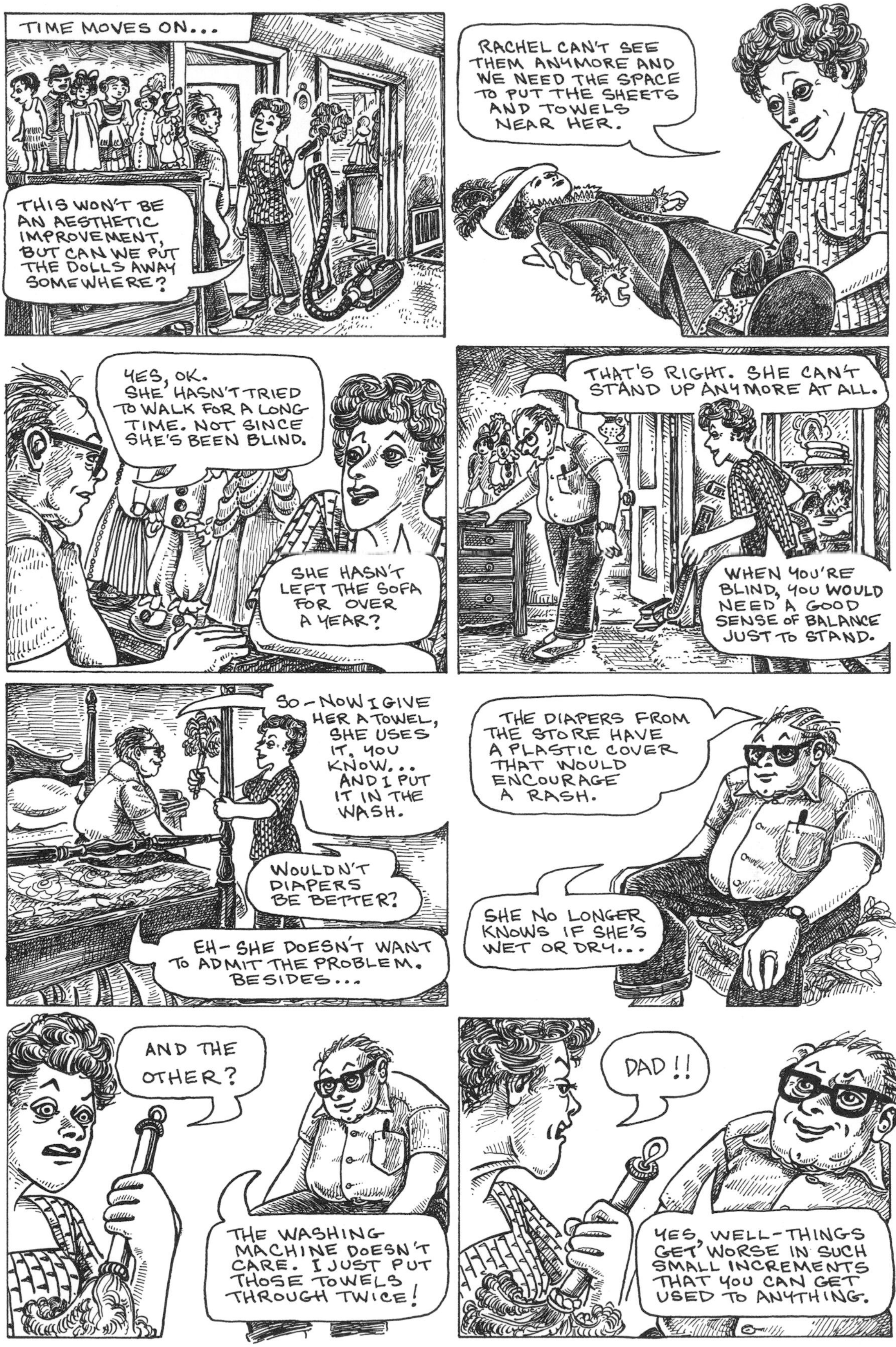
TIME MOVES ON...
THIS WON'T BE AN AESTHETIC IMPROVEMENT, BUT CAN WE PUT THE DOLLS AWAY SOMEWHERE?
RACHEL CAN'T SEE THEM ANYMORE AND WE NEED THE SPACE TO PUT THE SHEETS AND TOWELS NEAR HER.
YES, OK. SHE HASN'T TRIED TO WALK FOR A LONG TIME. NOT SINCE SHE'S BEEN BLIND.
SHE HASN'T LEFT THE SOFA FOR OVER A YEAR?
THAT'S RIGHT. SHE CAN'T STAND UP ANYMORE AT ALL.
WHEN YOU'RE BLIND, YOU WOULD NEED A GOOD SENSE OF BALANCE JUST TO STAND.
SO-NOW I GIVE HER A TOWEL, SHE USES IT, YOU KNOW... AND I PUT IT IN THE WASH.
WOULDN'T DIAPERS BE BETTER?
EH-SHE DOESN'T WANT TO ADMIT THE PROBLEM. BESIDES...
THE DIAPERS FROM THE STORE HAVE A PLASTIC COVER THAT WOULD ENCOURAGE A RASH.
SHE NO LONGER KNOWS IF SHE'S WET OR DRY...
AND THE OTHER?
THE WASHING MACHINE DOESN'T CARE. I JUST PUT THOSE TOWELS THROUGH TWICE!
DAD!!
YES, WELL-THINGS GET WORSE IN SUCH SMALL INCREMENTS THAT YOU CAN GET USED TO ANYTHING.

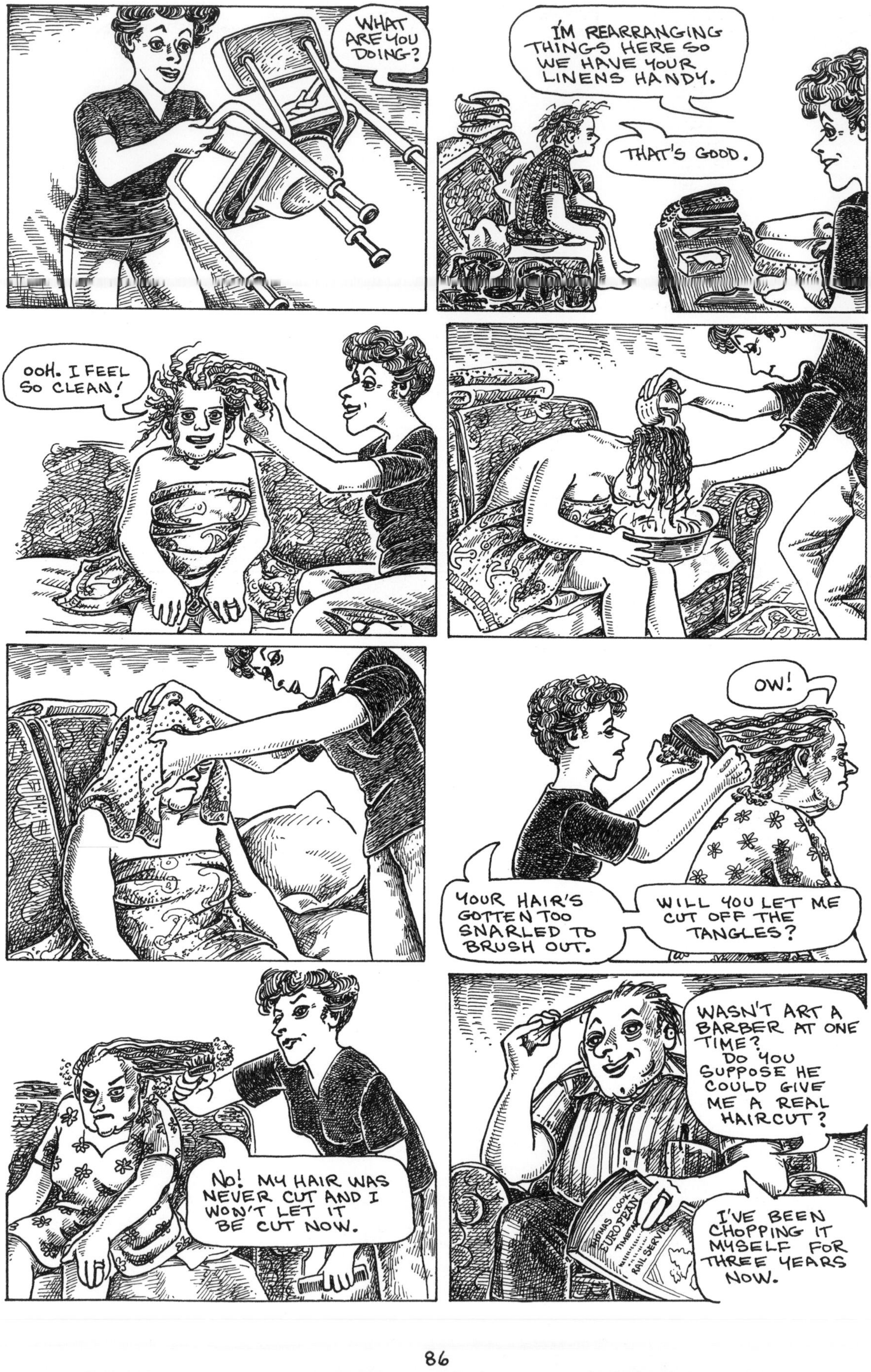
WHAT ARE YOU DOING?
I'M REARRANGING THINGS HERE SO WE HAVE YOUR LINENS HANDY.
THAT'S GOOD.
OOH. I FEEL SO CLEAN!
OW!
YOUR HAIR'S GOTTEN TOO SNARLED TO BRUSH OUT.
WILL YOU LET ME CUT OFF THE TANGLES?
NO! MY HAIR WAS NEVER CUT AND I WON'T LET IT BE CUT NOW.
WASN'T ART A BARBER AT ONE TIME? DO YOU SUPPOSE HE COULD GIVE ME A REAL HAIRCUT?
I'VE BEEN CHOPPING IT MYSELF FOR THREE YEARS NOW.

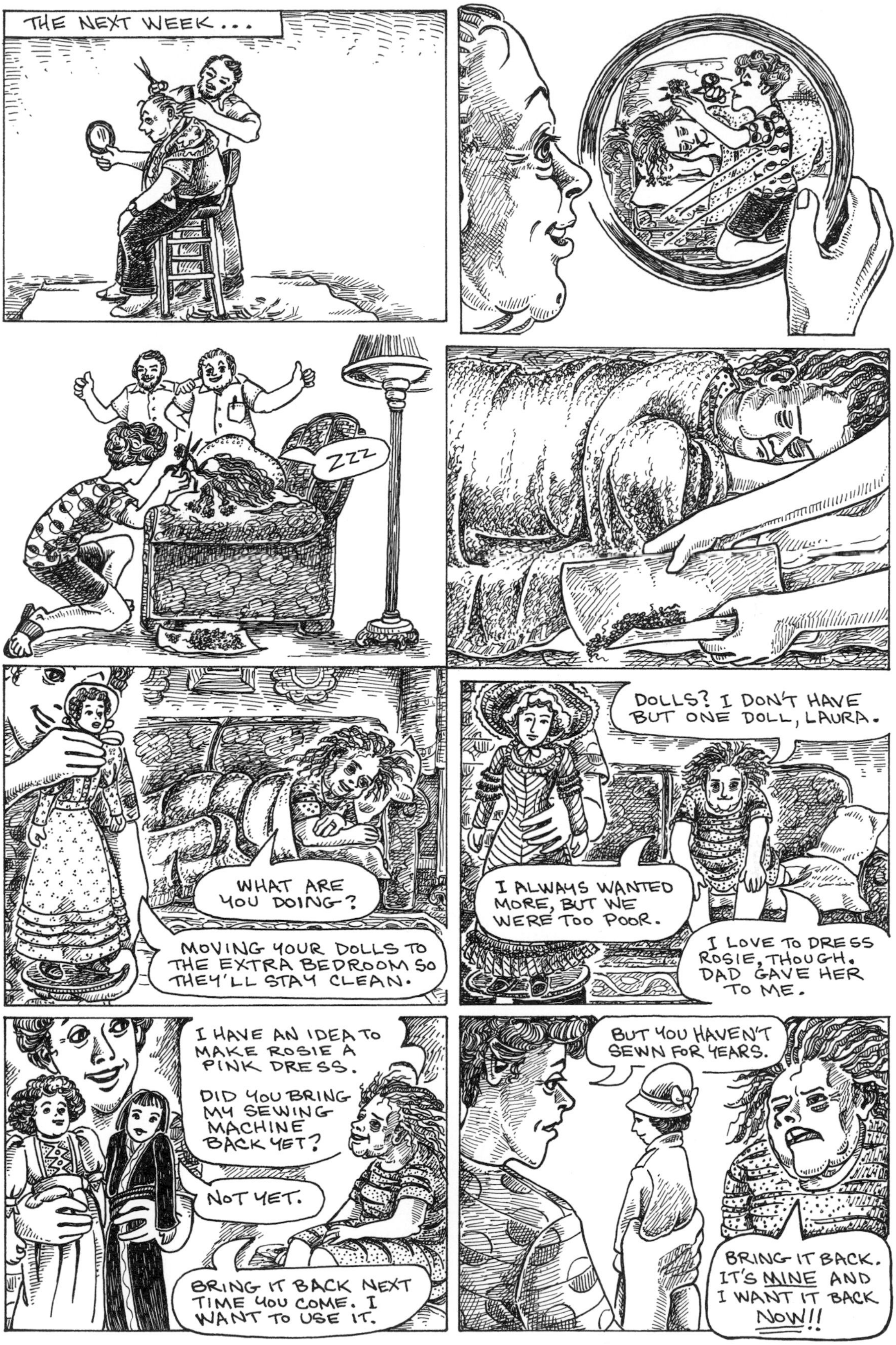
THE NEXT WEEK . . .
ZZZ
WHAT ARE YOU DOING?
MOVING YOUR DOLLS TO THE EXTRA BEDROOM SO THEY'LL STAY CLEAN.
DOLLS? I DON'T HAVE BUT ONE DOLL, LAURA.
I ALWAYS WANTED MORE, BUT WE WERE TOO POOR.
I LOVE TO DRESS ROSIE, THOUGH. DAD GAVE HER TO ME.
I HAVE AN IDEA TO MAKE ROSIE A PINK DRESS.
DID YOU BRING MY SEWING MACHINE BACK YET?
NOT YET.
BRING IT BACK NEXT TIME YOU COME. I WANT TO USE IT.
BUT YOU HAVEN'T SEWN FOR YEARS.
BRING IT BACK. IT'S MINE AND I WANT IT BACK NOW!!

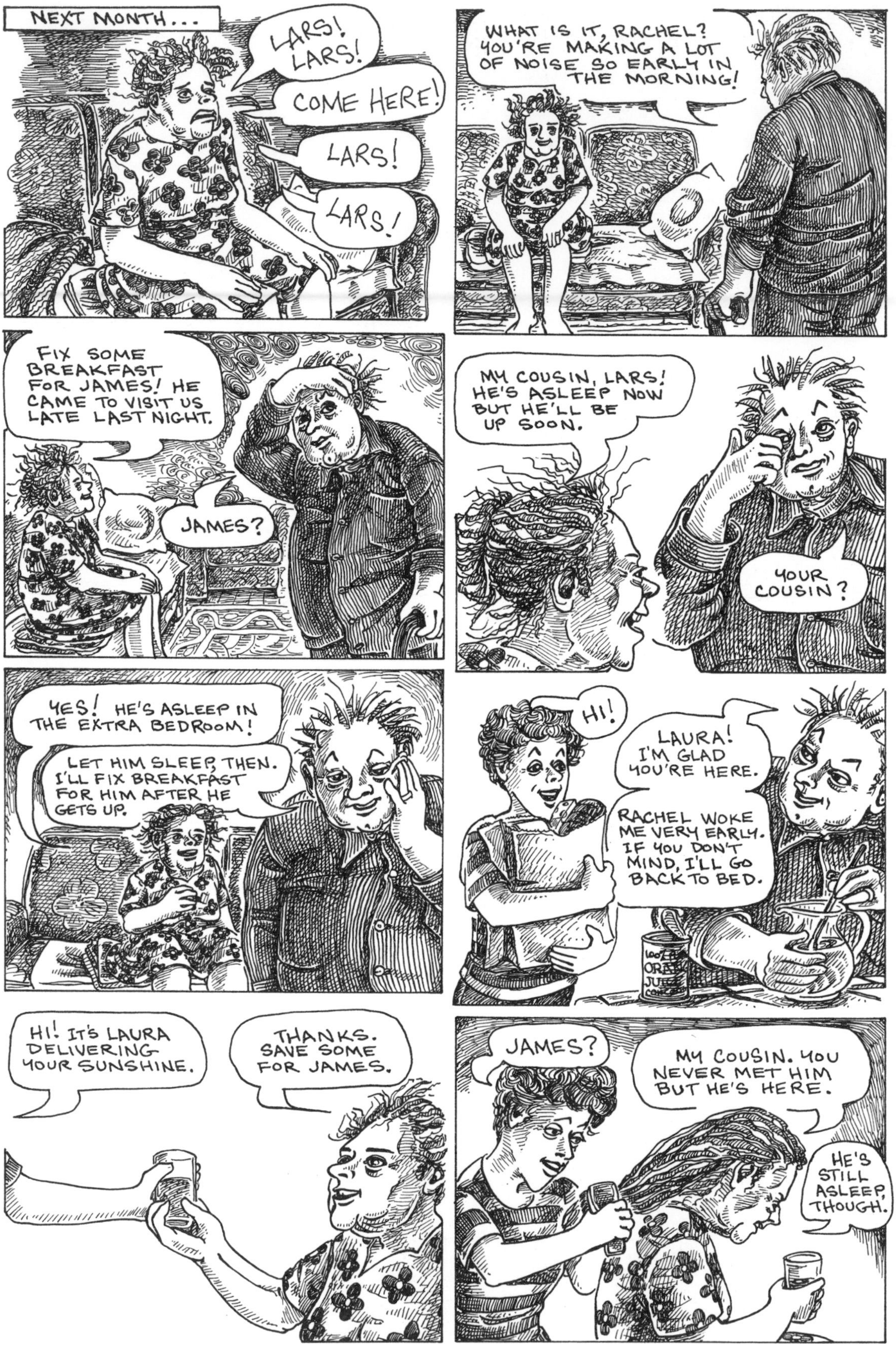
NEXT MONTH...
LARS! LARS!
COME HERE!
LARS!
LARS!
WHAT IS IT, RACHEL? YOU'RE MAKING A LOT OF NOISE SO EARLY IN THE MORNING!
FIX SOME BREAKFAST FOR JAMES! HE CAME TO VISIT US LATE LAST NIGHT.
JAMES?
MY COUSIN, LARS! HE'S ASLEEP NOW BUT HE'LL BE UP SOON.
YOUR COUSIN?
YES! HE'S ASLEEP IN THE EXTRA BEDROOM!
LET HIM SLEEP, THEN. I'LL FIX BREAKFAST FOR HIM AFTER HE GETS UP.
HI!
LAURA! I'M GLAD YOU'RE HERE.
RACHEL WOKE ME VERY EARLY. IF YOU DON'T MIND, I'LL GO BACK TO BED.
HI! IT'S LAURA DELIVERING YOUR SUNSHINE.
THANKS. SAVE SOME FOR JAMES.
JAMES?
MY COUSIN. YOU NEVER MET HIM BUT HE'S HERE.
HE'S STILL ASLEEP, THOUGH.

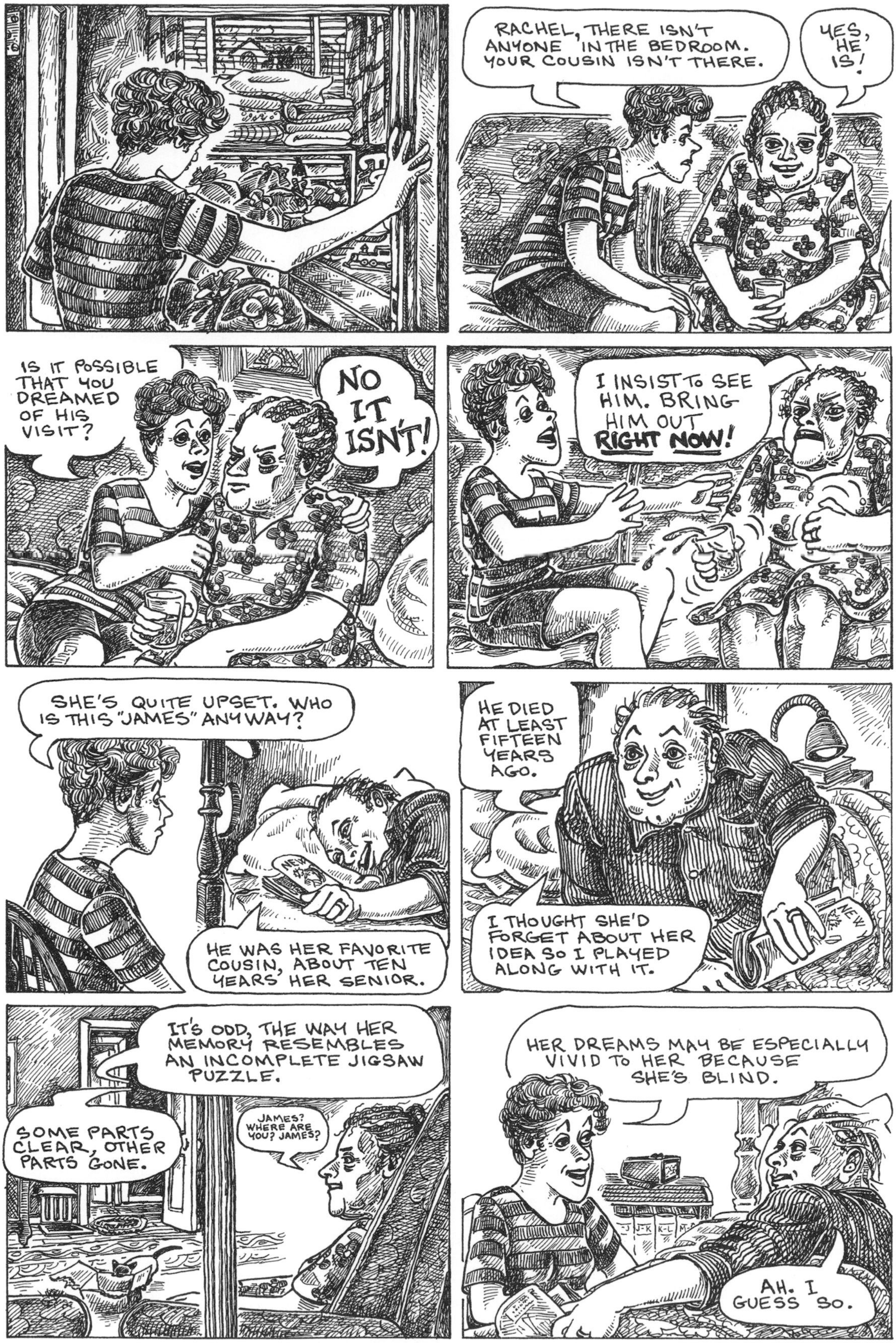
RACHEL, THERE ISN'T ANYONE IN THE BEDROOM. YOUR COUSIN ISN'T THERE.
YES, HE IS!
IS IT POSSIBLE THAT YOU DREAMED OF HIS VISIT?
NO IT ISN'T!
I INSIST TO SEE HIM. BRING HIM OUT RIGHT NOW!
SHE'S QUITE UPSET. WHO IS THIS "JAMES" ANYWAY?
HE WAS HER FAVORITE COUSIN, ABOUT TEN YEARS HER SENIOR.
HE DIED AT LEAST FIFTEEN YEARS AGO.
I THOUGHT SHE'D FORGET ABOUT HER IDEA SO I PLAYED ALONG WITH IT.
IT'S ODD, THE WAY HER MEMORY RESEMBLES AN INCOMPLETE JIGSAW PUZZLE.
SOME PARTS CLEAR, OTHER PARTS GONE.
JAMES? WHERE ARE YOU? JAMES?
HER DREAMS MAY BE ESPECIALLY VIVID TO HER BECAUSE SHE'S BLIND.
AH. I GUESS SO.

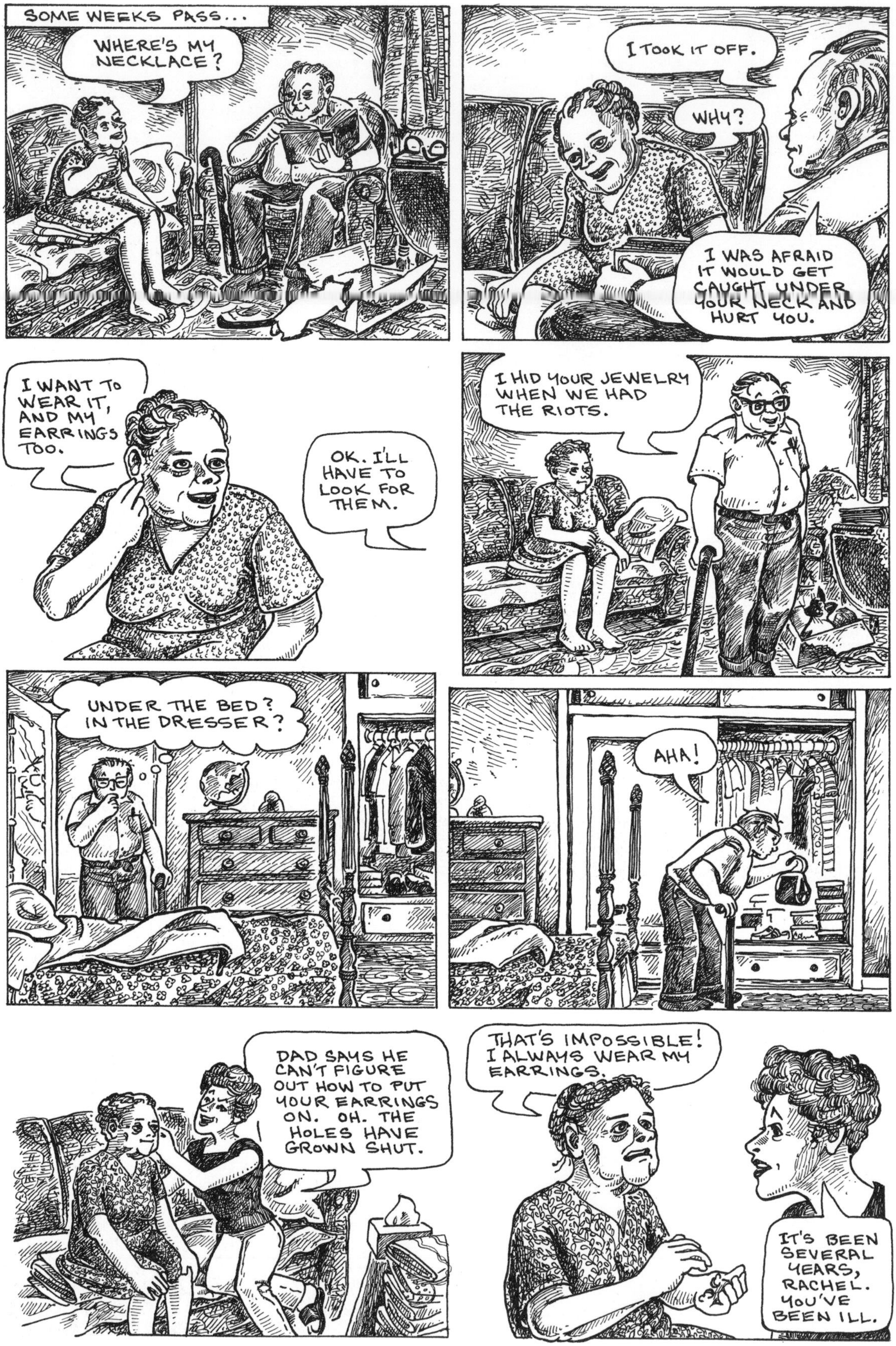

SOME WEEKS PASS...
WHERE'S MY NECKLACE?
I TOOK IT OFF.
WHY?
I WAS AFRAID IT WOULD GET CAUGHT UNDER YOUR NECK AND HURT YOU.
I WANT TO WEAR IT, AND MY EARRINGS TOO.
OK. I'LL HAVE TO LOOK FOR THEM.
I HID YOUR JEWELRY WHEN WE HAD THE RIOTS.
UNDER THE BED? IN THE DRESSER?
AHA!
DAD SAYS HE CAN'T FIGURE OUT HOW TO PUT YOUR EARRINGS ON. OH. THE HOLES HAVE GROWN SHUT.
THAT'S IMPOSSIBLE! I ALWAYS WEAR MY EARRINGS.
IT'S BEEN SEVERAL YEARS, RACHEL. YOU'VE BEEN ILL.

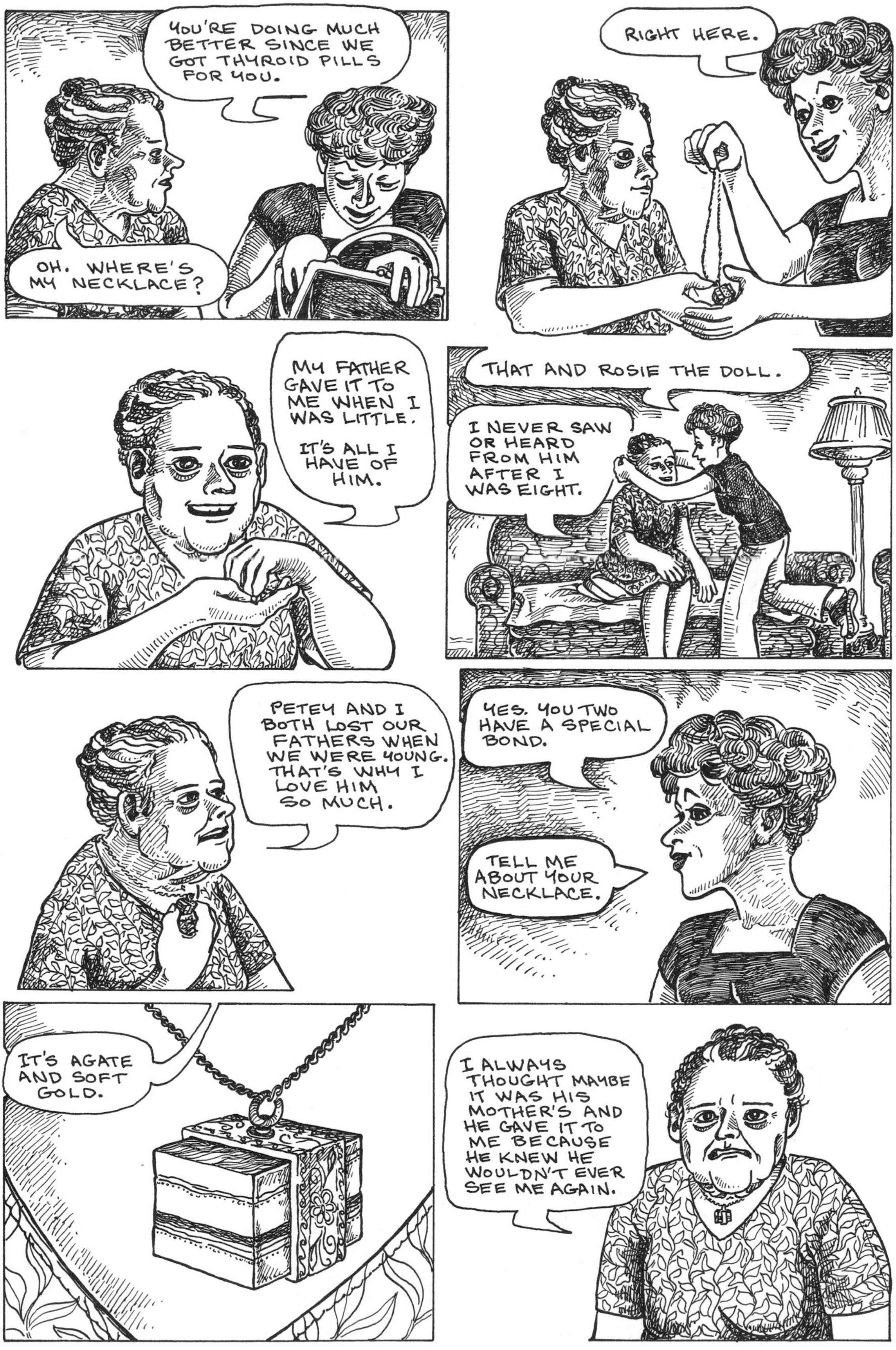
YOU'RE DOING MUCH BETTER SINCE WE GOT THYROID PILLS FOR YOU.
OH. WHERE'S MY NECKLACE?
RIGHT HERE.
MY FATHER GAVE IT TO ME WHEN I WAS LITTLE.
IT'S ALL I HAVE OF HIM.
THAT AND ROSIE THE DOLL.
I NEVER SAW OR HEARD FROM HIM AFTER I WAS EIGHT.
PETEY AND I BOTH LOST OUR FATHERS WHEN WE WERE YOUNG. THAT'S WHY I LOVE HIM SO MUCH.
YES. YOU TWO HAVE A SPECIAL BOND.
TELL ME ABOUT YOUR NECKLACE.
IT'S AGATE AND SOFT GOLD.
I ALWAYS THOUGHT MAYBE IT WAS HIS MOTHER'S AND HE GAVE IT TO ME BECAUSE HE KNEW HE WOULDN'T EVER SEE ME AGAIN.

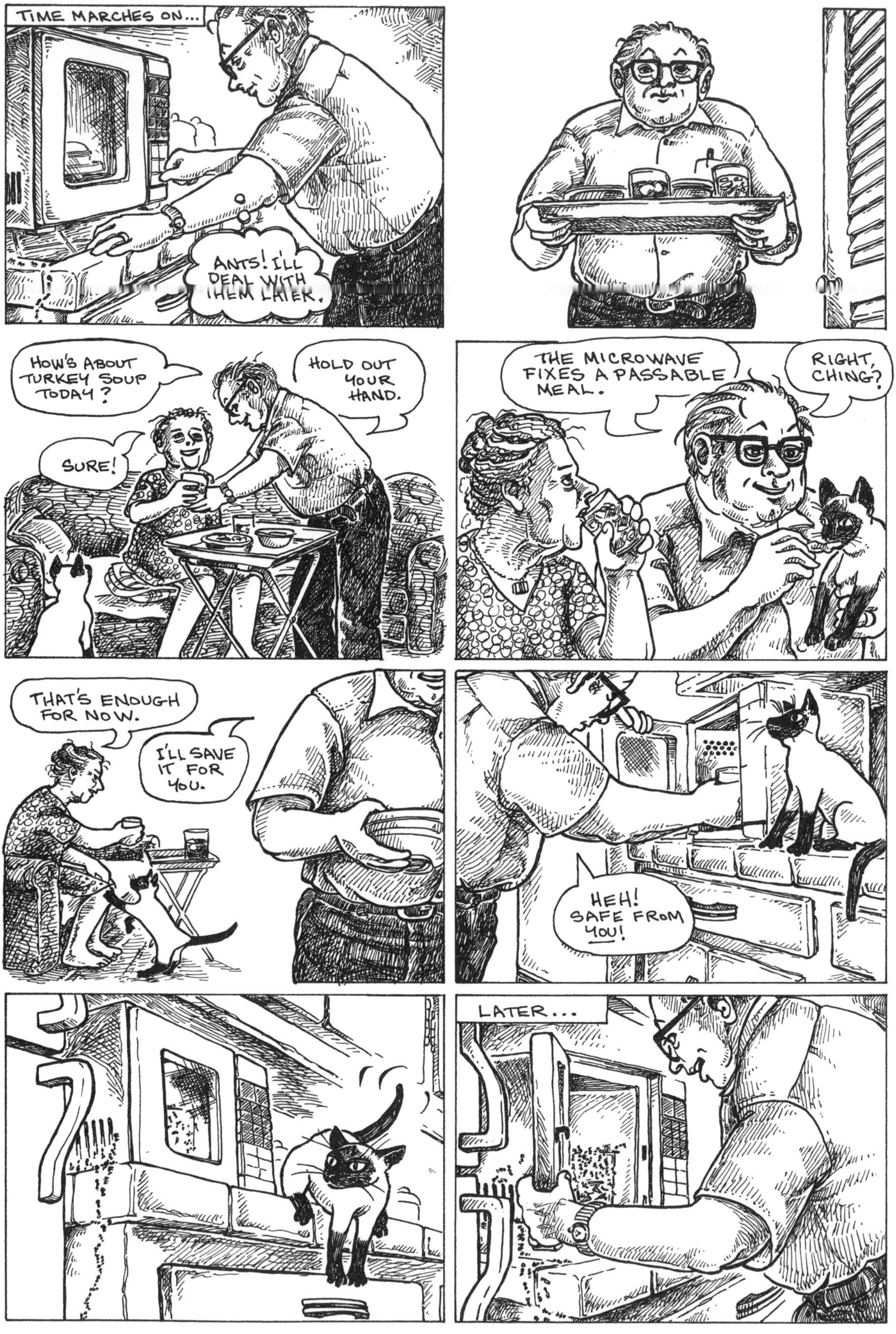
TIME MARCHES ON...
ANTS! I'LL DEAL WITH THEM LATER.
HOW'S ABOUT TURKEY SOUP TODAY?
SURE!
HOLD OUT YOUR HAND.
THE MICROWAVE FIXES A PASSABLE MEAL.
RIGHT, CHING?
THAT'S ENOUGH FOR NOW.
I'LL SAVE IT FOR YOU.
HEH! SAFE FROM YOU!
LATER...

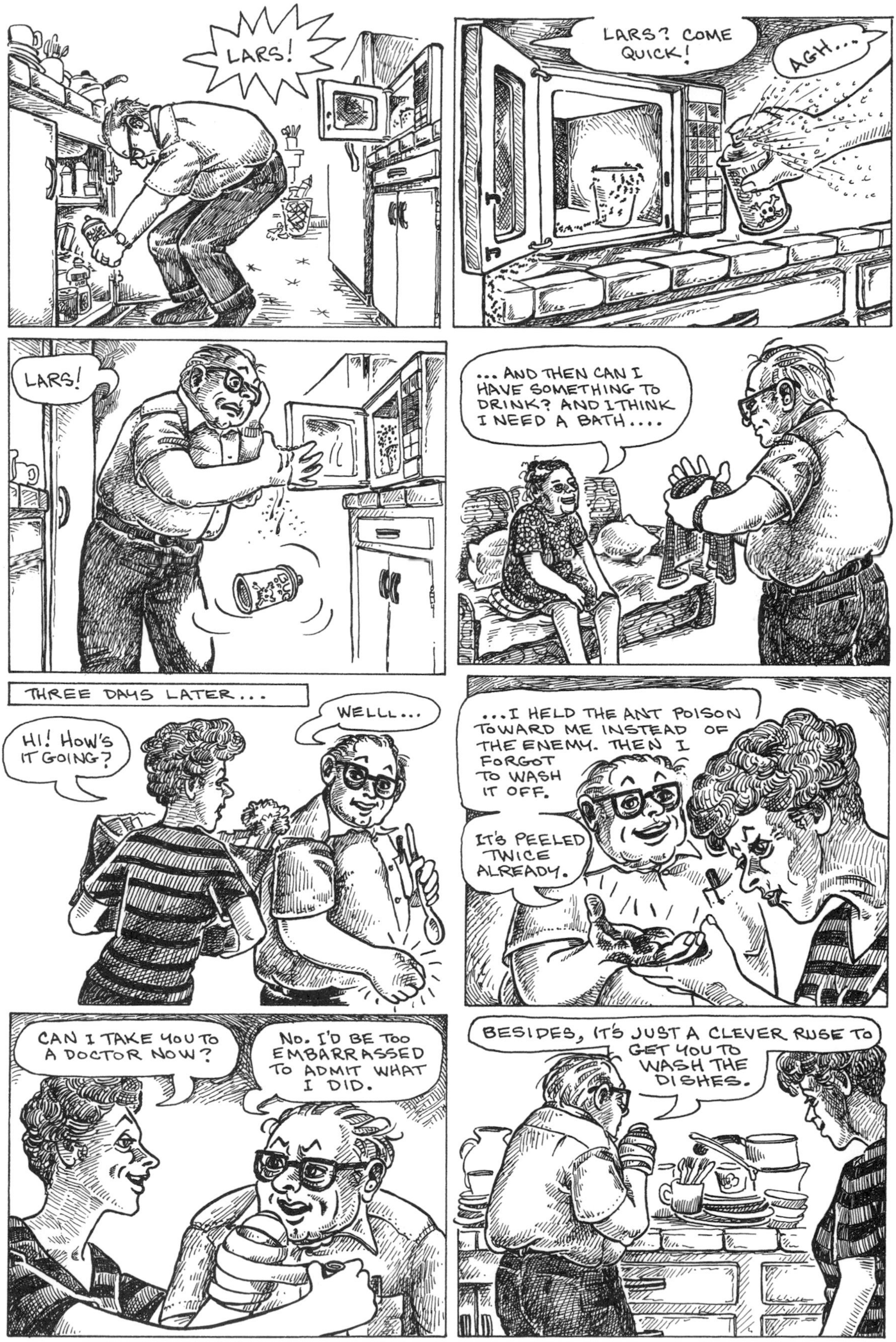
LARS!
LARS? COME QUICK!
AGH...
LARS!
...AND THEN CAN I HAVE SOMETHING TO DRINK? AND I THINK I NEED A BATH....
THREE DAYS LATER...
HI! HOW'S IT GOING?
WELLL...
...I HELD THE ANT POISON TOWARD ME INSTEAD OF THE ENEMY. THEN I FORGOT TO WASH IT OFF.
IT'S PEELED TWICE ALREADY.
CAN I TAKE YOU TO A DOCTOR NOW?
NO. I'D BE TOO EMBARRASSED TO ADMIT WHAT I DID.
BESIDES, IT'S JUST A CLEVER RUSE TO GET YOU TO WASH THE DISHES.

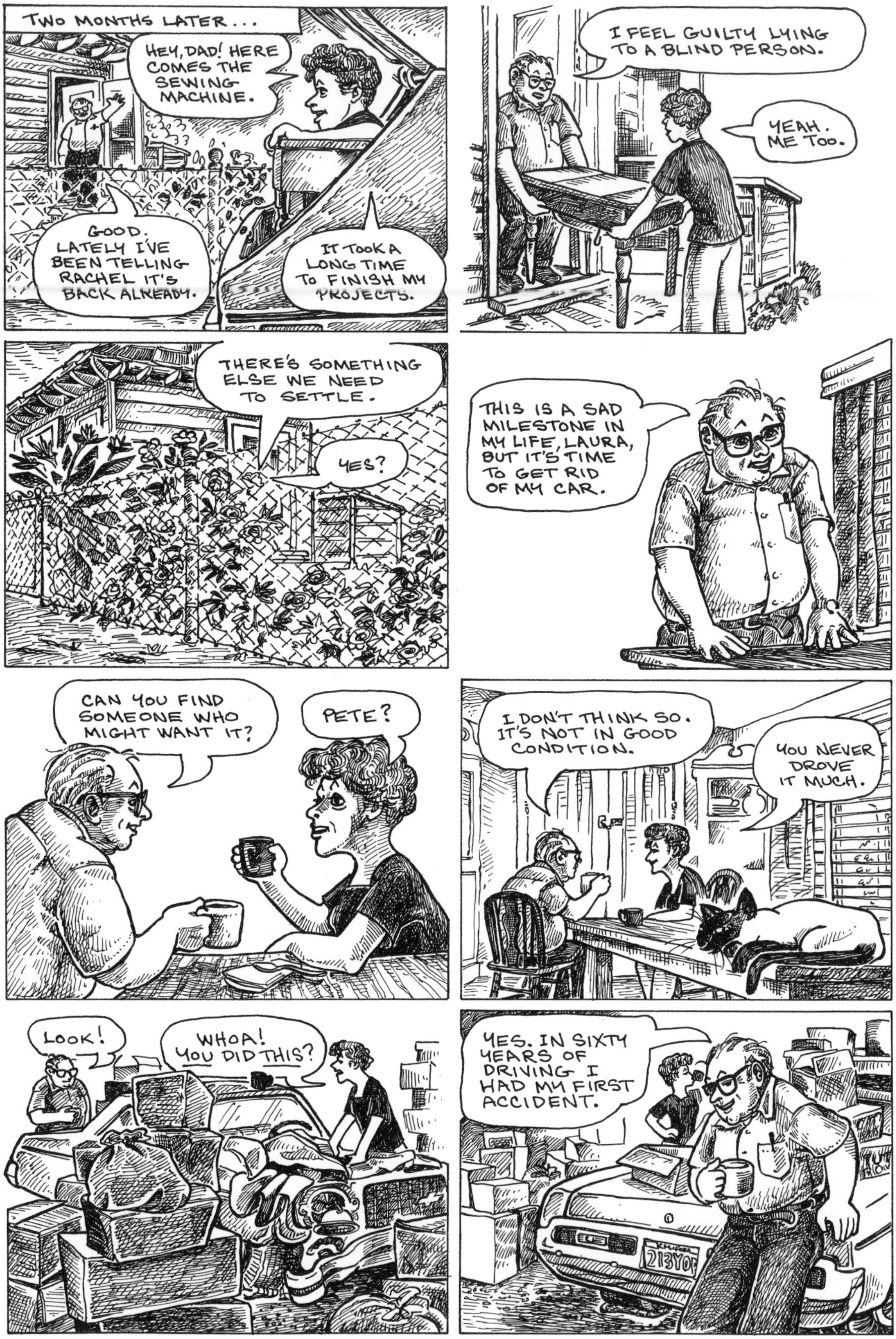
TWO MONTHS LATER...
HEY, DAD! HERE COMES THE SEWING MACHINE.
GOOD. LATELY I'VE BEEN TELLING RACHEL IT'S BACK ALREADY.
IT TOOK A LONG TIME TO FINISH MY PROJECTS.
I FEEL GUILTY LYING TO A BLIND PERSON.
YEAH. ME TOO.
THERE'S SOMETHING ELSE WE NEED TO SETTLE.
YES?
THIS IS A SAD MILESTONE IN MY LIFE, LAURA, BUT IT'S TIME TO GET RID OF MY CAR.
CAN YOU FIND SOMEONE WHO MIGHT WANT IT?
PETE?
I DON'T THINK SO. IT'S NOT IN GOOD CONDITION.
YOU NEVER DROVE IT MUCH.
LOOK!
WHOA! YOU DID THIS?
YES. IN SIXTY YEARS OF DRIVING I HAD MY FIRST ACCIDENT.
213YOC

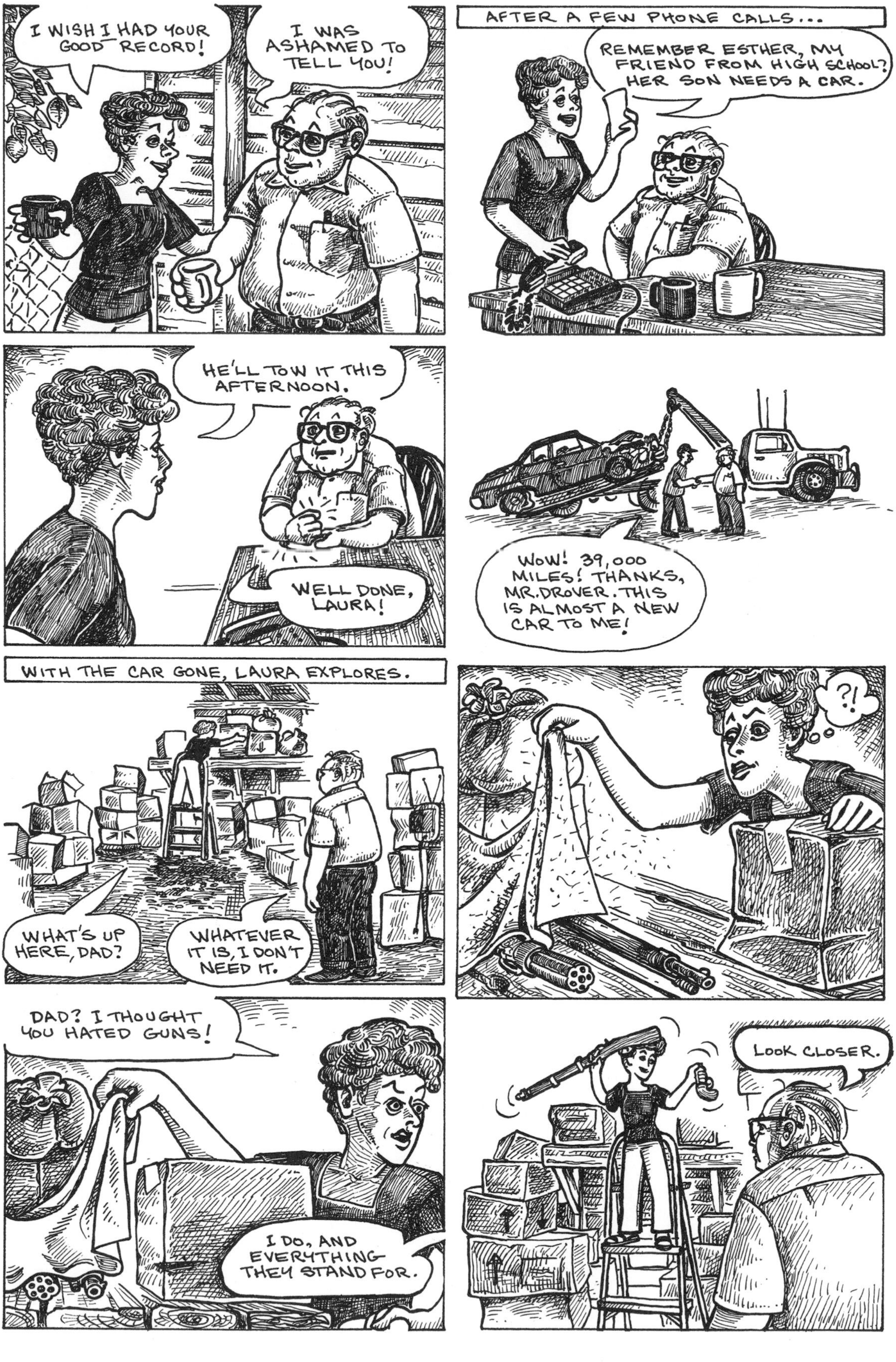
I WISH I HAD YOUR GOOD RECORD!
I WAS ASHAMED TO TELL YOU!
AFTER A FEW PHONE CALLS...
REMEMBER ESTHER, MY FRIEND FROM HIGH SCHOOL? HER SON NEEDS A CAR.
HE'LL TOW IT THIS AFTERNOON.
WELL DONE, LAURA!
WOW! 39,000 MILES! THANKS, MR. DROVER. THIS IS ALMOST A NEW CAR TO ME!
WITH THE CAR GONE, LAURA EXPLORES.
WHAT'S UP HERE, DAD?
WHATEVER IT IS, I DON'T NEED IT.
?!
DAD? I THOUGHT YOU HATED GUNS!
I DO, AND EVERYTHING THEY STAND FOR.
LOOK CLOSER.

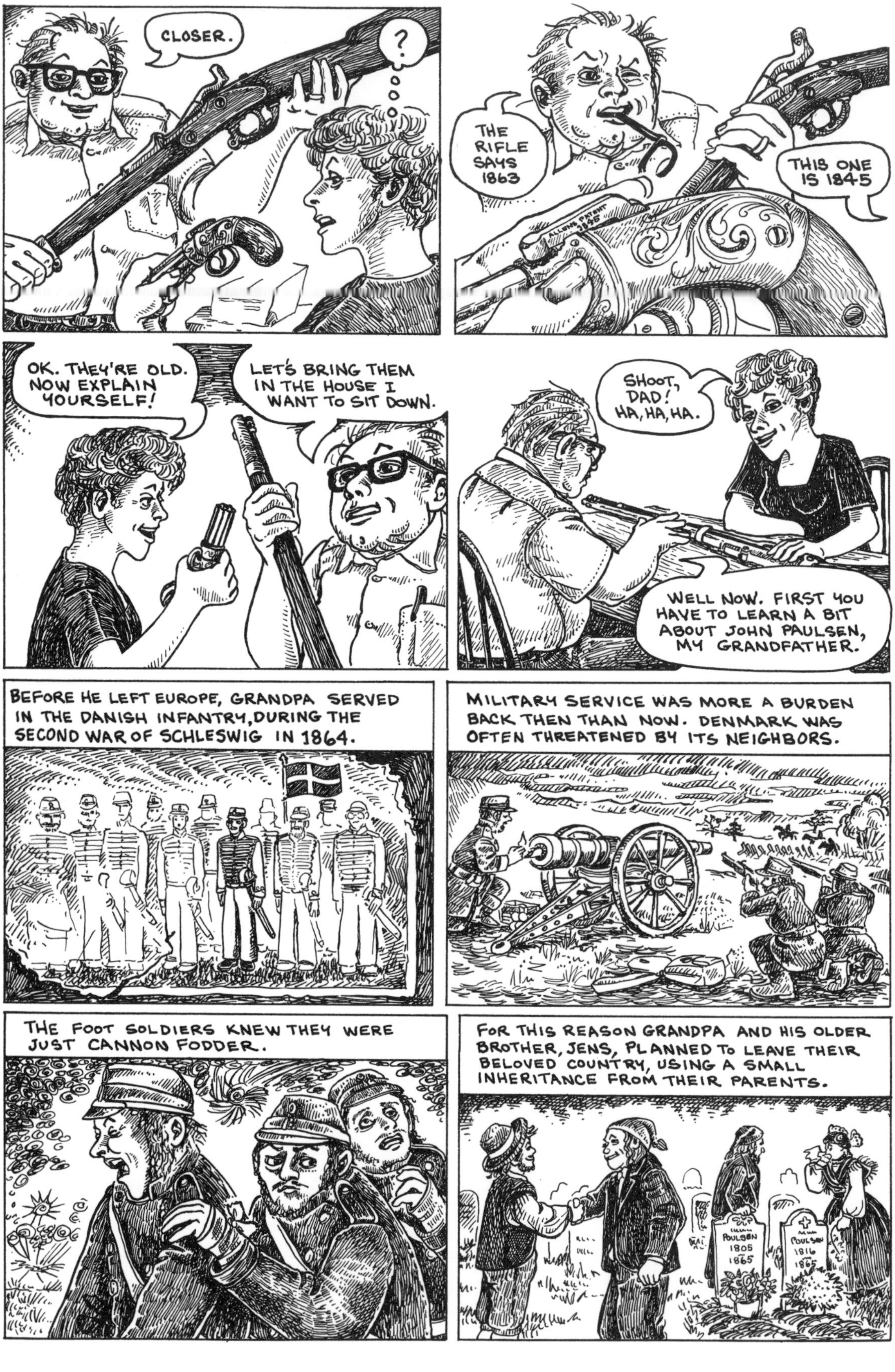

CLOSER.
?
THE RIFLE SAYS 1863
ALLENS PATENT 1845
THIS ONE IS 1845
OK. THEY'RE OLD. NOW EXPLAIN YOURSELF!
LET'S BRING THEM IN THE HOUSE I WANT TO SIT DOWN.
SHOOT, DAD! HA, HA, HA.
WELL NOW. FIRST YOU HAVE TO LEARN A BIT ABOUT JOHN PAULSEN, MY GRANDFATHER.
BEFORE HE LEFT EUROPE, GRANDPA SERVED IN THE DANISH INFANTRY, DURING THE SECOND WAR OF SCHLESWIG IN 1864.
MILITARY SERVICE WAS MORE A BURDEN BACK THEN THAN NOW. DENMARK WAS OFTEN THREATENED BY ITS NEIGHBORS.
THE FOOT SOLDIERS KNEW THEY WERE JUST CANNON FODDER.
FOR THIS REASON GRANDPA AND HIS OLDER BROTHER, JENS, PLANNED TO LEAVE THEIR BELOVED COUNTRY, USING A SMALL INHERITANCE FROM THEIR PARENTS.
PAULSEN 1805 1865
PAULSEN 1816 1865

JENS CAME TO AMERICA FIRST, SETTLING IN OREGON ABOUT 1866. HE PROMISED TO SEND PASSAGE MONEY TO GRANDPA AS SOON AS HE WAS ESTABLISHED.

MEANWHILE GRANDPA JOHN MARRIED GRANDMA HANSINE AND QUICKLY STARTED A FAMILY.

WHEN THE PASSAGE MONEY ARRIVED FROM JENS IN 1871, IT WAS BARELY ENOUGH TO GET THEM TO NEW YORK!

‹···› = DANISH

‹IF WE HURRY, WE'LL ONLY HAVE TO BUY FOUR FARES.›

THEY MANAGED THIRD-CLASS TICKETS WITH TWENTY-FIVE DOLLARS LEFT OVER.

‹I'VE STARTED LABOR, JOHN.›

JENS DIDN'T SEND THE REST OF THE MONEY FOR THE FAMILY TO TRAVEL TO OREGON.

‹I'LL NEVER SPEAK TO MY BROTHER AGAIN FOR STRANDING US HERE!›

THERE WERE NO JOBS FOR A DANISH GARDENER IN NEW YORK CITY.

‹IF WE TAKE THE TRAIN WEST, I'LL FIND WORK ALONG THE WAY.›

THAT'S WHEN GRANDPA BOUGHT THIS PISTOL.

PEPPERBOX... IS... NAME. USED. TWO... DOLLARS.

GOOD! I BUY! ...HOLD FAMILIEN SAFE!

THEIR MONEY RAN OUT IN IOWA. FORTUNATELY THERE WAS AN ESTABLISHED SCANDINAVIAN COMMUNITY IN WATERLOO, AND GRANDPA FOUND WORK.

‹OUR NEW HOME!›

‹HAVE PITY!›

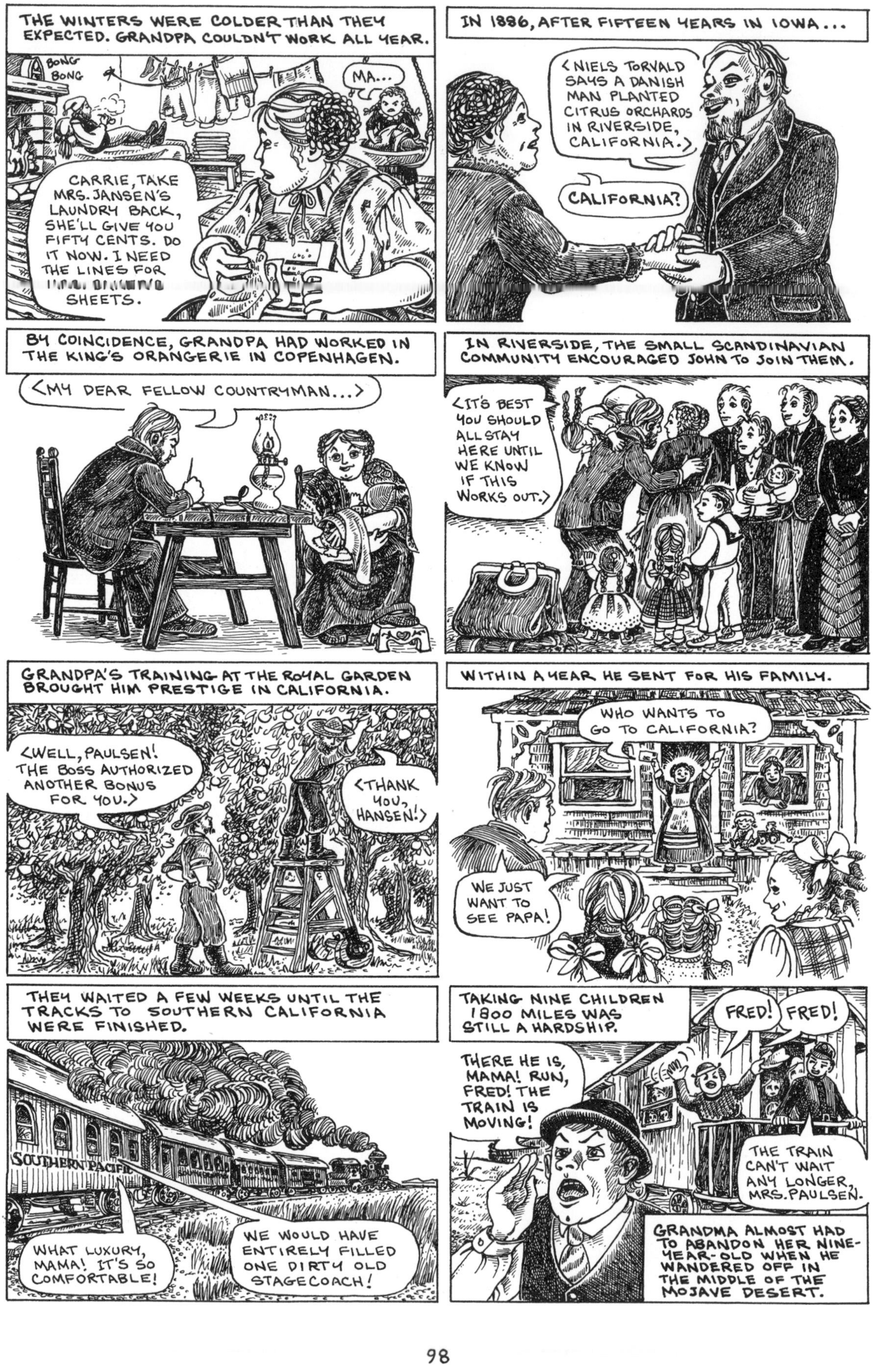

THE WINTERS WERE COLDER THAN THEY EXPECTED. GRANDPA COULDN'T WORK ALL YEAR.
BONG BONG
MA...
CARRIE, TAKE MRS. JANSEN'S LAUNDRY BACK, SHE'LL GIVE YOU FIFTY CENTS. DO IT NOW. I NEED THE LINES FOR
SHEETS.
IN 1886, AFTER FIFTEEN YEARS IN IOWA...
<NIELS TORVALD SAYS A DANISH MAN PLANTED CITRUS ORCHARDS IN RIVERSIDE, CALIFORNIA.>
CALIFORNIA?
BY COINCIDENCE, GRANDPA HAD WORKED IN THE KING'S ORANGERIE IN COPENHAGEN.
<MY DEAR FELLOW COUNTRYMAN...>
IN RIVERSIDE, THE SMALL SCANDINAVIAN COMMUNITY ENCOURAGED JOHN TO JOIN THEM.
<IT'S BEST YOU SHOULD ALL STAY HERE UNTIL WE KNOW IF THIS WORKS OUT.>
GRANDPA'S TRAINING AT THE ROYAL GARDEN BROUGHT HIM PRESTIGE IN CALIFORNIA.
<WELL, PAULSEN! THE BOSS AUTHORIZED ANOTHER BONUS FOR YOU.>
<THANK YOU, HANSEN!>
WITHIN A YEAR HE SENT FOR HIS FAMILY.
WHO WANTS TO GO TO CALIFORNIA?
WE JUST WANT TO SEE PAPA!
THEY WAITED A FEW WEEKS UNTIL THE TRACKS TO SOUTHERN CALIFORNIA WERE FINISHED.
SOUTHERN PACIFIC
WHAT LUXURY, MAMA! IT'S SO COMFORTABLE!
WE WOULD HAVE ENTIRELY FILLED ONE DIRTY OLD STAGECOACH!
TAKING NINE CHILDREN 1800 MILES WAS STILL A HARDSHIP.
FRED!
FRED!
THERE HE IS, MAMA! RUN, FRED! THE TRAIN IS MOVING!
THE TRAIN CAN'T WAIT ANY LONGER, MRS. PAULSEN.
GRANDMA ALMOST HAD TO ABANDON HER NINE-YEAR-OLD WHEN HE WANDERED OFF IN THE MIDDLE OF THE MOJAVE DESERT.

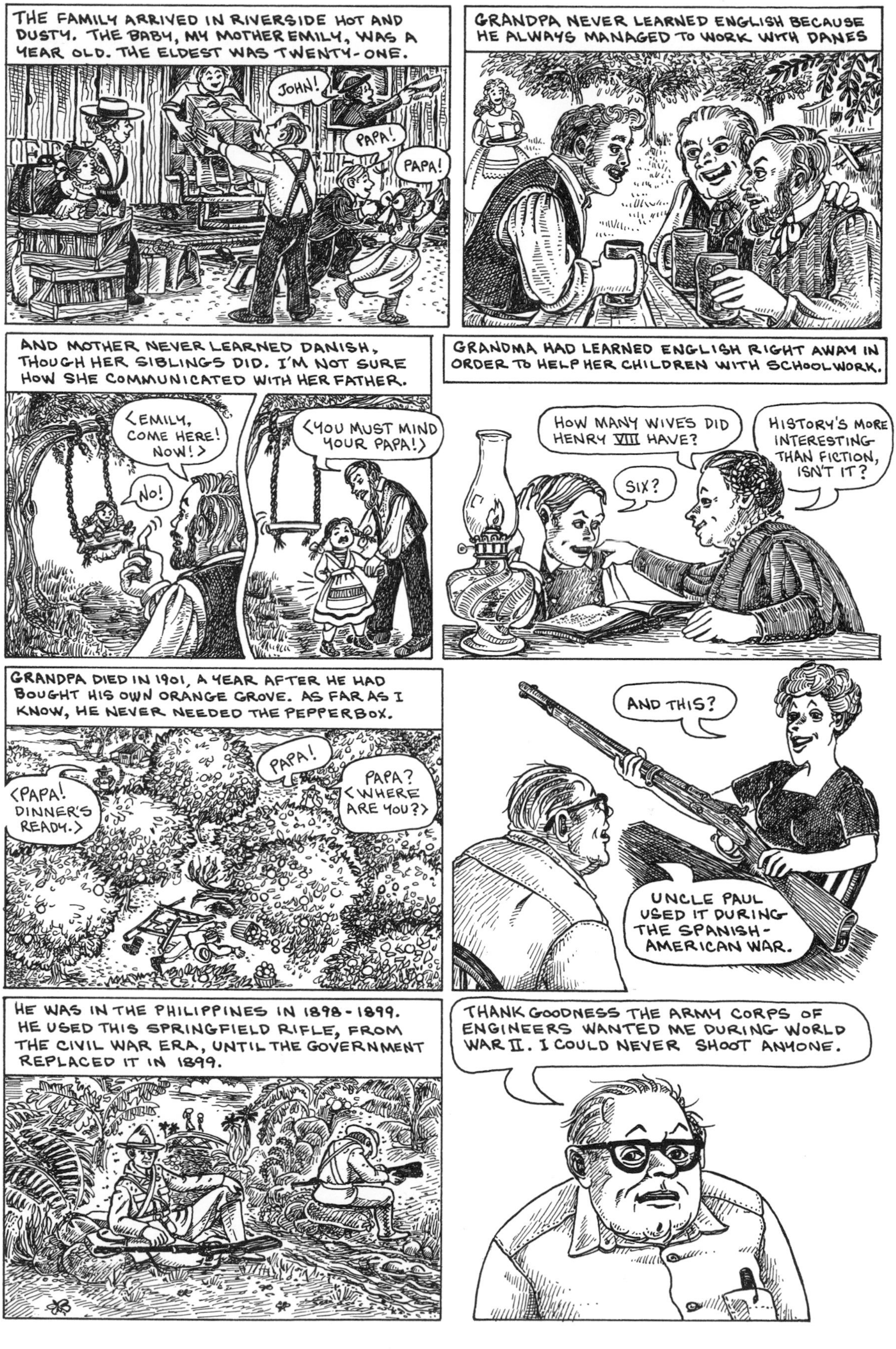
THE FAMILY ARRIVED IN RIVERSIDE HOT AND DUSTY. THE BABY, MY MOTHER EMILY, WAS A YEAR OLD. THE ELDEST WAS TWENTY-ONE.
JOHN!
PAPA!
PAPA!
GRANDPA NEVER LEARNED ENGLISH BECAUSE HE ALWAYS MANAGED TO WORK WITH DANES
AND MOTHER NEVER LEARNED DANISH, THOUGH HER SIBLINGS DID. I'M NOT SURE HOW SHE COMMUNICATED WITH HER FATHER.
<EMILY, COME HERE! NOW!>
NO!
<YOU MUST MIND YOUR PAPA!>
GRANDMA HAD LEARNED ENGLISH RIGHT AWAY IN ORDER TO HELP HER CHILDREN WITH SCHOOLWORK.
HOW MANY WIVES DID HENRY VIII HAVE?
SIX?
HISTORY'S MORE INTERESTING THAN FICTION, ISN'T IT?
GRANDPA DIED IN 1901, A YEAR AFTER HE HAD BOUGHT HIS OWN ORANGE GROVE. AS FAR AS I KNOW, HE NEVER NEEDED THE PEPPERBOX.
<PAPA! DINNER'S READY.>
PAPA!
PAPA? <WHERE ARE YOU?>
AND THIS?
UNCLE PAUL USED IT DURING THE SPANISH-AMERICAN WAR.
HE WAS IN THE PHILIPPINES IN 1898-1899. HE USED THIS SPRINGFIELD RIFLE, FROM THE CIVIL WAR ERA, UNTIL THE GOVERNMENT REPLACED IT IN 1899.
THANK GOODNESS THE ARMY CORPS OF ENGINEERS WANTED ME DURING WORLD WAR II. I COULD NEVER SHOOT ANYONE.

7

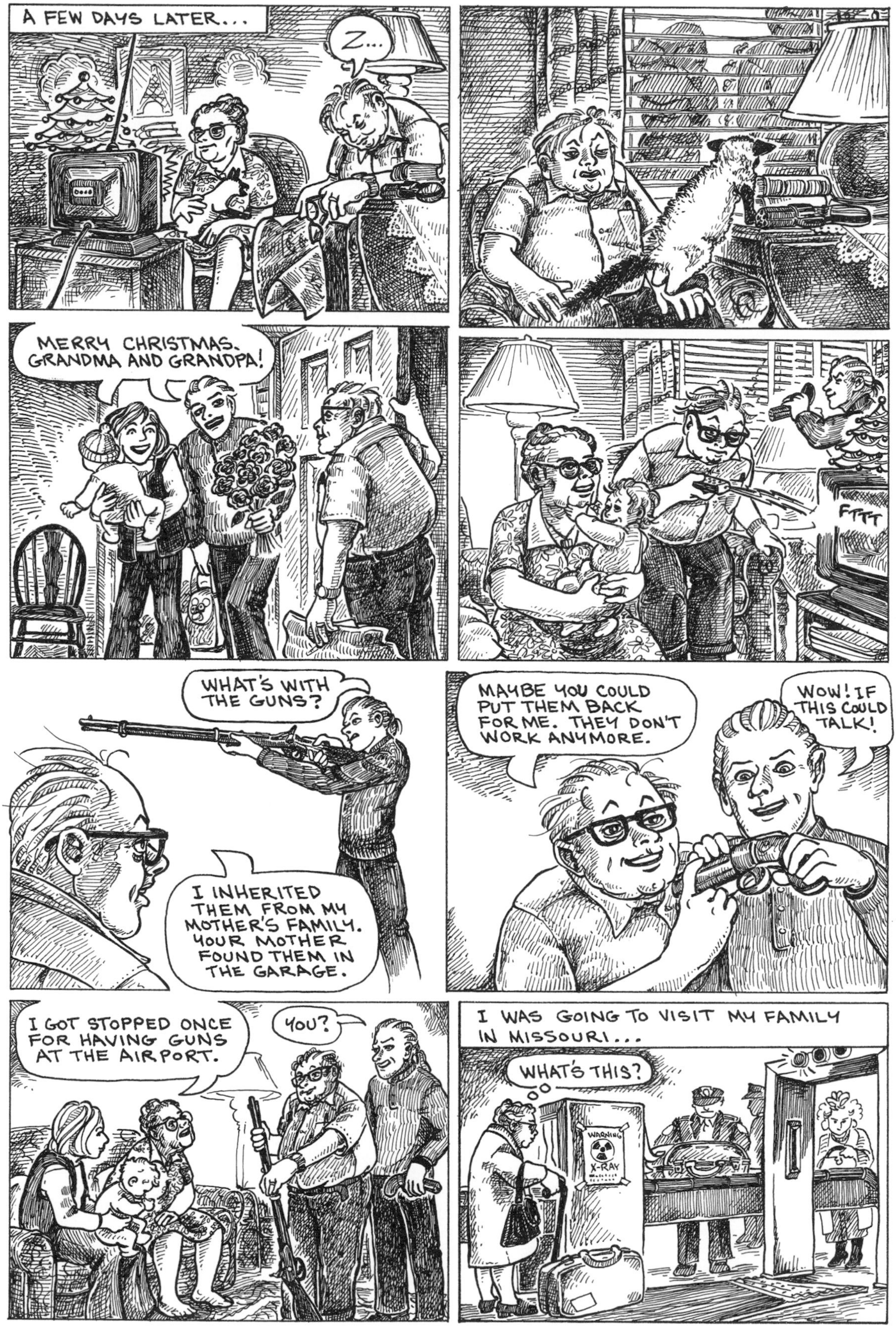
A FEW DAYS LATER...
Z...
MERRY CHRISTMAS. GRANDMA AND GRANDPA!
FTTT
WHAT'S WITH THE GUNS?
I INHERITED THEM FROM MY MOTHER'S FAMILY. YOUR MOTHER FOUND THEM IN THE GARAGE.
MAYBE YOU COULD PUT THEM BACK FOR ME. THEY DON'T WORK ANYMORE.
WOW! IF THIS COULD TALK!
I GOT STOPPED ONCE FOR HAVING GUNS AT THE AIRPORT.
YOU?
I WAS GOING TO VISIT MY FAMILY IN MISSOURI...
WHAT'S THIS?
WARNING
X-RAY

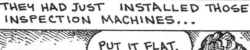

THEY HAD JUST INSTALLED THOSE INSPECTION MACHINES...

PUT IT FLAT, LADY!

YOU HAVE GUNS IN YOUR BAG!

STEP OVER HERE!

AT FIRST I THOUGHT THEY WERE LOOKING AT SOMEONE ELSE'S BAG.

OPEN IT.

BUT... I HAVE UNDERWEAR IN THERE!

I WONDERED IF THEY WERE JOKING.

IF YOU INSIST.

OK, NOW STEP OVER THERE, MA'AM.

HERE THEY ARE!

I WASN'T EXACTLY SCARED, BUT I NOTICED I HAD BEEN THE CENTER OF ATTENTION.

AFTERSHAVE!

GUN SHAPE!

METALLIC GLASS!

AVON BOTTLES CALLING!

I JUST BARELY MADE THE PLANE.

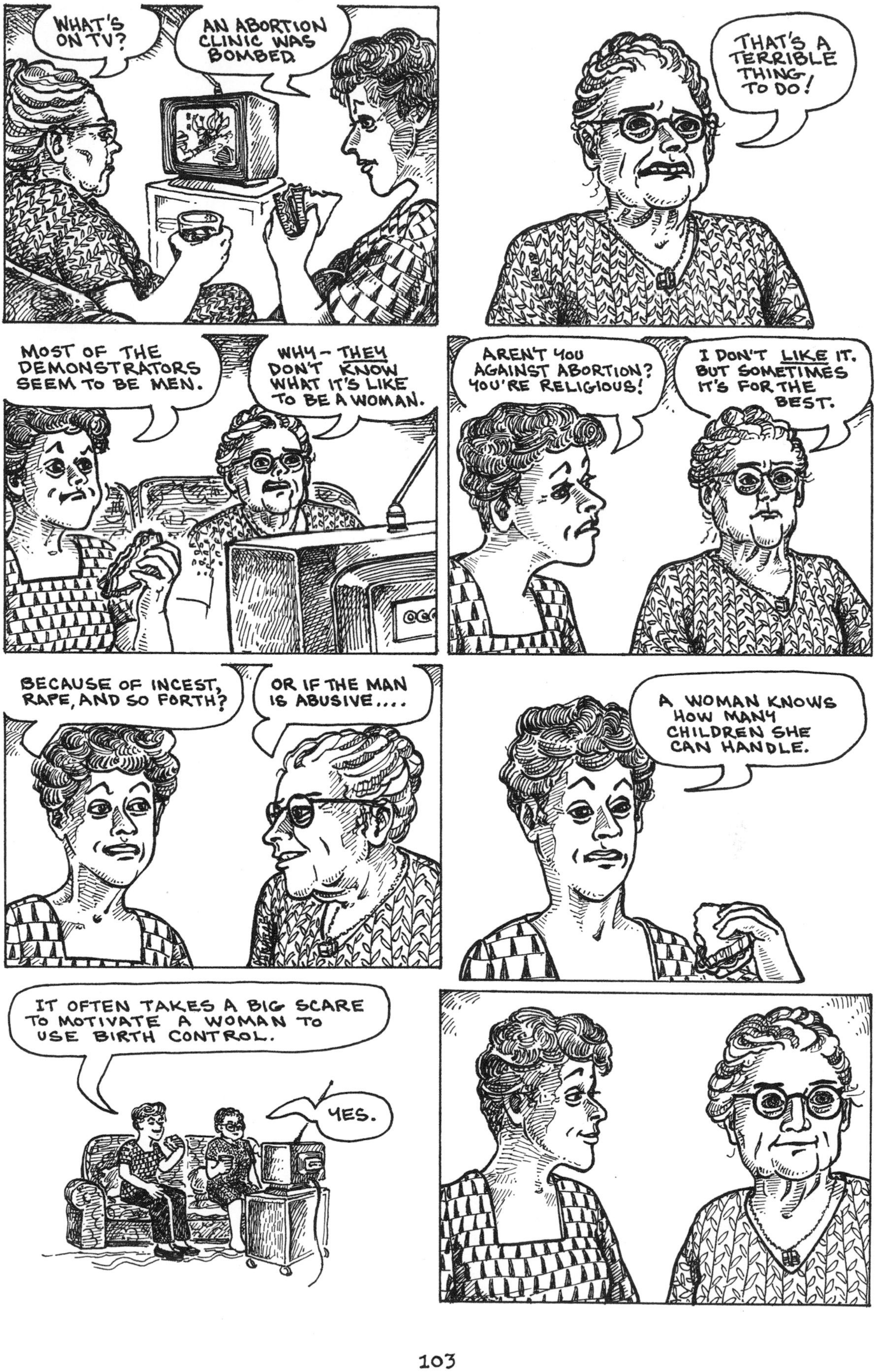
WHAT'S ON TV?
AN ABORTION CLINIC WAS BOMBED.
THAT'S A TERRIBLE THING TO DO!
MOST OF THE DEMONSTRATORS SEEM TO BE MEN.
WHY- THEY DON'T KNOW WHAT IT'S LIKE TO BE A WOMAN.
AREN'T YOU AGAINST ABORTION? YOU'RE RELIGIOUS!
I DON'T LIKE IT. BUT SOMETIMES IT'S FOR THE BEST.
BECAUSE OF INCEST, RAPE, AND SO FORTH?
OR IF THE MAN IS ABUSIVE....
A WOMAN KNOWS HOW MANY CHILDREN SHE CAN HANDLE.
IT OFTEN TAKES A BIG SCARE TO MOTIVATE A WOMAN TO USE BIRTH CONTROL.
YES.

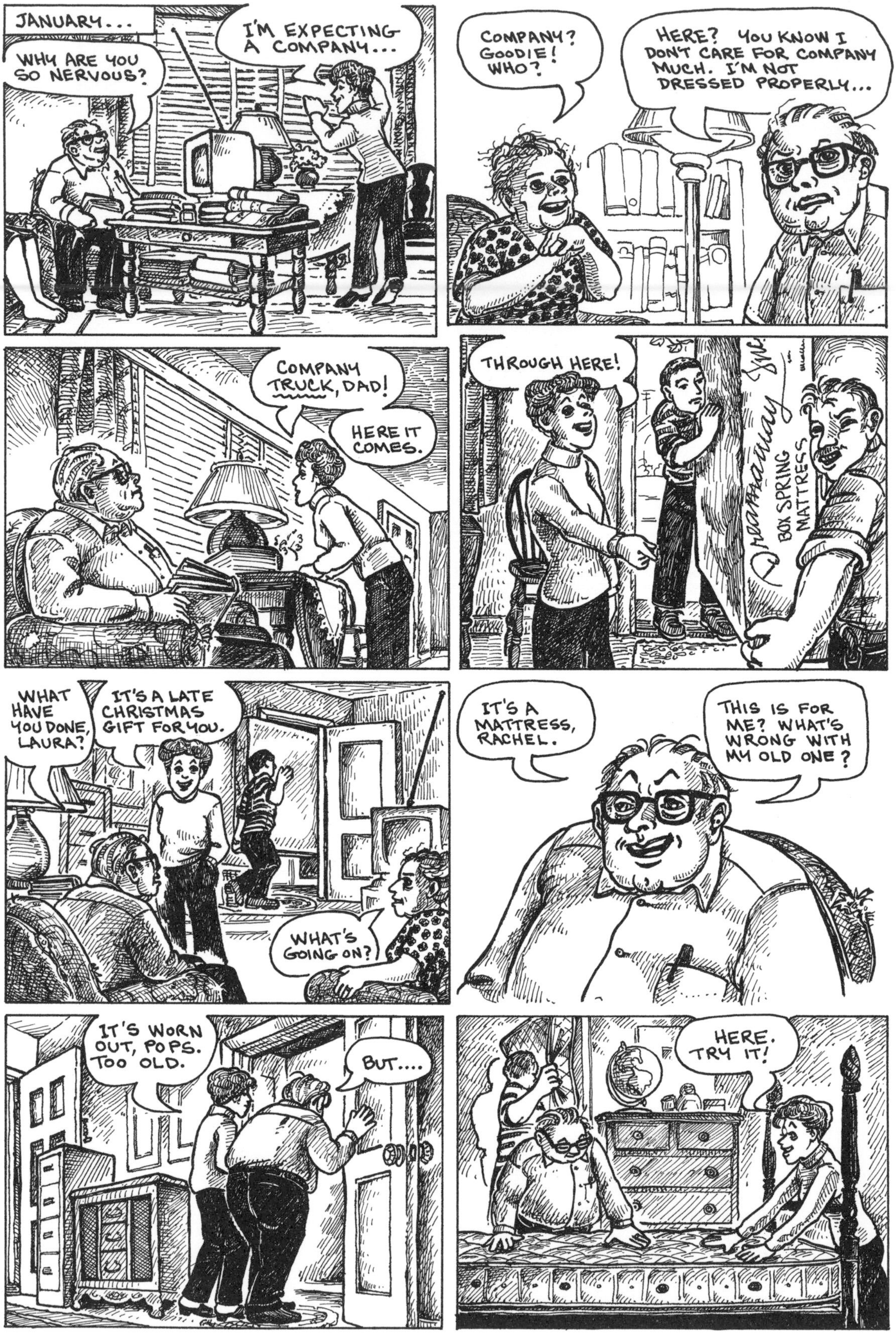
JANUARY...
WHY ARE YOU SO NERVOUS?
I'M EXPECTING A COMPANY...
COMPANY? GOODIE! WHO?
HERE? YOU KNOW I DON'T CARE FOR COMPANY MUCH. I'M NOT DRESSED PROPERLY...
COMPANY TRUCK, DAD!
HERE IT COMES.
THROUGH HERE!
Dreamaway Inc.
BOX SPRING MATTRESS
WHAT HAVE YOU DONE, LAURA?
IT'S A LATE CHRISTMAS GIFT FOR YOU.
WHAT'S GOING ON?
IT'S A MATTRESS, RACHEL.
THIS IS FOR ME? WHAT'S WRONG WITH MY OLD ONE?
IT'S WORN OUT, POPS. TOO OLD.
BUT....
HERE. TRY IT!

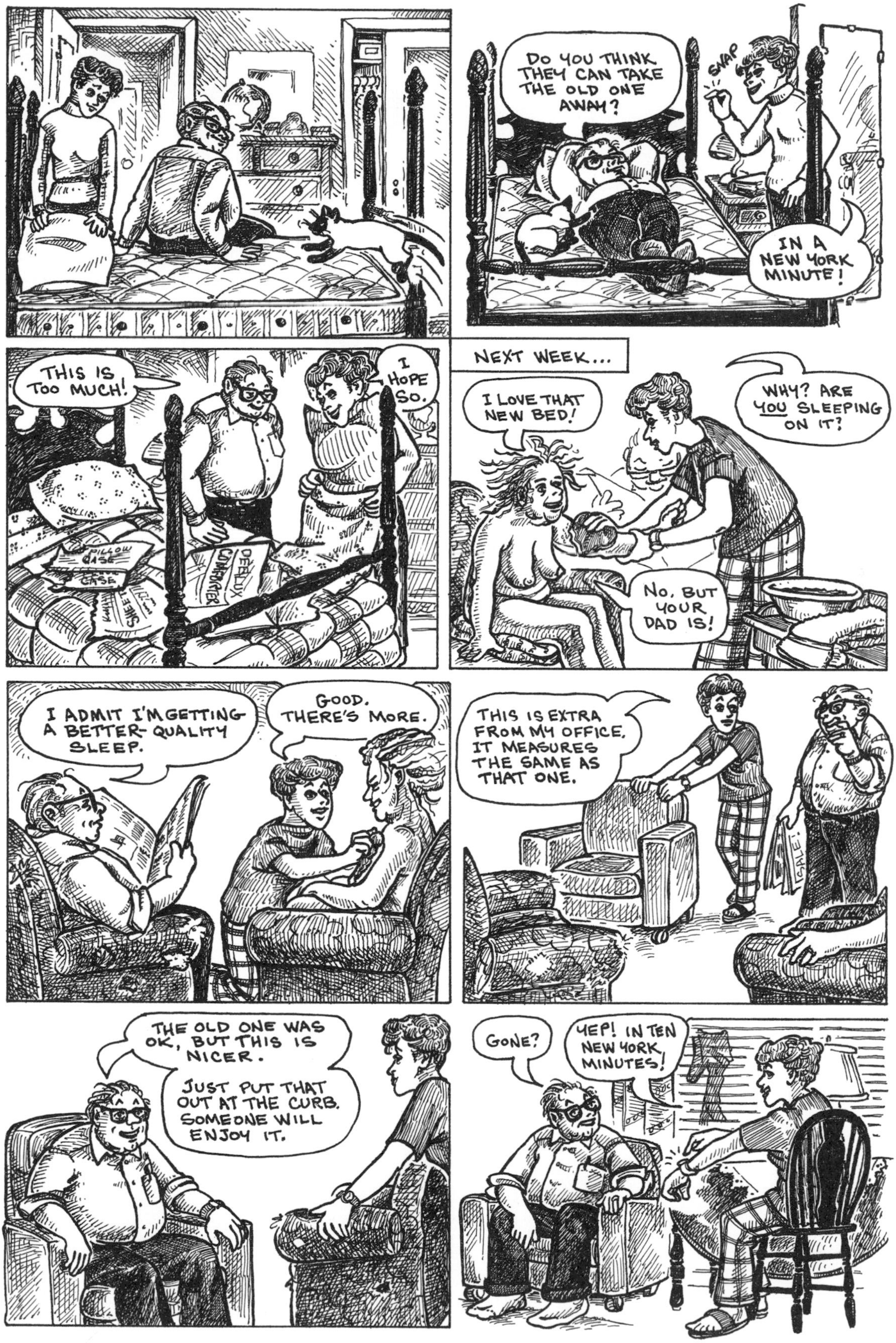
DO YOU THINK THEY CAN TAKE THE OLD ONE AWAY?
SNAP
IN A NEW YORK MINUTE!
THIS IS TOO MUCH!
I HOPE SO.
PILLOW CASE
CASE
SHEET
DEELUX COMFORTER
NEXT WEEK...
I LOVE THAT NEW BED!
WHY? ARE YOU SLEEPING ON IT?
NO, BUT YOUR DAD IS!
I ADMIT I'M GETTING A BETTER-QUALITY SLEEP.
GOOD. THERE'S MORE.
THIS IS EXTRA FROM MY OFFICE. IT MEASURES THE SAME AS THAT ONE.
SALE
THE OLD ONE WAS OK, BUT THIS IS NICER.
JUST PUT THAT OUT AT THE CURB. SOMEONE WILL ENJOY IT.
GONE?
YEP! IN TEN NEW YORK MINUTES!

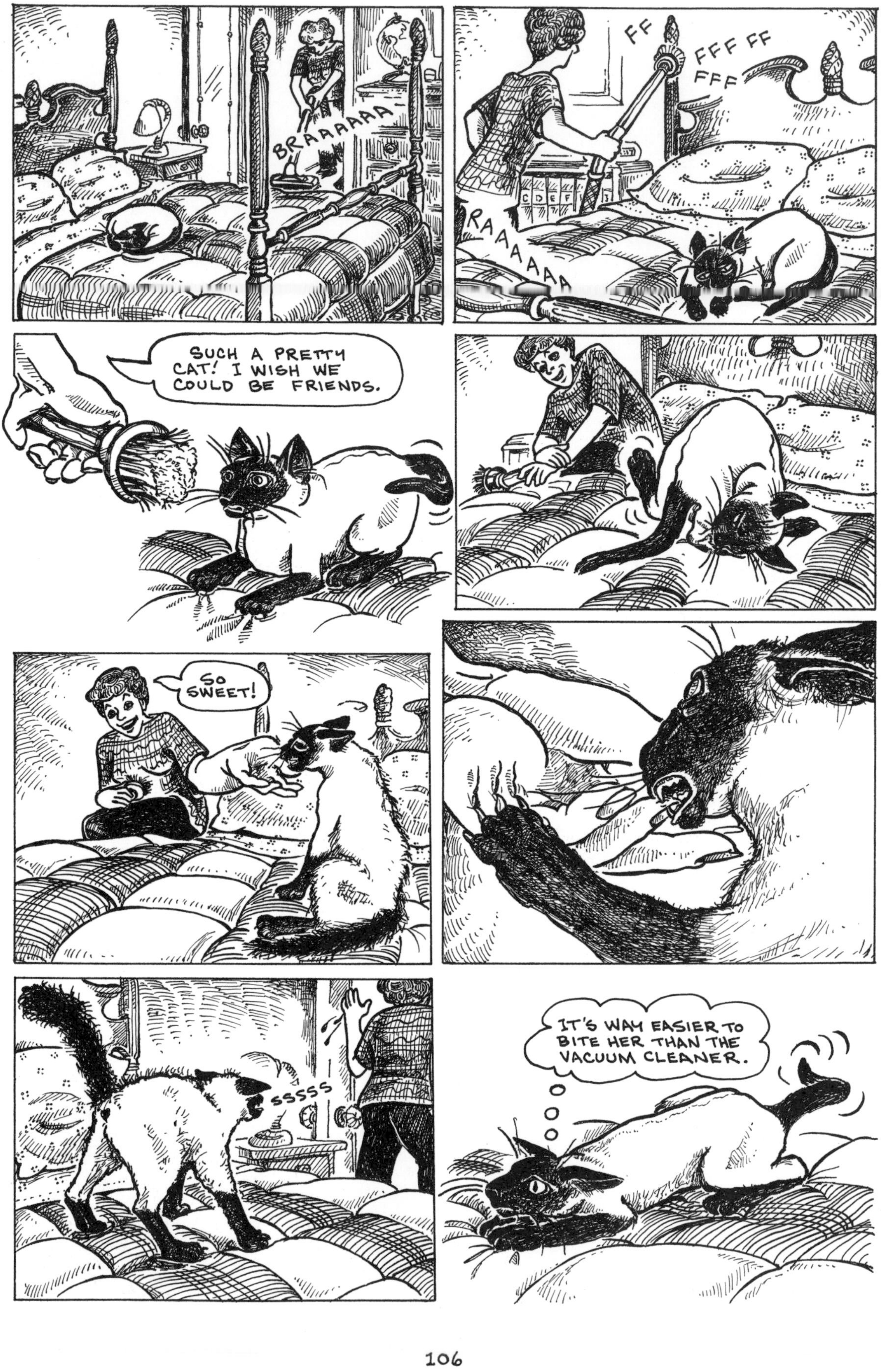
BRAAAAAA
FF
FFF FF
FFF
RAAAAAAA
SUCH A PRETTY CAT! I WISH WE COULD BE FRIENDS.
SO SWEET!
SSSSS
IT'S WAY EASIER TO BITE HER THAN THE VACUUM CLEANER.

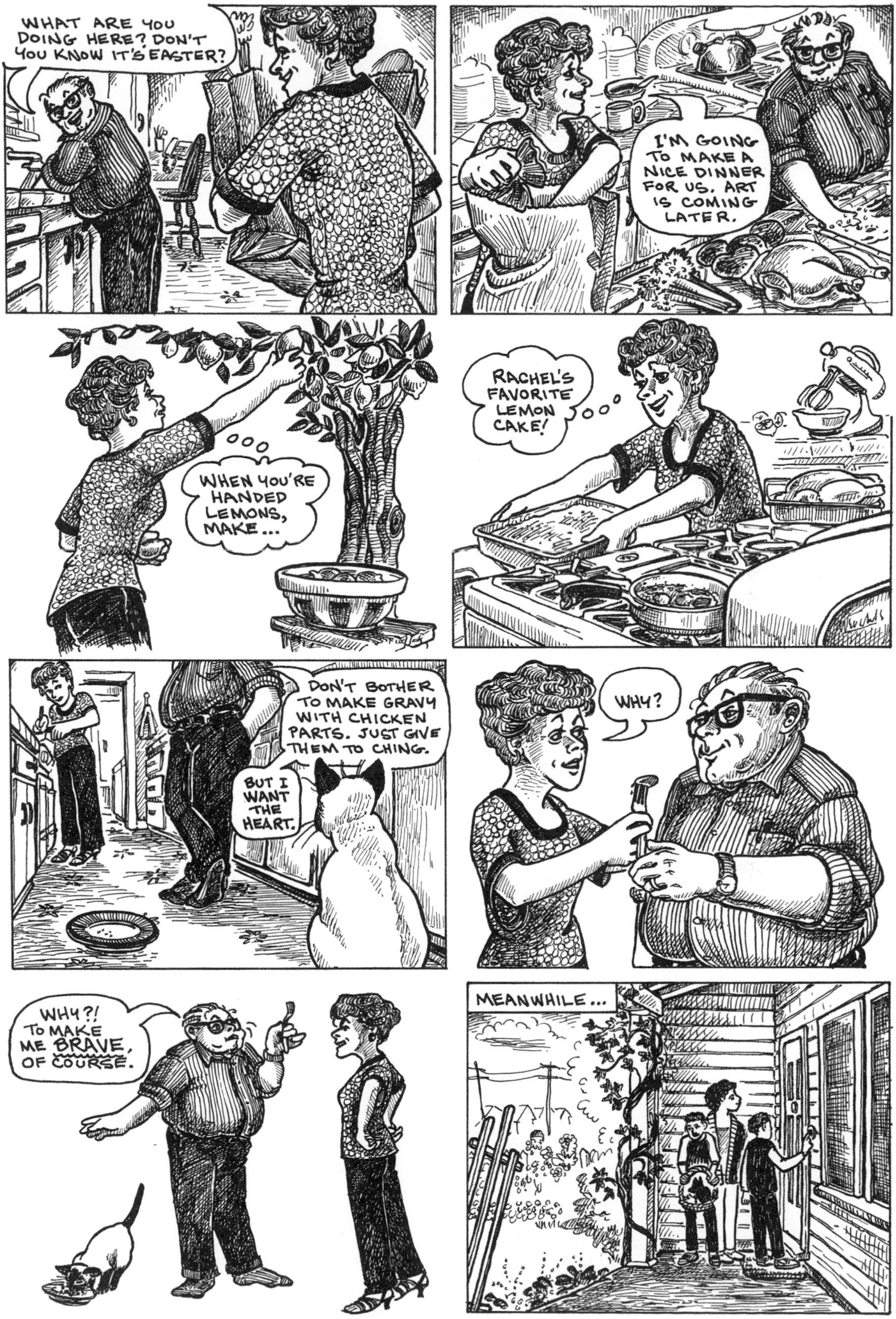
WHAT ARE YOU DOING HERE? DON'T YOU KNOW IT'S EASTER?
I'M GOING TO MAKE A NICE DINNER FOR US. ART IS COMING LATER.
WHEN YOU'RE HANDED LEMONS, MAKE...
RACHEL'S FAVORITE LEMON CAKE!
DON'T BOTHER TO MAKE GRAVY WITH CHICKEN PARTS. JUST GIVE THEM TO CHING.
BUT I WANT THE HEART.
WHY?
WHY?! TO MAKE ME BRAVE, OF COURSE.
MEANWHILE...

8

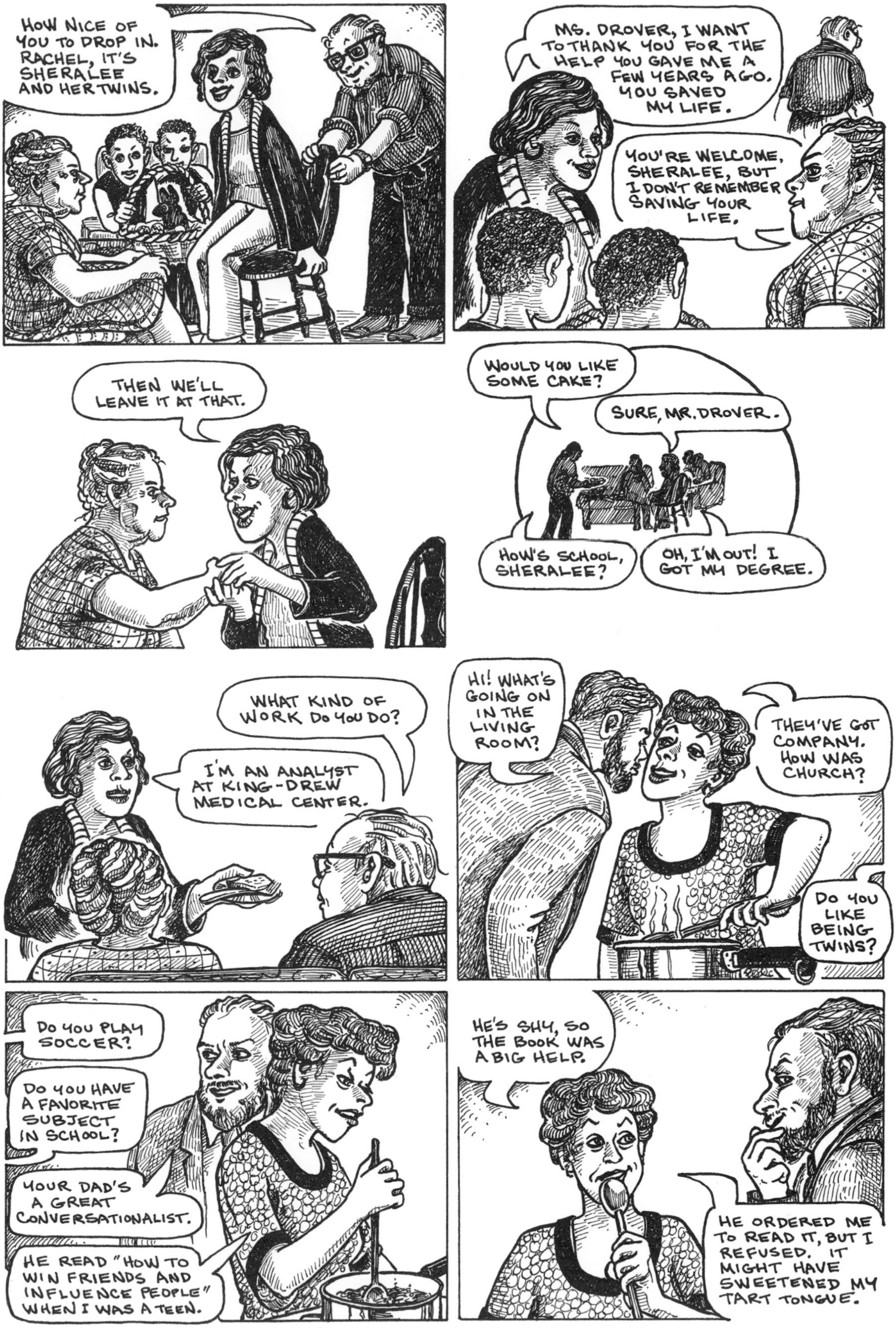
HOW NICE OF YOU TO DROP IN. RACHEL, IT'S SHERALEE AND HER TWINS.
MS. DROVER, I WANT TO THANK YOU FOR THE HELP YOU GAVE ME A FEW YEARS AGO. YOU SAVED MY LIFE.
YOU'RE WELCOME, SHERALEE, BUT I DON'T REMEMBER SAVING YOUR LIFE.
THEN WE'LL LEAVE IT AT THAT.
WOULD YOU LIKE SOME CAKE?
SURE, MR. DROVER.
HOW'S SCHOOL, SHERALEE?
OH, I'M OUT! I GOT MY DEGREE.
WHAT KIND OF WORK DO YOU DO?
I'M AN ANALYST AT KING-DREW MEDICAL CENTER.
HI! WHAT'S GOING ON IN THE LIVING ROOM?
THEY'VE GOT COMPANY. HOW WAS CHURCH?
DO YOU LIKE BEING TWINS?
DO YOU PLAY SOCCER?
DO YOU HAVE A FAVORITE SUBJECT IN SCHOOL?
YOUR DAD'S A GREAT CONVERSATIONALIST.
HE READ "HOW TO WIN FRIENDS AND INFLUENCE PEOPLE" WHEN I WAS A TEEN.
HE'S SHY, SO THE BOOK WAS A BIG HELP.
HE ORDERED ME TO READ IT, BUT I REFUSED. IT MIGHT HAVE SWEETENED MY TART TONGUE.

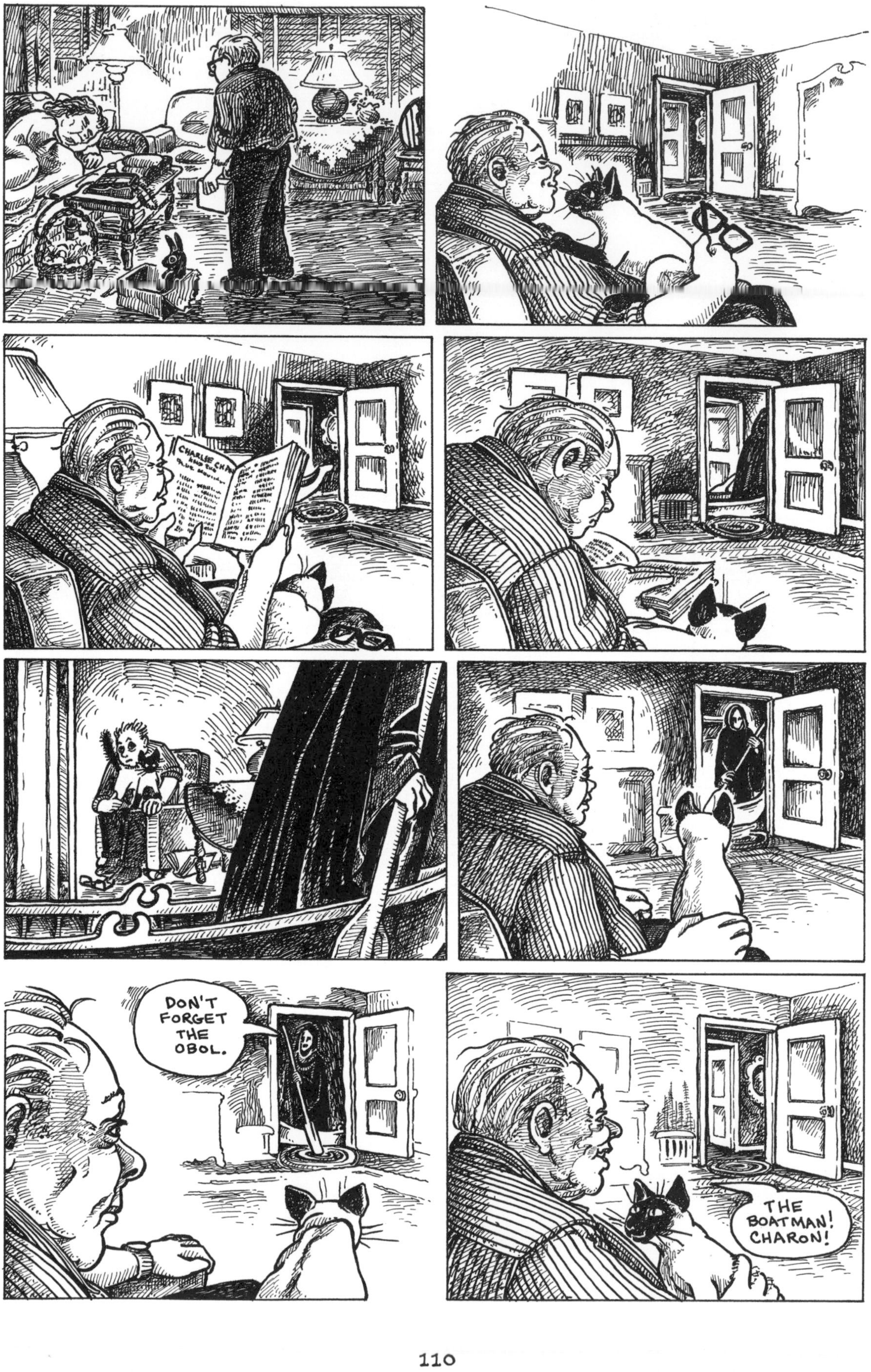
DON'T FORGET THE OBOL.
THE BOATMAN! CHARON!

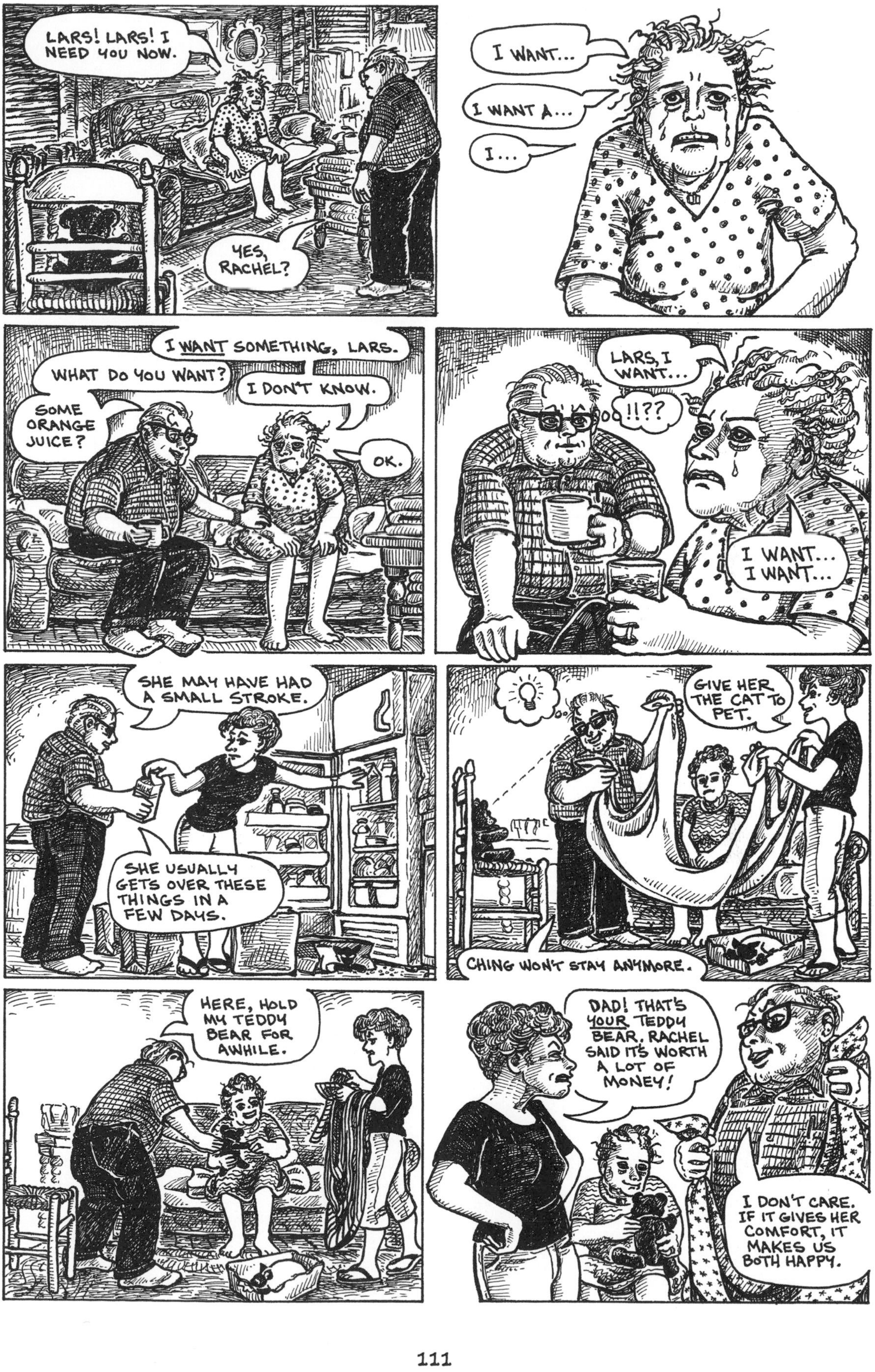

LARS! LARS! I NEED YOU NOW.
YES, RACHEL?
I WANT...
I WANT A...
I...
I WANT SOMETHING, LARS.
WHAT DO YOU WANT?
I DON'T KNOW.
SOME ORANGE JUICE?
OK.
LARS, I WANT...
!!??
I WANT... I WANT...
SHE MAY HAVE HAD A SMALL STROKE.
SHE USUALLY GETS OVER THESE THINGS IN A FEW DAYS.
GIVE HER THE CAT TO PET.
CHING WON'T STAY ANYMORE.
HERE, HOLD MY TEDDY BEAR FOR AWHILE.
DAD! THAT'S YOUR TEDDY BEAR. RACHEL SAID IT'S WORTH A LOT OF MONEY!
I DON'T CARE. IF IT GIVES HER COMFORT, IT MAKES US BOTH HAPPY.

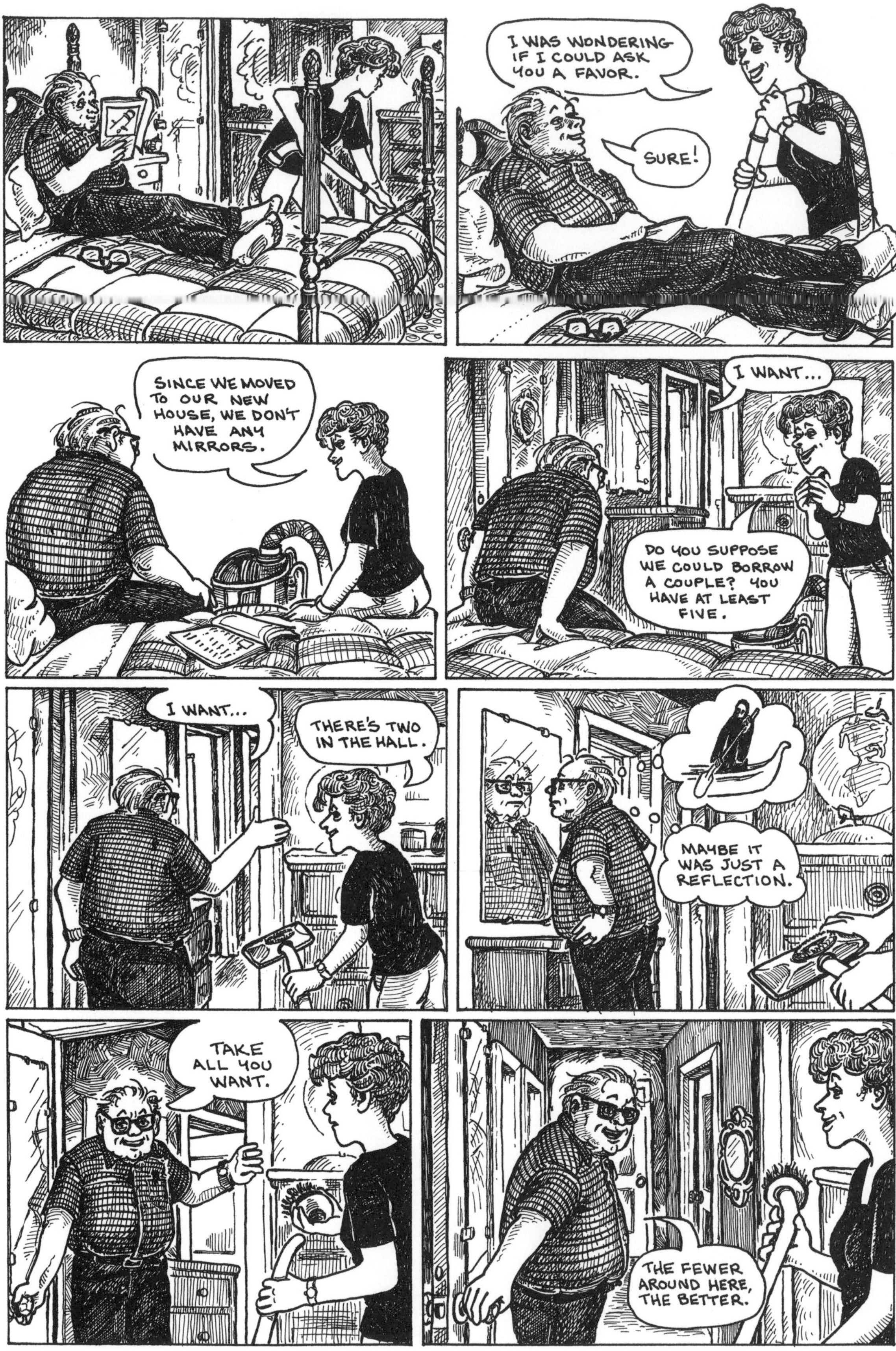
I WAS WONDERING IF I COULD ASK YOU A FAVOR.
SURE!
SINCE WE MOVED TO OUR NEW HOUSE, WE DON'T HAVE ANY MIRRORS.
I WANT...
DO YOU SUPPOSE WE COULD BORROW A COUPLE? YOU HAVE AT LEAST FIVE.
I WANT...
THERE'S TWO IN THE HALL.
MAYBE IT WAS JUST A REFLECTION.
TAKE ALL YOU WANT.
THE FEWER AROUND HERE, THE BETTER.

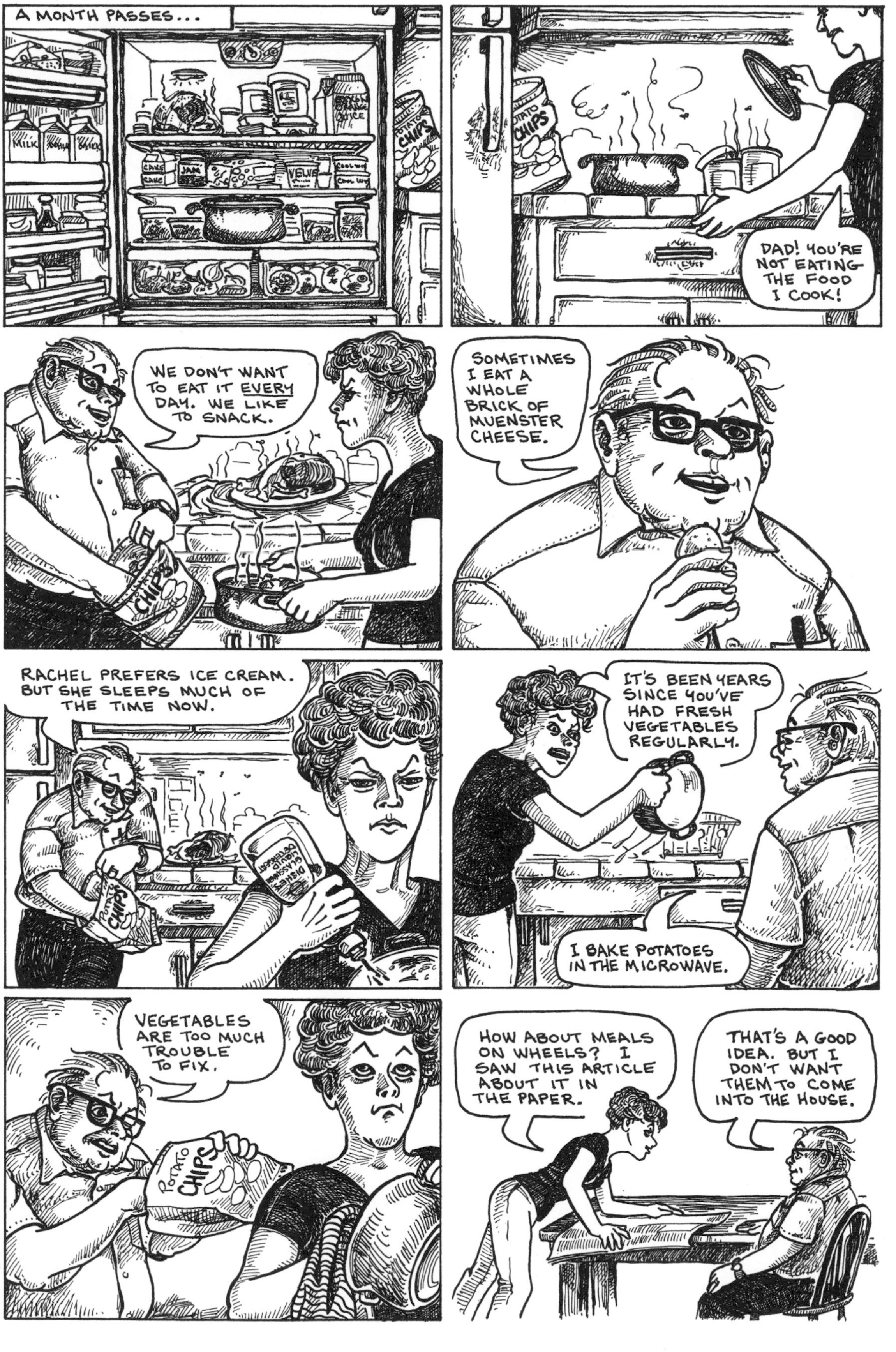
A MONTH PASSES...
MILK
POTATO CHIPS
DAD! YOU'RE NOT EATING THE FOOD I COOK!
WE DON'T WANT TO EAT IT EVERY DAY. WE LIKE TO SNACK.
CHIPS
SOMETIMES I EAT A WHOLE BRICK OF MUENSTER CHEESE.
RACHEL PREFERS ICE CREAM. BUT SHE SLEEPS MUCH OF THE TIME NOW.
POTATO CHIPS
IT'S BEEN YEARS SINCE YOU'VE HAD FRESH VEGETABLES REGULARLY.
I BAKE POTATOES IN THE MICROWAVE.
VEGETABLES ARE TOO MUCH TROUBLE TO FIX.
POTATO CHIPS
HOW ABOUT MEALS ON WHEELS? I SAW THIS ARTICLE ABOUT IT IN THE PAPER.
THAT'S A GOOD IDEA. BUT I DON'T WANT THEM TO COME INTO THE HOUSE.

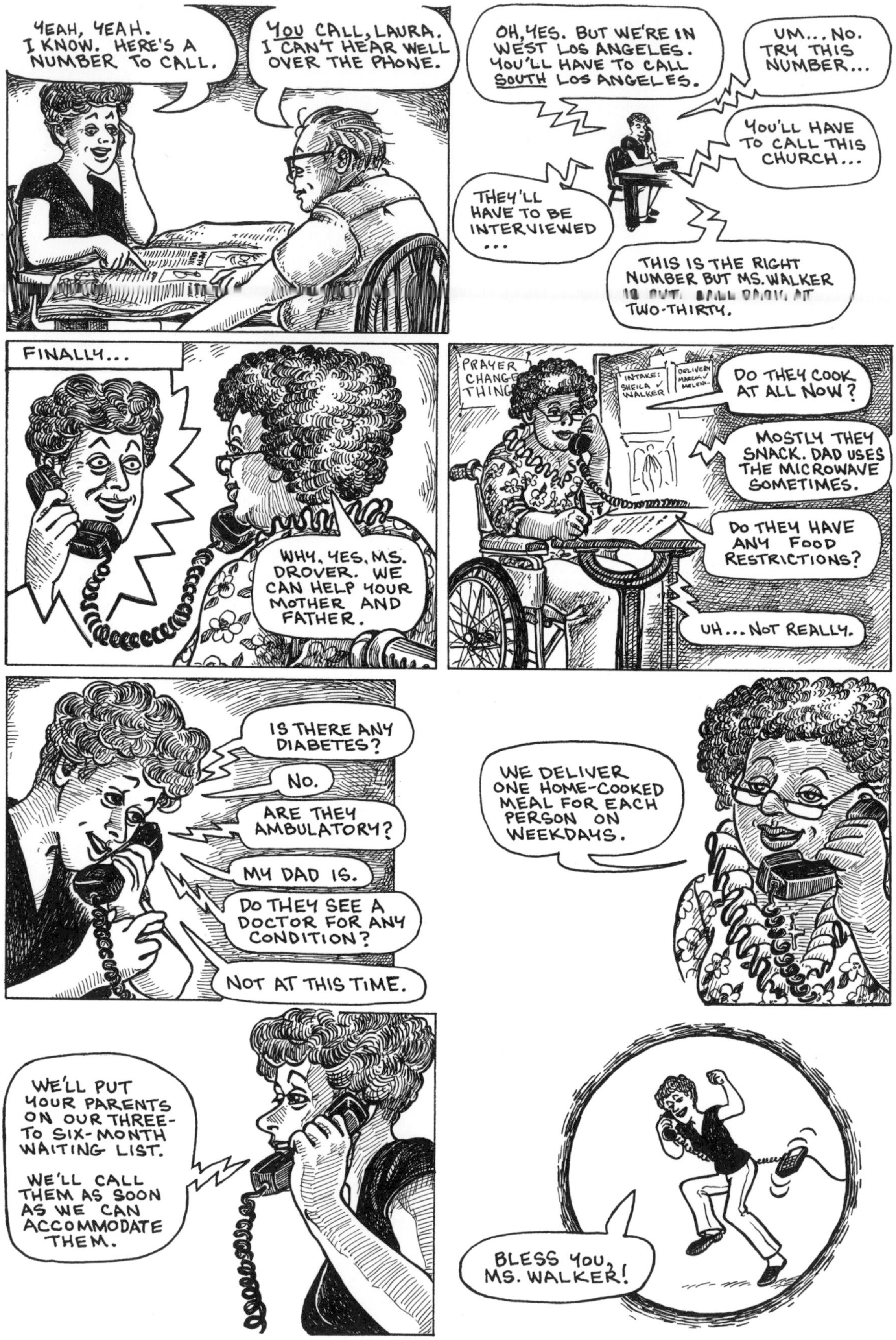
YEAH, YEAH. I KNOW. HERE'S A NUMBER TO CALL.
YOU CALL, LAURA. I CAN'T HEAR WELL OVER THE PHONE.
OH, YES. BUT WE'RE IN WEST LOS ANGELES. YOU'LL HAVE TO CALL SOUTH LOS ANGELES.
UM... NO. TRY THIS NUMBER...
YOU'LL HAVE TO CALL THIS CHURCH...
THEY'LL HAVE TO BE INTERVIEWED ...
THIS IS THE RIGHT NUMBER BUT MS. WALKER IS OUT. CALL BACK AT TWO-THIRTY.
FINALLY...
WHY, YES, MS. DROVER. WE CAN HELP YOUR MOTHER AND FATHER.
PRAYER CHANGE THING
INTAKE: SHEILA ✓ WALKER
DO THEY COOK AT ALL NOW?
MOSTLY THEY SNACK. DAD USES THE MICROWAVE SOMETIMES.
DO THEY HAVE ANY FOOD RESTRICTIONS?
UH... NOT REALLY.
IS THERE ANY DIABETES?
NO.
ARE THEY AMBULATORY?
MY DAD IS.
DO THEY SEE A DOCTOR FOR ANY CONDITION?
NOT AT THIS TIME.
WE DELIVER ONE HOME-COOKED MEAL FOR EACH PERSON ON WEEKDAYS.
WE'LL PUT YOUR PARENTS ON OUR THREE- TO SIX-MONTH WAITING LIST.
WE'LL CALL THEM AS SOON AS WE CAN ACCOMMODATE THEM.
BLESS YOU, MS. WALKER!

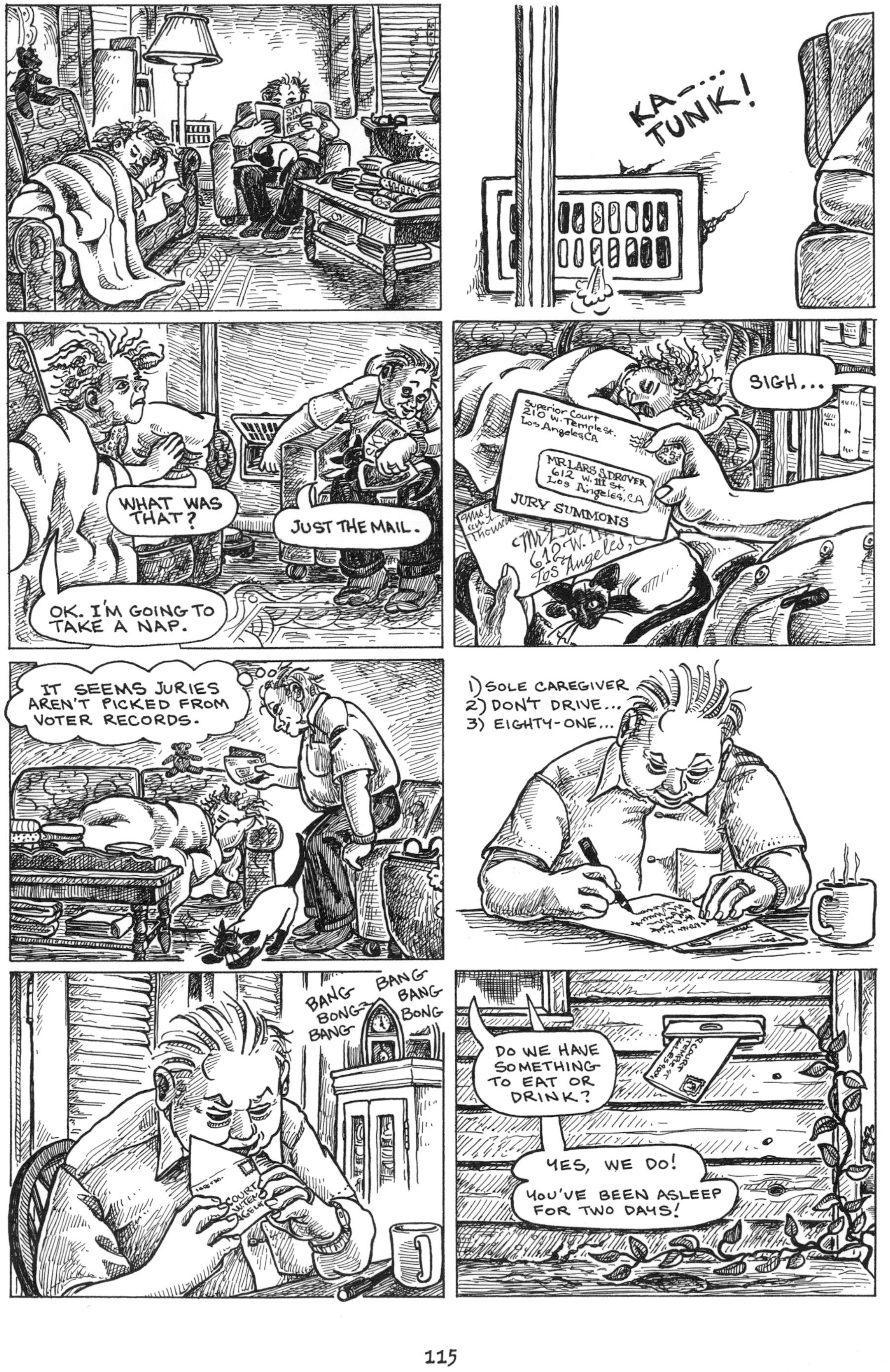
KA-... TUNK!
WHAT WAS THAT?
JUST THE MAIL.
OK. I'M GOING TO TAKE A NAP.
Superior Court 210 W. Temple St. Los Angeles CA
MR LARS S.DROVER 612 W. 111 St. Los Angeles, CA
JURY SUMMONS
SIGH...
IT SEEMS JURIES AREN'T PICKED FROM VOTER RECORDS.
1) SOLE CAREGIVER
2) DON'T DRIVE...
3) EIGHTY-ONE...
BANG BONG BANG BANG BANG BONG
DO WE HAVE SOMETHING TO EAT OR DRINK?
YES, WE DO!
YOU'VE BEEN ASLEEP FOR TWO DAYS!

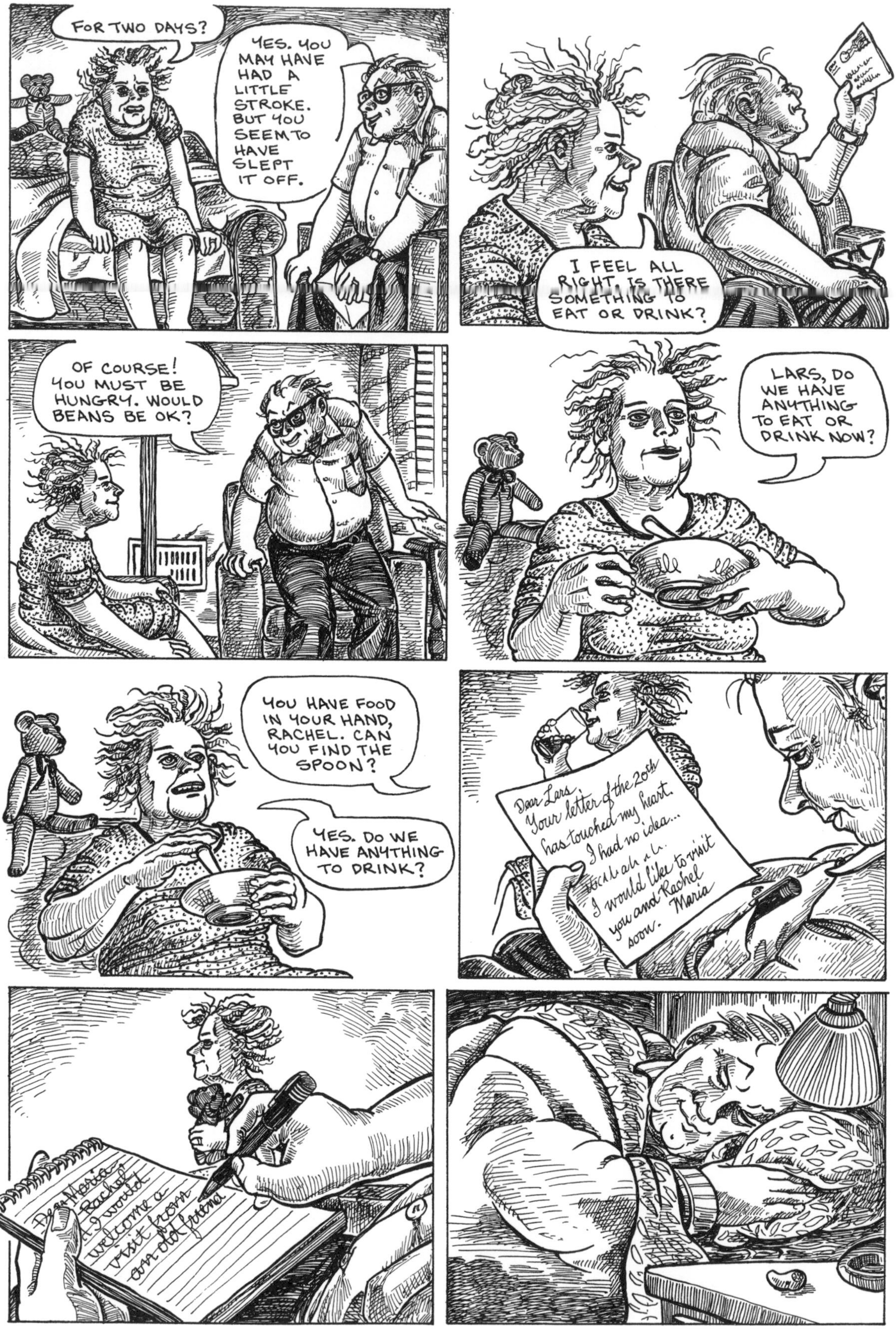
FOR TWO DAYS?
YES. YOU MAY HAVE HAD A LITTLE STROKE. BUT YOU SEEM TO HAVE SLEPT IT OFF.
I FEEL ALL RIGHT. IS THERE SOMETHING TO EAT OR DRINK?
OF COURSE! YOU MUST BE HUNGRY. WOULD BEANS BE OK?
LARS, DO WE HAVE ANYTHING TO EAT OR DRINK NOW?
YOU HAVE FOOD IN YOUR HAND, RACHEL. CAN YOU FIND THE SPOON?
YES. DO WE HAVE ANYTHING TO DRINK?
Dear Lars,
Your letter of the 20th has touched my heart.
I had no idea...
I would like to visit you and Rachel soon. Maria
Dear Maria
Rachel
I would welcome a visit from an old friend

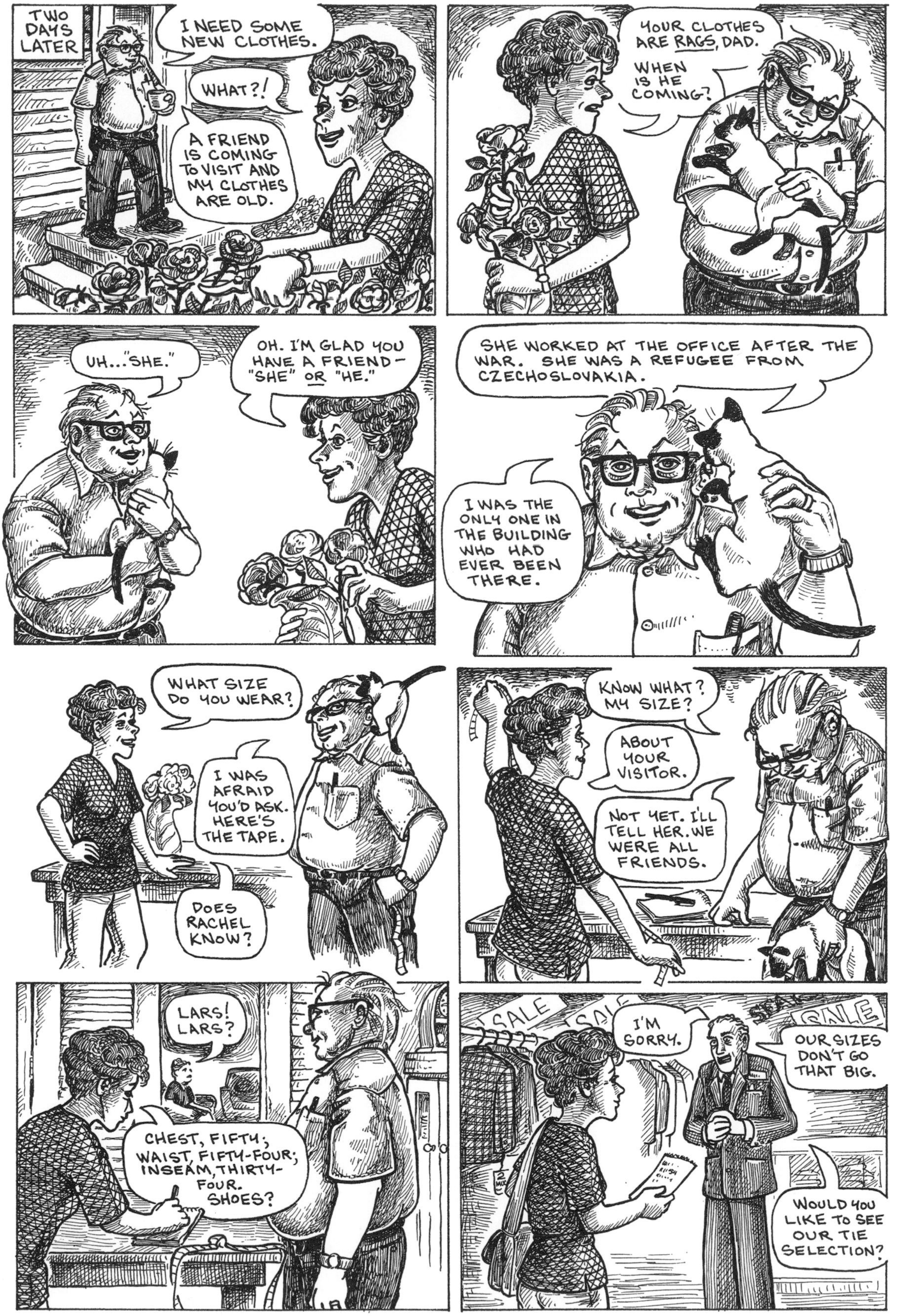

TWO DAYS LATER
I NEED SOME NEW CLOTHES.
WHAT?!
A FRIEND IS COMING TO VISIT AND MY CLOTHES ARE OLD.
YOUR CLOTHES ARE RAGS, DAD.
WHEN IS HE COMING?
UH..."SHE."
OH. I'M GLAD YOU HAVE A FRIEND— "SHE" OR "HE."
SHE WORKED AT THE OFFICE AFTER THE WAR. SHE WAS A REFUGEE FROM CZECHOSLOVAKIA.
I WAS THE ONLY ONE IN THE BUILDING WHO HAD EVER BEEN THERE.
WHAT SIZE DO YOU WEAR?
I WAS AFRAID YOU'D ASK. HERE'S THE TAPE.
DOES RACHEL KNOW?
KNOW WHAT? MY SIZE?
ABOUT YOUR VISITOR.
NOT YET. I'LL TELL HER. WE WERE ALL FRIENDS.
LARS! LARS?
CHEST, FIFTY; WAIST, FIFTY-FOUR; INSEAM, THIRTY-FOUR. SHOES?
SALE
SALE
SALE
I'M SORRY.
OUR SIZES DON'T GO THAT BIG.
WOULD YOU LIKE TO SEE OUR TIE SELECTION?

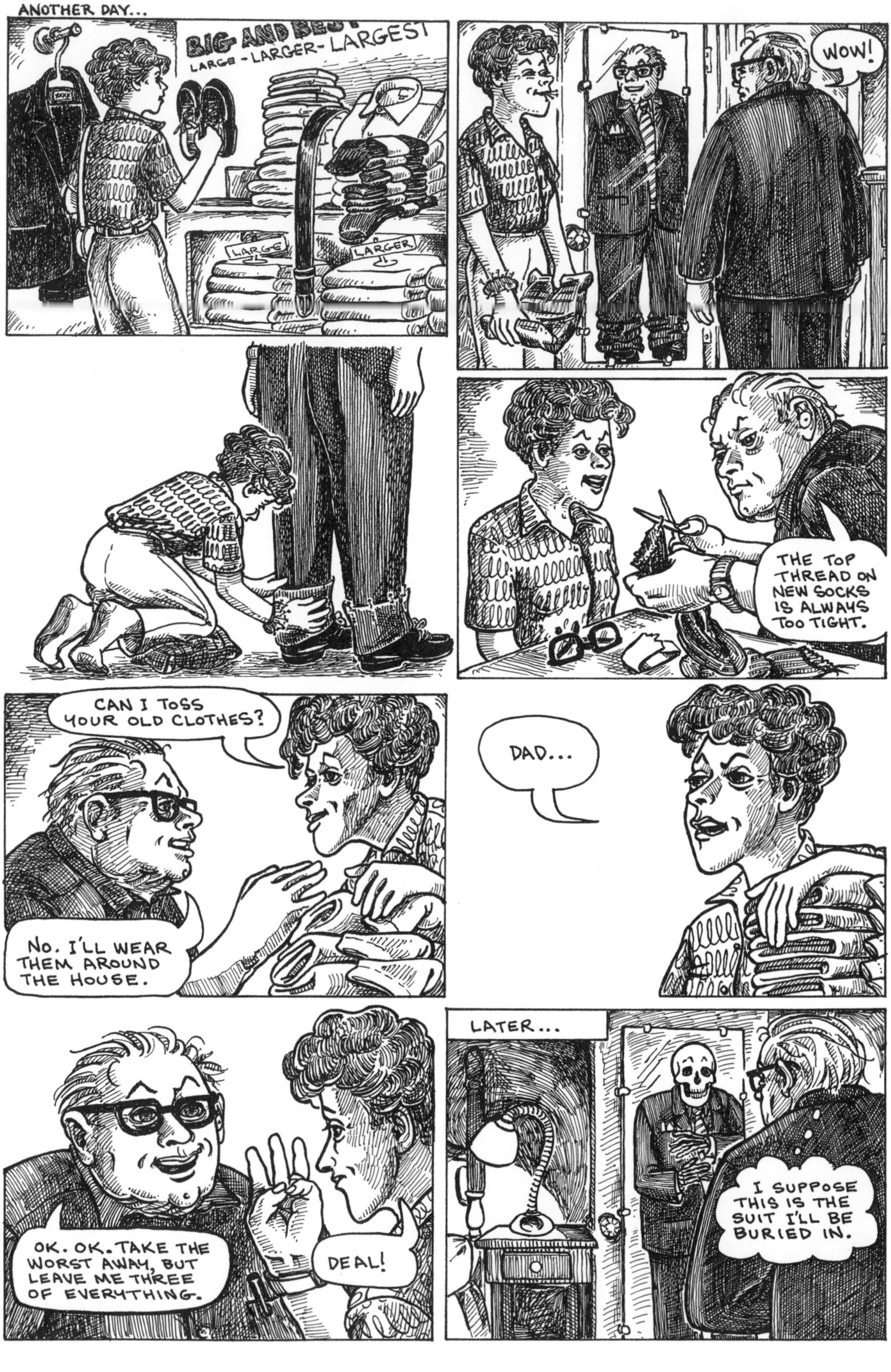
ANOTHER DAY...
LARGE - LARGER - LARGEST
LARGE
LARGER
WOW!
THE TOP THREAD ON NEW SOCKS IS ALWAYS TOO TIGHT.
CAN I TOSS YOUR OLD CLOTHES?
NO. I'LL WEAR THEM AROUND THE HOUSE.
DAD...
OK. OK. TAKE THE WORST AWAY, BUT LEAVE ME THREE OF EVERYTHING.
DEAL!
LATER...
I SUPPOSE THIS IS THE SUIT I'LL BE BURIED IN.

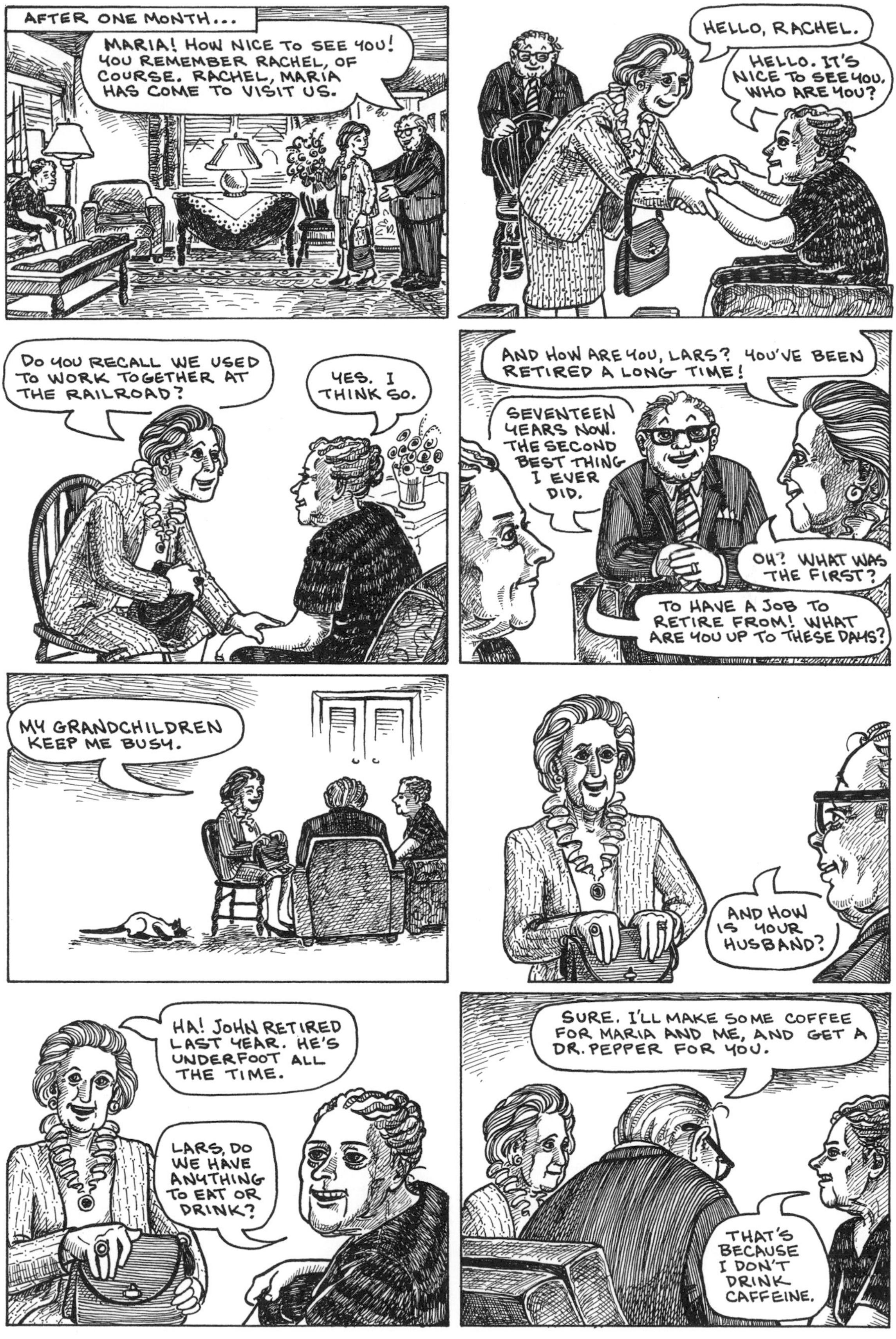
AFTER ONE MONTH...
MARIA! HOW NICE TO SEE YOU! YOU REMEMBER RACHEL, OF COURSE. RACHEL, MARIA HAS COME TO VISIT US.
HELLO, RACHEL.
HELLO. IT'S NICE TO SEE YOU. WHO ARE YOU?
DO YOU RECALL WE USED TO WORK TOGETHER AT THE RAILROAD?
YES. I THINK SO.
AND HOW ARE YOU, LARS? YOU'VE BEEN RETIRED A LONG TIME!
SEVENTEEN YEARS NOW. THE SECOND BEST THING I EVER DID.
OH? WHAT WAS THE FIRST?
TO HAVE A JOB TO RETIRE FROM! WHAT ARE YOU UP TO THESE DAYS?
MY GRANDCHILDREN KEEP ME BUSY.
AND HOW IS YOUR HUSBAND?
HA! JOHN RETIRED LAST YEAR. HE'S UNDERFOOT ALL THE TIME.
LARS, DO WE HAVE ANYTHING TO EAT OR DRINK?
SURE. I'LL MAKE SOME COFFEE FOR MARIA AND ME, AND GET A DR. PEPPER FOR YOU.
THAT'S BECAUSE I DON'T DRINK CAFFEINE.

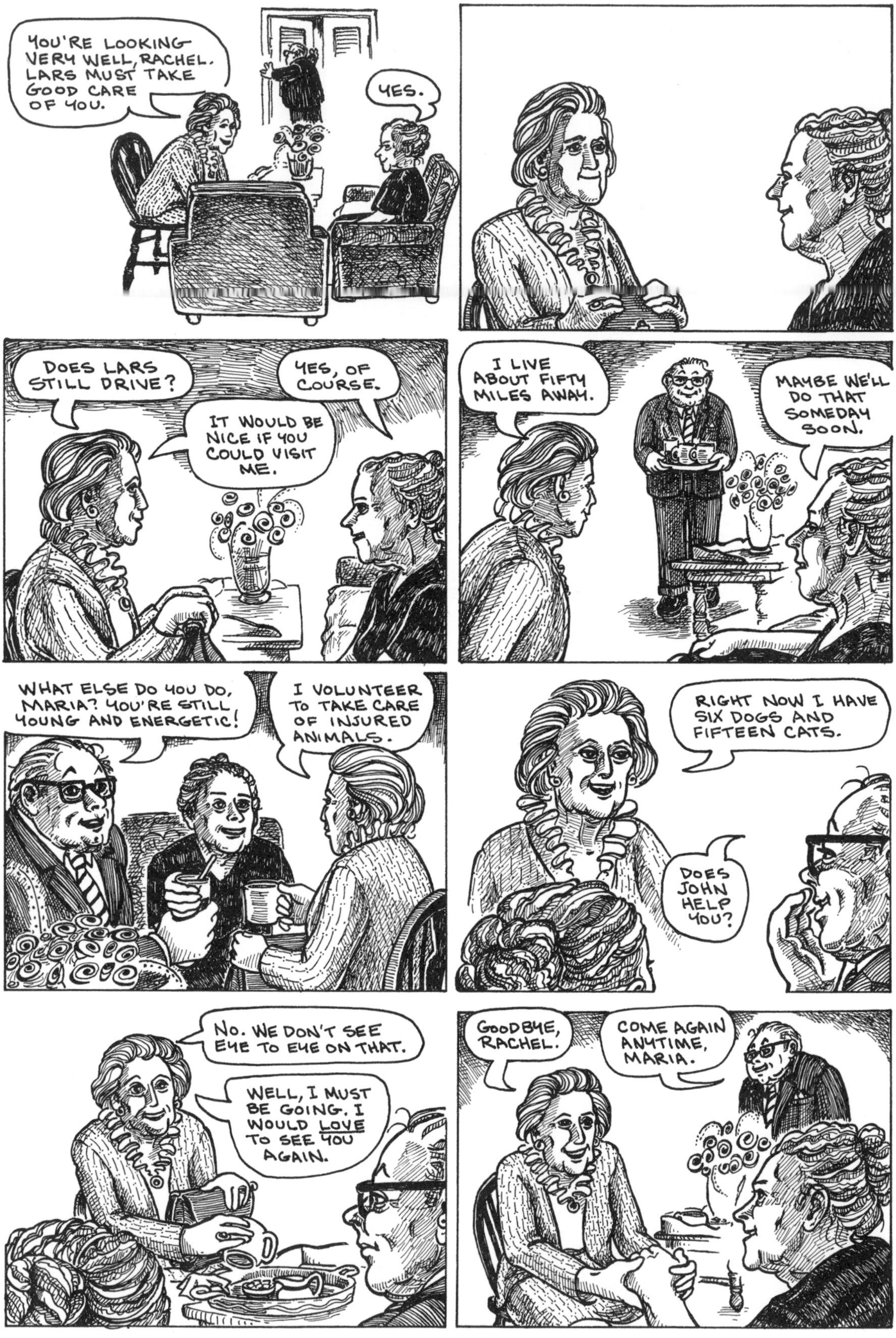
YOU'RE LOOKING VERY WELL, RACHEL. LARS MUST TAKE GOOD CARE OF YOU.
YES.
DOES LARS STILL DRIVE?
YES, OF COURSE.
IT WOULD BE NICE IF YOU COULD VISIT ME.
I LIVE ABOUT FIFTY MILES AWAY.
MAYBE WE'LL DO THAT SOMEDAY SOON.
WHAT ELSE DO YOU DO, MARIA? YOU'RE STILL YOUNG AND ENERGETIC!
I VOLUNTEER TO TAKE CARE OF INJURED ANIMALS.
RIGHT NOW I HAVE SIX DOGS AND FIFTEEN CATS.
DOES JOHN HELP YOU?
NO. WE DON'T SEE EYE TO EYE ON THAT.
WELL, I MUST BE GOING. I WOULD LOVE TO SEE YOU AGAIN.
GOODBYE, RACHEL.
COME AGAIN ANYTIME, MARIA.

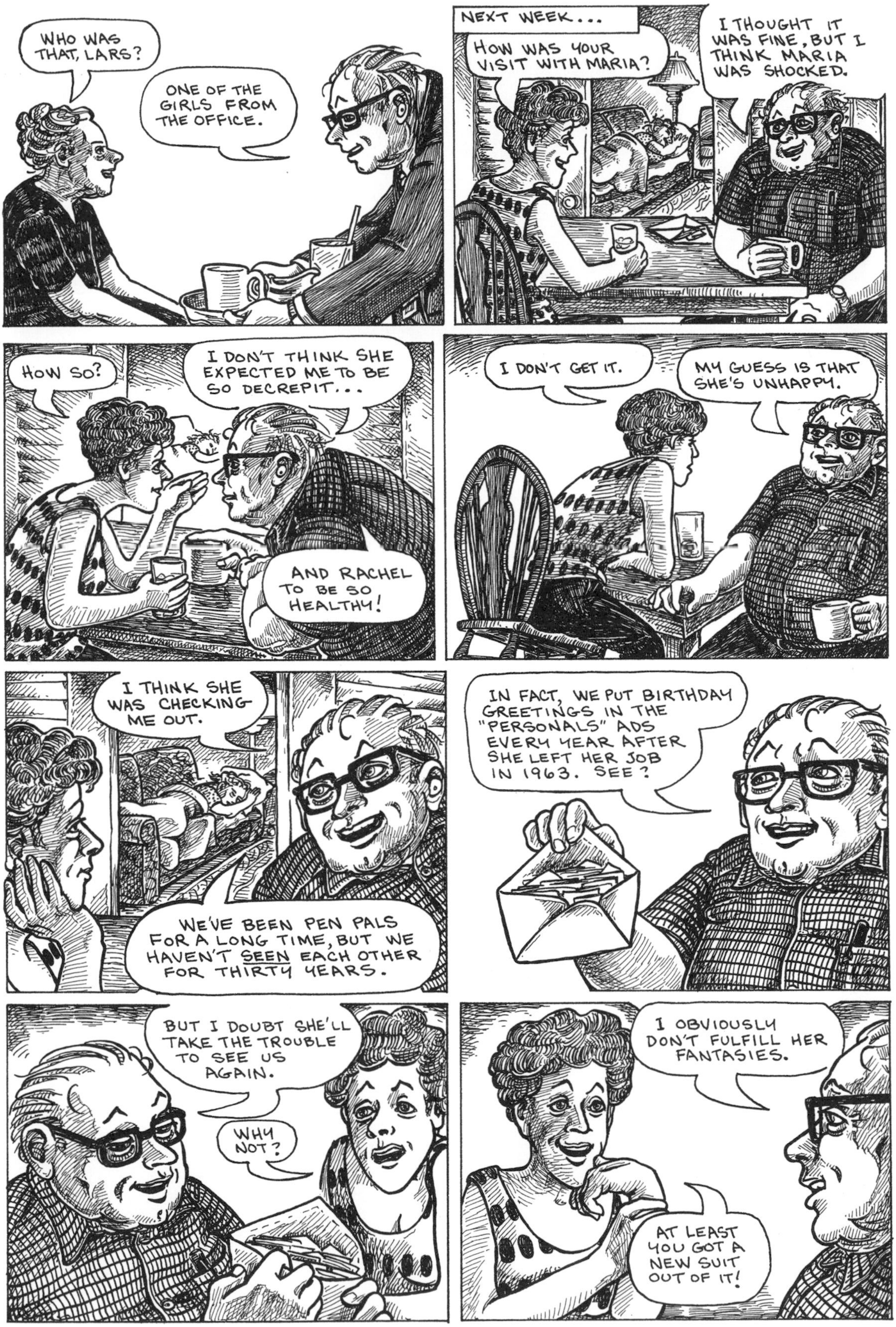
WHO WAS THAT, LARS?
ONE OF THE GIRLS FROM THE OFFICE.
NEXT WEEK...
HOW WAS YOUR VISIT WITH MARIA?
I THOUGHT IT WAS FINE, BUT I THINK MARIA WAS SHOCKED.
HOW SO?
I DON'T THINK SHE EXPECTED ME TO BE SO DECREPIT...
AND RACHEL TO BE SO HEALTHY!
I DON'T GET IT.
MY GUESS IS THAT SHE'S UNHAPPY.
I THINK SHE WAS CHECKING ME OUT.
WE'VE BEEN PEN PALS FOR A LONG TIME, BUT WE HAVEN'T SEEN EACH OTHER FOR THIRTY YEARS.
IN FACT, WE PUT BIRTHDAY GREETINGS IN THE "PERSONALS" ADS EVERY YEAR AFTER SHE LEFT HER JOB IN 1963. SEE?
BUT I DOUBT SHE'LL TAKE THE TROUBLE TO SEE US AGAIN.
WHY NOT?
I OBVIOUSLY DON'T FULFILL HER FANTASIES.
AT LEAST YOU GOT A NEW SUIT OUT OF IT!

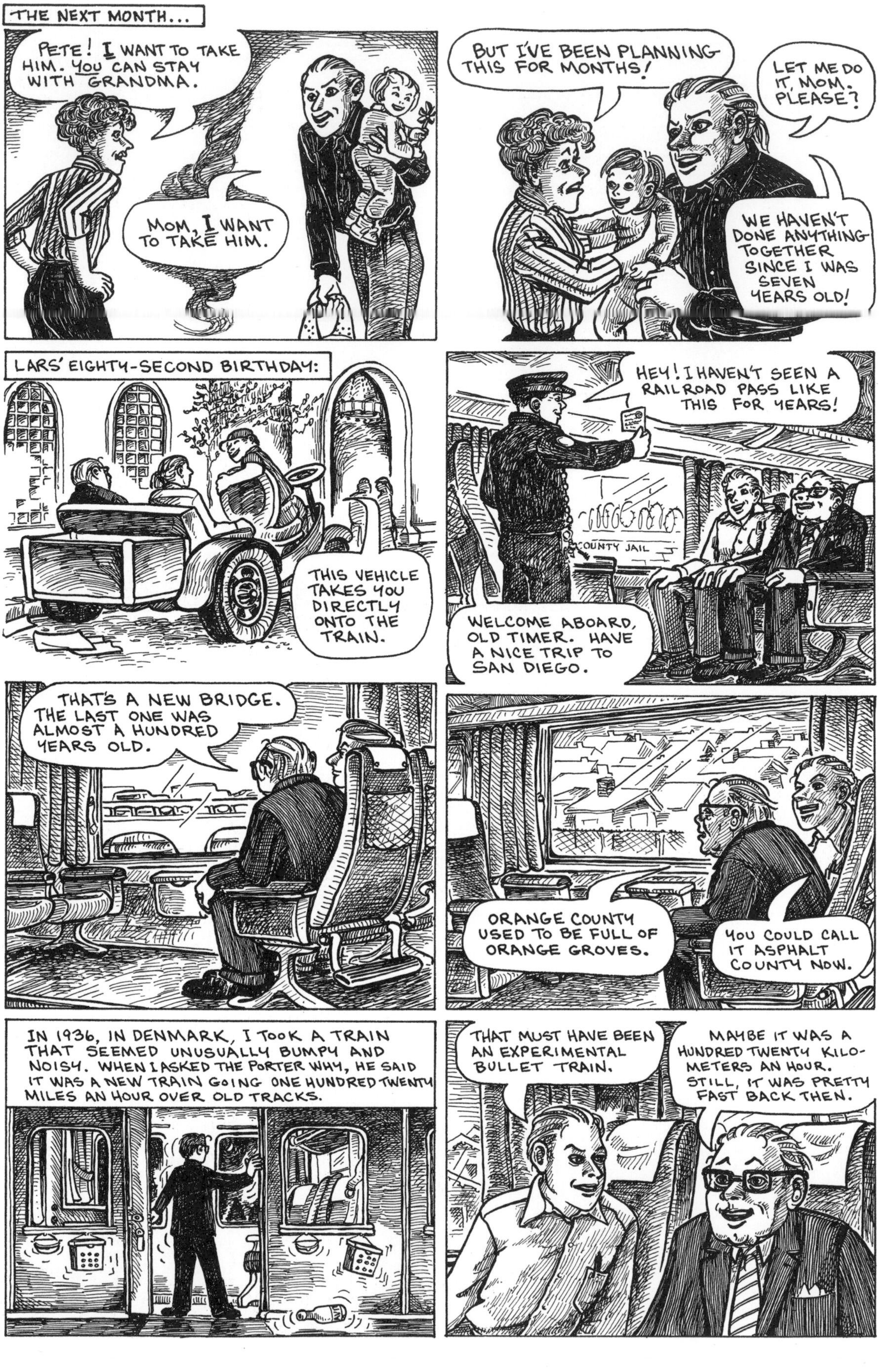
THE NEXT MONTH...
PETE! I WANT TO TAKE HIM. YOU CAN STAY WITH GRANDMA.
MOM, I WANT TO TAKE HIM.
BUT I'VE BEEN PLANNING THIS FOR MONTHS!
LET ME DO IT, MOM. PLEASE?
WE HAVEN'T DONE ANYTHING TOGETHER SINCE I WAS SEVEN YEARS OLD!
LARS' EIGHTY-SECOND BIRTHDAY:
THIS VEHICLE TAKES YOU DIRECTLY ONTO THE TRAIN.
HEY! I HAVEN'T SEEN A RAILROAD PASS LIKE THIS FOR YEARS!
COUNTY JAIL
WELCOME ABOARD, OLD TIMER. HAVE A NICE TRIP TO SAN DIEGO.
THAT'S A NEW BRIDGE. THE LAST ONE WAS ALMOST A HUNDRED YEARS OLD.
ORANGE COUNTY USED TO BE FULL OF ORANGE GROVES.
YOU COULD CALL IT ASPHALT COUNTY NOW.
IN 1936, IN DENMARK, I TOOK A TRAIN THAT SEEMED UNUSUALLY BUMPY AND NOISY. WHEN I ASKED THE PORTER WHY, HE SAID IT WAS A NEW TRAIN GOING ONE HUNDRED TWENTY MILES AN HOUR OVER OLD TRACKS.
THAT MUST HAVE BEEN AN EXPERIMENTAL BULLET TRAIN.
MAYBE IT WAS A HUNDRED TWENTY KILOMETERS AN HOUR. STILL, IT WAS PRETTY FAST BACK THEN.

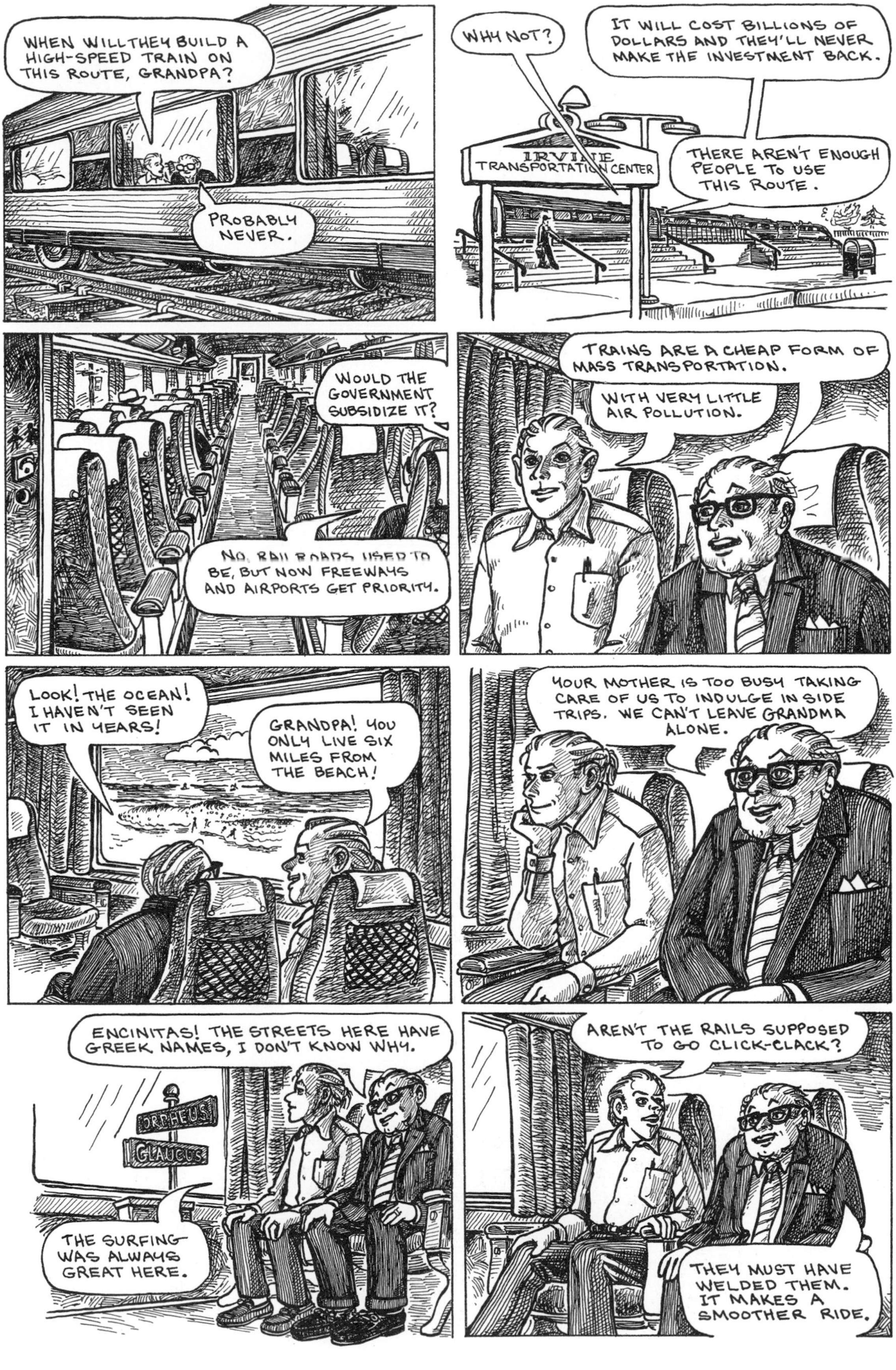
WHEN WILL THEY BUILD A HIGH-SPEED TRAIN ON THIS ROUTE, GRANDPA?
PROBABLY NEVER.
WHY NOT?
IT WILL COST BILLIONS OF DOLLARS AND THEY'LL NEVER MAKE THE INVESTMENT BACK.
IRVINE TRANSPORTATION CENTER
THERE AREN'T ENOUGH PEOPLE TO USE THIS ROUTE.
WOULD THE GOVERNMENT SUBSIDIZE IT?
NO. RAILROADS USED TO BE, BUT NOW FREEWAYS AND AIRPORTS GET PRIORITY.
TRAINS ARE A CHEAP FORM OF MASS TRANSPORTATION.
WITH VERY LITTLE AIR POLLUTION.
LOOK! THE OCEAN! I HAVEN'T SEEN IT IN YEARS!
GRANDPA! YOU ONLY LIVE SIX MILES FROM THE BEACH!
YOUR MOTHER IS TOO BUSY TAKING CARE OF US TO INDULGE IN SIDE TRIPS. WE CAN'T LEAVE GRANDMA ALONE.
ENCINITAS! THE STREETS HERE HAVE GREEK NAMES, I DON'T KNOW WHY.
ORPHEUS
GLAUCUS
THE SURFING WAS ALWAYS GREAT HERE.
AREN'T THE RAILS SUPPOSED TO GO CLICK-CLACK?
THEY MUST HAVE WELDED THEM. IT MAKES A SMOOTHER RIDE.

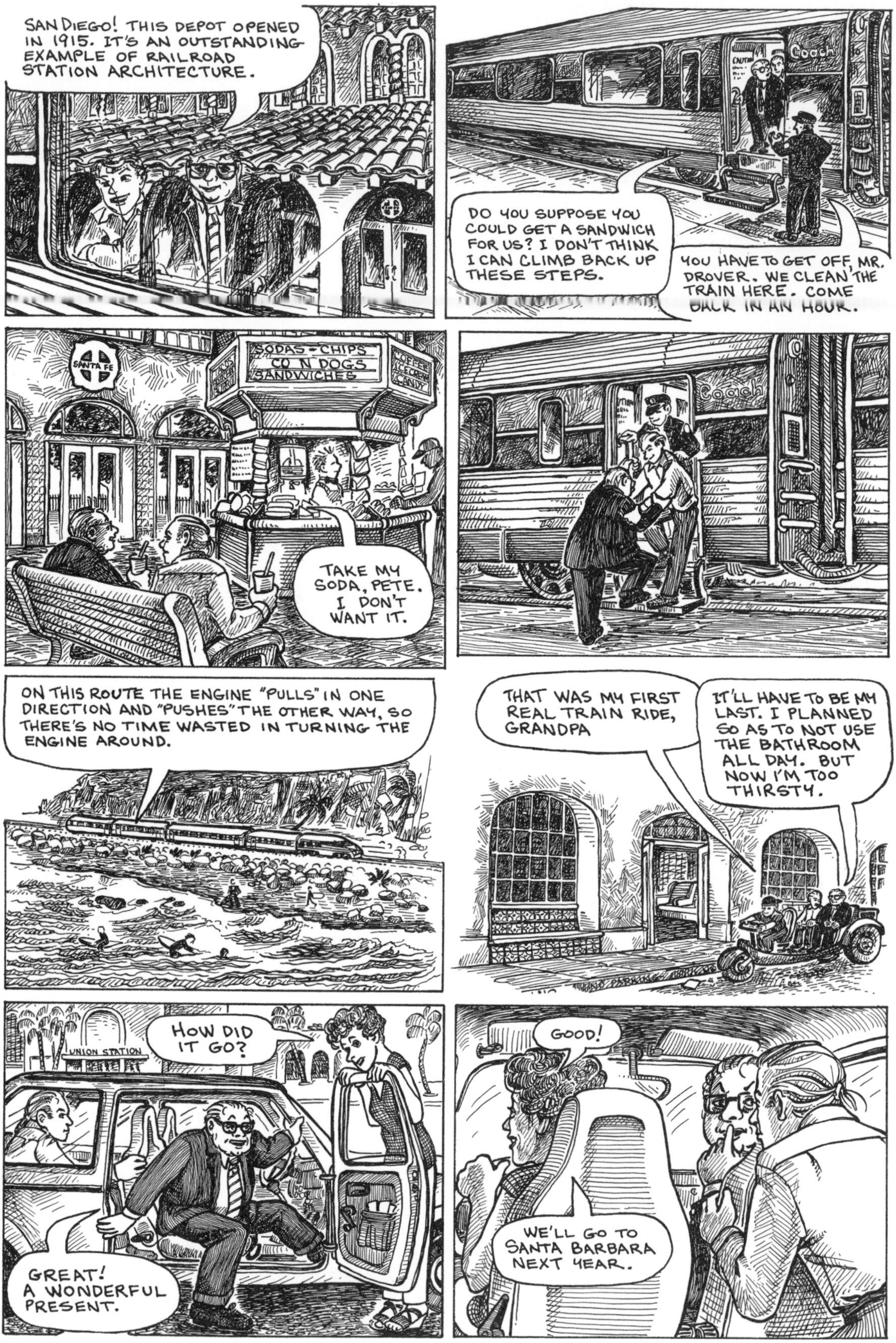
SAN DIEGO! THIS DEPOT OPENED IN 1915. IT'S AN OUTSTANDING EXAMPLE OF RAILROAD STATION ARCHITECTURE.
DO YOU SUPPOSE YOU COULD GET A SANDWICH FOR US? I DON'T THINK I CAN CLIMB BACK UP THESE STEPS.
YOU HAVE TO GET OFF, MR. DROVER. WE CLEAN THE TRAIN HERE. COME BACK IN AN HOUR.
SODAS - CHIPS
CO N DOGS
SANDWICHES
SANTA FE
TAKE MY SODA, PETE. I DON'T WANT IT.
Coach
ON THIS ROUTE THE ENGINE "PULLS" IN ONE DIRECTION AND "PUSHES" THE OTHER WAY, SO THERE'S NO TIME WASTED IN TURNING THE ENGINE AROUND.
THAT WAS MY FIRST REAL TRAIN RIDE, GRANDPA
IT'LL HAVE TO BE MY LAST. I PLANNED SO AS TO NOT USE THE BATHROOM ALL DAY. BUT NOW I'M TOO THIRSTY.
UNION STATION
HOW DID IT GO?
GREAT! A WONDERFUL PRESENT.
GOOD!
WE'LL GO TO SANTA BARBARA NEXT YEAR.

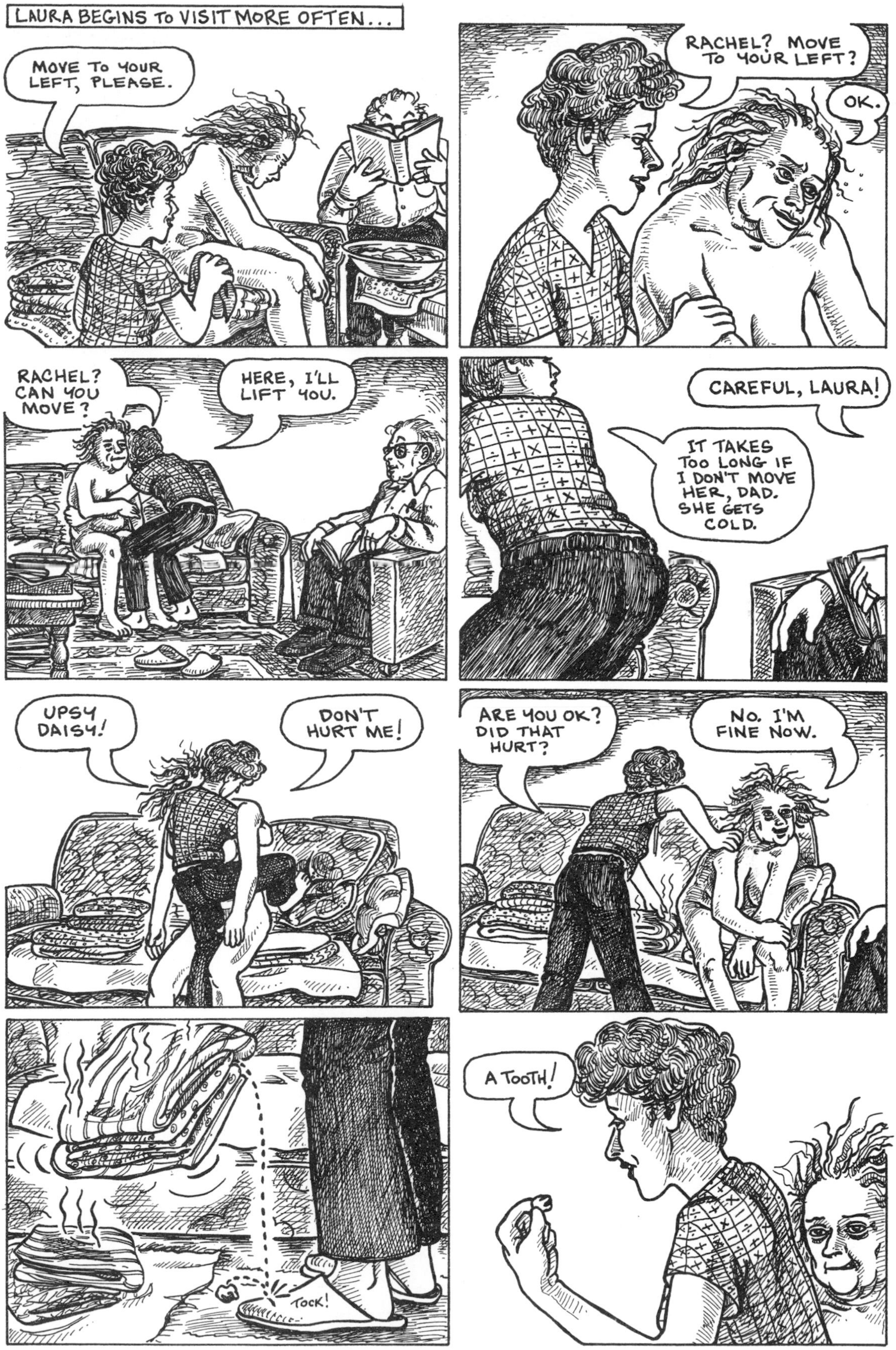
LAURA BEGINS TO VISIT MORE OFTEN...
MOVE TO YOUR LEFT, PLEASE.
RACHEL? MOVE TO YOUR LEFT?
OK.
RACHEL? CAN YOU MOVE?
HERE, I'LL LIFT YOU.
CAREFUL, LAURA!
IT TAKES TOO LONG IF I DON'T MOVE HER, DAD. SHE GETS COLD.
UPSY DAISY!
DON'T HURT ME!
ARE YOU OK? DID THAT HURT?
NO. I'M FINE NOW.
TOCK!
A TOOTH!

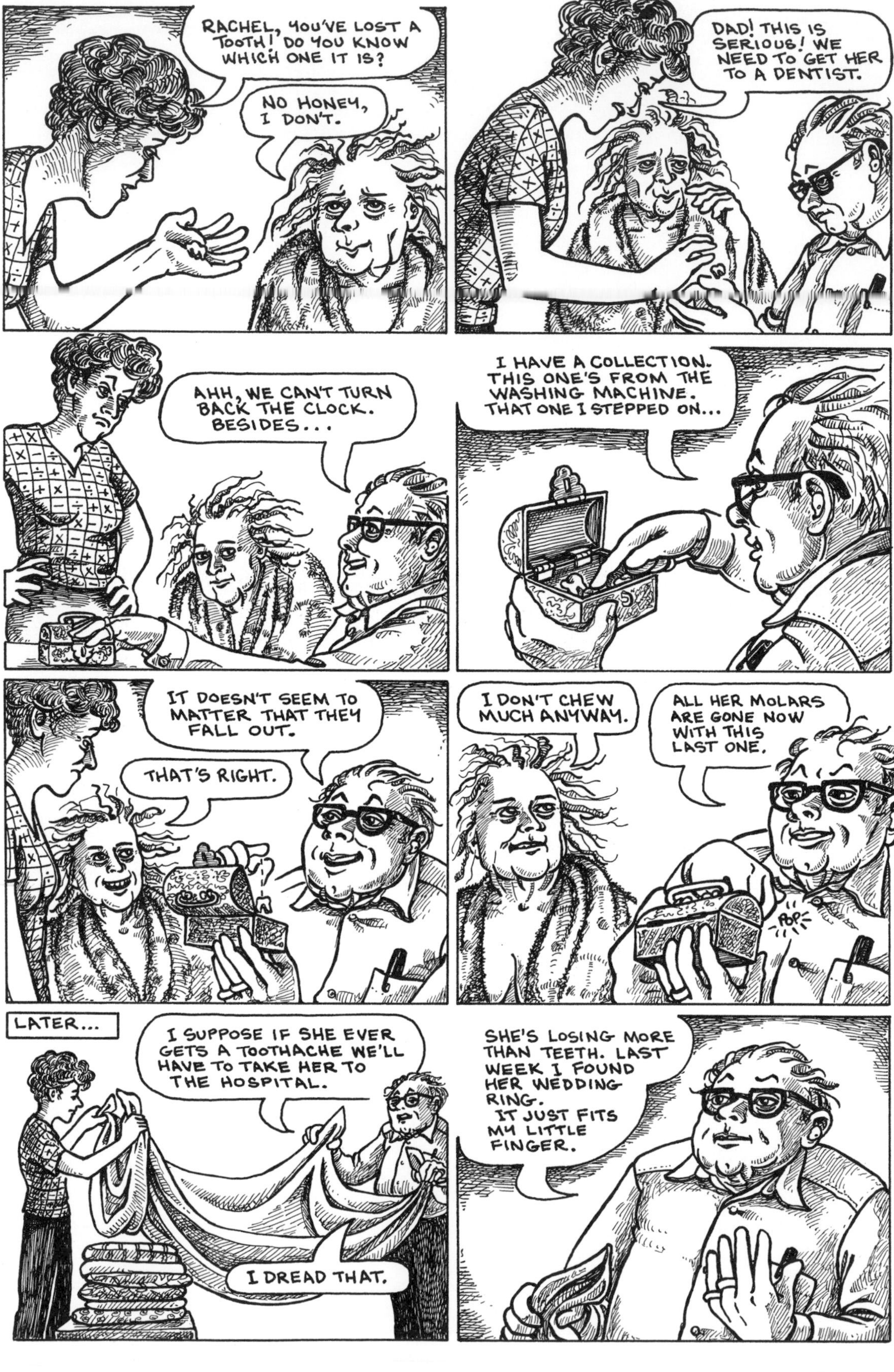
RACHEL, YOU'VE LOST A TOOTH! DO YOU KNOW WHICH ONE IT IS?
NO HONEY, I DON'T.
DAD! THIS IS SERIOUS! WE NEED TO GET HER TO A DENTIST.
AHH, WE CAN'T TURN BACK THE CLOCK. BESIDES...
I HAVE A COLLECTION. THIS ONE'S FROM THE WASHING MACHINE. THAT ONE I STEPPED ON...
IT DOESN'T SEEM TO MATTER THAT THEY FALL OUT.
THAT'S RIGHT.
I DON'T CHEW MUCH ANYWAY.
ALL HER MOLARS ARE GONE NOW WITH THIS LAST ONE.
POP
LATER...
I SUPPOSE IF SHE EVER GETS A TOOTHACHE WE'LL HAVE TO TAKE HER TO THE HOSPITAL.
I DREAD THAT.
SHE'S LOSING MORE THAN TEETH. LAST WEEK I FOUND HER WEDDING RING.
IT JUST FITS MY LITTLE FINGER.

9

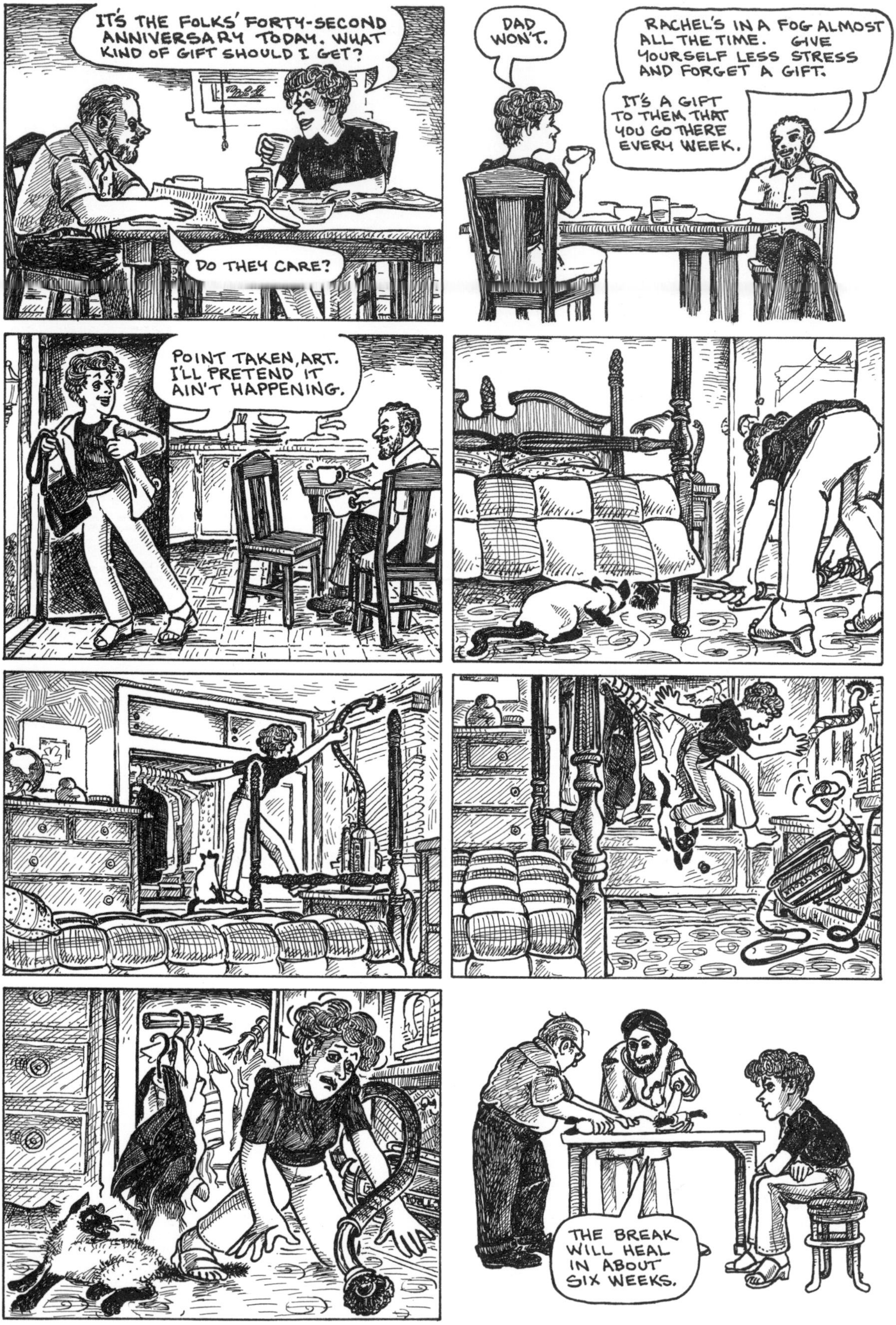
IT'S THE FOLKS' FORTY-SECOND ANNIVERSARY TODAY. WHAT KIND OF GIFT SHOULD I GET?
DO THEY CARE?
DAD WON'T.
RACHEL'S IN A FOG ALMOST ALL THE TIME. GIVE YOURSELF LESS STRESS AND FORGET A GIFT.
IT'S A GIFT TO THEM THAT YOU GO THERE EVERY WEEK.
POINT TAKEN, ART. I'LL PRETEND IT AIN'T HAPPENING.
THE BREAK WILL HEAL IN ABOUT SIX WEEKS.

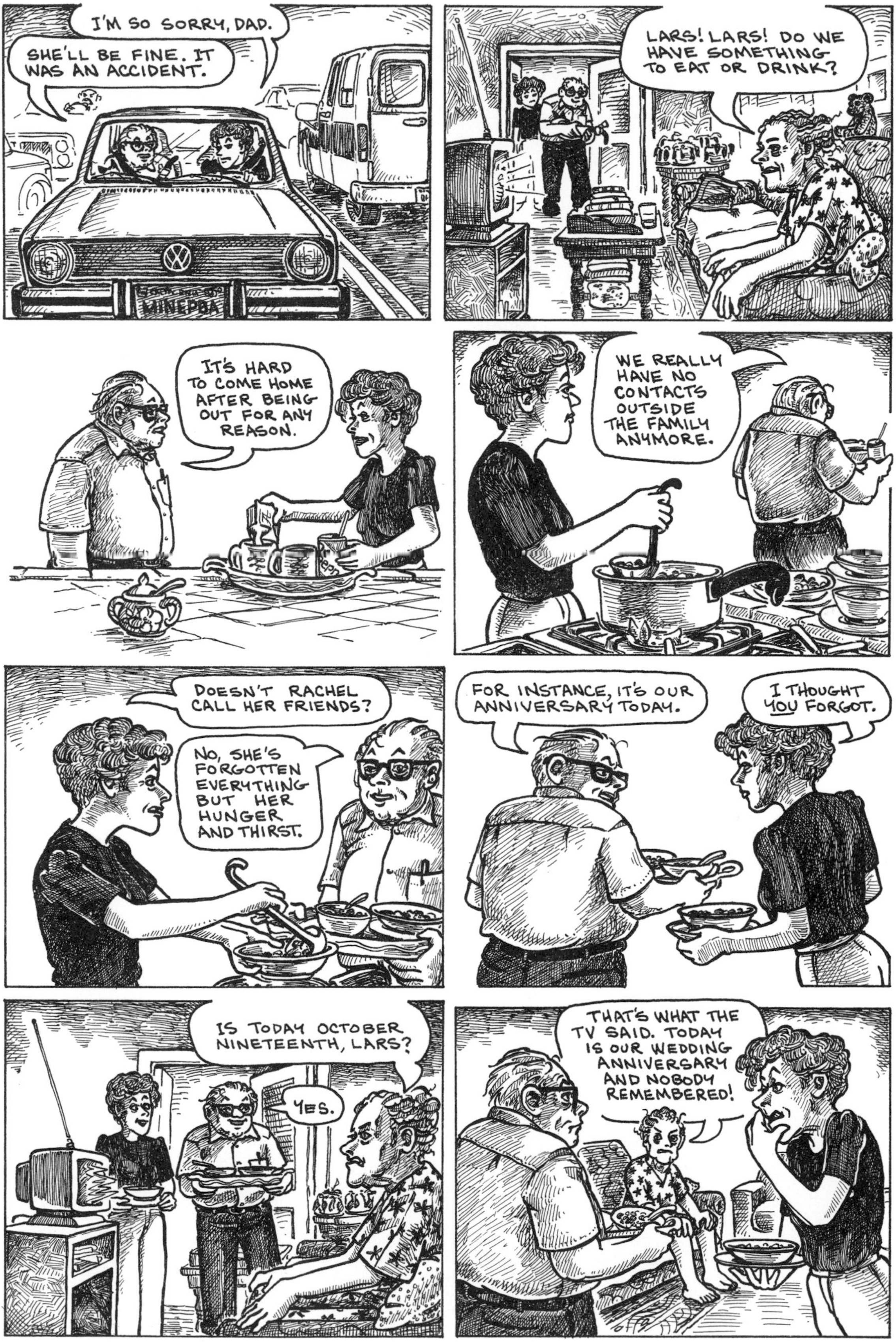
I'M SO SORRY, DAD.
SHE'LL BE FINE. IT WAS AN ACCIDENT.
LARS! LARS! DO WE HAVE SOMETHING TO EAT OR DRINK?
IT'S HARD TO COME HOME AFTER BEING OUT FOR ANY REASON.
WE REALLY HAVE NO CONTACTS OUTSIDE THE FAMILY ANYMORE.
DOESN'T RACHEL CALL HER FRIENDS?
NO, SHE'S FORGOTTEN EVERYTHING BUT HER HUNGER AND THIRST.
FOR INSTANCE, IT'S OUR ANNIVERSARY TODAY.
I THOUGHT YOU FORGOT.
IS TODAY OCTOBER NINETEENTH, LARS?
YES.
THAT'S WHAT THE TV SAID. TODAY IS OUR WEDDING ANNIVERSARY AND NOBODY REMEMBERED!

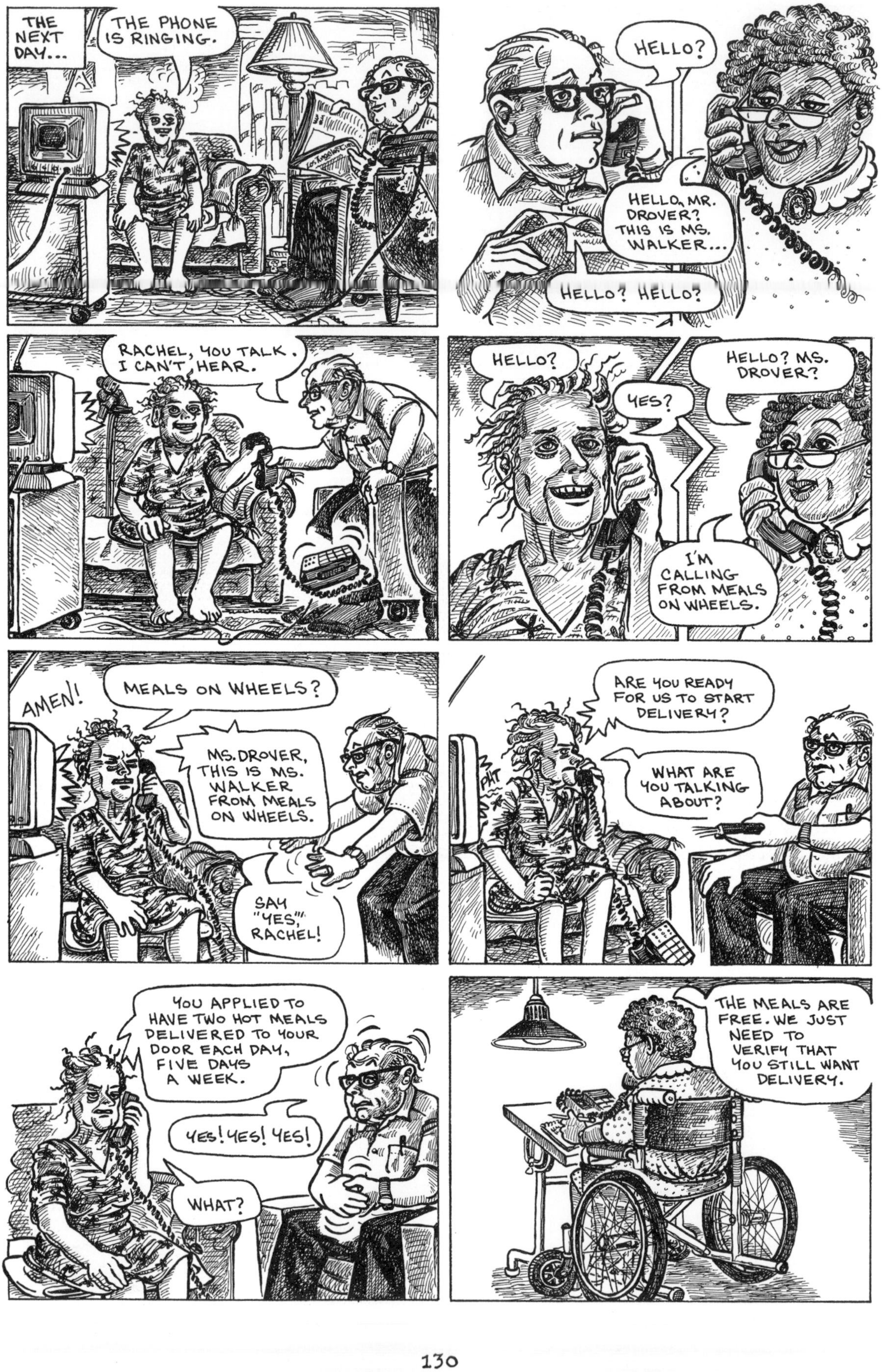
THE NEXT DAY...
THE PHONE IS RINGING.
HELLO?
HELLO, MR. DROVER? THIS IS MS. WALKER...
HELLO? HELLO?
RACHEL, YOU TALK. I CAN'T HEAR.
HELLO?
HELLO? MS. DROVER?
YES?
I'M CALLING FROM MEALS ON WHEELS.
AMEN!
MEALS ON WHEELS?
MS. DROVER, THIS IS MS. WALKER FROM MEALS ON WHEELS.
SAY "YES," RACHEL!
ARE YOU READY FOR US TO START DELIVERY?
WHAT ARE YOU TALKING ABOUT?
YOU APPLIED TO HAVE TWO HOT MEALS DELIVERED TO YOUR DOOR EACH DAY, FIVE DAYS A WEEK.
YES! YES! YES!
WHAT?
THE MEALS ARE FREE. WE JUST NEED TO VERIFY THAT YOU STILL WANT DELIVERY.

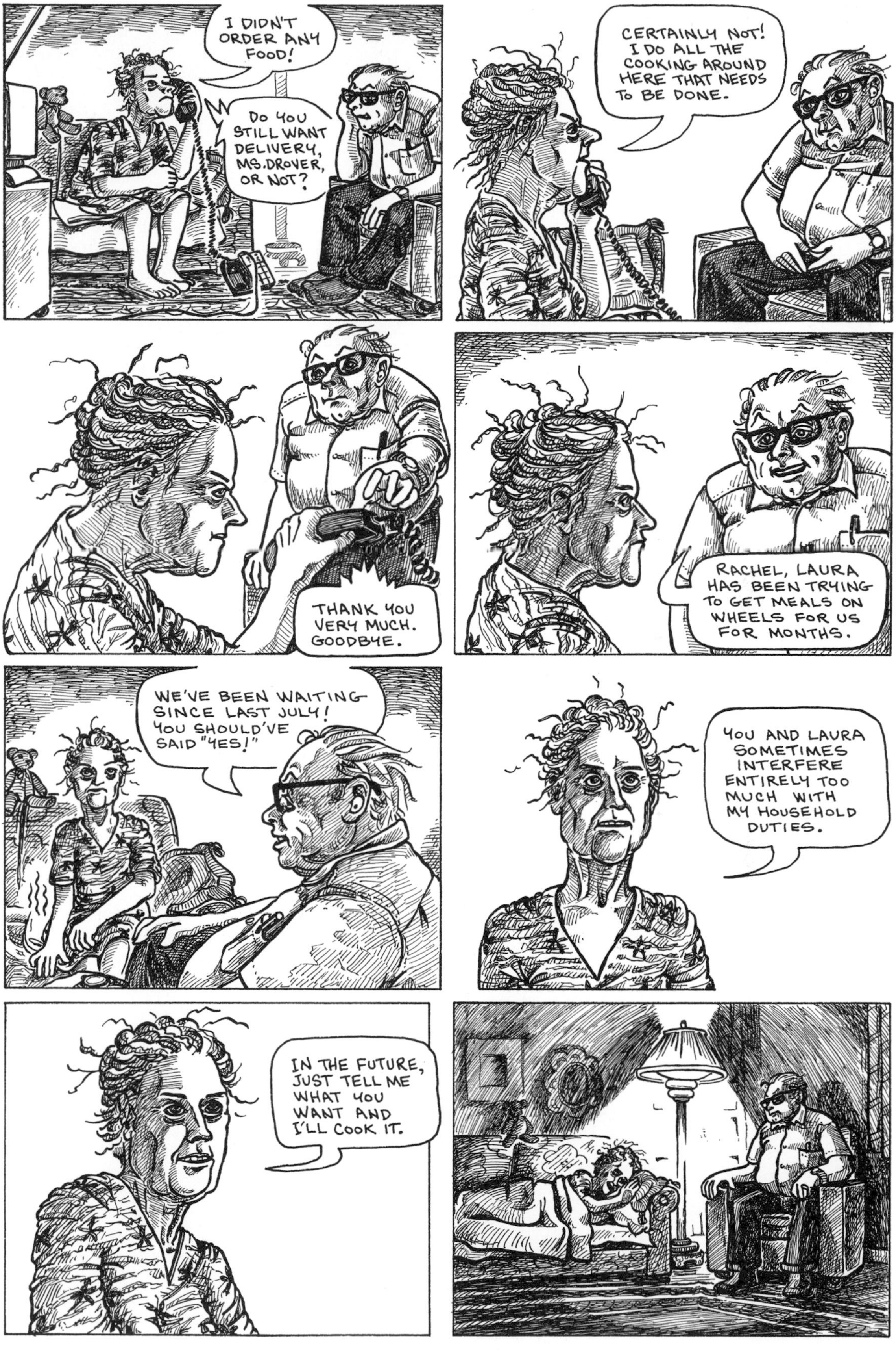
I DIDN'T ORDER ANY FOOD!
DO YOU STILL WANT DELIVERY, MS. DROVER, OR NOT?
CERTAINLY NOT! I DO ALL THE COOKING AROUND HERE THAT NEEDS TO BE DONE.
THANK YOU VERY MUCH. GOODBYE.
RACHEL, LAURA HAS BEEN TRYING TO GET MEALS ON WHEELS FOR US FOR MONTHS.
WE'VE BEEN WAITING SINCE LAST JULY! YOU SHOULD'VE SAID "YES!"
YOU AND LAURA SOMETIMES INTERFERE ENTIRELY TOO MUCH WITH MY HOUSEHOLD DUTIES.
IN THE FUTURE, JUST TELL ME WHAT YOU WANT AND I'LL COOK IT.

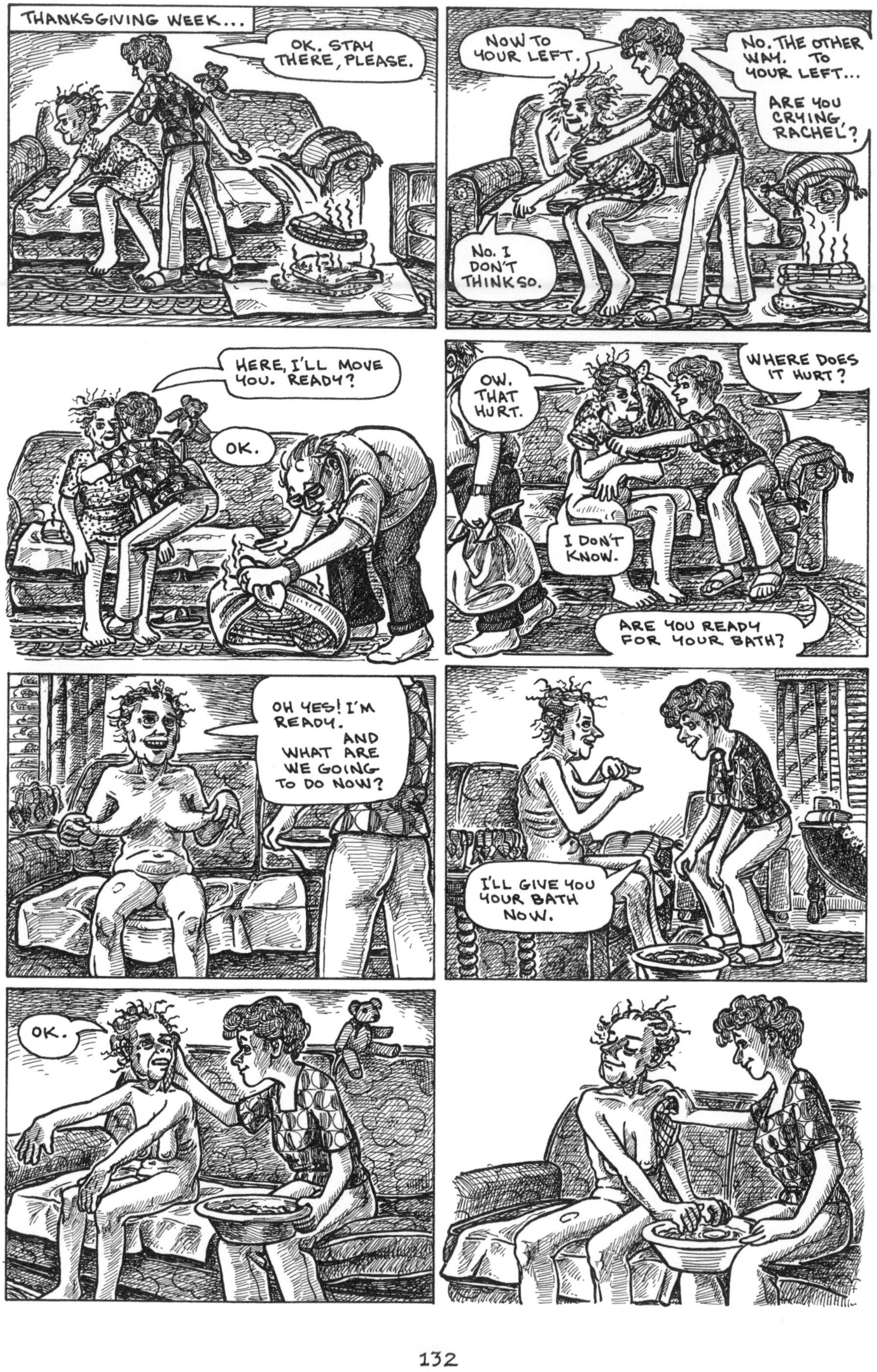
THANKSGIVING WEEK...
OK. STAY THERE, PLEASE.
NOW TO YOUR LEFT.
NO. THE OTHER WAY. TO YOUR LEFT...
ARE YOU CRYING, RACHEL?
NO. I DON'T THINK SO.
HERE, I'LL MOVE YOU. READY?
OK.
OW. THAT HURT.
WHERE DOES IT HURT?
I DON'T KNOW.
ARE YOU READY FOR YOUR BATH?
OH YES! I'M READY. AND WHAT ARE WE GOING TO DO NOW?
I'LL GIVE YOU YOUR BATH NOW.
OK.

RACHEL, I SEE YOU HAVE A BLISTER.

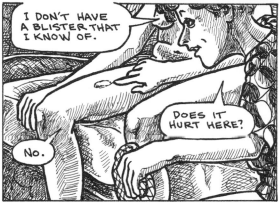

I DON'T HAVE A BLISTER THAT I KNOW OF.

DOES IT HURT HERE?

NO.

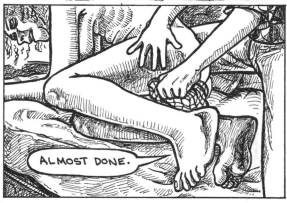

ALMOST DONE.

THERE! CLEAN AND SHINY. NOW SOME LOTION TO MAKE YOU PERFECT.

WHAT COLOR DRESS DO YOU WANT?

PINK!

SUCH LONG, PRETTY HAIR.

IT WAS NEVER CUT.

RACHEL'S GOT A BLISTER ON HER LEG.

YES, I FORGOT TO TELL YOU BUT I KNEW YOU'D SEE IT.

I'VE GOT A BLISTER! I'VE GOT A BLISTER!

IS THERE ANYTHING TO EAT OR DRINK IN THIS HOUSE?

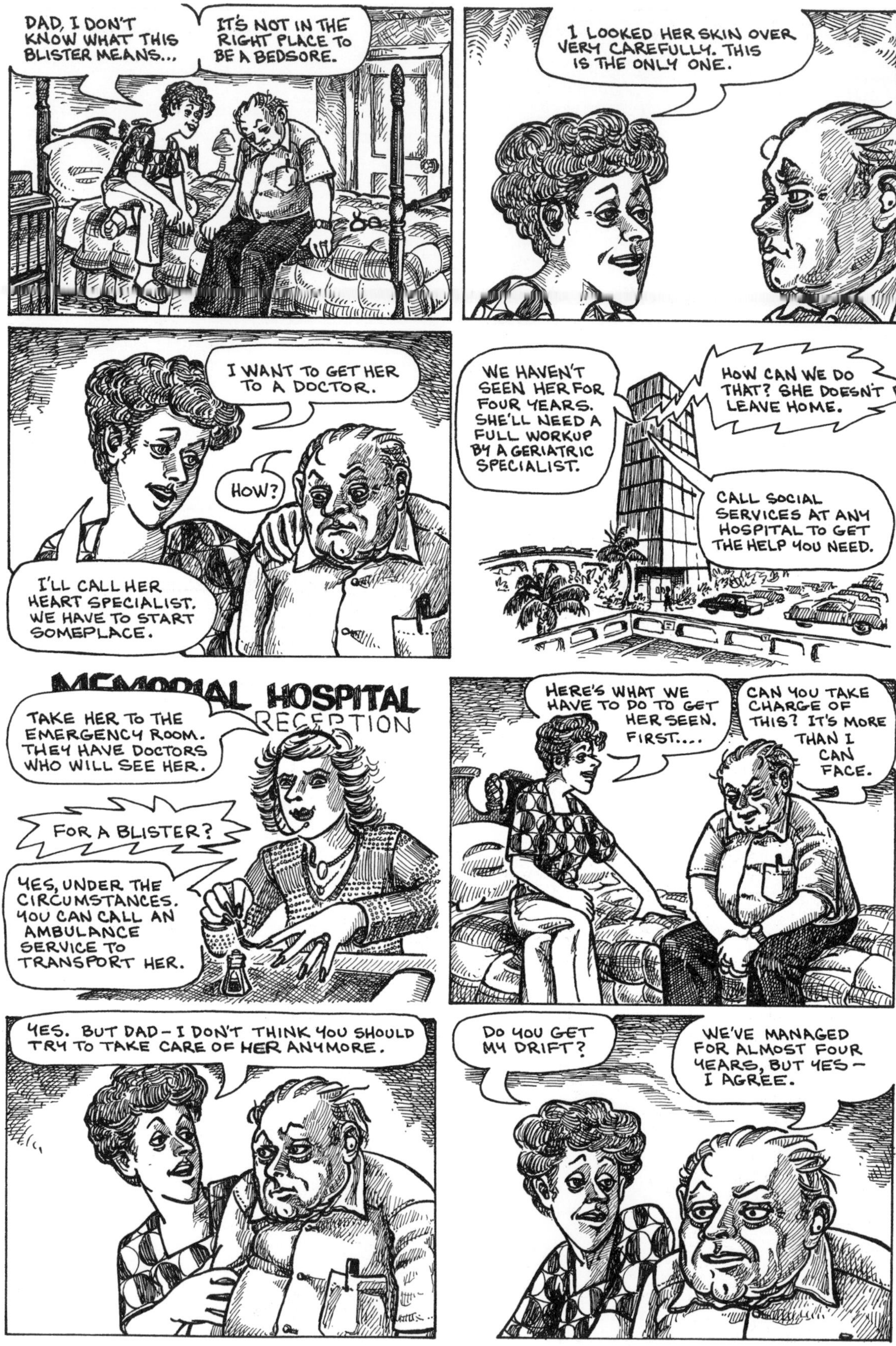
DAD, I DON'T KNOW WHAT THIS BLISTER MEANS...
IT'S NOT IN THE RIGHT PLACE TO BE A BEDSORE.
I LOOKED HER SKIN OVER VERY CAREFULLY. THIS IS THE ONLY ONE.
I WANT TO GET HER TO A DOCTOR.
HOW?
I'LL CALL HER HEART SPECIALIST. WE HAVE TO START SOMEPLACE.
WE HAVEN'T SEEN HER FOR FOUR YEARS. SHE'LL NEED A FULL WORKUP BY A GERIATRIC SPECIALIST.
HOW CAN WE DO THAT? SHE DOESN'T LEAVE HOME.
CALL SOCIAL SERVICES AT ANY HOSPITAL TO GET THE HELP YOU NEED.
MEMORIAL HOSPITAL
RECEPTION
TAKE HER TO THE EMERGENCY ROOM. THEY HAVE DOCTORS WHO WILL SEE HER.
FOR A BLISTER?
YES, UNDER THE CIRCUMSTANCES. YOU CAN CALL AN AMBULANCE SERVICE TO TRANSPORT HER.
HERE'S WHAT WE HAVE TO DO TO GET HER SEEN. FIRST....
CAN YOU TAKE CHARGE OF THIS? IT'S MORE THAN I CAN FACE.
YES. BUT DAD - I DON'T THINK YOU SHOULD TRY TO TAKE CARE OF HER ANYMORE.
DO YOU GET MY DRIFT?
WE'VE MANAGED FOR ALMOST FOUR YEARS, BUT YES - I AGREE.

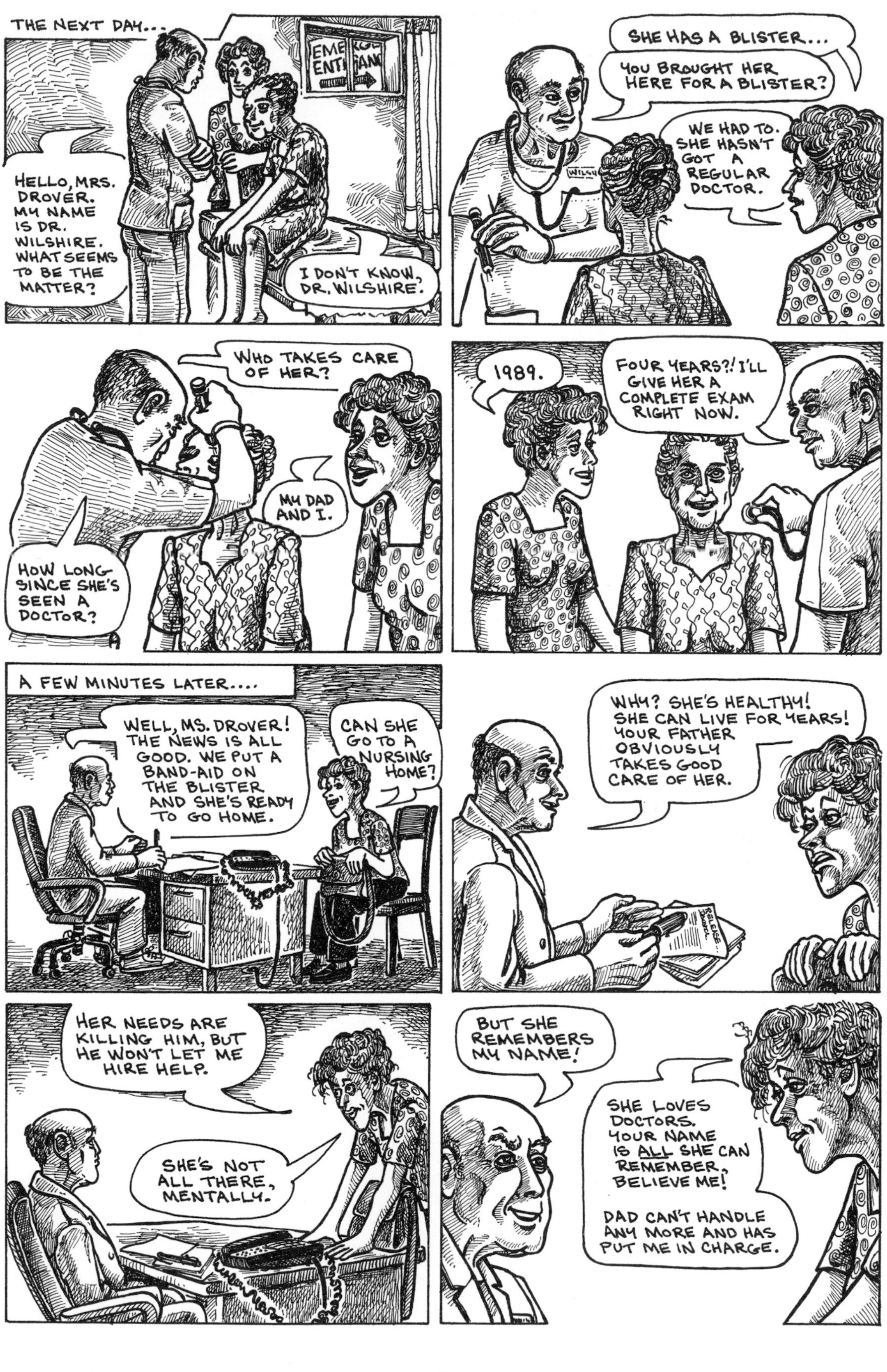
THE NEXT DAY...
HELLO, MRS. DROVER. MY NAME IS DR. WILSHIRE. WHAT SEEMS TO BE THE MATTER?
I DON'T KNOW, DR. WILSHIRE.
SHE HAS A BLISTER...
YOU BROUGHT HER HERE FOR A BLISTER?
WE HAD TO. SHE HASN'T GOT A REGULAR DOCTOR.
WHO TAKES CARE OF HER?
MY DAD AND I.
HOW LONG SINCE SHE'S SEEN A DOCTOR?
1989.
FOUR YEARS?! I'LL GIVE HER A COMPLETE EXAM RIGHT NOW.
A FEW MINUTES LATER....
WELL, MS. DROVER! THE NEWS IS ALL GOOD. WE PUT A BAND-AID ON THE BLISTER AND SHE'S READY TO GO HOME.
CAN SHE GO TO A NURSING HOME?
WHY? SHE'S HEALTHY! SHE CAN LIVE FOR YEARS! YOUR FATHER OBVIOUSLY TAKES GOOD CARE OF HER.
HER NEEDS ARE KILLING HIM, BUT HE WON'T LET ME HIRE HELP.
SHE'S NOT ALL THERE, MENTALLY.
BUT SHE REMEMBERS MY NAME!
SHE LOVES DOCTORS. YOUR NAME IS ALL SHE CAN REMEMBER, BELIEVE ME!
DAD CAN'T HANDLE ANY MORE AND HAS PUT ME IN CHARGE.

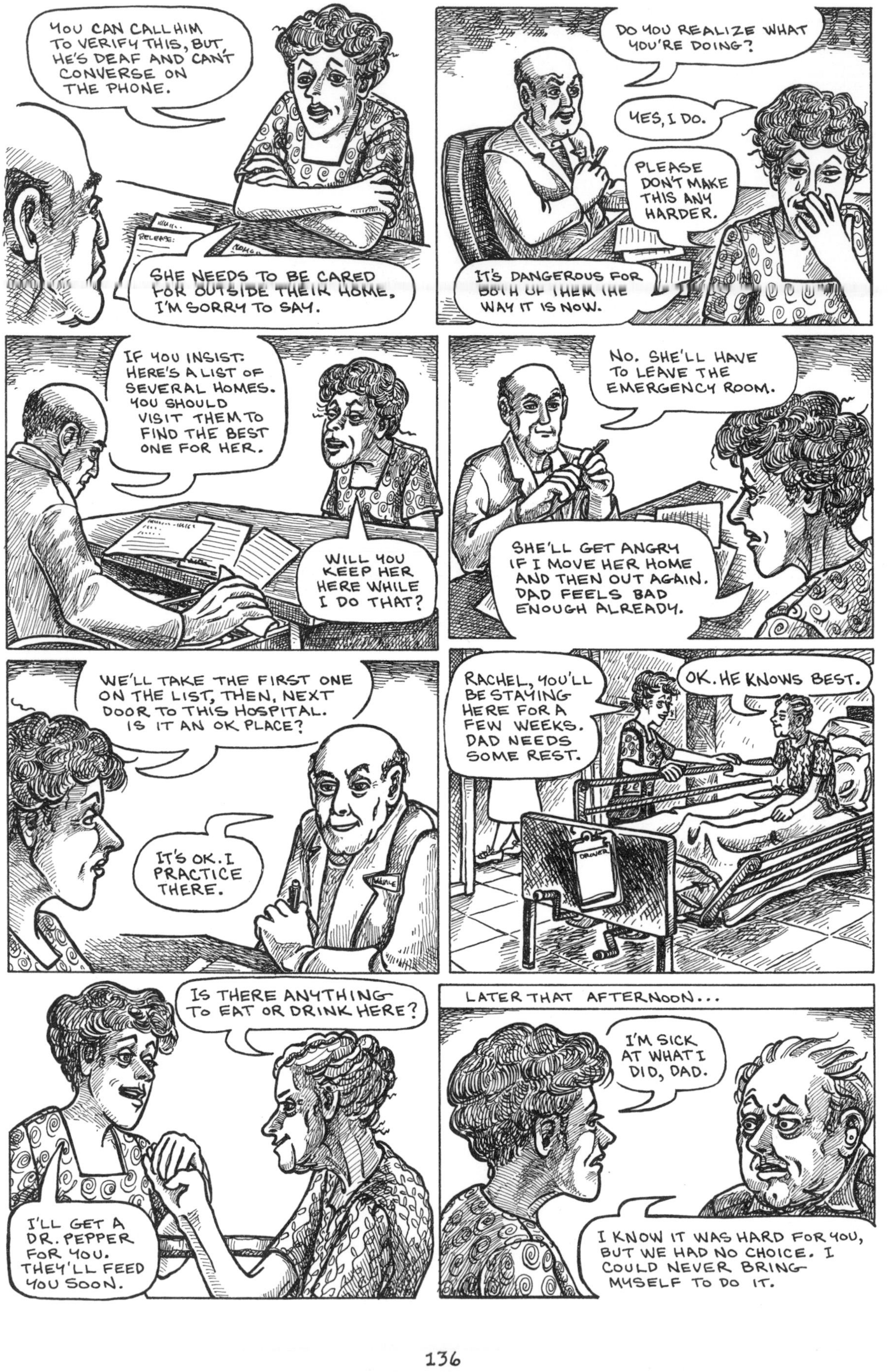

YOU CAN CALL HIM TO VERIFY THIS, BUT HE'S DEAF AND CAN'T CONVERSE ON THE PHONE.
SHE NEEDS TO BE CARED FOR OUTSIDE THEIR HOME, I'M SORRY TO SAY.
DO YOU REALIZE WHAT YOU'RE DOING?
YES, I DO.
PLEASE DON'T MAKE THIS ANY HARDER.
IT'S DANGEROUS FOR BOTH OF THEM THE WAY IT IS NOW.
IF YOU INSIST: HERE'S A LIST OF SEVERAL HOMES. YOU SHOULD VISIT THEM TO FIND THE BEST ONE FOR HER.
WILL YOU KEEP HER HERE WHILE I DO THAT?
NO. SHE'LL HAVE TO LEAVE THE EMERGENCY ROOM.
SHE'LL GET ANGRY IF I MOVE HER HOME AND THEN OUT AGAIN. DAD FEELS BAD ENOUGH ALREADY.
WE'LL TAKE THE FIRST ONE ON THE LIST, THEN. NEXT DOOR TO THIS HOSPITAL. IS IT AN OK PLACE?
IT'S OK. I PRACTICE THERE.
RACHEL, YOU'LL BE STAYING HERE FOR A FEW WEEKS. DAD NEEDS SOME REST.
OK. HE KNOWS BEST.
IS THERE ANYTHING TO EAT OR DRINK HERE?
I'LL GET A DR. PEPPER FOR YOU. THEY'LL FEED YOU SOON.
LATER THAT AFTERNOON...
I'M SICK AT WHAT I DID, DAD.
I KNOW IT WAS HARD FOR YOU, BUT WE HAD NO CHOICE. I COULD NEVER BRING MYSELF TO DO IT.

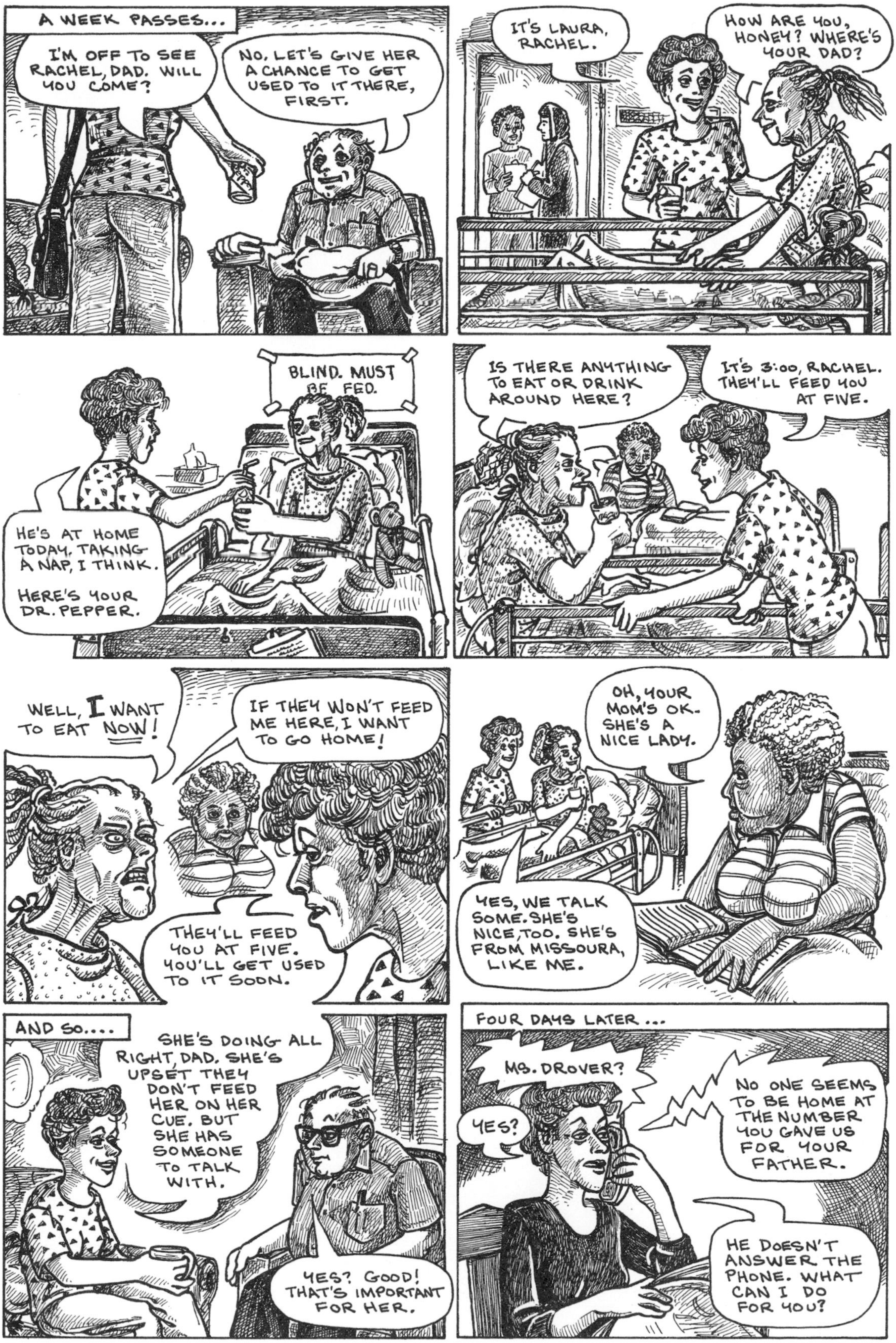
A WEEK PASSES...
I'M OFF TO SEE RACHEL, DAD. WILL YOU COME?
NO, LET'S GIVE HER A CHANCE TO GET USED TO IT THERE, FIRST.
IT'S LAURA, RACHEL.
HOW ARE YOU, HONEY? WHERE'S YOUR DAD?
BLIND. MUST BE FED.
HE'S AT HOME TODAY, TAKING A NAP, I THINK.
HERE'S YOUR DR. PEPPER.
IS THERE ANYTHING TO EAT OR DRINK AROUND HERE?
IT'S 3:00, RACHEL. THEY'LL FEED YOU AT FIVE.
WELL, I WANT TO EAT NOW!
IF THEY WON'T FEED ME HERE, I WANT TO GO HOME!
THEY'LL FEED YOU AT FIVE. YOU'LL GET USED TO IT SOON.
OH, YOUR MOM'S OK. SHE'S A NICE LADY.
YES, WE TALK SOME. SHE'S NICE, TOO. SHE'S FROM MISSOURA, LIKE ME.
AND SO....
SHE'S DOING ALL RIGHT, DAD. SHE'S UPSET THEY DON'T FEED HER ON HER CUE. BUT SHE HAS SOMEONE TO TALK WITH.
YES? GOOD! THAT'S IMPORTANT FOR HER.
FOUR DAYS LATER...
MS. DROVER?
YES?
NO ONE SEEMS TO BE HOME AT THE NUMBER YOU GAVE US FOR YOUR FATHER.
HE DOESN'T ANSWER THE PHONE. WHAT CAN I DO FOR YOU?

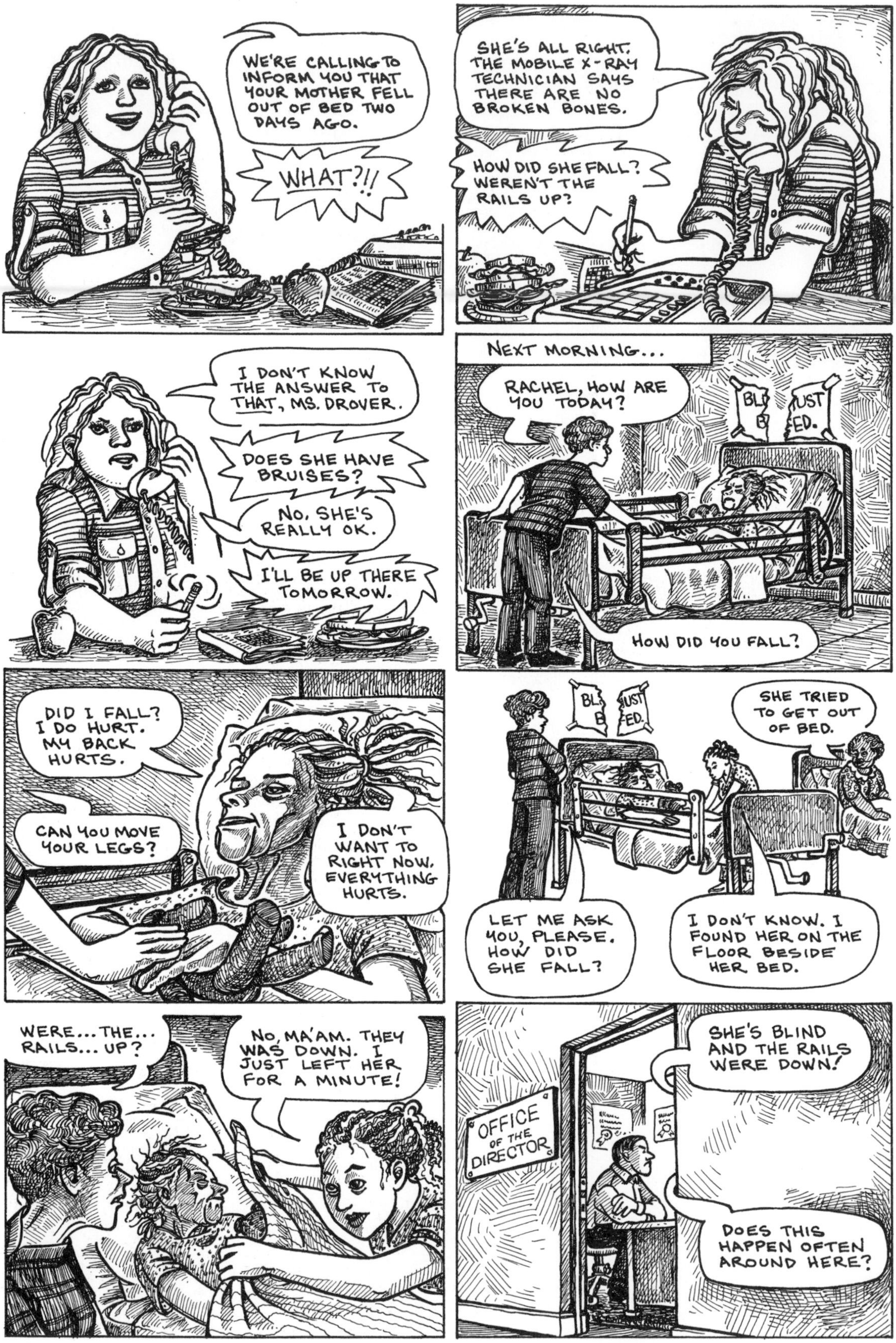
WE'RE CALLING TO INFORM YOU THAT YOUR MOTHER FELL OUT OF BED TWO DAYS AGO.
WHAT?!!
SHE'S ALL RIGHT. THE MOBILE X-RAY TECHNICIAN SAYS THERE ARE NO BROKEN BONES.
HOW DID SHE FALL? WEREN'T THE RAILS UP?
I DON'T KNOW THE ANSWER TO THAT, MS. DROVER.
DOES SHE HAVE BRUISES?
NO, SHE'S REALLY OK.
I'LL BE UP THERE TOMORROW.
NEXT MORNING...
RACHEL, HOW ARE YOU TODAY?
HOW DID YOU FALL?
DID I FALL? I DO HURT. MY BACK HURTS.
CAN YOU MOVE YOUR LEGS?
I DON'T WANT TO RIGHT NOW. EVERYTHING HURTS.
SHE TRIED TO GET OUT OF BED.
LET ME ASK YOU, PLEASE. HOW DID SHE FALL?
I DON'T KNOW. I FOUND HER ON THE FLOOR BESIDE HER BED.
WERE... THE... RAILS... UP?
NO, MA'AM. THEY WAS DOWN. I JUST LEFT HER FOR A MINUTE!
OFFICE OF THE DIRECTOR
SHE'S BLIND AND THE RAILS WERE DOWN!
DOES THIS HAPPEN OFTEN AROUND HERE?

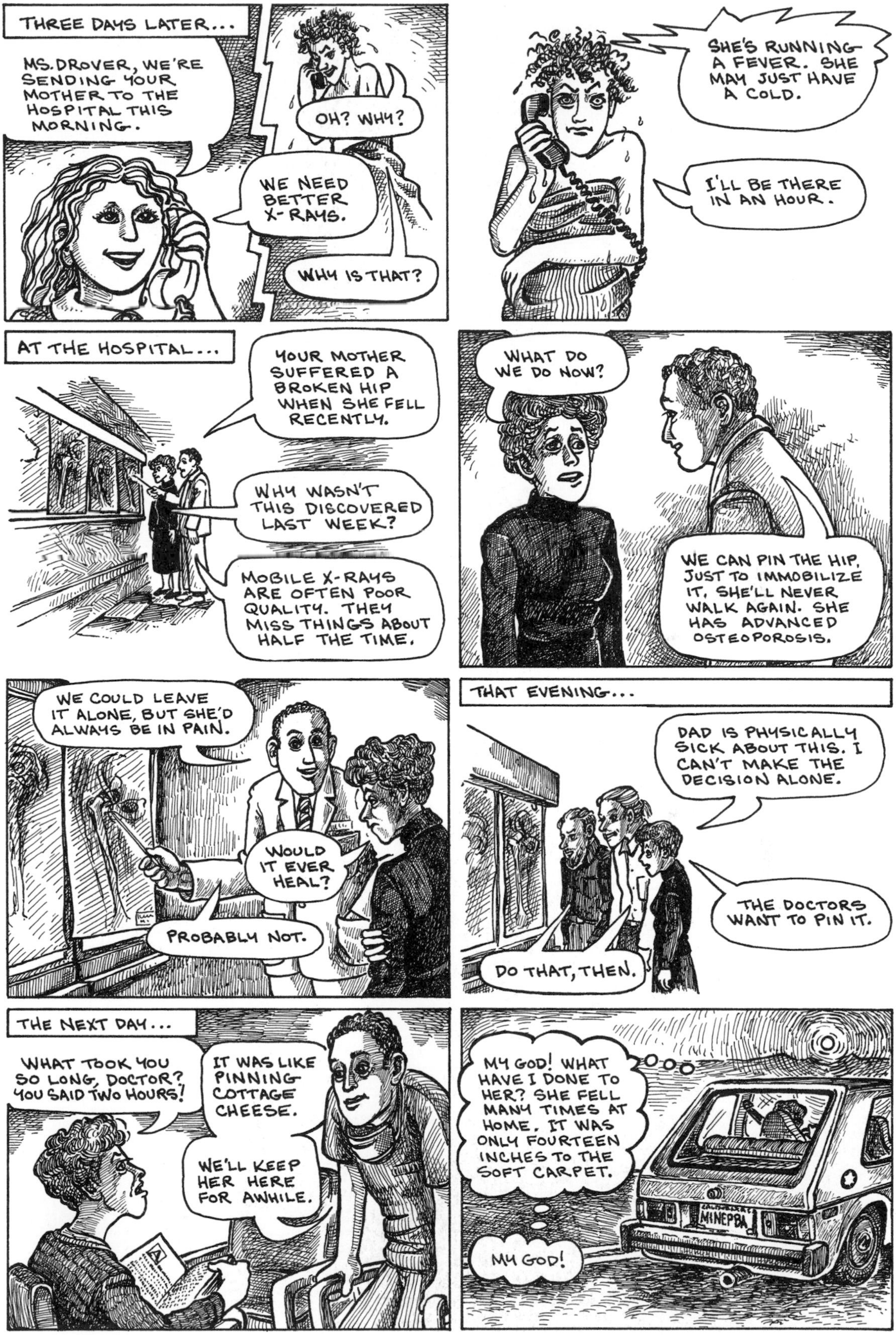
THREE DAYS LATER...
MS. DROVER, WE'RE SENDING YOUR MOTHER TO THE HOSPITAL THIS MORNING.
OH? WHY?
WE NEED BETTER X-RAYS.
WHY IS THAT?
SHE'S RUNNING A FEVER. SHE MAY JUST HAVE A COLD.
I'LL BE THERE IN AN HOUR.
AT THE HOSPITAL...
YOUR MOTHER SUFFERED A BROKEN HIP WHEN SHE FELL RECENTLY.
WHY WASN'T THIS DISCOVERED LAST WEEK?
MOBILE X-RAYS ARE OFTEN POOR QUALITY. THEY MISS THINGS ABOUT HALF THE TIME.
WHAT DO WE DO NOW?
WE CAN PIN THE HIP, JUST TO IMMOBILIZE IT. SHE'LL NEVER WALK AGAIN. SHE HAS ADVANCED OSTEOPOROSIS.
WE COULD LEAVE IT ALONE, BUT SHE'D ALWAYS BE IN PAIN.
WOULD IT EVER HEAL?
PROBABLY NOT.
THAT EVENING...
DAD IS PHYSICALLY SICK ABOUT THIS. I CAN'T MAKE THE DECISION ALONE.
THE DOCTORS WANT TO PIN IT.
DO THAT, THEN.
THE NEXT DAY...
WHAT TOOK YOU SO LONG, DOCTOR? YOU SAID TWO HOURS!
IT WAS LIKE PINNING COTTAGE CHEESE.
WE'LL KEEP HER HERE FOR AWHILE.
MY GOD! WHAT HAVE I DONE TO HER? SHE FELL MANY TIMES AT HOME. IT WAS ONLY FOURTEEN INCHES TO THE SOFT CARPET.
MY GOD!

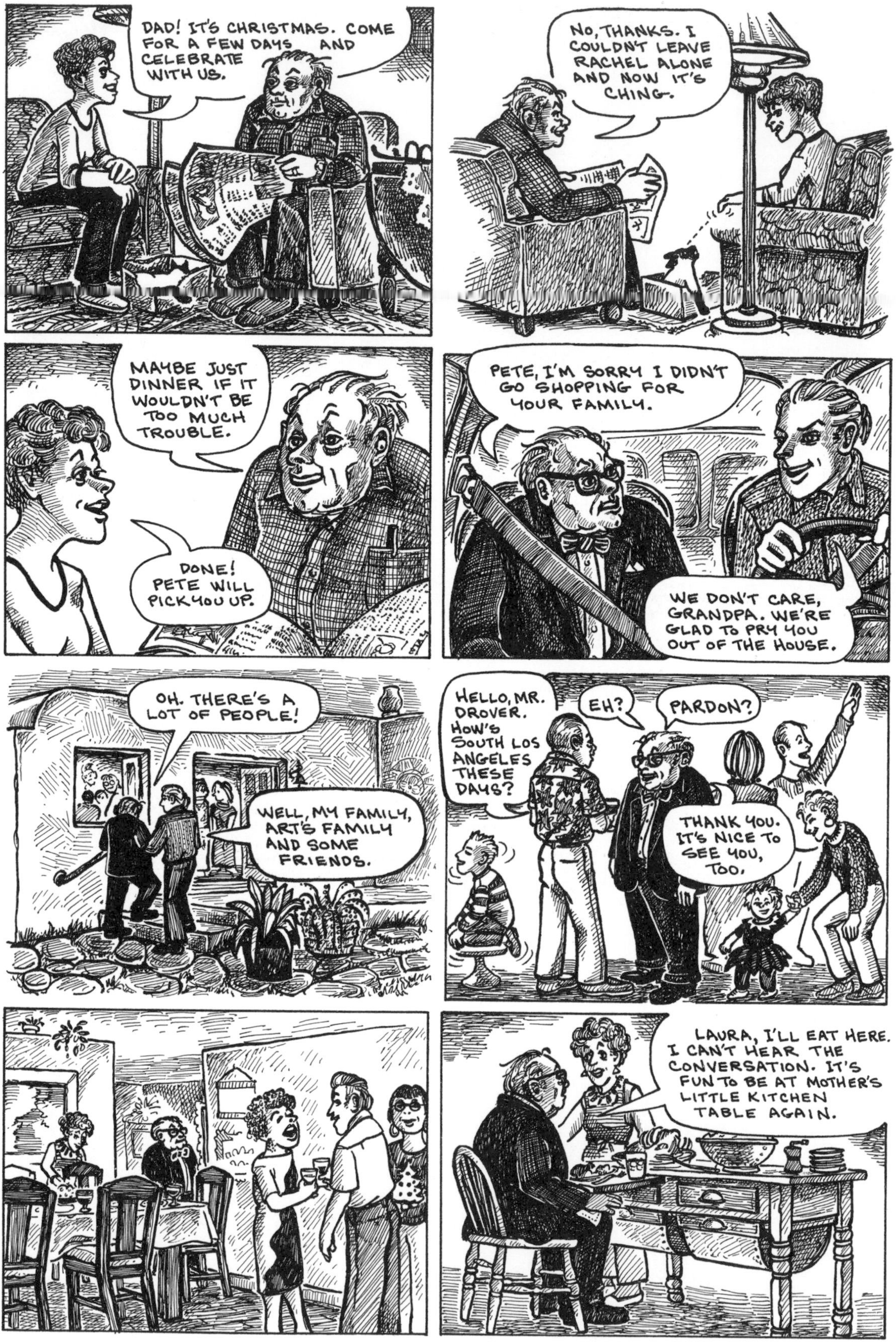
DAD! IT'S CHRISTMAS. COME FOR A FEW DAYS AND CELEBRATE WITH US.
NO, THANKS. I COULDN'T LEAVE RACHEL ALONE AND NOW IT'S CHING.
MAYBE JUST DINNER IF IT WOULDN'T BE TOO MUCH TROUBLE.
DONE! PETE WILL PICK YOU UP.
PETE, I'M SORRY I DIDN'T GO SHOPPING FOR YOUR FAMILY.
WE DON'T CARE, GRANDPA. WE'RE GLAD TO PRY YOU OUT OF THE HOUSE.
OH. THERE'S A LOT OF PEOPLE!
WELL, MY FAMILY, ART'S FAMILY AND SOME FRIENDS.
HELLO, MR. DROVER. HOW'S SOUTH LOS ANGELES THESE DAYS?
EH?
PARDON?
THANK YOU. IT'S NICE TO SEE YOU, TOO.
LAURA, I'LL EAT HERE. I CAN'T HEAR THE CONVERSATION. IT'S FUN TO BE AT MOTHER'S LITTLE KITCHEN TABLE AGAIN.

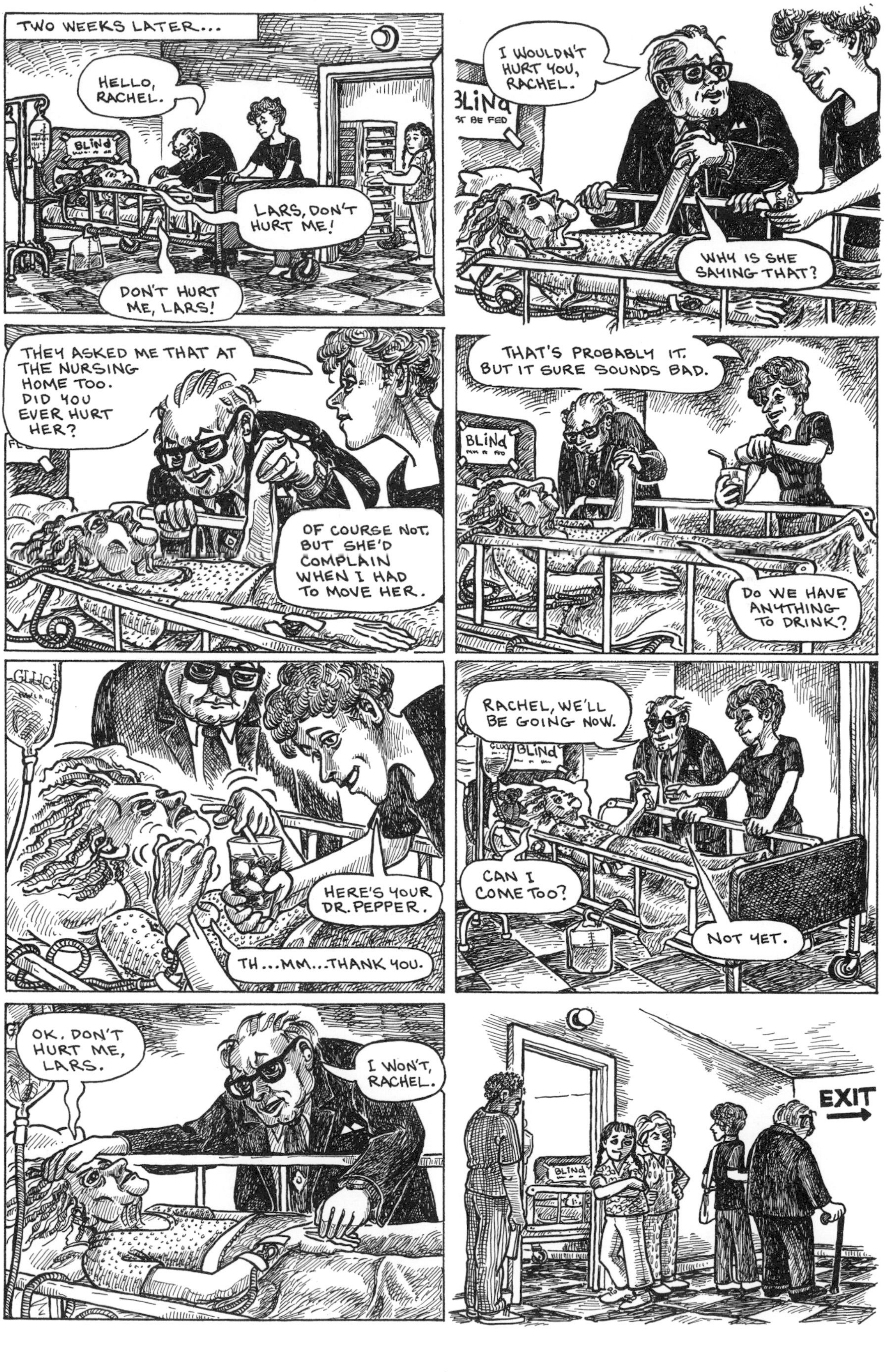

TWO WEEKS LATER...
HELLO, RACHEL.
LARS, DON'T HURT ME!
DON'T HURT ME, LARS!
I WOULDN'T HURT YOU, RACHEL.
WHY IS SHE SAYING THAT?
THEY ASKED ME THAT AT THE NURSING HOME TOO. DID YOU EVER HURT HER?
OF COURSE NOT. BUT SHE'D COMPLAIN WHEN I HAD TO MOVE HER.
THAT'S PROBABLY IT. BUT IT SURE SOUNDS BAD.
DO WE HAVE ANYTHING TO DRINK?
HERE'S YOUR DR. PEPPER.
TH...MM...THANK YOU.
RACHEL, WE'LL BE GOING NOW.
CAN I COME TOO?
NOT YET.
OK. DON'T HURT ME, LARS.
I WON'T, RACHEL.
EXIT

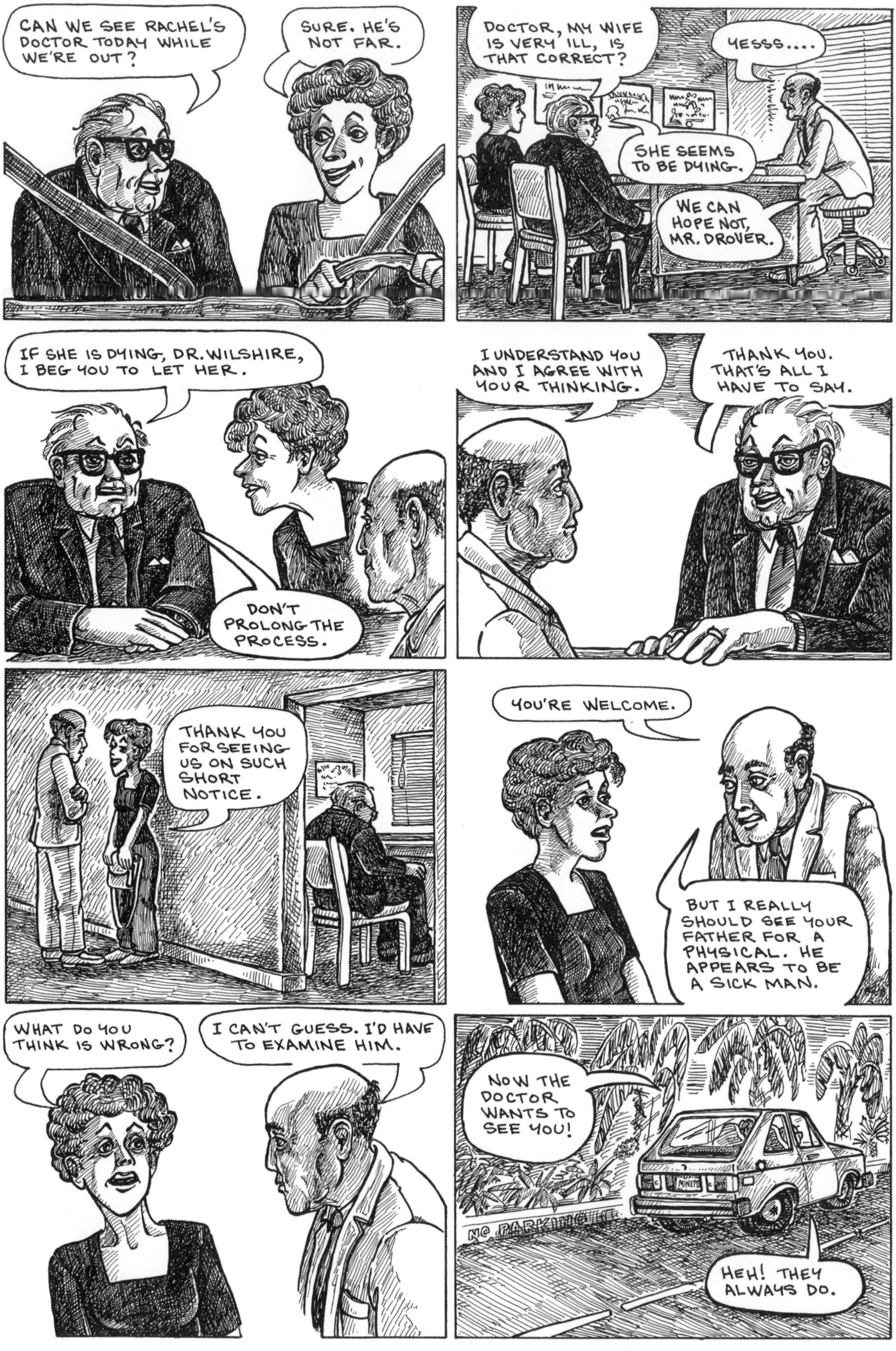
CAN WE SEE RACHEL'S DOCTOR TODAY WHILE WE'RE OUT?
SURE. HE'S NOT FAR.
DOCTOR, MY WIFE IS VERY ILL, IS THAT CORRECT?
YESSS....
SHE SEEMS TO BE DYING.
WE CAN HOPE NOT, MR. DROVER.
IF SHE IS DYING, DR. WILSHIRE, I BEG YOU TO LET HER.
DON'T PROLONG THE PROCESS.
I UNDERSTAND YOU AND I AGREE WITH YOUR THINKING.
THANK YOU. THAT'S ALL I HAVE TO SAY.
THANK YOU FOR SEEING US ON SUCH SHORT NOTICE.
YOU'RE WELCOME.
BUT I REALLY SHOULD SEE YOUR FATHER FOR A PHYSICAL. HE APPEARS TO BE A SICK MAN.
WHAT DO YOU THINK IS WRONG?
I CAN'T GUESS. I'D HAVE TO EXAMINE HIM.
NOW THE DOCTOR WANTS TO SEE YOU!
HEH! THEY ALWAYS DO.

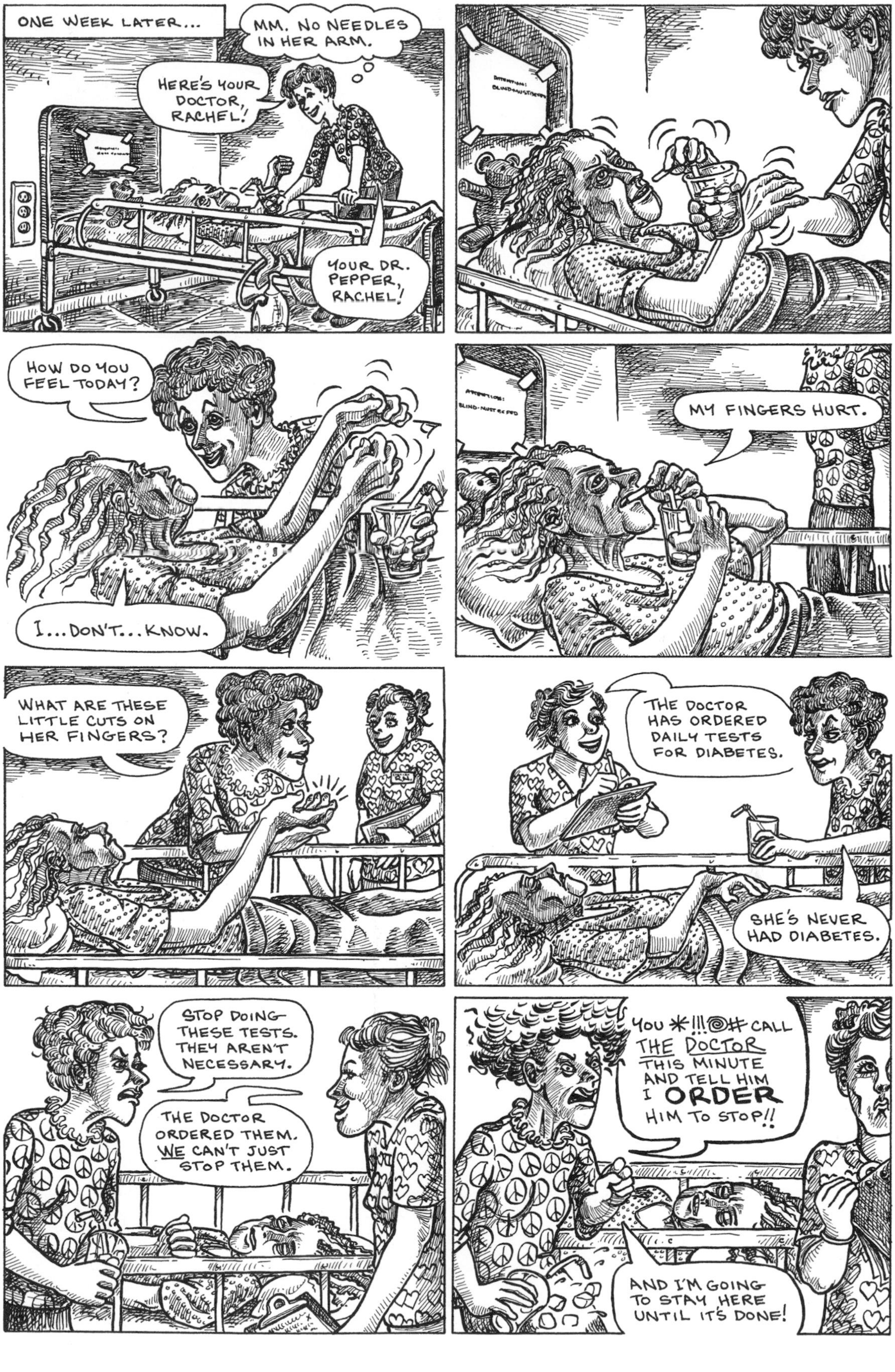

ONE WEEK LATER...
MM. NO NEEDLES IN HER ARM.
HERE'S YOUR DOCTOR, RACHEL!
YOUR DR. PEPPER, RACHEL!
HOW DO YOU FEEL TODAY?
I...DON'T...KNOW.
MY FINGERS HURT.
WHAT ARE THESE LITTLE CUTS ON HER FINGERS?
THE DOCTOR HAS ORDERED DAILY TESTS FOR DIABETES.
SHE'S NEVER HAD DIABETES.
STOP DOING THESE TESTS. THEY AREN'T NECESSARY.
THE DOCTOR ORDERED THEM. WE CAN'T JUST STOP THEM.
YOU *!!!@# CALL THE DOCTOR THIS MINUTE AND TELL HIM I ORDER HIM TO STOP!!
AND I'M GOING TO STAY HERE UNTIL IT'S DONE!

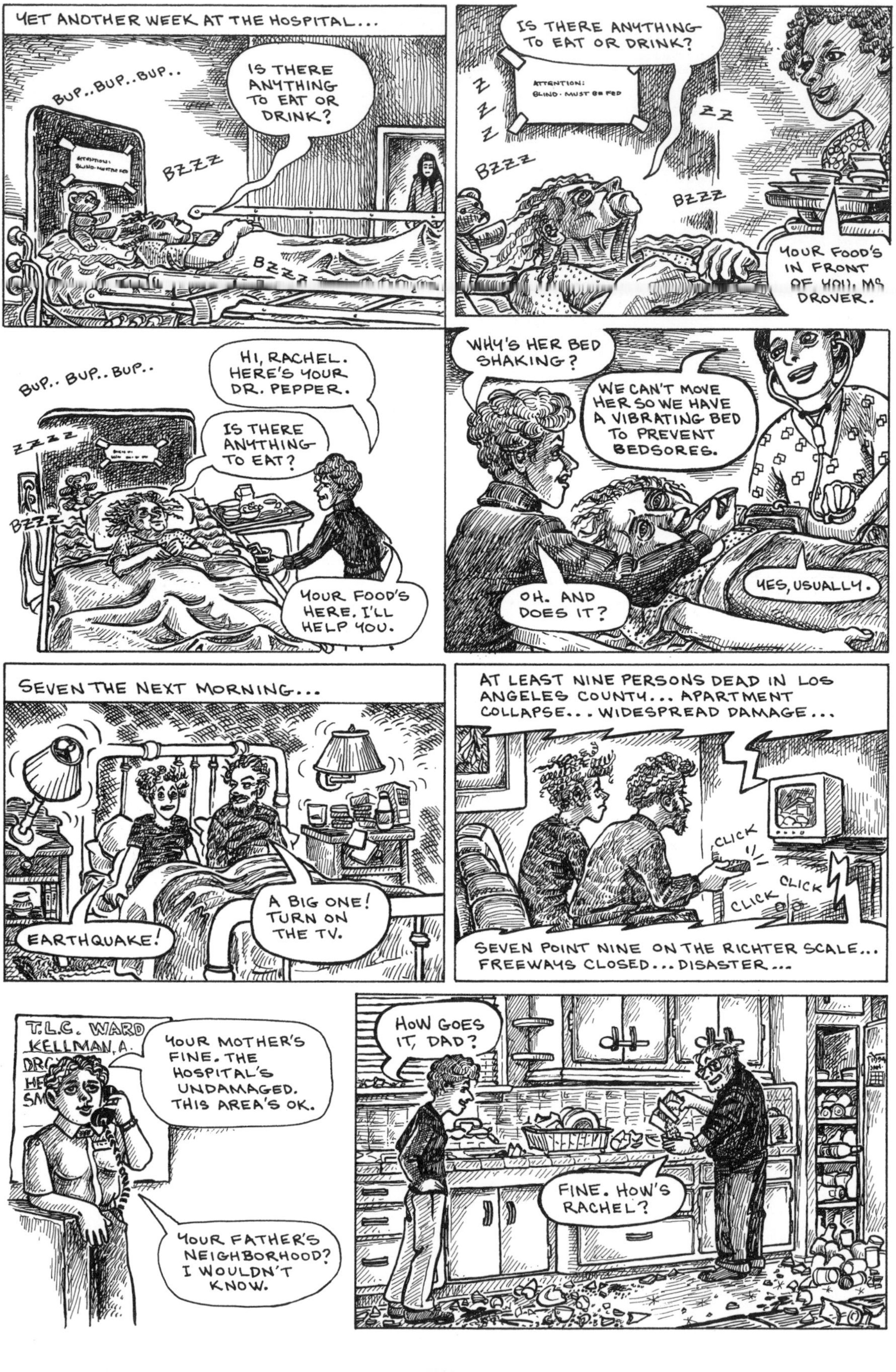
YET ANOTHER WEEK AT THE HOSPITAL...
BUP.. BUP.. BUP..
IS THERE ANYTHING TO EAT OR DRINK?
ATTENTION: BLIND - MUST BE FED
BZZZ
BZZZ
IS THERE ANYTHING TO EAT OR DRINK?
Z Z Z
ZZ
BZZZ
BZZZ
YOUR FOOD'S IN FRONT OF YOU, MS DROVER.
BUP.. BUP.. BUP..
HI, RACHEL. HERE'S YOUR DR. PEPPER.
ZZZZ
IS THERE ANYTHING TO EAT?
BZZZ
YOUR FOOD'S HERE. I'LL HELP YOU.
WHY'S HER BED SHAKING?
WE CAN'T MOVE HER SO WE HAVE A VIBRATING BED TO PREVENT BEDSORES.
OH. AND DOES IT?
YES, USUALLY.
SEVEN THE NEXT MORNING...
EARTHQUAKE!
A BIG ONE! TURN ON THE TV.
AT LEAST NINE PERSONS DEAD IN LOS ANGELES COUNTY... APARTMENT COLLAPSE... WIDESPREAD DAMAGE...
CLICK
CLICK
CLICK
SEVEN POINT NINE ON THE RICHTER SCALE... FREEWAYS CLOSED... DISASTER...
T.L.C. WARD
KELLMAN, A.
YOUR MOTHER'S FINE. THE HOSPITAL'S UNDAMAGED. THIS AREA'S OK.
YOUR FATHER'S NEIGHBORHOOD? I WOULDN'T KNOW.
HOW GOES IT, DAD?
FINE. HOW'S RACHEL?

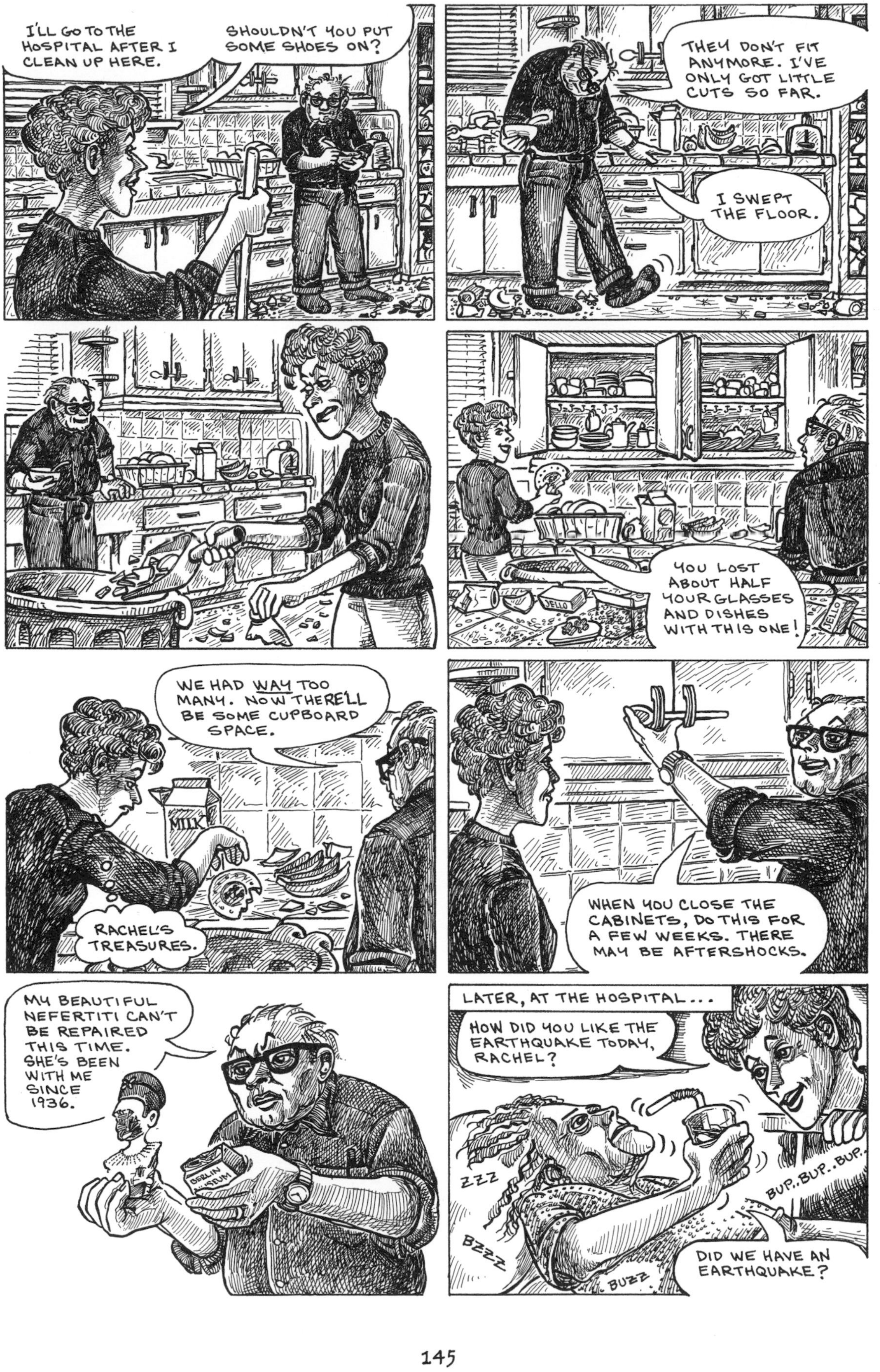
I'LL GO TO THE HOSPITAL AFTER I CLEAN UP HERE.
SHOULDN'T YOU PUT SOME SHOES ON?
THEY DON'T FIT ANYMORE. I'VE ONLY GOT LITTLE CUTS SO FAR.
I SWEPT THE FLOOR.
JELLO
YOU LOST ABOUT HALF YOUR GLASSES AND DISHES WITH THIS ONE!
WE HAD WAY TOO MANY. NOW THERE'LL BE SOME CUPBOARD SPACE.
MILK
RACHEL'S TREASURES.
WHEN YOU CLOSE THE CABINETS, DO THIS FOR A FEW WEEKS. THERE MAY BE AFTERSHOCKS.
MY BEAUTIFUL NEFERTITI CAN'T BE REPAIRED THIS TIME. SHE'S BEEN WITH ME SINCE 1936.
LATER, AT THE HOSPITAL...
HOW DID YOU LIKE THE EARTHQUAKE TODAY, RACHEL?
ZZZ
BZZZ
BUZZ
BUP.. BUP.. BUP.
DID WE HAVE AN EARTHQUAKE?

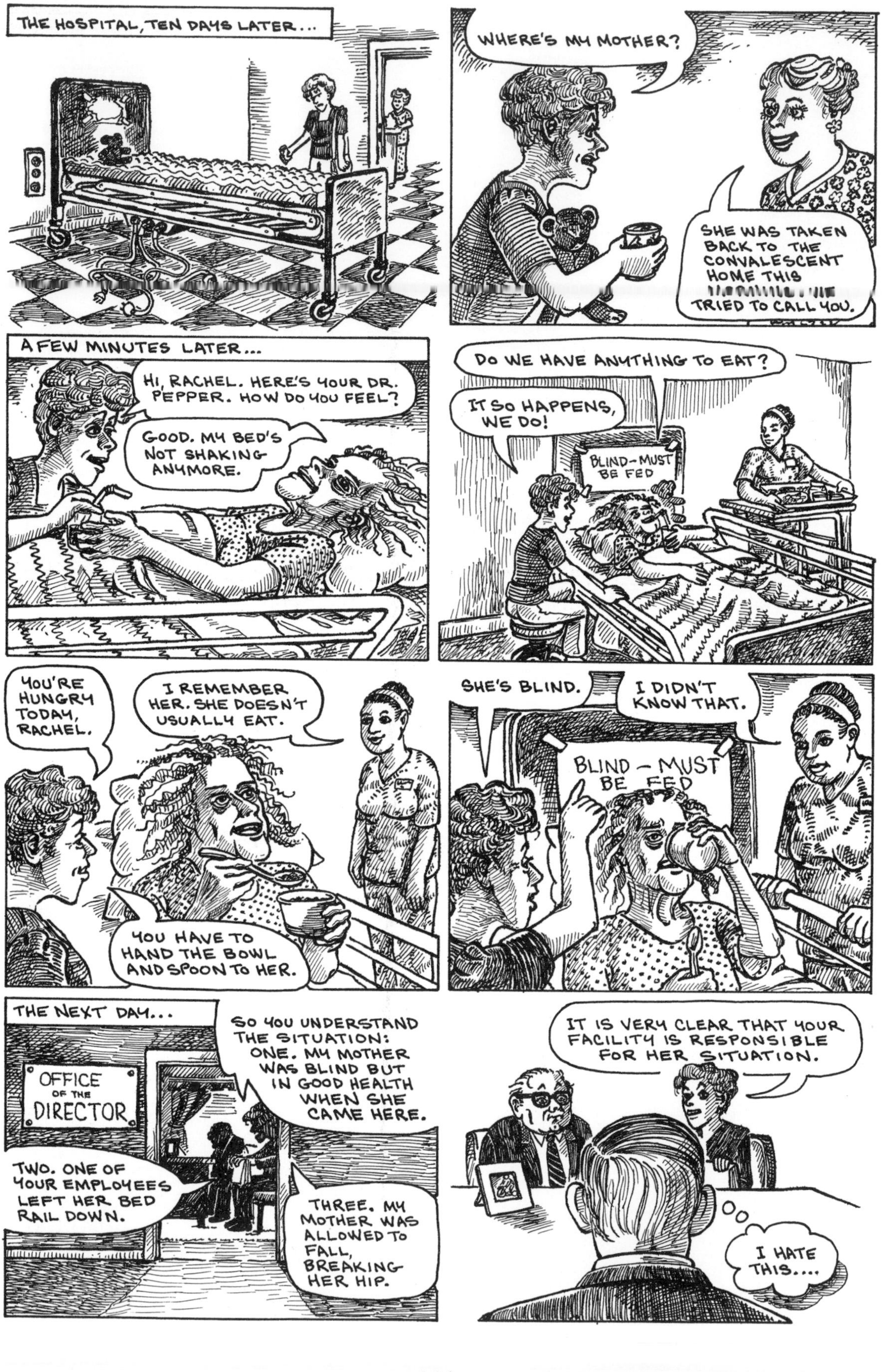
THE HOSPITAL, TEN DAYS LATER...
WHERE'S MY MOTHER?
SHE WAS TAKEN BACK TO THE CONVALESCENT HOME THIS TRIED TO CALL YOU.
A FEW MINUTES LATER...
HI, RACHEL. HERE'S YOUR DR. PEPPER. HOW DO YOU FEEL?
GOOD. MY BED'S NOT SHAKING ANYMORE.
DO WE HAVE ANYTHING TO EAT?
IT SO HAPPENS, WE DO!
BLIND - MUST BE FED
YOU'RE HUNGRY TODAY, RACHEL.
I REMEMBER HER. SHE DOESN'T USUALLY EAT.
YOU HAVE TO HAND THE BOWL AND SPOON TO HER.
SHE'S BLIND.
I DIDN'T KNOW THAT.
BLIND - MUST BE FED
THE NEXT DAY...
OFFICE OF THE DIRECTOR
SO YOU UNDERSTAND THE SITUATION: ONE. MY MOTHER WAS BLIND BUT IN GOOD HEALTH WHEN SHE CAME HERE.
TWO. ONE OF YOUR EMPLOYEES LEFT HER BED RAIL DOWN.
THREE. MY MOTHER WAS ALLOWED TO FALL, BREAKING HER HIP.
IT IS VERY CLEAR THAT YOUR FACILITY IS RESPONSIBLE FOR HER SITUATION.
I HATE THIS....

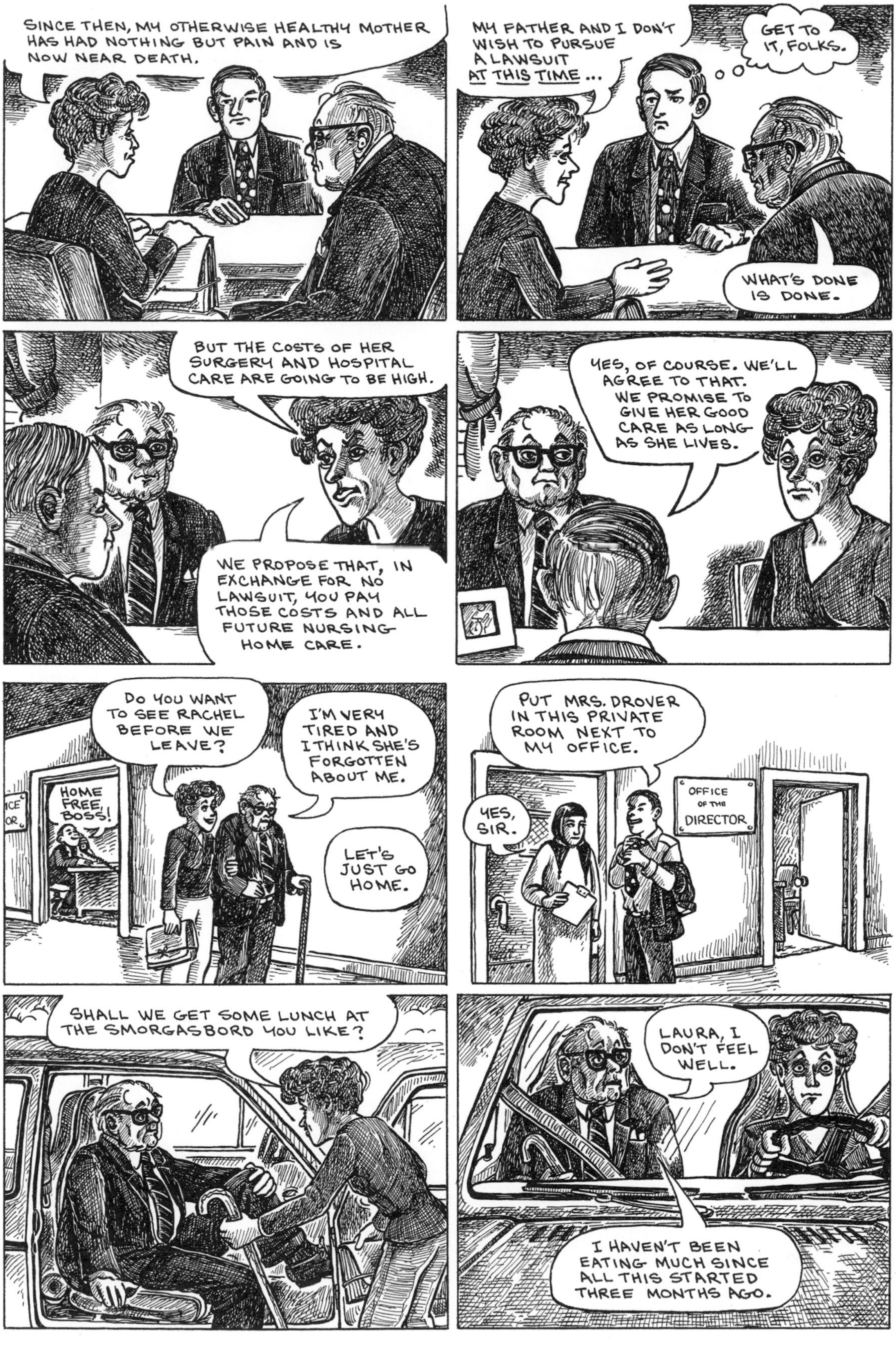
SINCE THEN, MY OTHERWISE HEALTHY MOTHER HAS HAD NOTHING BUT PAIN AND IS NOW NEAR DEATH.
MY FATHER AND I DON'T WISH TO PURSUE A LAWSUIT AT THIS TIME ...
GET TO IT, FOLKS.
WHAT'S DONE IS DONE.
BUT THE COSTS OF HER SURGERY AND HOSPITAL CARE ARE GOING TO BE HIGH.
WE PROPOSE THAT, IN EXCHANGE FOR NO LAWSUIT, YOU PAY THOSE COSTS AND ALL FUTURE NURSING-HOME CARE.
YES, OF COURSE. WE'LL AGREE TO THAT. WE PROMISE TO GIVE HER GOOD CARE AS LONG AS SHE LIVES.
DO YOU WANT TO SEE RACHEL BEFORE WE LEAVE?
I'M VERY TIRED AND I THINK SHE'S FORGOTTEN ABOUT ME.
HOME FREE, BOSS!
LET'S JUST GO HOME.
PUT MRS. DROVER IN THIS PRIVATE ROOM NEXT TO MY OFFICE.
YES, SIR.
OFFICE OF THE DIRECTOR
SHALL WE GET SOME LUNCH AT THE SMORGASBORD YOU LIKE?
LAURA, I DON'T FEEL WELL.
I HAVEN'T BEEN EATING MUCH SINCE ALL THIS STARTED THREE MONTHS AGO.

10

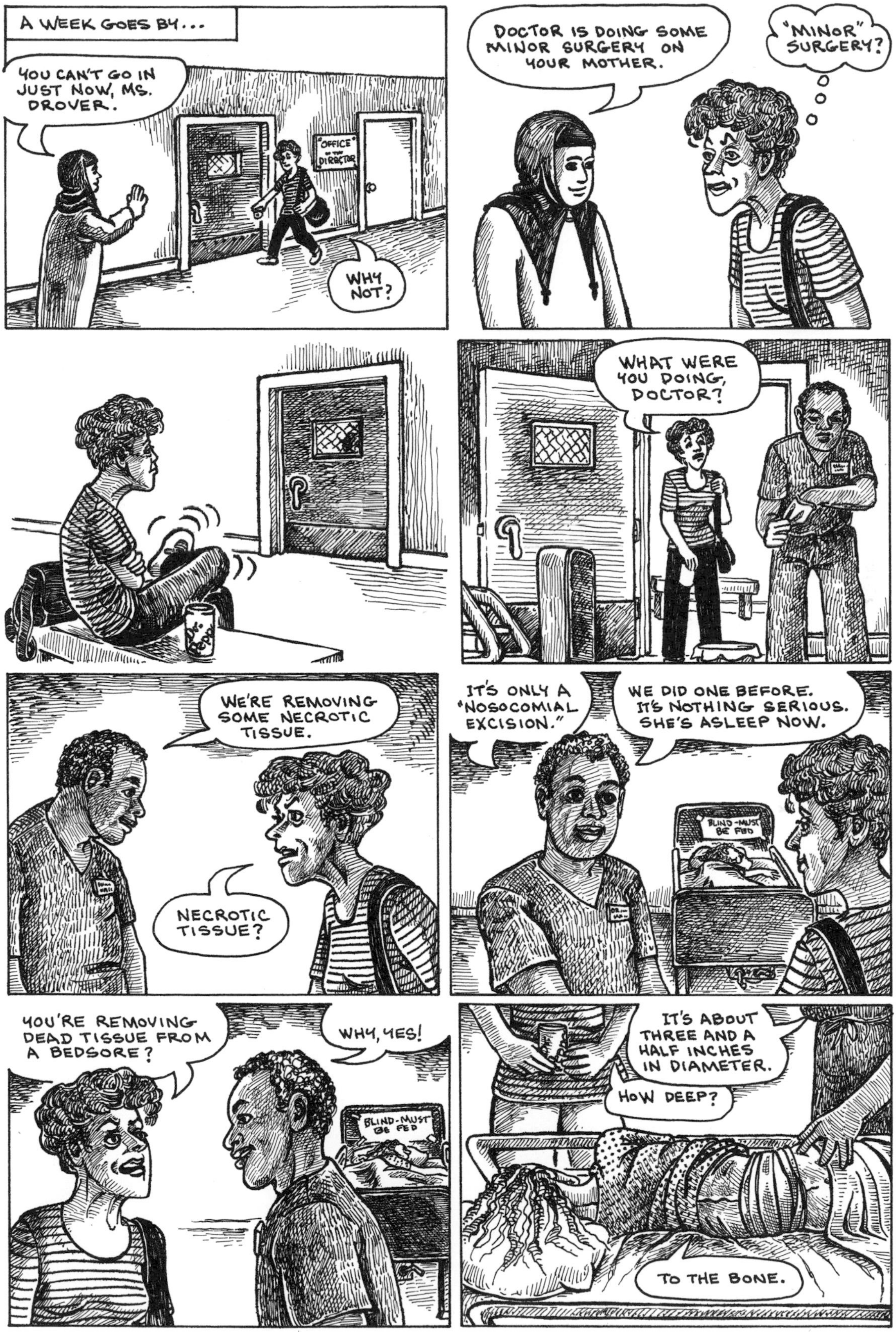
A WEEK GOES BY...
YOU CAN'T GO IN JUST NOW, MS. DROVER.
"OFFICE OF THE DIRECTOR"
WHY NOT?
DOCTOR IS DOING SOME MINOR SURGERY ON YOUR MOTHER.
"MINOR" SURGERY?
WHAT WERE YOU DOING, DOCTOR?
WE'RE REMOVING SOME NECROTIC TISSUE.
NECROTIC TISSUE?
IT'S ONLY A "NOSOCOMIAL EXCISION."
WE DID ONE BEFORE. IT'S NOTHING SERIOUS. SHE'S ASLEEP NOW.
BLIND-MUST BE FED
YOU'RE REMOVING DEAD TISSUE FROM A BEDSORE?
WHY, YES!
BLIND-MUST BE FED
IT'S ABOUT THREE AND A HALF INCHES IN DIAMETER.
HOW DEEP?
TO THE BONE.

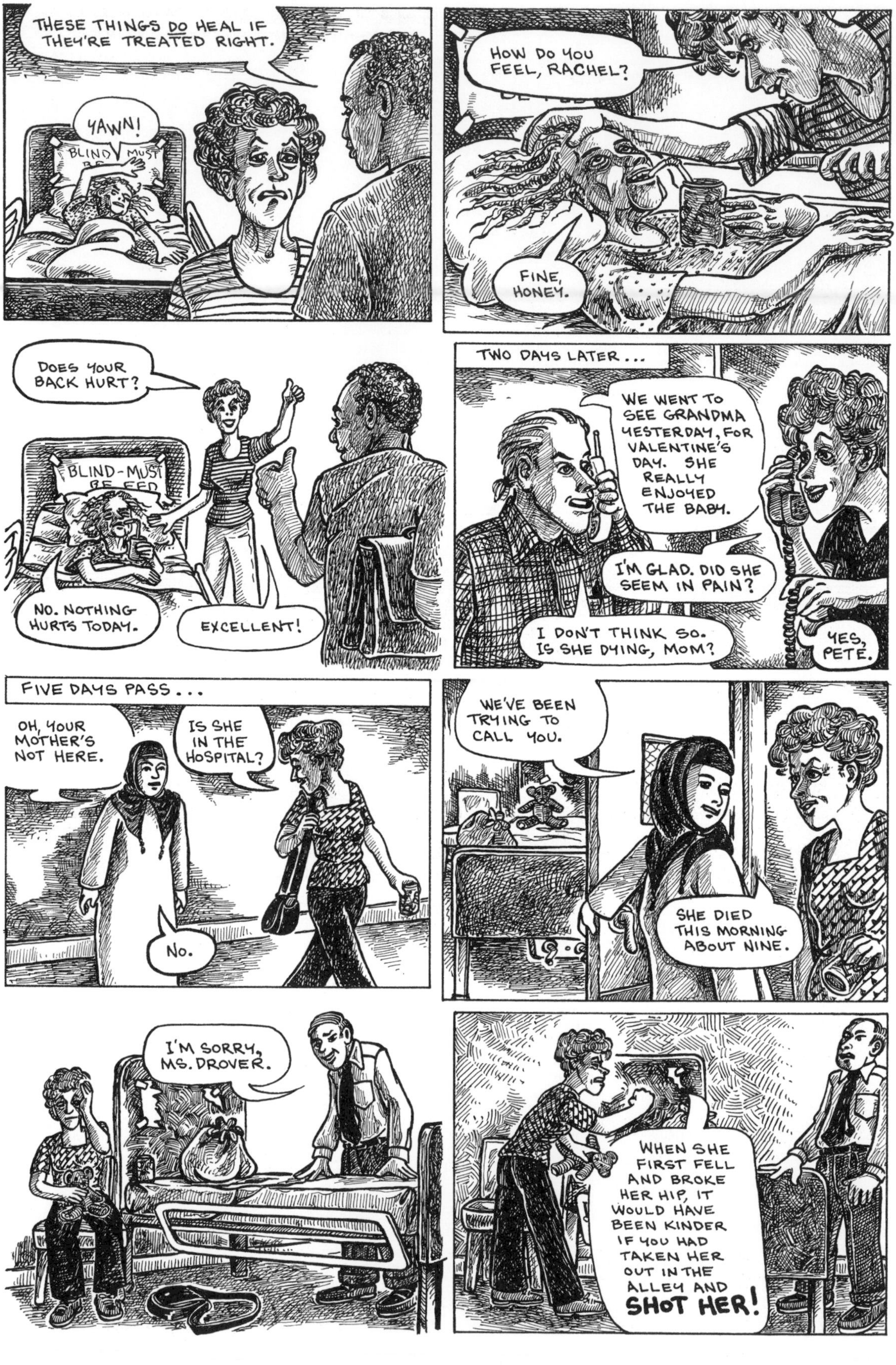

THESE THINGS DO HEAL IF THEY'RE TREATED RIGHT.
YAWN!
BLIND MUST
HOW DO YOU FEEL, RACHEL?
FINE, HONEY.
DOES YOUR BACK HURT?
BLIND-MUST
NO. NOTHING HURTS TODAY.
EXCELLENT!
TWO DAYS LATER...
WE WENT TO SEE GRANDMA YESTERDAY, FOR VALENTINE'S DAY. SHE REALLY ENJOYED THE BABY.
I'M GLAD. DID SHE SEEM IN PAIN?
I DON'T THINK SO. IS SHE DYING, MOM?
YES, PETE.
FIVE DAYS PASS...
OH, YOUR MOTHER'S NOT HERE.
IS SHE IN THE HOSPITAL?
NO.
WE'VE BEEN TRYING TO CALL YOU.
SHE DIED THIS MORNING ABOUT NINE.
I'M SORRY, MS. DROVER.
WHEN SHE FIRST FELL AND BROKE HER HIP, IT WOULD HAVE BEEN KINDER IF YOU HAD TAKEN HER OUT IN THE ALLEY AND SHOT HER!

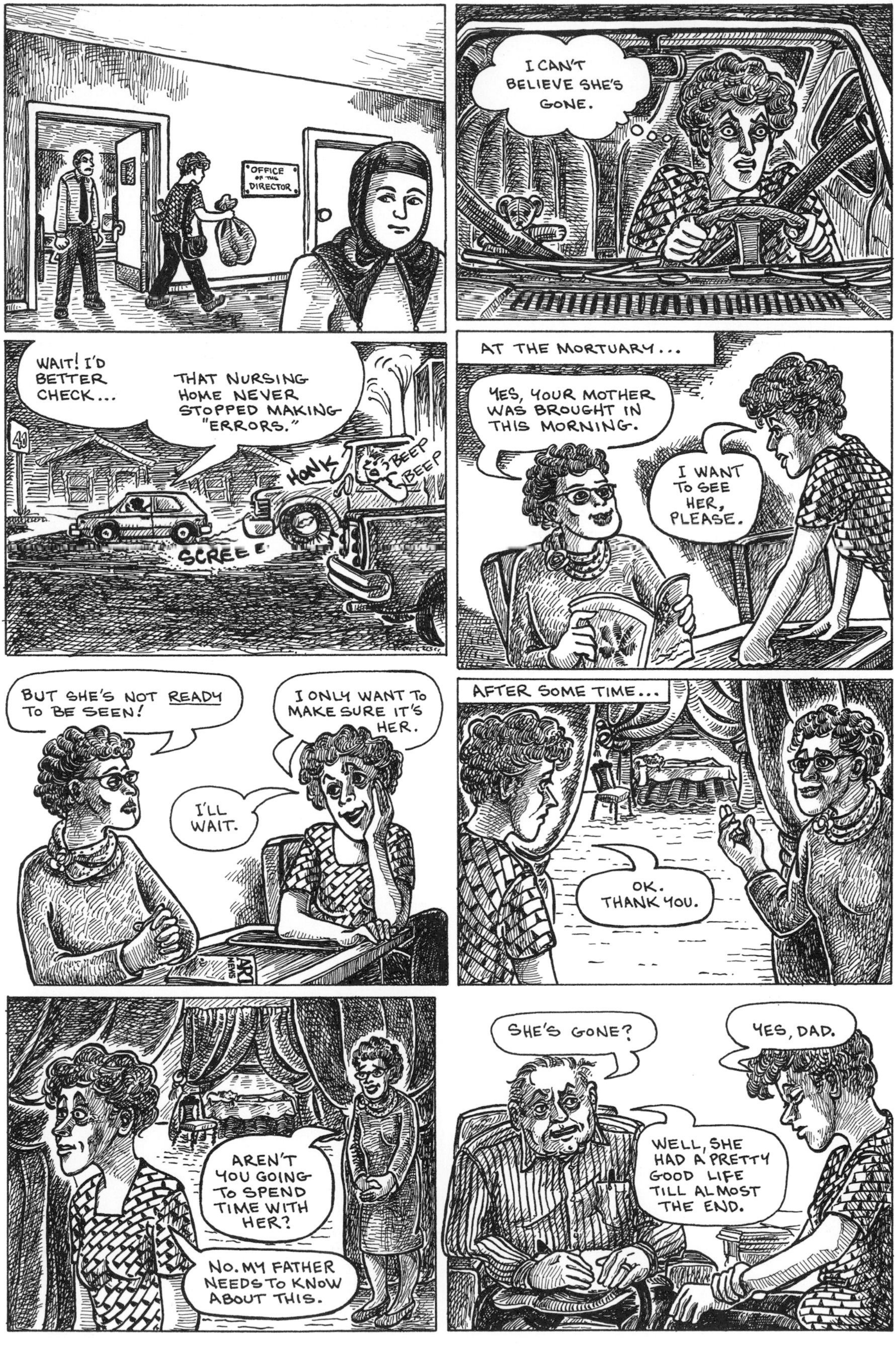
OFFICE OF THE DIRECTOR
I CAN'T BELIEVE SHE'S GONE.
WAIT! I'D BETTER CHECK...
THAT NURSING HOME NEVER STOPPED MAKING "ERRORS."
HONK
BEEP BEEP
SCREE
AT THE MORTUARY...
YES, YOUR MOTHER WAS BROUGHT IN THIS MORNING.
I WANT TO SEE HER, PLEASE.
BUT SHE'S NOT READY TO BE SEEN!
I ONLY WANT TO MAKE SURE IT'S HER.
I'LL WAIT.
AFTER SOME TIME...
OK. THANK YOU.
AREN'T YOU GOING TO SPEND TIME WITH HER?
NO. MY FATHER NEEDS TO KNOW ABOUT THIS.
SHE'S GONE?
YES, DAD.
WELL, SHE HAD A PRETTY GOOD LIFE TILL ALMOST THE END.

11

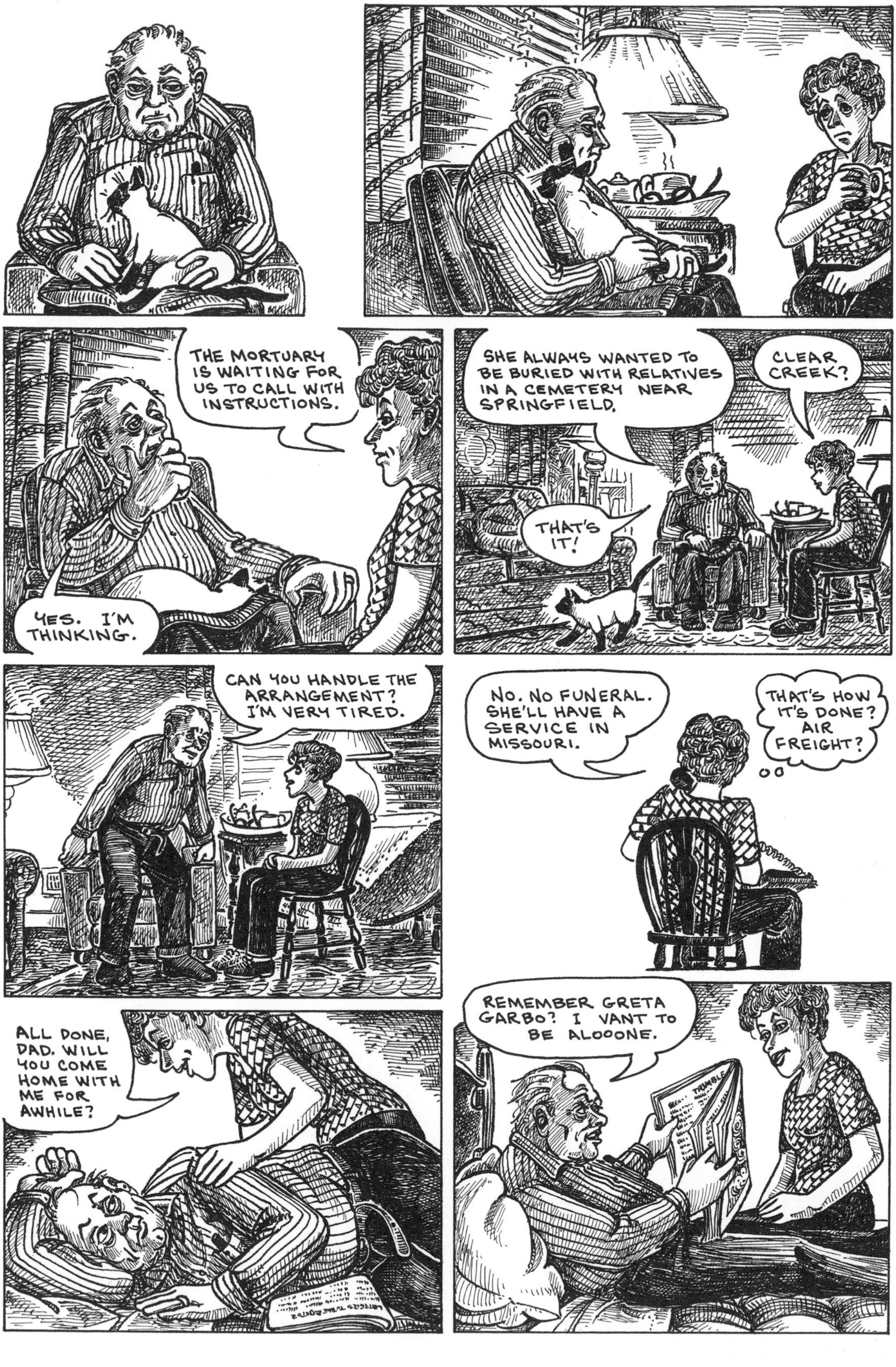
THE MORTUARY IS WAITING FOR US TO CALL WITH INSTRUCTIONS.
YES. I'M THINKING.
SHE ALWAYS WANTED TO BE BURIED WITH RELATIVES IN A CEMETERY NEAR SPRINGFIELD.
CLEAR CREEK?
THAT'S IT!
CAN YOU HANDLE THE ARRANGEMENT? I'M VERY TIRED.
NO. NO FUNERAL. SHE'LL HAVE A SERVICE IN MISSOURI.
THAT'S HOW IT'S DONE? AIR FREIGHT?
ALL DONE, DAD. WILL YOU COME HOME WITH ME FOR AWHILE?
REMEMBER GRETA GARBO? I VANT TO BE ALOOONE.

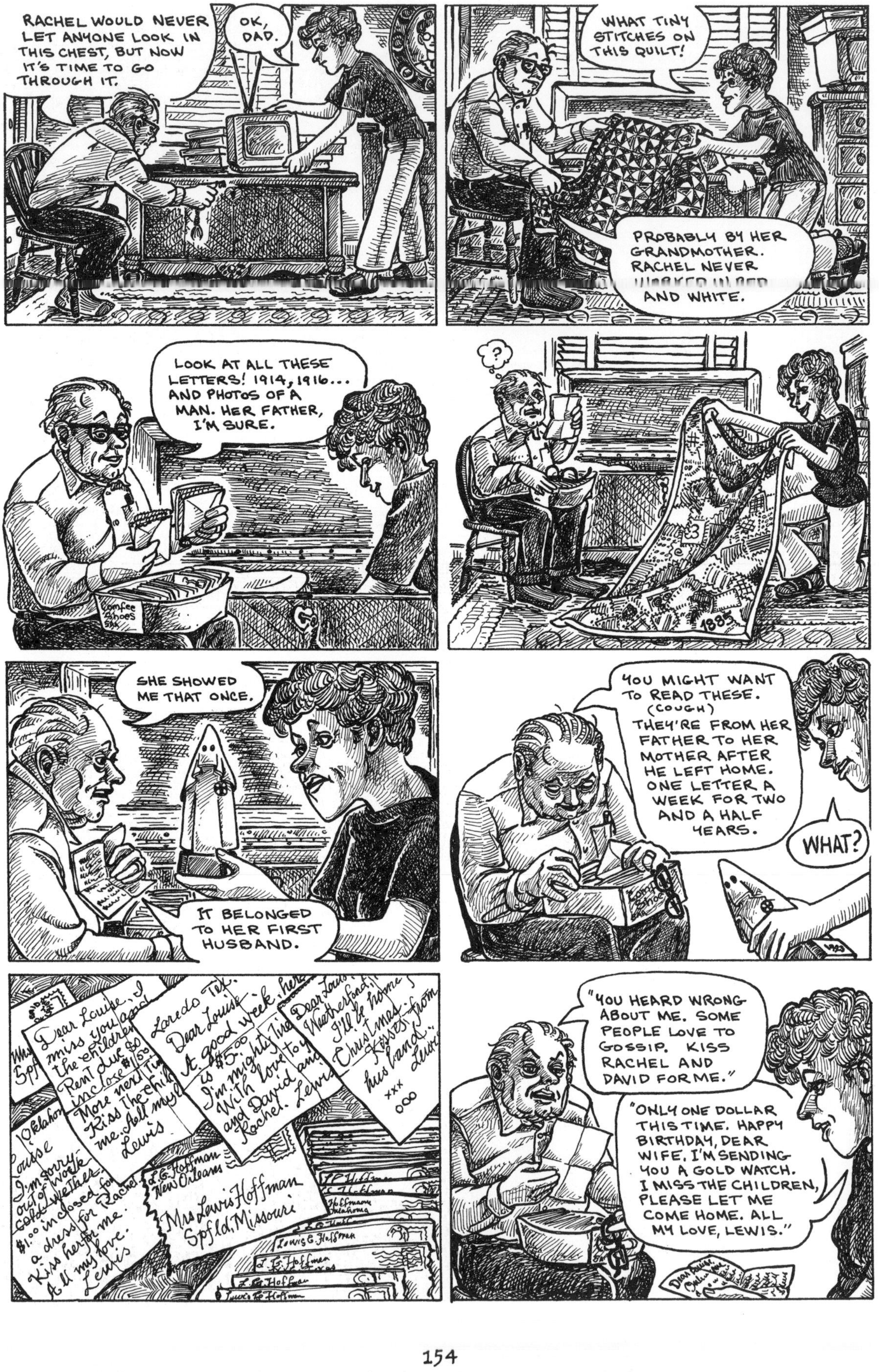
RACHEL WOULD NEVER LET ANYONE LOOK IN THIS CHEST, BUT NOW IT'S TIME TO GO THROUGH IT.
OK, DAD.
WHAT TINY STITCHES ON THIS QUILT!
PROBABLY BY HER GRANDMOTHER. RACHEL NEVER
AND WHITE.
LOOK AT ALL THESE LETTERS! 1914, 1916... AND PHOTOS OF A MAN. HER FATHER, I'M SURE.
?
1885
SHE SHOWED ME THAT ONCE.
IT BELONGED TO HER FIRST HUSBAND.
YOU MIGHT WANT TO READ THESE. (COUGH) THEY'RE FROM HER FATHER TO HER MOTHER AFTER HE LEFT HOME. ONE LETTER A WEEK FOR TWO AND A HALF YEARS.
WHAT?
L.G. Hoffman New Orleans
Mrs Lewis Hoffman Spfld. Missouri
"YOU HEARD WRONG ABOUT ME. SOME PEOPLE LOVE TO GOSSIP. KISS RACHEL AND DAVID FOR ME."
"ONLY ONE DOLLAR THIS TIME. HAPPY BIRTHDAY, DEAR WIFE. I'M SENDING YOU A GOLD WATCH. I MISS THE CHILDREN, PLEASE LET ME COME HOME. ALL MY LOVE, LEWIS."

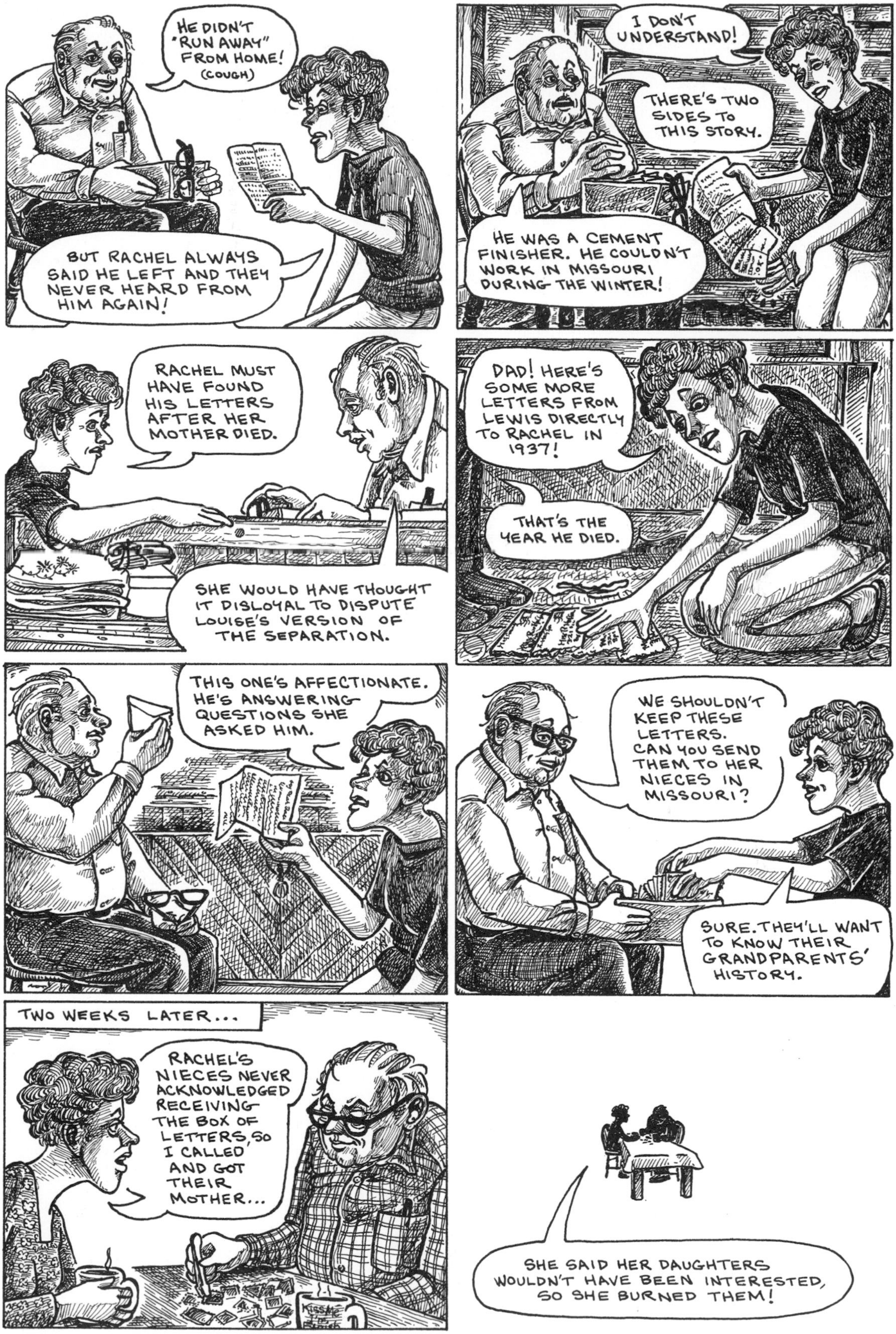
HE DIDN'T "RUN AWAY" FROM HOME! (COUGH)
BUT RACHEL ALWAYS SAID HE LEFT AND THEY NEVER HEARD FROM HIM AGAIN!
I DON'T UNDERSTAND!
THERE'S TWO SIDES TO THIS STORY.
HE WAS A CEMENT FINISHER. HE COULDN'T WORK IN MISSOURI DURING THE WINTER!
RACHEL MUST HAVE FOUND HIS LETTERS AFTER HER MOTHER DIED.
SHE WOULD HAVE THOUGHT IT DISLOYAL TO DISPUTE LOUISE'S VERSION OF THE SEPARATION.
DAD! HERE'S SOME MORE LETTERS FROM LEWIS DIRECTLY TO RACHEL IN 1937!
THAT'S THE YEAR HE DIED.
THIS ONE'S AFFECTIONATE. HE'S ANSWERING QUESTIONS SHE ASKED HIM.
WE SHOULDN'T KEEP THESE LETTERS. CAN YOU SEND THEM TO HER NIECES IN MISSOURI?
SURE. THEY'LL WANT TO KNOW THEIR GRANDPARENTS' HISTORY.
TWO WEEKS LATER...
RACHEL'S NIECES NEVER ACKNOWLEDGED RECEIVING THE BOX OF LETTERS, SO I CALLED AND GOT THEIR MOTHER...
SHE SAID HER DAUGHTERS WOULDN'T HAVE BEEN INTERESTED, SO SHE BURNED THEM!

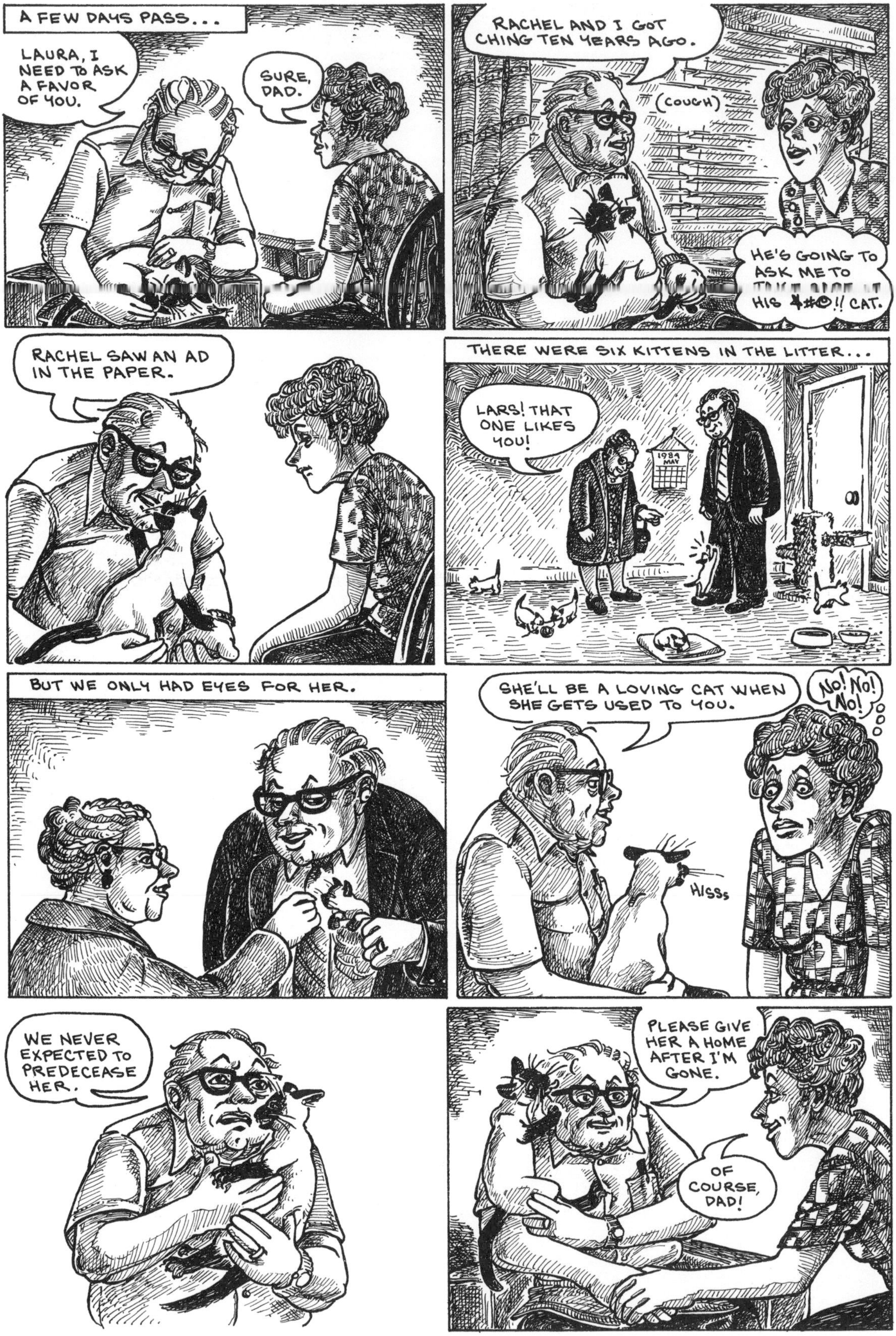
A FEW DAYS PASS...
LAURA, I NEED TO ASK A FAVOR OF YOU.
SURE, DAD.
RACHEL AND I GOT CHING TEN YEARS AGO.
(COUGH)
HE'S GOING TO ASK ME TO
HIS $#©!! CAT.
RACHEL SAW AN AD IN THE PAPER.
THERE WERE SIX KITTENS IN THE LITTER...
LARS! THAT ONE LIKES YOU!
1984 MAY
BUT WE ONLY HAD EYES FOR HER.
SHE'LL BE A LOVING CAT WHEN SHE GETS USED TO YOU.
NO! NO! NO!
HISSS
WE NEVER EXPECTED TO PREDECEASE HER.
PLEASE GIVE HER A HOME AFTER I'M GONE.
OF COURSE, DAD!

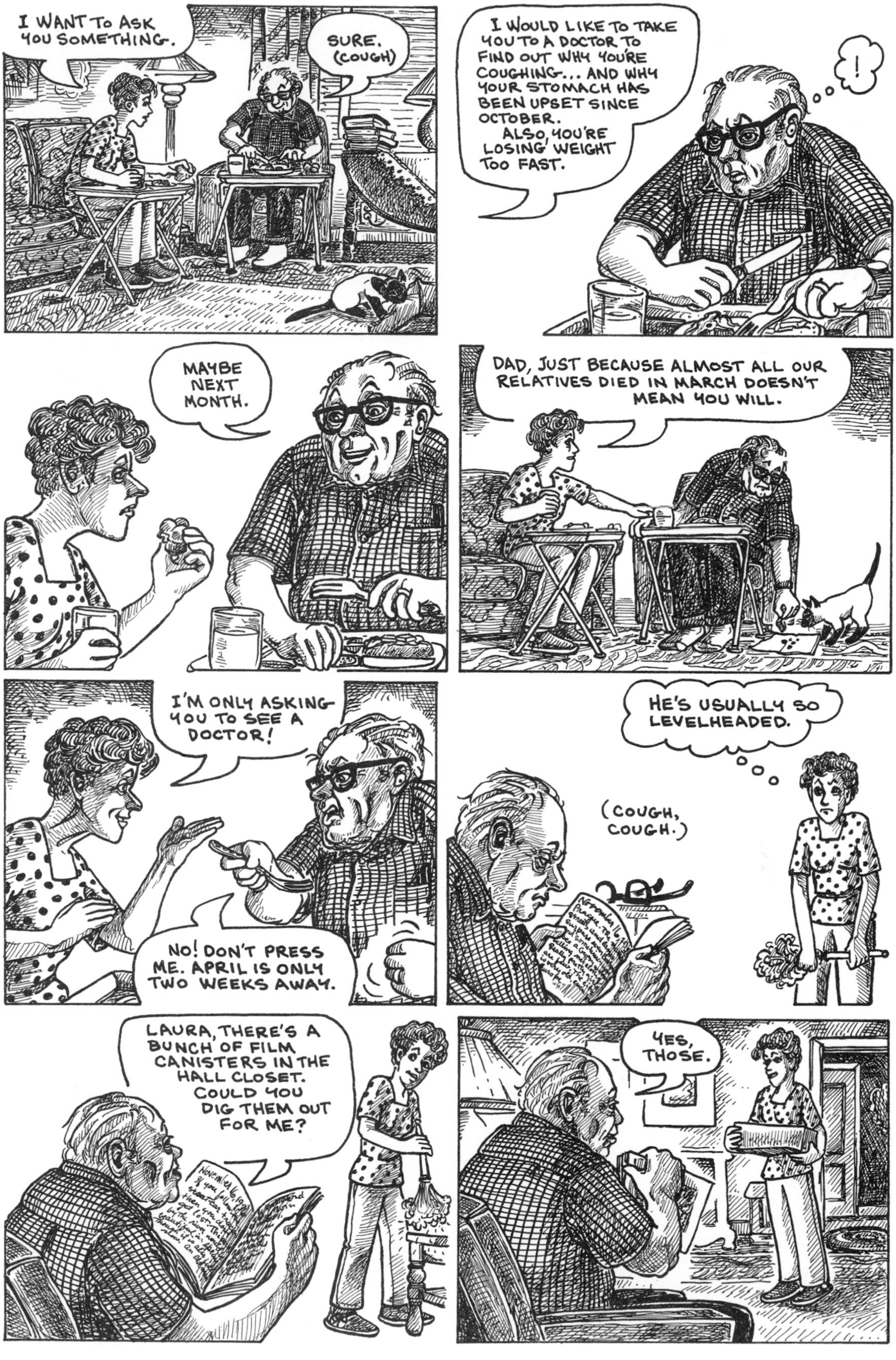
I WANT TO ASK YOU SOMETHING.
SURE. (COUGH)
I WOULD LIKE TO TAKE YOU TO A DOCTOR TO FIND OUT WHY YOU'RE COUGHING... AND WHY YOUR STOMACH HAS BEEN UPSET SINCE OCTOBER. ALSO, YOU'RE LOSING WEIGHT TOO FAST.
!
MAYBE NEXT MONTH.
DAD, JUST BECAUSE ALMOST ALL OUR RELATIVES DIED IN MARCH DOESN'T MEAN YOU WILL.
I'M ONLY ASKING YOU TO SEE A DOCTOR!
NO! DON'T PRESS ME. APRIL IS ONLY TWO WEEKS AWAY.
HE'S USUALLY SO LEVELHEADED.
(COUGH, COUGH.)
LAURA, THERE'S A BUNCH OF FILM CANISTERS IN THE HALL CLOSET. COULD YOU DIG THEM OUT FOR ME?
YES, THOSE.

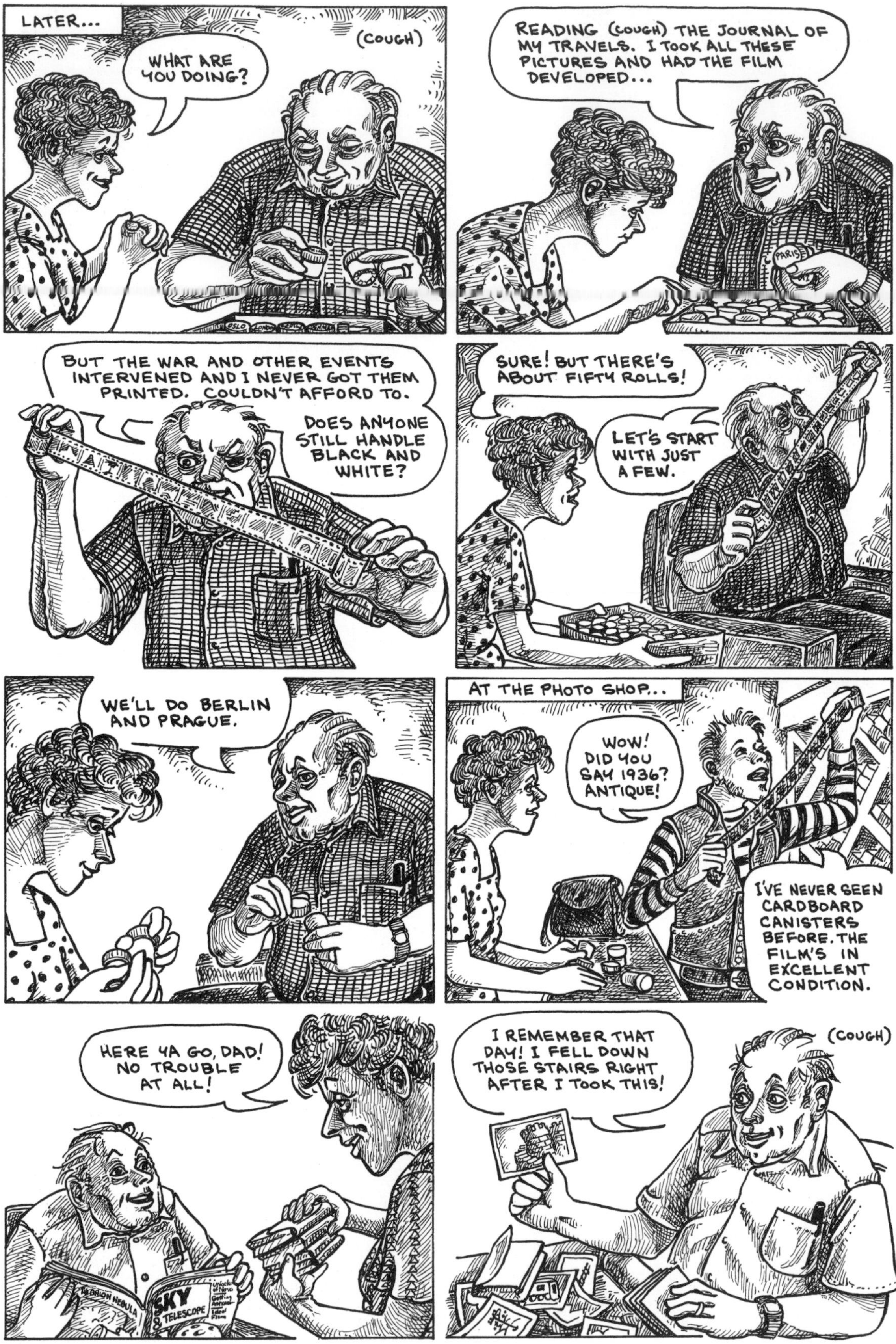
LATER...
(COUGH)
WHAT ARE YOU DOING?
READING (COUGH) THE JOURNAL OF MY TRAVELS. I TOOK ALL THESE PICTURES AND HAD THE FILM DEVELOPED...
PARIS
BUT THE WAR AND OTHER EVENTS INTERVENED AND I NEVER GOT THEM PRINTED. COULDN'T AFFORD TO.
DOES ANYONE STILL HANDLE BLACK AND WHITE?
SURE! BUT THERE'S ABOUT FIFTY ROLLS!
LET'S START WITH JUST A FEW.
WE'LL DO BERLIN AND PRAGUE.
AT THE PHOTO SHOP...
WOW! DID YOU SAY 1936? ANTIQUE!
I'VE NEVER SEEN CARDBOARD CANISTERS BEFORE. THE FILM'S IN EXCELLENT CONDITION.
HERE YA GO, DAD! NO TROUBLE AT ALL!
SKY TELESCOPE
I REMEMBER THAT DAY! I FELL DOWN THOSE STAIRS RIGHT AFTER I TOOK THIS!
(COUGH)

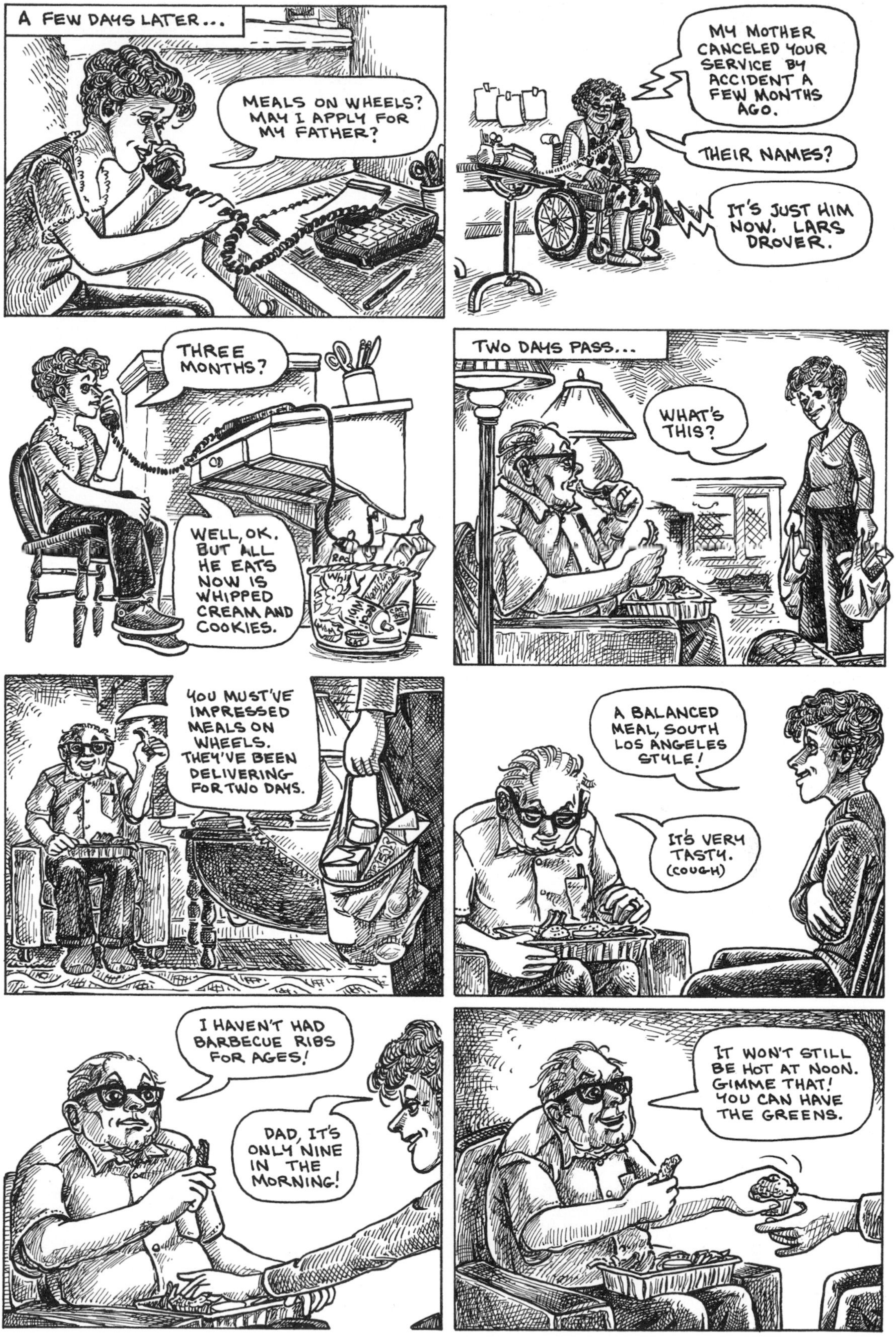

A FEW DAYS LATER...
MEALS ON WHEELS? MAY I APPLY FOR MY FATHER?
MY MOTHER CANCELED YOUR SERVICE BY ACCIDENT A FEW MONTHS AGO.
THEIR NAMES?
IT'S JUST HIM NOW. LARS DROVER.
THREE MONTHS?
WELL, OK. BUT ALL HE EATS NOW IS WHIPPED CREAM AND COOKIES.
TWO DAYS PASS...
WHAT'S THIS?
YOU MUST'VE IMPRESSED MEALS ON WHEELS. THEY'VE BEEN DELIVERING FOR TWO DAYS.
A BALANCED MEAL, SOUTH LOS ANGELES STYLE!
IT'S VERY TASTY. (COUGH)
I HAVEN'T HAD BARBECUE RIBS FOR AGES!
DAD, IT'S ONLY NINE IN THE MORNING!
IT WON'T STILL BE HOT AT NOON. GIMME THAT! YOU CAN HAVE THE GREENS.

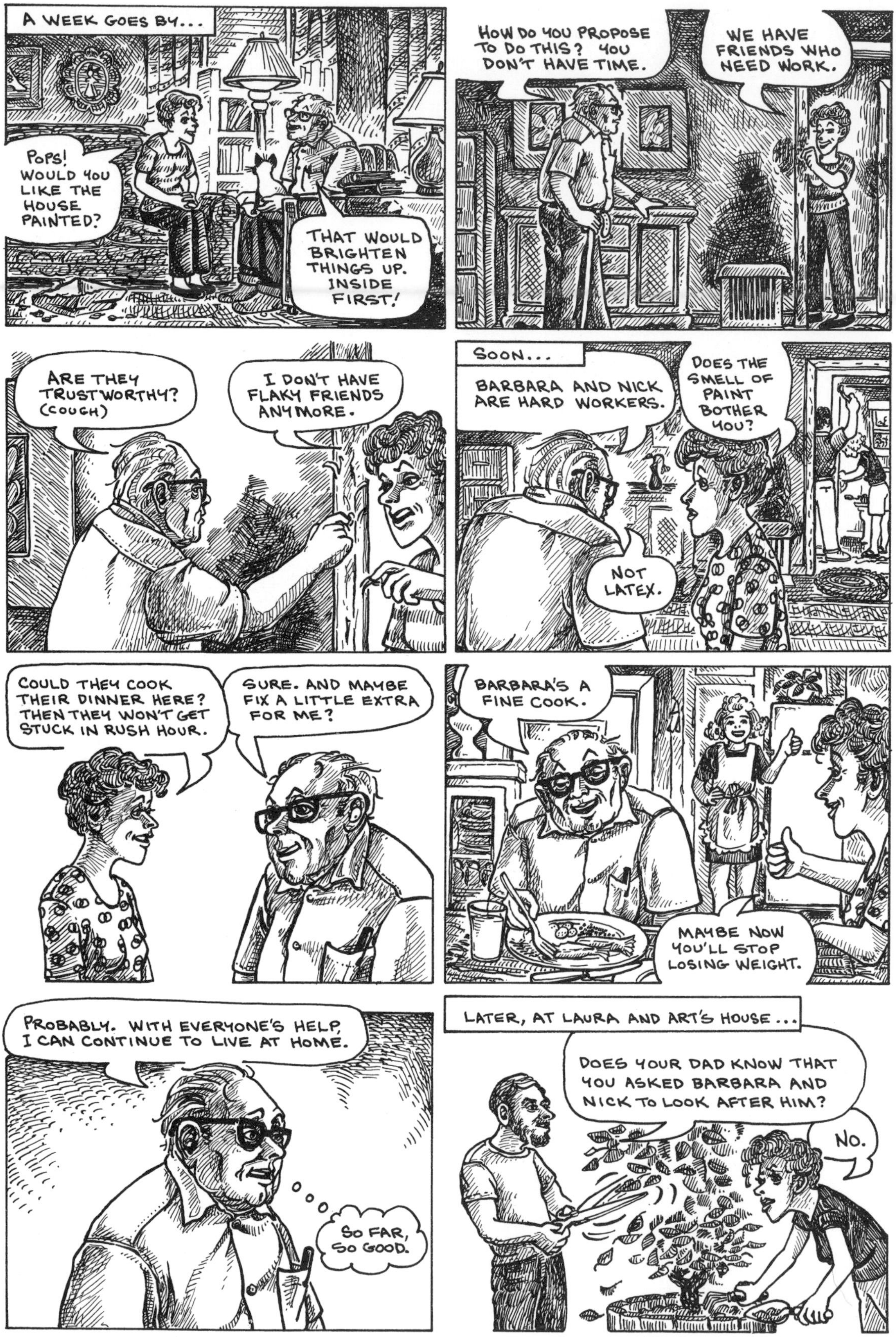
A WEEK GOES BY...
POPS! WOULD YOU LIKE THE HOUSE PAINTED?
THAT WOULD BRIGHTEN THINGS UP. INSIDE FIRST!
HOW DO YOU PROPOSE TO DO THIS? YOU DON'T HAVE TIME.
WE HAVE FRIENDS WHO NEED WORK.
ARE THEY TRUSTWORTHY? (COUGH)
I DON'T HAVE FLAKY FRIENDS ANYMORE.
SOON...
BARBARA AND NICK ARE HARD WORKERS.
DOES THE SMELL OF PAINT BOTHER YOU?
NOT LATEX.
COULD THEY COOK THEIR DINNER HERE? THEN THEY WON'T GET STUCK IN RUSH HOUR.
SURE. AND MAYBE FIX A LITTLE EXTRA FOR ME?
BARBARA'S A FINE COOK.
MAYBE NOW YOU'LL STOP LOSING WEIGHT.
PROBABLY. WITH EVERYONE'S HELP, I CAN CONTINUE TO LIVE AT HOME.
SO FAR, SO GOOD.
LATER, AT LAURA AND ART'S HOUSE...
DOES YOUR DAD KNOW THAT YOU ASKED BARBARA AND NICK TO LOOK AFTER HIM?
NO.

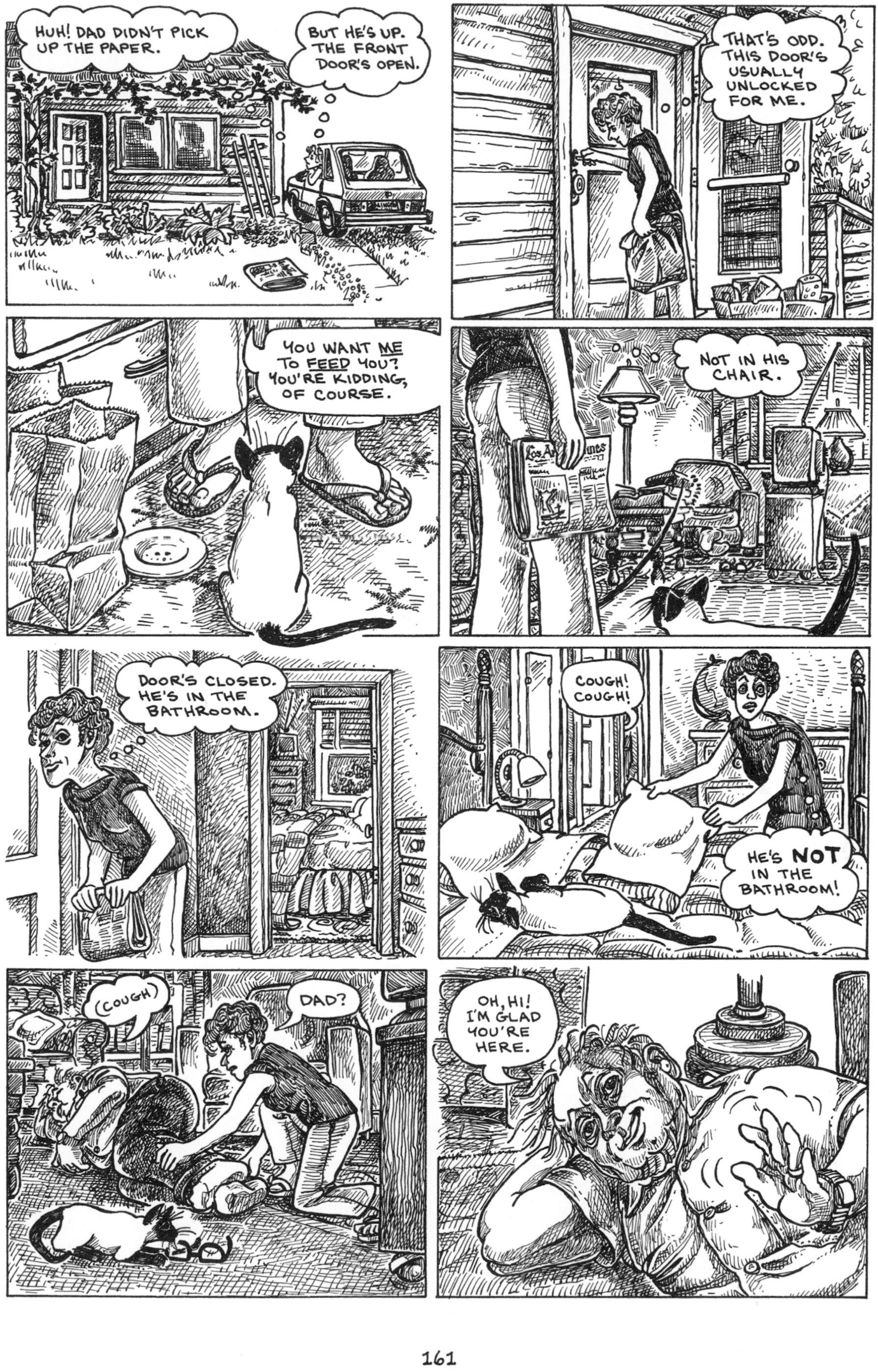
HUH! DAD DIDN'T PICK UP THE PAPER.
BUT HE'S UP. THE FRONT DOOR'S OPEN.
THAT'S ODD. THIS DOOR'S USUALLY UNLOCKED FOR ME.
YOU WANT ME TO FEED YOU? YOU'RE KIDDING, OF COURSE.
NOT IN HIS CHAIR.
DOOR'S CLOSED. HE'S IN THE BATHROOM.
COUGH! COUGH!
HE'S **NOT** IN THE BATHROOM!
(COUGH)
DAD?
OH, HI! I'M GLAD YOU'RE HERE.

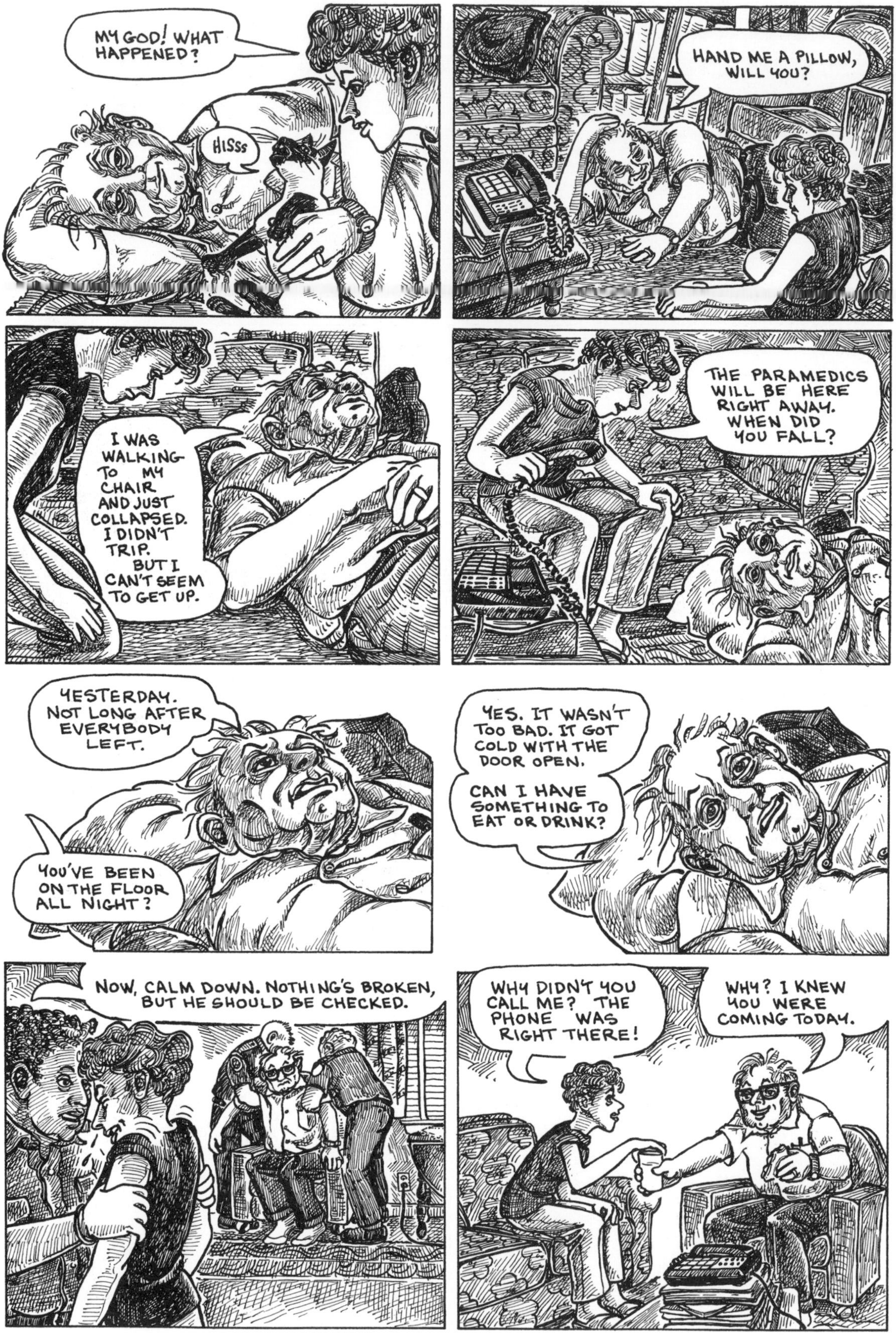
MY GOD! WHAT HAPPENED?
HISSS
HAND ME A PILLOW, WILL YOU?
I WAS WALKING TO MY CHAIR AND JUST COLLAPSED. I DIDN'T TRIP. BUT I CAN'T SEEM TO GET UP.
THE PARAMEDICS WILL BE HERE RIGHT AWAY. WHEN DID YOU FALL?
YESTERDAY. NOT LONG AFTER EVERYBODY LEFT.
YOU'VE BEEN ON THE FLOOR ALL NIGHT?
YES. IT WASN'T TOO BAD. IT GOT COLD WITH THE DOOR OPEN.
CAN I HAVE SOMETHING TO EAT OR DRINK?
NOW, CALM DOWN. NOTHING'S BROKEN, BUT HE SHOULD BE CHECKED.
WHY DIDN'T YOU CALL ME? THE PHONE WAS RIGHT THERE!
WHY? I KNEW YOU WERE COMING TODAY.

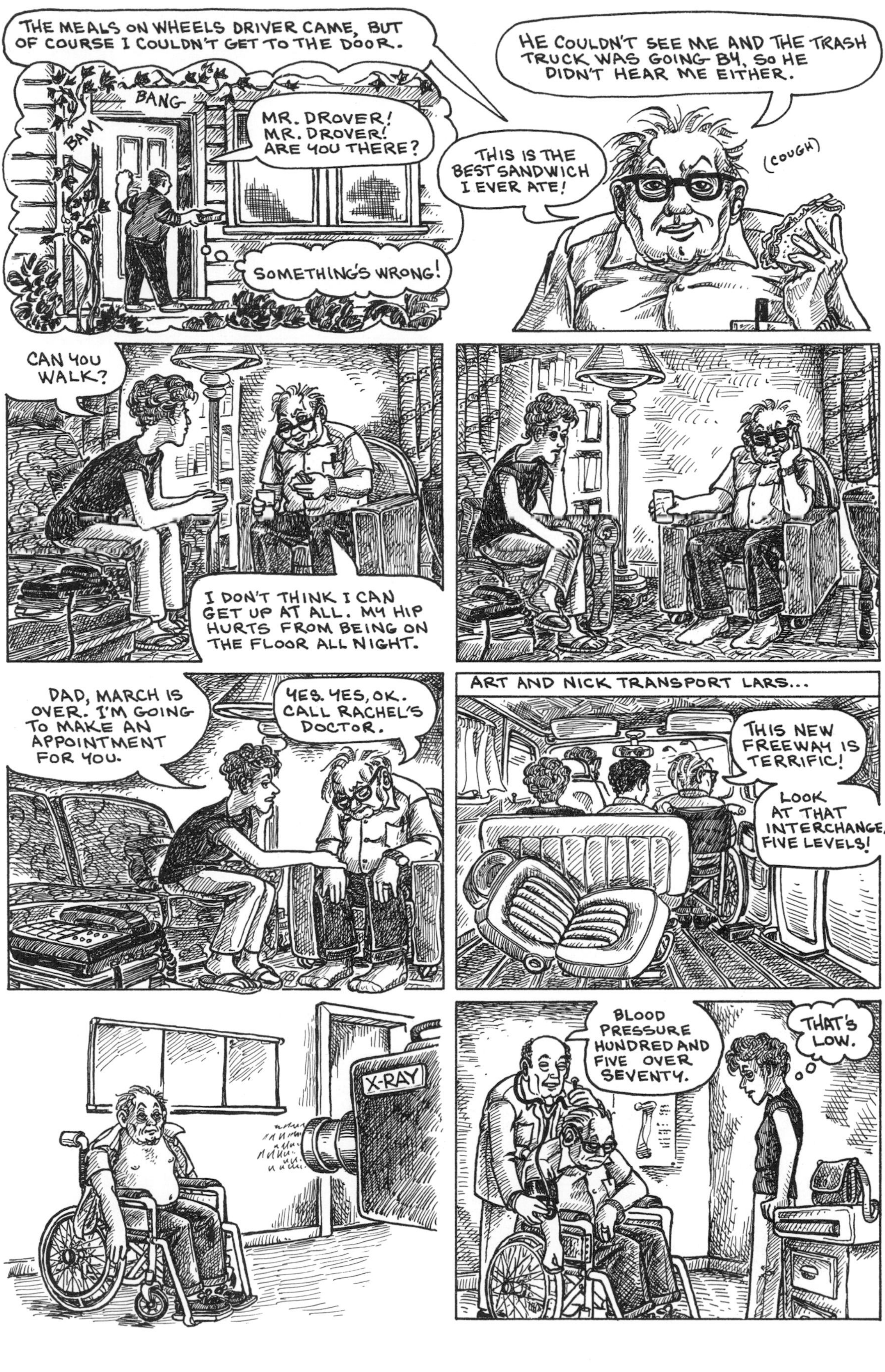
THE MEALS ON WHEELS DRIVER CAME, BUT OF COURSE I COULDN'T GET TO THE DOOR.
BANG
BAM
MR. DROVER! MR. DROVER! ARE YOU THERE?
SOMETHING'S WRONG!
HE COULDN'T SEE ME AND THE TRASH TRUCK WAS GOING BY, SO HE DIDN'T HEAR ME EITHER.
THIS IS THE BEST SANDWICH I EVER ATE!
(COUGH)
CAN YOU WALK?
I DON'T THINK I CAN GET UP AT ALL. MY HIP HURTS FROM BEING ON THE FLOOR ALL NIGHT.
DAD, MARCH IS OVER. I'M GOING TO MAKE AN APPOINTMENT FOR YOU.
YES. YES, OK. CALL RACHEL'S DOCTOR.
ART AND NICK TRANSPORT LARS...
THIS NEW FREEWAY IS TERRIFIC!
LOOK AT THAT INTERCHANGE. FIVE LEVELS!
X-RAY
BLOOD PRESSURE HUNDRED AND FIVE OVER SEVENTY.
THAT'S LOW.

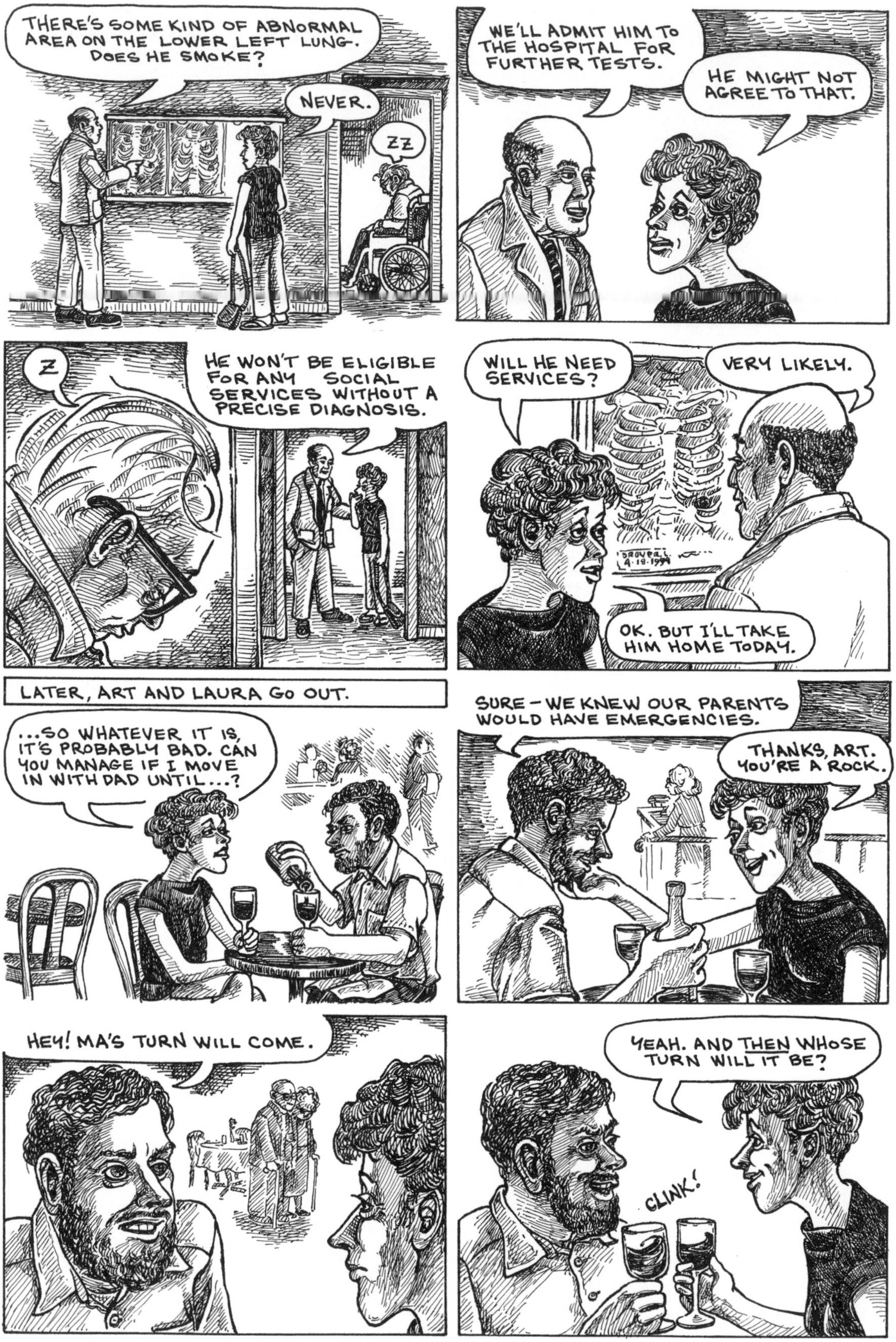
THERE'S SOME KIND OF ABNORMAL AREA ON THE LOWER LEFT LUNG. DOES HE SMOKE?
NEVER.
ZZ
WE'LL ADMIT HIM TO THE HOSPITAL FOR FURTHER TESTS.
HE MIGHT NOT AGREE TO THAT.
Z
HE WON'T BE ELIGIBLE FOR ANY SOCIAL SERVICES WITHOUT A PRECISE DIAGNOSIS.
WILL HE NEED SERVICES?
VERY LIKELY.
DROVER L. 4-18-1994
OK. BUT I'LL TAKE HIM HOME TODAY.
LATER, ART AND LAURA GO OUT.
...SO WHATEVER IT IS, IT'S PROBABLY BAD. CAN YOU MANAGE IF I MOVE IN WITH DAD UNTIL...?
SURE – WE KNEW OUR PARENTS WOULD HAVE EMERGENCIES.
THANKS, ART. YOU'RE A ROCK.
HEY! MA'S TURN WILL COME.
YEAH. AND THEN WHOSE TURN WILL IT BE?
CLINK!

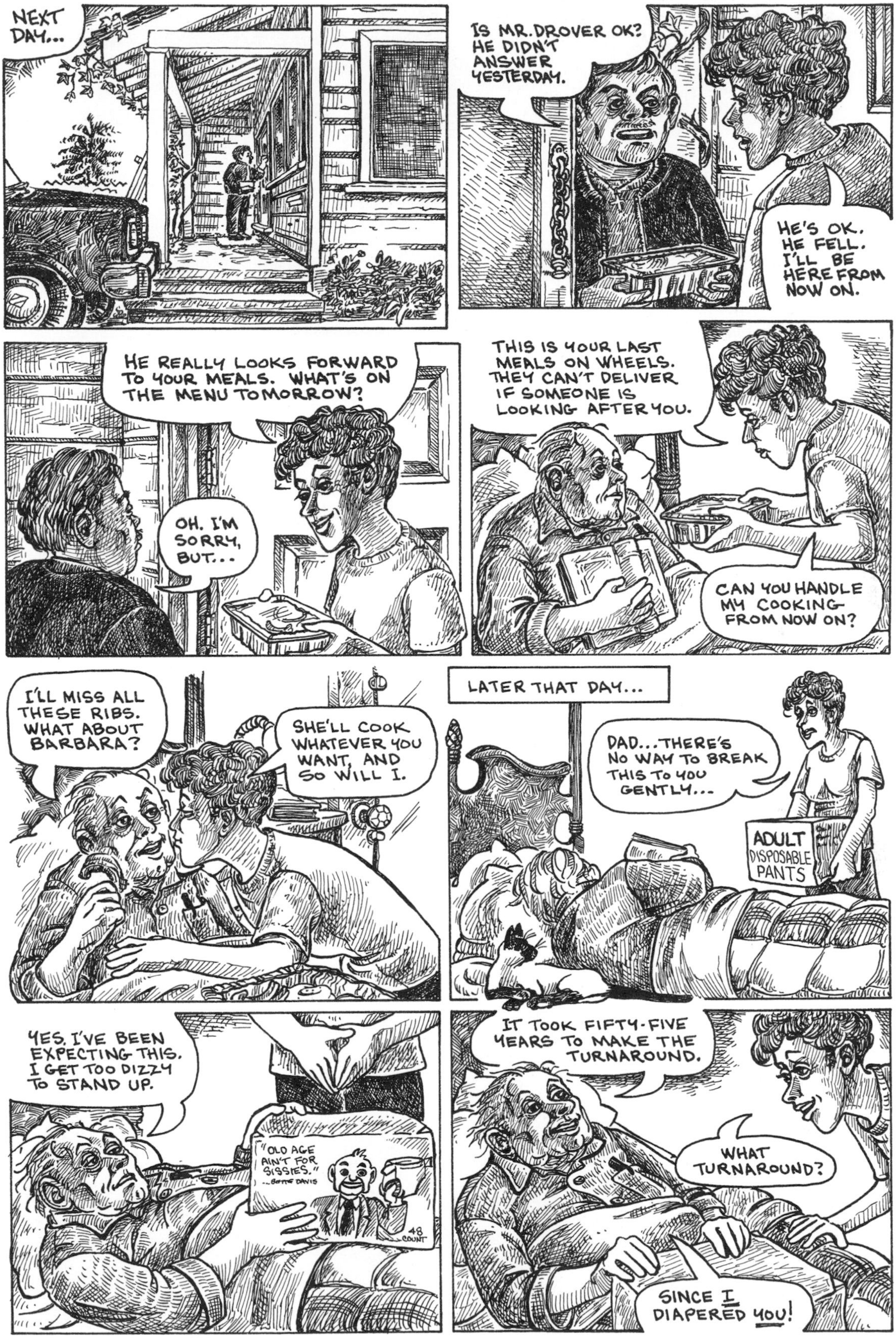
NEXT DAY...
IS MR. DROVER OK? HE DIDN'T ANSWER YESTERDAY.
HE'S OK. HE FELL. I'LL BE HERE FROM NOW ON.
HE REALLY LOOKS FORWARD TO YOUR MEALS. WHAT'S ON THE MENU TOMORROW?
OH. I'M SORRY, BUT...
THIS IS YOUR LAST MEALS ON WHEELS. THEY CAN'T DELIVER IF SOMEONE IS LOOKING AFTER YOU.
CAN YOU HANDLE MY COOKING FROM NOW ON?
I'LL MISS ALL THESE RIBS. WHAT ABOUT BARBARA?
SHE'LL COOK WHATEVER YOU WANT, AND SO WILL I.
LATER THAT DAY...
DAD... THERE'S NO WAY TO BREAK THIS TO YOU GENTLY...
ADULT DISPOSABLE PANTS
YES, I'VE BEEN EXPECTING THIS. I GET TOO DIZZY TO STAND UP.
"OLD AGE AIN'T FOR SISSIES." ...BETTE DAVIS
48 COUNT
IT TOOK FIFTY-FIVE YEARS TO MAKE THE TURNAROUND.
WHAT TURNAROUND?
SINCE I DIAPERED YOU!

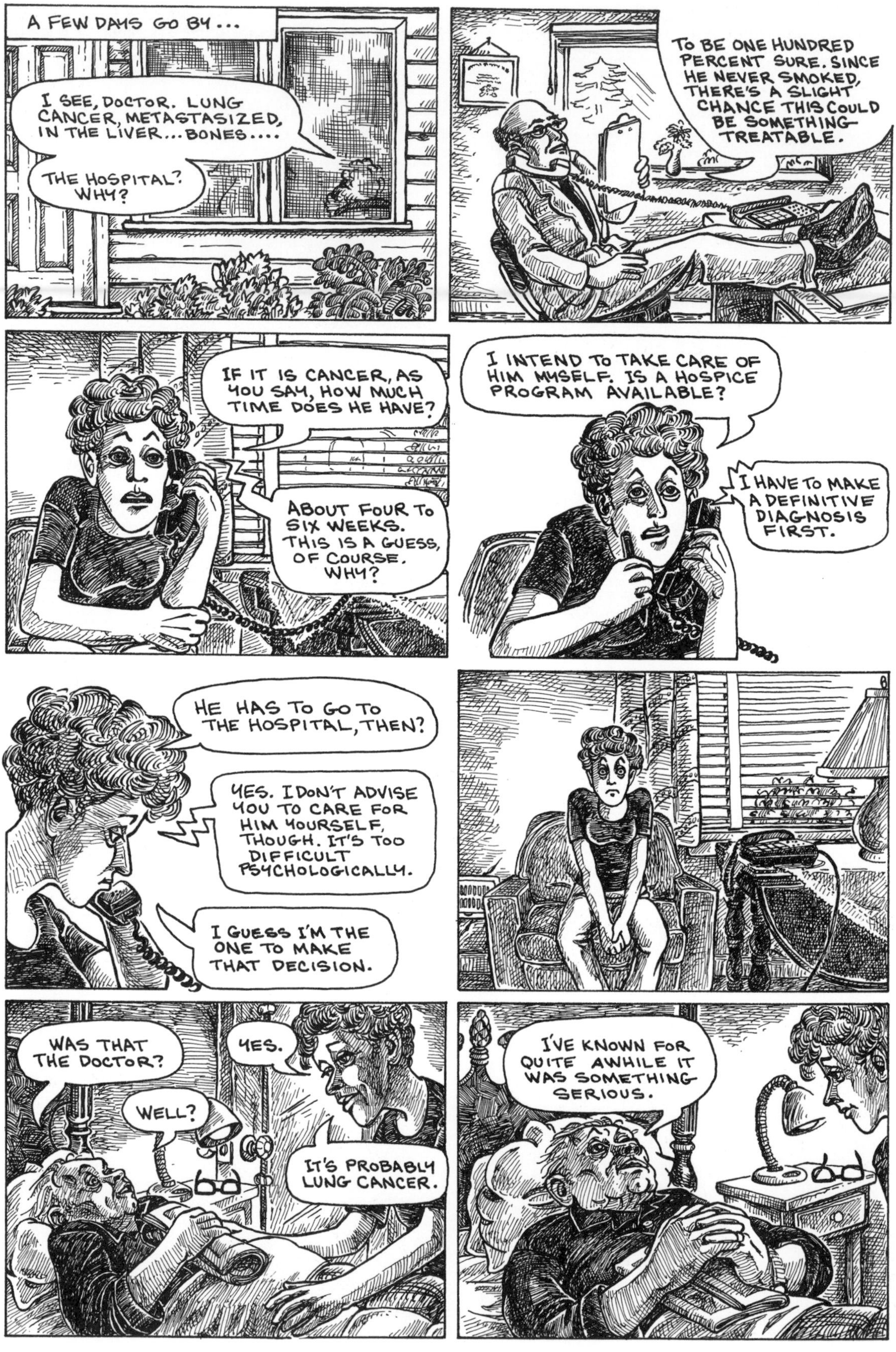
A FEW DAYS GO BY...
I SEE, DOCTOR. LUNG CANCER, METASTASIZED, IN THE LIVER... BONES....
THE HOSPITAL? WHY?
TO BE ONE HUNDRED PERCENT SURE. SINCE HE NEVER SMOKED, THERE'S A SLIGHT CHANCE THIS COULD BE SOMETHING TREATABLE.
IF IT IS CANCER, AS YOU SAY, HOW MUCH TIME DOES HE HAVE?
ABOUT FOUR TO SIX WEEKS. THIS IS A GUESS, OF COURSE. WHY?
I INTEND TO TAKE CARE OF HIM MYSELF. IS A HOSPICE PROGRAM AVAILABLE?
I HAVE TO MAKE A DEFINITIVE DIAGNOSIS FIRST.
HE HAS TO GO TO THE HOSPITAL, THEN?
YES. I DON'T ADVISE YOU TO CARE FOR HIM YOURSELF, THOUGH. IT'S TOO DIFFICULT PSYCHOLOGICALLY.
I GUESS I'M THE ONE TO MAKE THAT DECISION.
WAS THAT THE DOCTOR?
YES.
WELL?
IT'S PROBABLY LUNG CANCER.
I'VE KNOWN FOR QUITE AWHILE IT WAS SOMETHING SERIOUS.

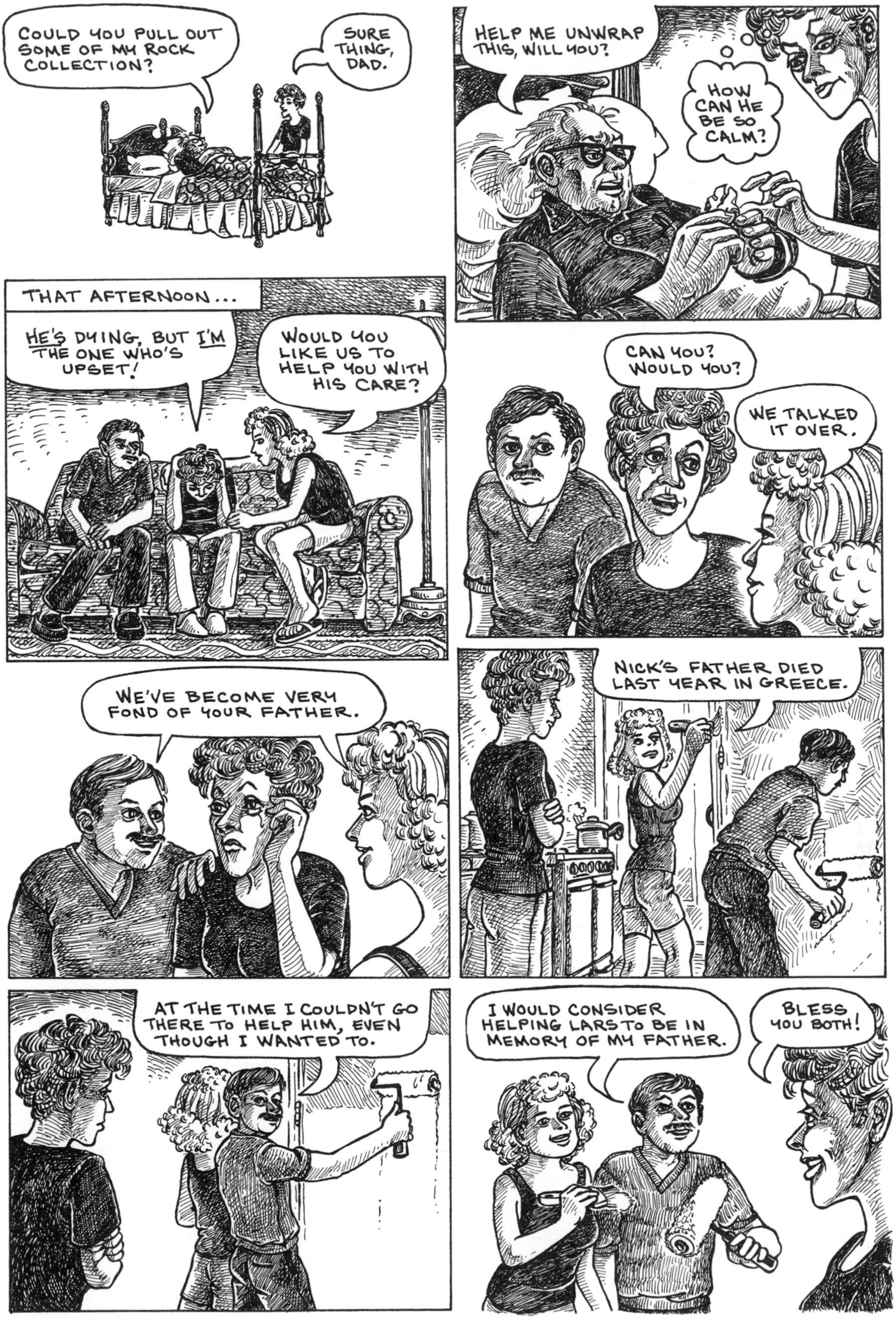
COULD YOU PULL OUT SOME OF MY ROCK COLLECTION?
SURE THING, DAD.
HELP ME UNWRAP THIS, WILL YOU?
HOW CAN HE BE SO CALM?
THAT AFTERNOON...
HE'S DYING, BUT I'M THE ONE WHO'S UPSET!
WOULD YOU LIKE US TO HELP YOU WITH HIS CARE?
CAN YOU? WOULD YOU?
WE TALKED IT OVER.
WE'VE BECOME VERY FOND OF YOUR FATHER.
NICK'S FATHER DIED LAST YEAR IN GREECE.
AT THE TIME I COULDN'T GO THERE TO HELP HIM, EVEN THOUGH I WANTED TO.
I WOULD CONSIDER HELPING LARS TO BE IN MEMORY OF MY FATHER.
BLESS YOU BOTH!

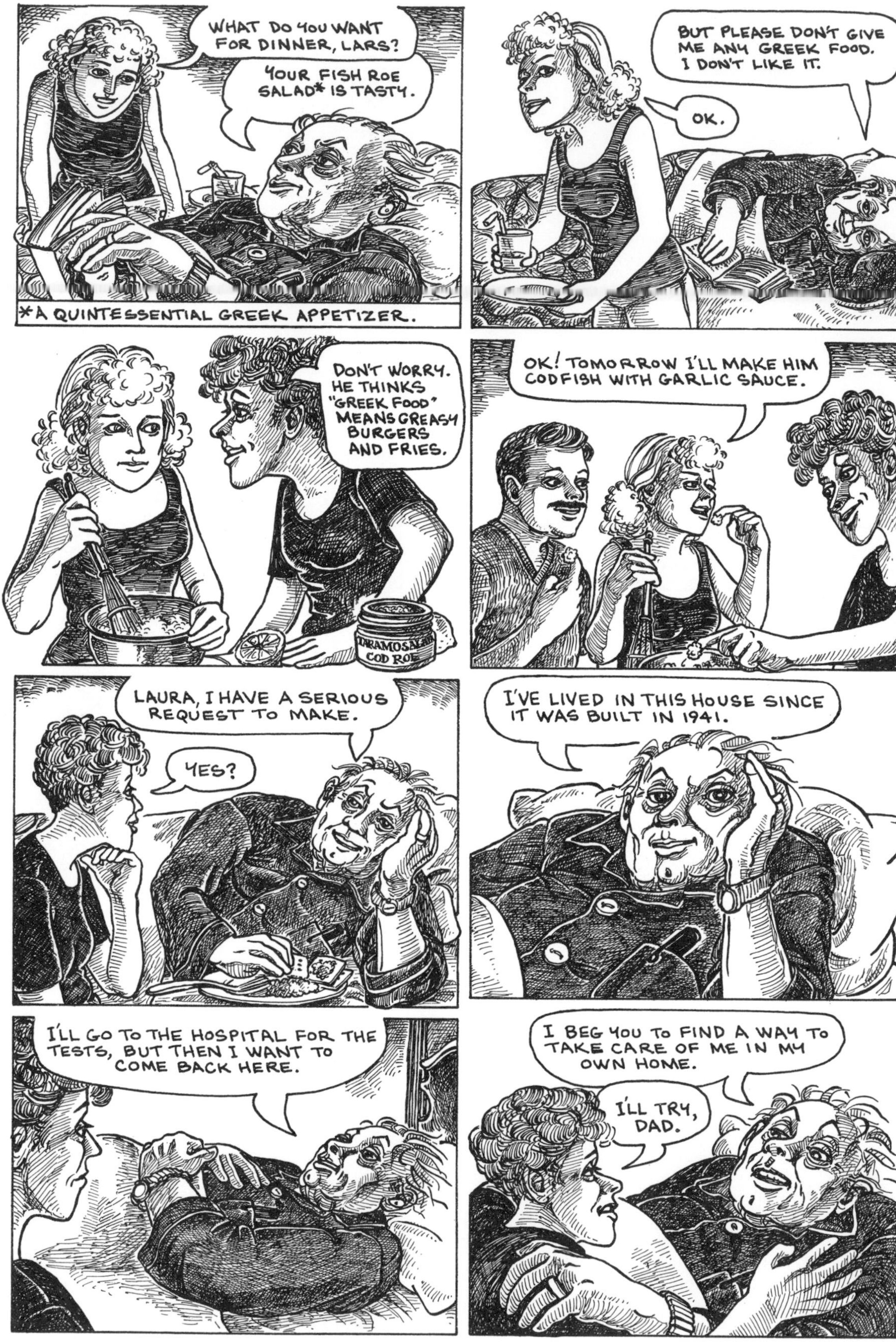
WHAT DO YOU WANT FOR DINNER, LARS?
YOUR FISH ROE SALAD* IS TASTY.
*A QUINTESSENTIAL GREEK APPETIZER.
BUT PLEASE DON'T GIVE ME ANY GREEK FOOD. I DON'T LIKE IT.
OK.
DON'T WORRY. HE THINKS "GREEK FOOD" MEANS GREASY BURGERS AND FRIES.
TARAMOSALATA COD ROE
OK! TOMORROW I'LL MAKE HIM CODFISH WITH GARLIC SAUCE.
LAURA, I HAVE A SERIOUS REQUEST TO MAKE.
YES?
I'VE LIVED IN THIS HOUSE SINCE IT WAS BUILT IN 1941.
I'LL GO TO THE HOSPITAL FOR THE TESTS, BUT THEN I WANT TO COME BACK HERE.
I BEG YOU TO FIND A WAY TO TAKE CARE OF ME IN MY OWN HOME.
I'LL TRY, DAD.

12

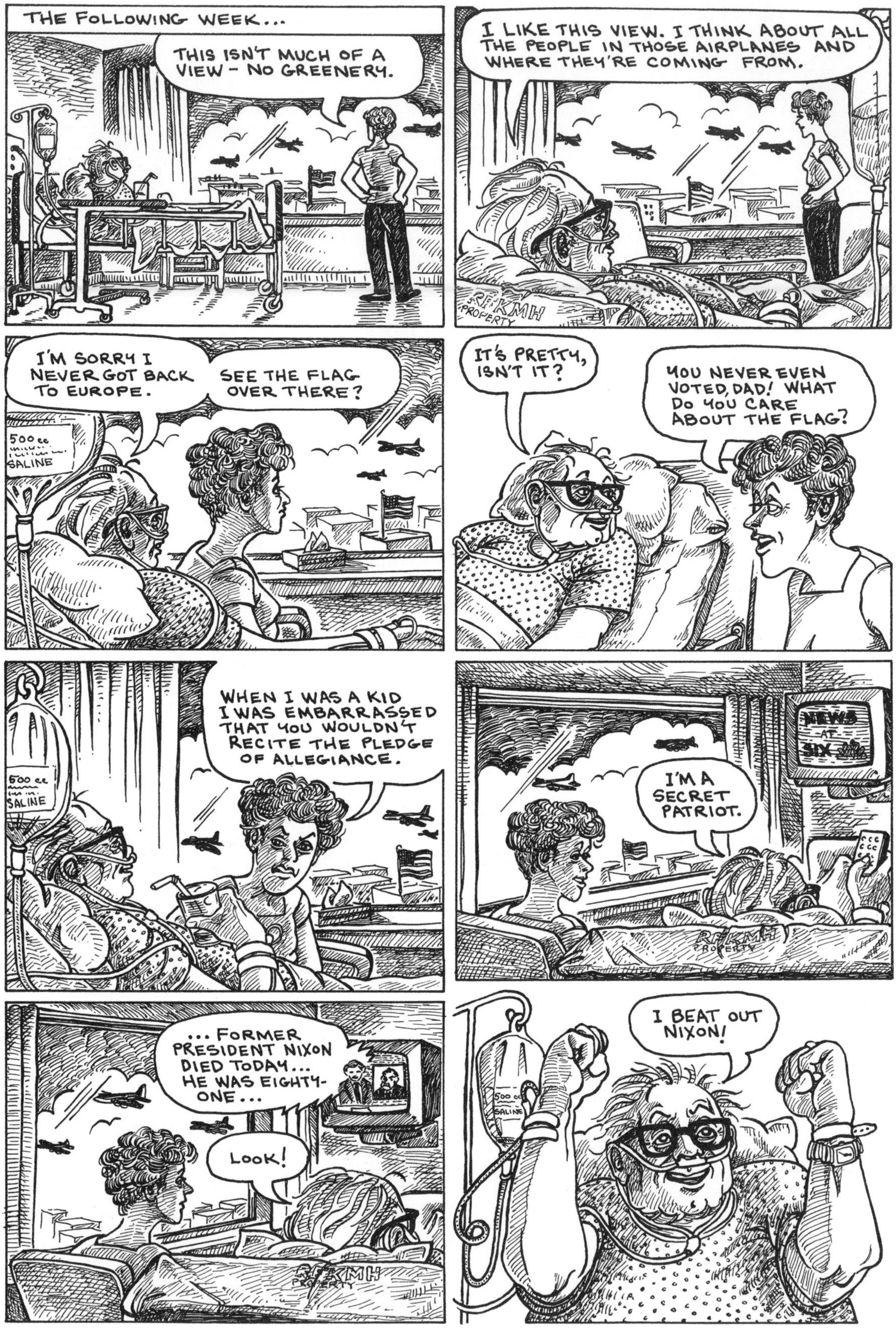
THE FOLLOWING WEEK...
THIS ISN'T MUCH OF A VIEW – NO GREENERY.
I LIKE THIS VIEW. I THINK ABOUT ALL THE PEOPLE IN THOSE AIRPLANES AND WHERE THEY'RE COMING FROM.
I'M SORRY I NEVER GOT BACK TO EUROPE.
SEE THE FLAG OVER THERE?
SALINE
IT'S PRETTY, ISN'T IT?
YOU NEVER EVEN VOTED, DAD! WHAT DO YOU CARE ABOUT THE FLAG?
WHEN I WAS A KID I WAS EMBARRASSED THAT YOU WOULDN'T RECITE THE PLEDGE OF ALLEGIANCE.
SALINE
NEWS AT SIX
I'M A SECRET PATRIOT.
...FORMER PRESIDENT NIXON DIED TODAY... HE WAS EIGHTY-ONE...
LOOK!
I BEAT OUT NIXON!

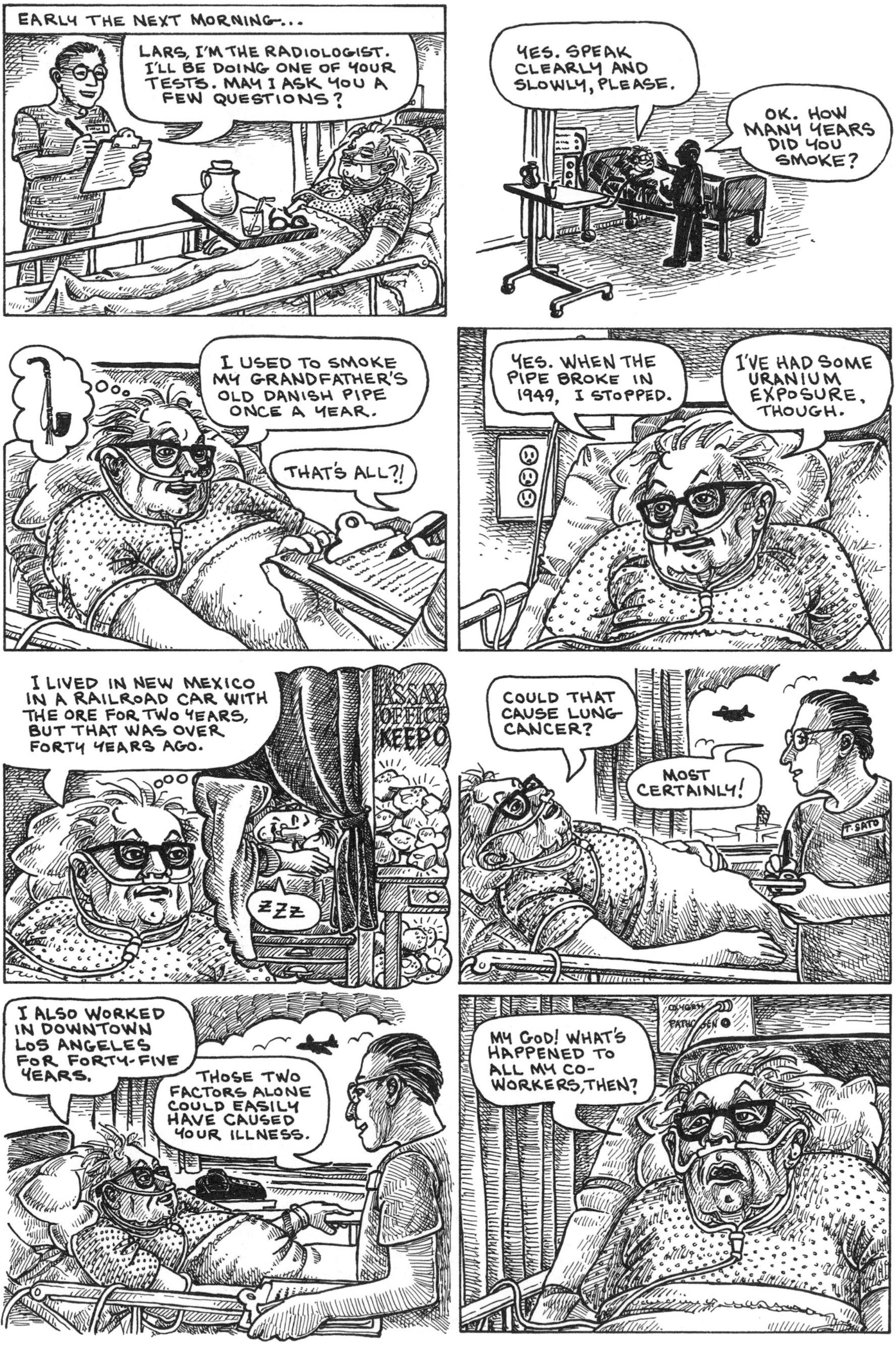
EARLY THE NEXT MORNING...
LARS, I'M THE RADIOLOGIST. I'LL BE DOING ONE OF YOUR TESTS. MAY I ASK YOU A FEW QUESTIONS?
YES. SPEAK CLEARLY AND SLOWLY, PLEASE.
OK. HOW MANY YEARS DID YOU SMOKE?
I USED TO SMOKE MY GRANDFATHER'S OLD DANISH PIPE ONCE A YEAR.
THAT'S ALL?!
YES. WHEN THE PIPE BROKE IN 1949, I STOPPED.
I'VE HAD SOME URANIUM EXPOSURE, THOUGH.
I LIVED IN NEW MEXICO IN A RAILROAD CAR WITH THE ORE FOR TWO YEARS, BUT THAT WAS OVER FORTY YEARS AGO.
ASSAY OFFICE KEEP O
ZZZ
COULD THAT CAUSE LUNG CANCER?
MOST CERTAINLY!
T. SATO
I ALSO WORKED IN DOWNTOWN LOS ANGELES FOR FORTY-FIVE YEARS.
THOSE TWO FACTORS ALONE COULD EASILY HAVE CAUSED YOUR ILLNESS.
MY GOD! WHAT'S HAPPENED TO ALL MY CO-WORKERS, THEN?

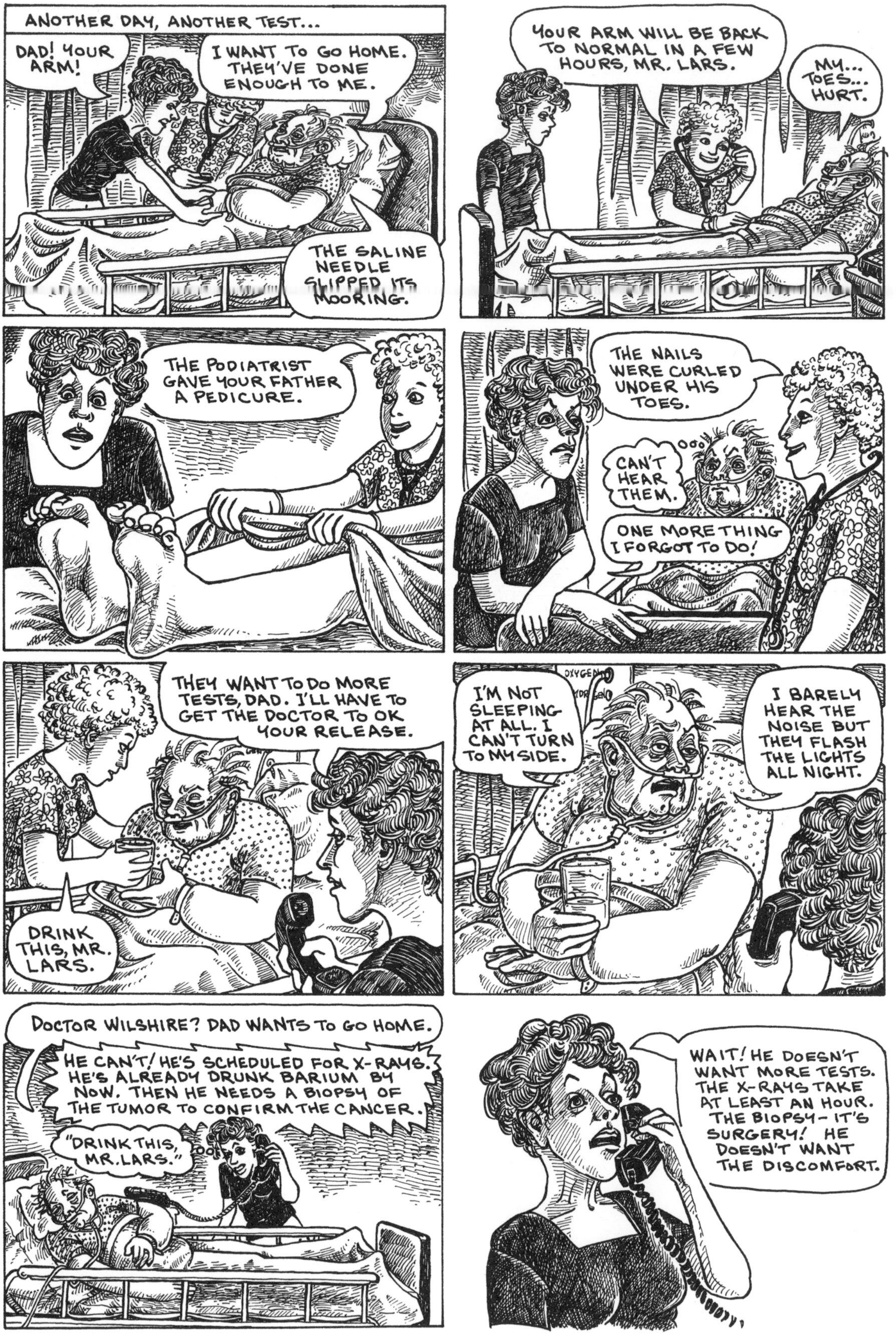

ANOTHER DAY, ANOTHER TEST...
DAD! YOUR ARM!
I WANT TO GO HOME. THEY'VE DONE ENOUGH TO ME.
THE SALINE NEEDLE SLIPPED ITS MOORING.
YOUR ARM WILL BE BACK TO NORMAL IN A FEW HOURS, MR. LARS.
MY... TOES... HURT.
THE PODIATRIST GAVE YOUR FATHER A PEDICURE.
THE NAILS WERE CURLED UNDER HIS TOES.
CAN'T HEAR THEM.
ONE MORE THING I FORGOT TO DO!
THEY WANT TO DO MORE TESTS, DAD. I'LL HAVE TO GET THE DOCTOR TO OK YOUR RELEASE.
DRINK THIS, MR. LARS.
OXYGEN
I'M NOT SLEEPING AT ALL. I CAN'T TURN TO MY SIDE.
I BARELY HEAR THE NOISE BUT THEY FLASH THE LIGHTS ALL NIGHT.
DOCTOR WILSHIRE? DAD WANTS TO GO HOME.
HE CAN'T! HE'S SCHEDULED FOR X-RAYS. HE'S ALREADY DRUNK BARIUM BY NOW. THEN HE NEEDS A BIOPSY OF THE TUMOR TO CONFIRM THE CANCER.
"DRINK THIS, MR. LARS."
WAIT! HE DOESN'T WANT MORE TESTS. THE X-RAYS TAKE AT LEAST AN HOUR. THE BIOPSY- IT'S SURGERY! HE DOESN'T WANT THE DISCOMFORT.

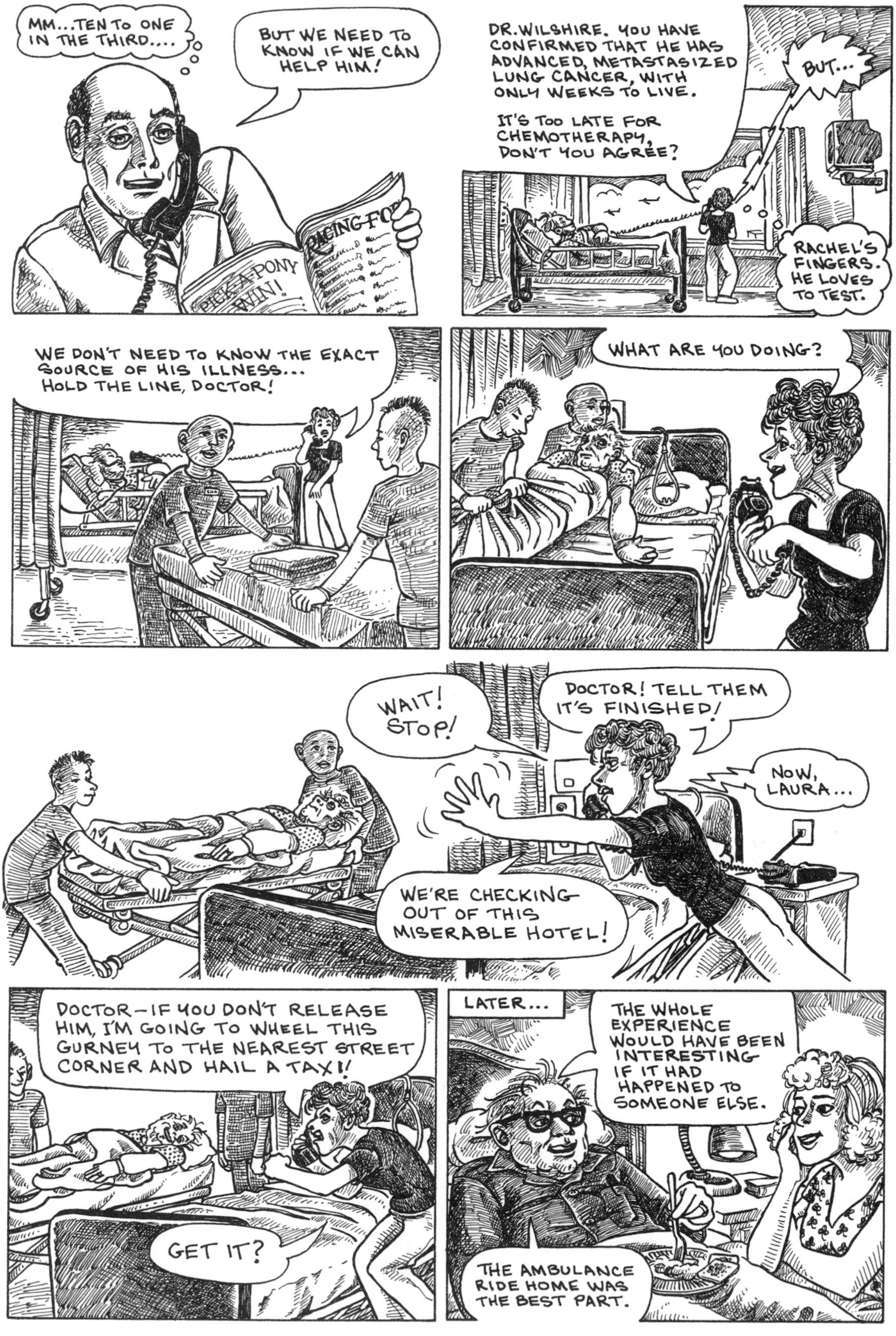
MM...TEN TO ONE IN THE THIRD....
BUT WE NEED TO KNOW IF WE CAN HELP HIM!
PICK A PONY WIN!
RACING FO
DR. WILSHIRE. YOU HAVE CONFIRMED THAT HE HAS ADVANCED, METASTASIZED LUNG CANCER, WITH ONLY WEEKS TO LIVE.
IT'S TOO LATE FOR CHEMOTHERAPY, DON'T YOU AGREE?
BUT...
RACHEL'S FINGERS. HE LOVES TO TEST.
WE DON'T NEED TO KNOW THE EXACT SOURCE OF HIS ILLNESS... HOLD THE LINE, DOCTOR!
WHAT ARE YOU DOING?
WAIT! STOP!
DOCTOR! TELL THEM IT'S FINISHED!
NOW, LAURA...
WE'RE CHECKING OUT OF THIS MISERABLE HOTEL!
DOCTOR—IF YOU DON'T RELEASE HIM, I'M GOING TO WHEEL THIS GURNEY TO THE NEAREST STREET CORNER AND HAIL A TAXI!
GET IT?
LATER...
THE WHOLE EXPERIENCE WOULD HAVE BEEN INTERESTING IF IT HAD HAPPENED TO SOMEONE ELSE.
THE AMBULANCE RIDE HOME WAS THE BEST PART.

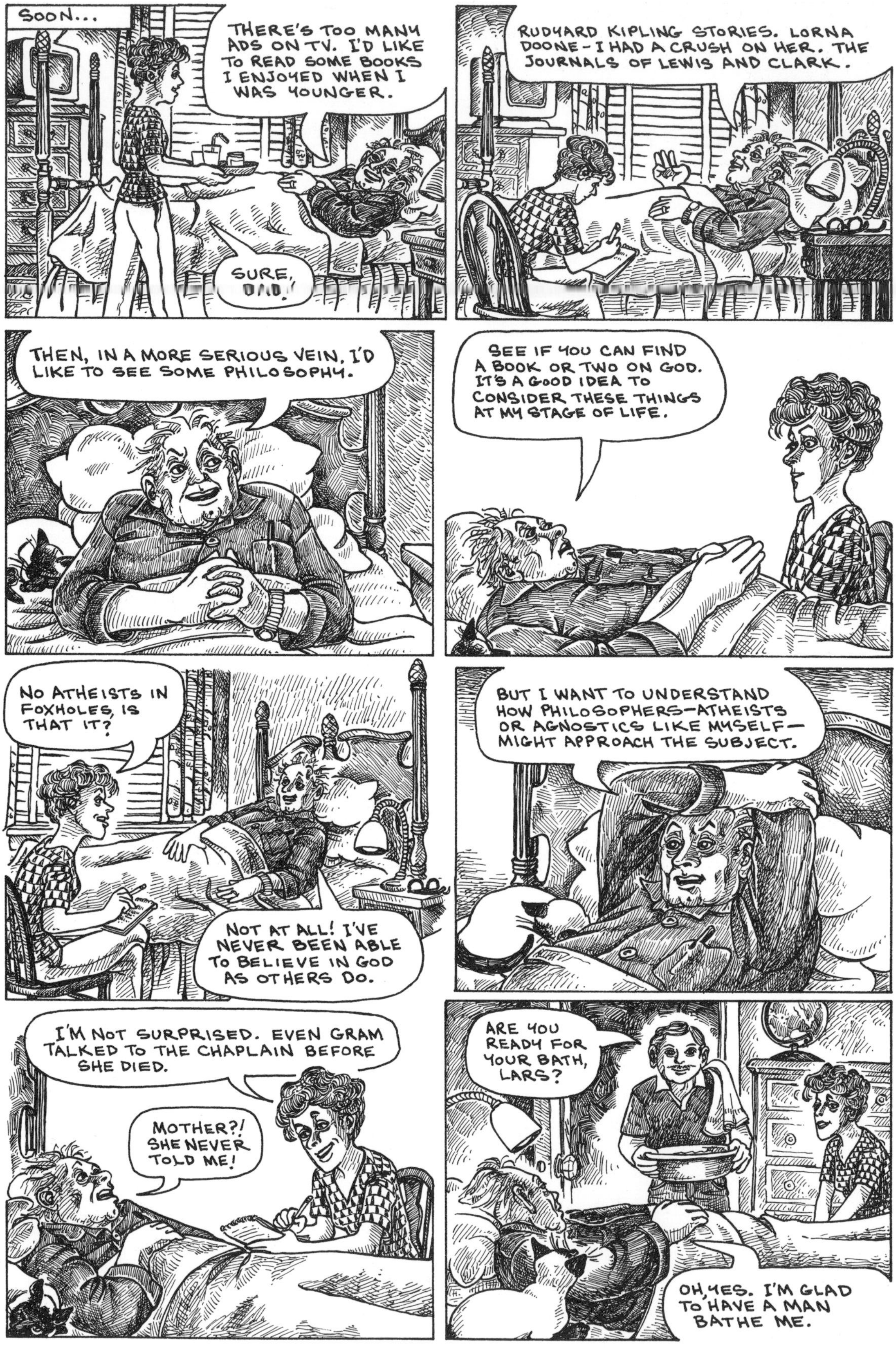
SOON...
THERE'S TOO MANY ADS ON TV. I'D LIKE TO READ SOME BOOKS I ENJOYED WHEN I WAS YOUNGER.
SURE, DAD.
RUDYARD KIPLING STORIES. LORNA DOONE–I HAD A CRUSH ON HER. THE JOURNALS OF LEWIS AND CLARK.
THEN, IN A MORE SERIOUS VEIN, I'D LIKE TO SEE SOME PHILOSOPHY.
SEE IF YOU CAN FIND A BOOK OR TWO ON GOD. IT'S A GOOD IDEA TO CONSIDER THESE THINGS AT MY STAGE OF LIFE.
NO ATHEISTS IN FOXHOLES, IS THAT IT?
NOT AT ALL! I'VE NEVER BEEN ABLE TO BELIEVE IN GOD AS OTHERS DO.
BUT I WANT TO UNDERSTAND HOW PHILOSOPHERS–ATHEISTS OR AGNOSTICS LIKE MYSELF–MIGHT APPROACH THE SUBJECT.
I'M NOT SURPRISED. EVEN GRAM TALKED TO THE CHAPLAIN BEFORE SHE DIED.
MOTHER?! SHE NEVER TOLD ME!
ARE YOU READY FOR YOUR BATH, LARS?
OH, YES. I'M GLAD TO HAVE A MAN BATHE ME.

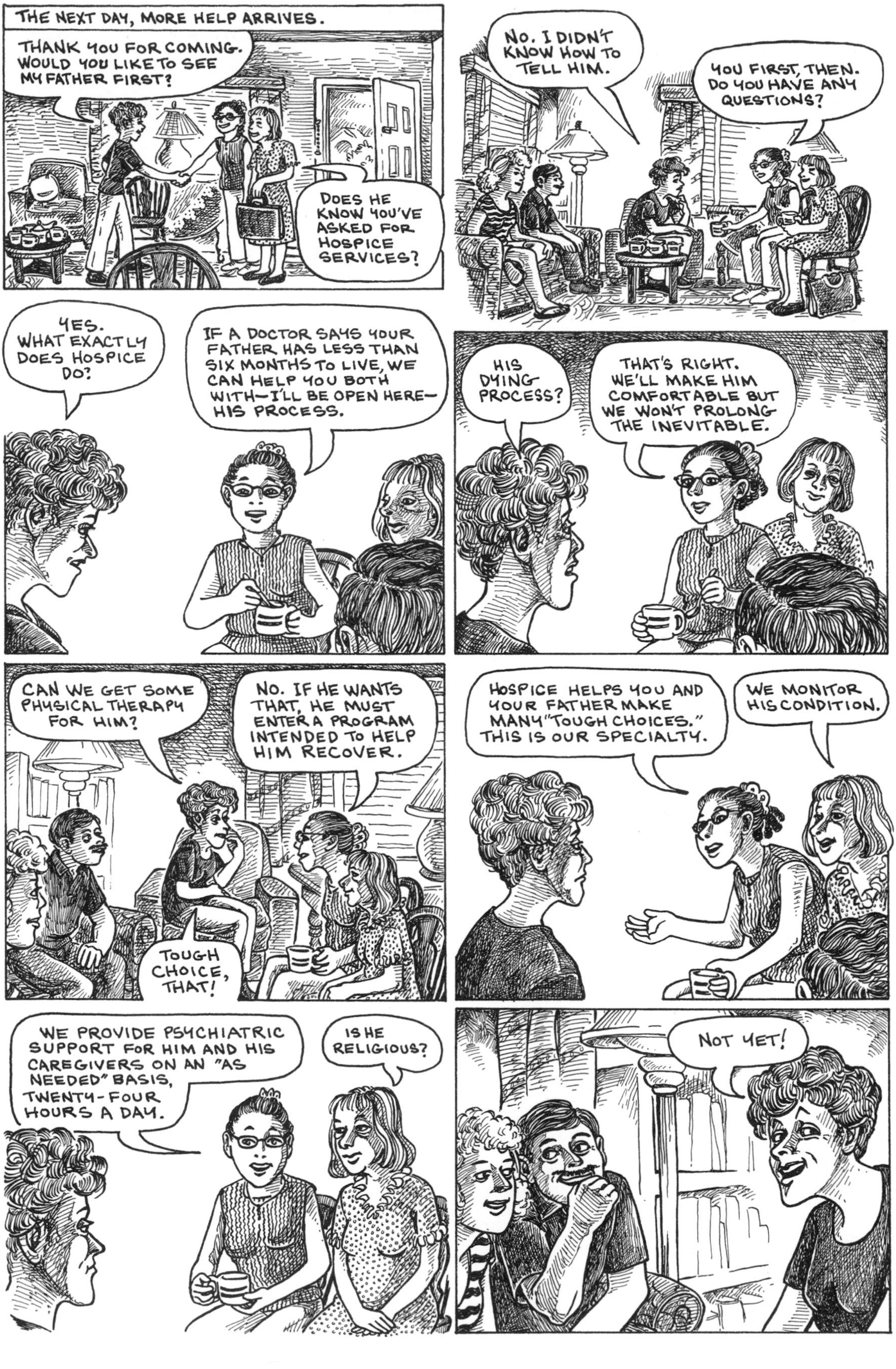
THE NEXT DAY, MORE HELP ARRIVES.
THANK YOU FOR COMING. WOULD YOU LIKE TO SEE MY FATHER FIRST?
DOES HE KNOW YOU'VE ASKED FOR HOSPICE SERVICES?
NO. I DIDN'T KNOW HOW TO TELL HIM.
YOU FIRST, THEN. DO YOU HAVE ANY QUESTIONS?
YES. WHAT EXACTLY DOES HOSPICE DO?
IF A DOCTOR SAYS YOUR FATHER HAS LESS THAN SIX MONTHS TO LIVE, WE CAN HELP YOU BOTH WITH—I'LL BE OPEN HERE—HIS PROCESS.
HIS DYING PROCESS?
THAT'S RIGHT. WE'LL MAKE HIM COMFORTABLE BUT WE WON'T PROLONG THE INEVITABLE.
CAN WE GET SOME PHYSICAL THERAPY FOR HIM?
NO. IF HE WANTS THAT, HE MUST ENTER A PROGRAM INTENDED TO HELP HIM RECOVER.
TOUGH CHOICE, THAT!
HOSPICE HELPS YOU AND YOUR FATHER MAKE MANY "TOUGH CHOICES." THIS IS OUR SPECIALTY.
WE MONITOR HIS CONDITION.
WE PROVIDE PSYCHIATRIC SUPPORT FOR HIM AND HIS CAREGIVERS ON AN "AS NEEDED" BASIS, TWENTY-FOUR HOURS A DAY.
IS HE RELIGIOUS?
NOT YET!

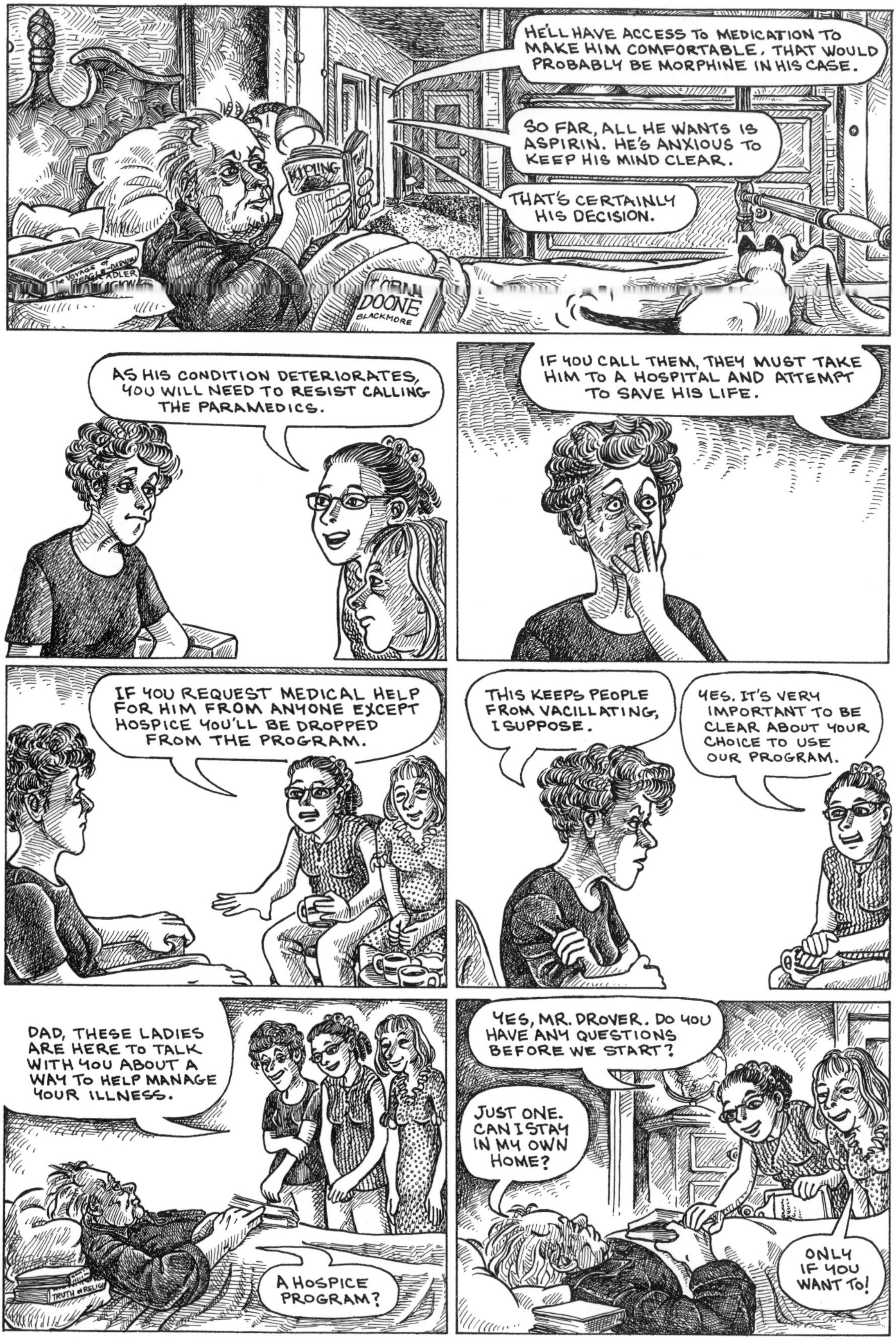
HE'LL HAVE ACCESS TO MEDICATION TO MAKE HIM COMFORTABLE. THAT WOULD PROBABLY BE MORPHINE IN HIS CASE.
SO FAR, ALL HE WANTS IS ASPIRIN. HE'S ANXIOUS TO KEEP HIS MIND CLEAR.
THAT'S CERTAINLY HIS DECISION.
KIPLING
LORNA DOONE BLACKMORE
AS HIS CONDITION DETERIORATES, YOU WILL NEED TO RESIST CALLING THE PARAMEDICS.
IF YOU CALL THEM, THEY MUST TAKE HIM TO A HOSPITAL AND ATTEMPT TO SAVE HIS LIFE.
IF YOU REQUEST MEDICAL HELP FOR HIM FROM ANYONE EXCEPT HOSPICE YOU'LL BE DROPPED FROM THE PROGRAM.
THIS KEEPS PEOPLE FROM VACILLATING, I SUPPOSE.
YES. IT'S VERY IMPORTANT TO BE CLEAR ABOUT YOUR CHOICE TO USE OUR PROGRAM.
DAD, THESE LADIES ARE HERE TO TALK WITH YOU ABOUT A WAY TO HELP MANAGE YOUR ILLNESS.
A HOSPICE PROGRAM?
YES, MR. DROVER. DO YOU HAVE ANY QUESTIONS BEFORE WE START?
JUST ONE. CAN I STAY IN MY OWN HOME?
ONLY IF YOU WANT TO!

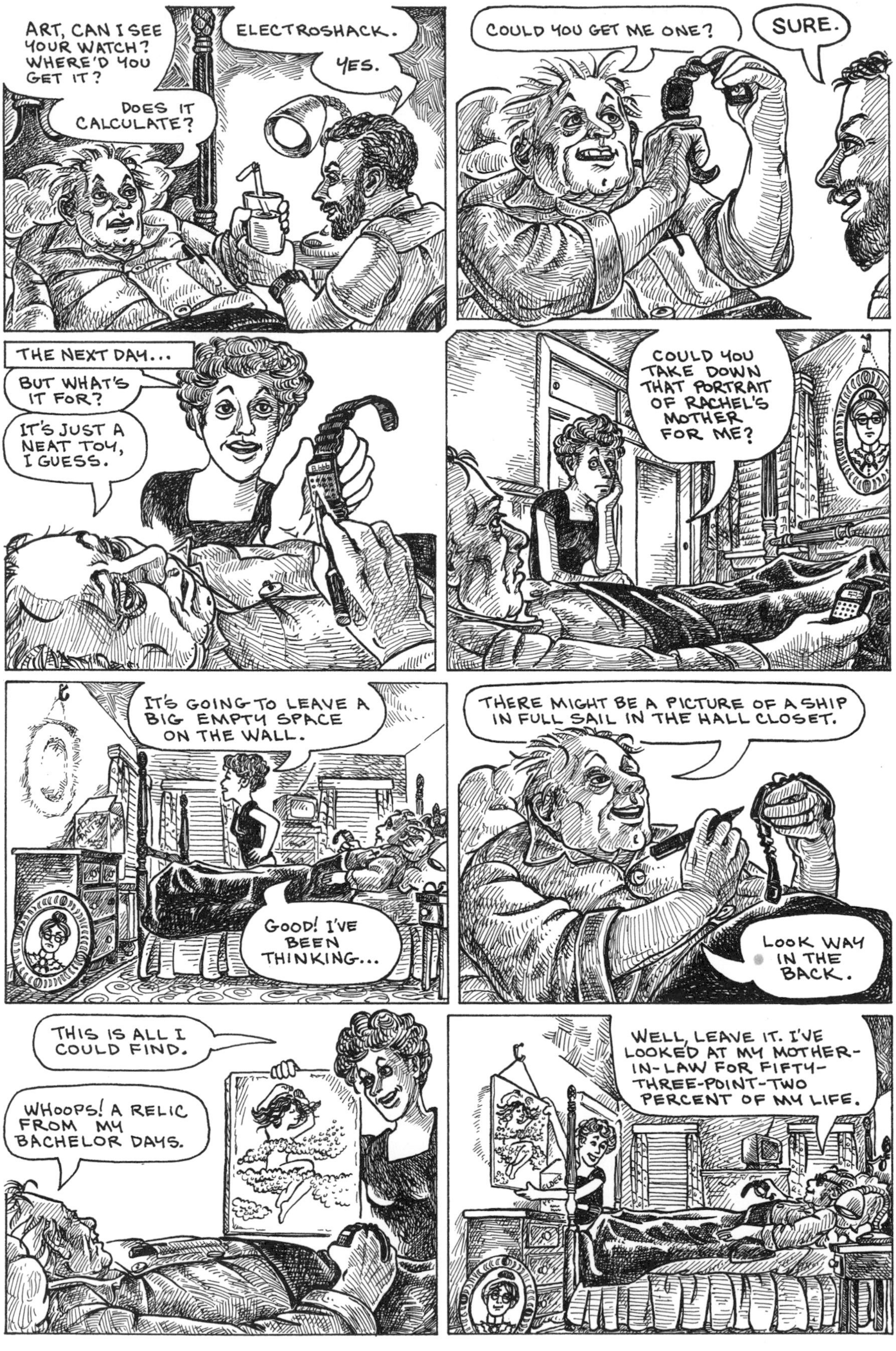
ART, CAN I SEE YOUR WATCH? WHERE'D YOU GET IT?
ELECTROSHACK.
DOES IT CALCULATE?
YES.
COULD YOU GET ME ONE?
SURE.
THE NEXT DAY...
BUT WHAT'S IT FOR?
IT'S JUST A NEAT TOY, I GUESS.
COULD YOU TAKE DOWN THAT PORTRAIT OF RACHEL'S MOTHER FOR ME?
IT'S GOING TO LEAVE A BIG EMPTY SPACE ON THE WALL.
GOOD! I'VE BEEN THINKING...
THERE MIGHT BE A PICTURE OF A SHIP IN FULL SAIL IN THE HALL CLOSET.
LOOK WAY IN THE BACK.
THIS IS ALL I COULD FIND.
WHOOPS! A RELIC FROM MY BACHELOR DAYS.
WELL, LEAVE IT. I'VE LOOKED AT MY MOTHER-IN-LAW FOR FIFTY-THREE-POINT-TWO PERCENT OF MY LIFE.

13

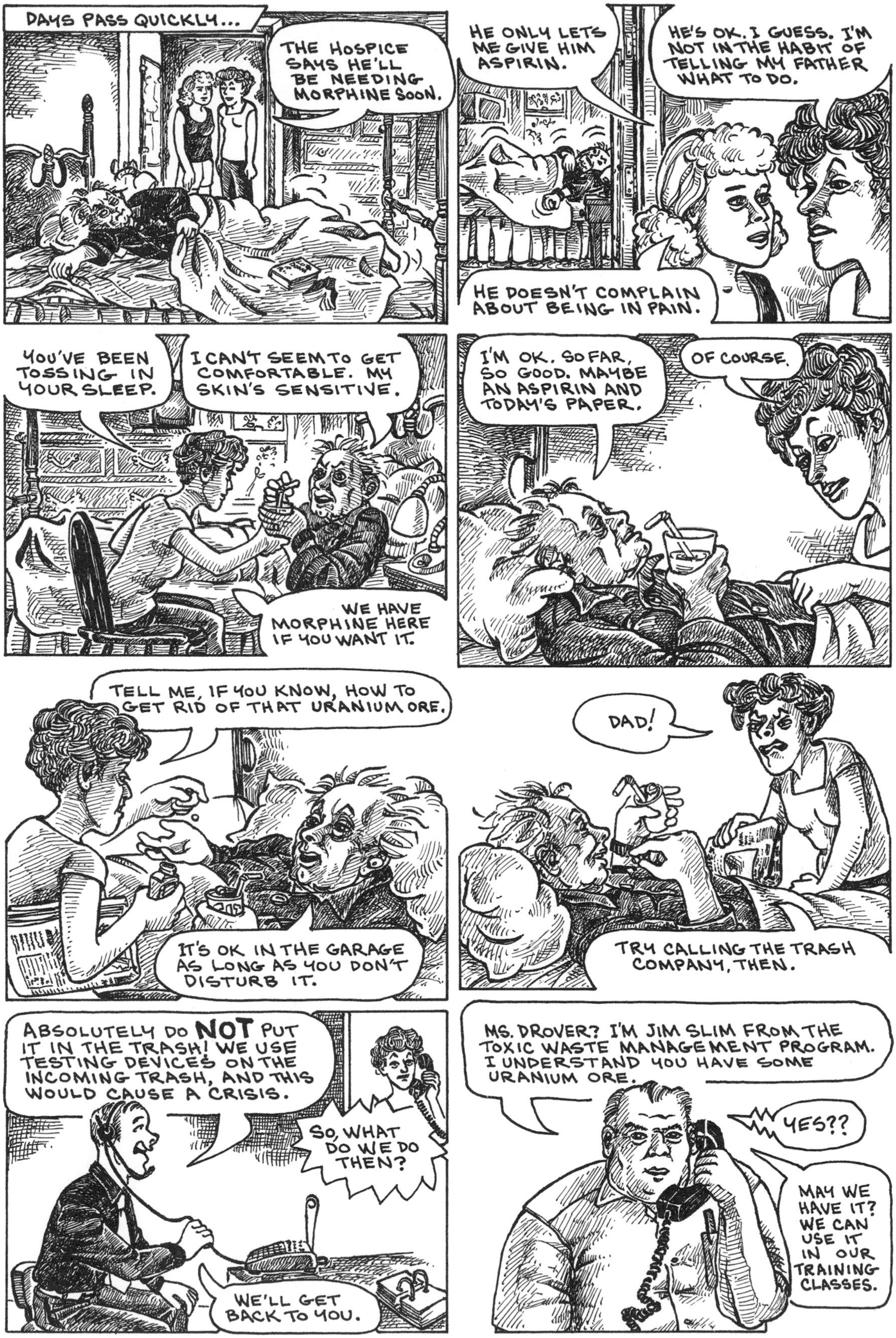
DAYS PASS QUICKLY...
THE HOSPICE SAYS HE'LL BE NEEDING MORPHINE SOON.
HE ONLY LETS ME GIVE HIM ASPIRIN.
HE'S OK, I GUESS. I'M NOT IN THE HABIT OF TELLING MY FATHER WHAT TO DO.
HE DOESN'T COMPLAIN ABOUT BEING IN PAIN.
YOU'VE BEEN TOSSING IN YOUR SLEEP.
I CAN'T SEEM TO GET COMFORTABLE. MY SKIN'S SENSITIVE.
WE HAVE MORPHINE HERE IF YOU WANT IT.
I'M OK. SO FAR, SO GOOD. MAYBE AN ASPIRIN AND TODAY'S PAPER.
OF COURSE.
TELL ME, IF YOU KNOW, HOW TO GET RID OF THAT URANIUM ORE.
IT'S OK IN THE GARAGE AS LONG AS YOU DON'T DISTURB IT.
DAD!
TRY CALLING THE TRASH COMPANY, THEN.
ABSOLUTELY DO NOT PUT IT IN THE TRASH! WE USE TESTING DEVICES ON THE INCOMING TRASH, AND THIS WOULD CAUSE A CRISIS.
SO, WHAT DO WE DO THEN?
WE'LL GET BACK TO YOU.
MS. DROVER? I'M JIM SLIM FROM THE TOXIC WASTE MANAGEMENT PROGRAM. I UNDERSTAND YOU HAVE SOME URANIUM ORE.
YES??
MAY WE HAVE IT? WE CAN USE IT IN OUR TRAINING CLASSES.

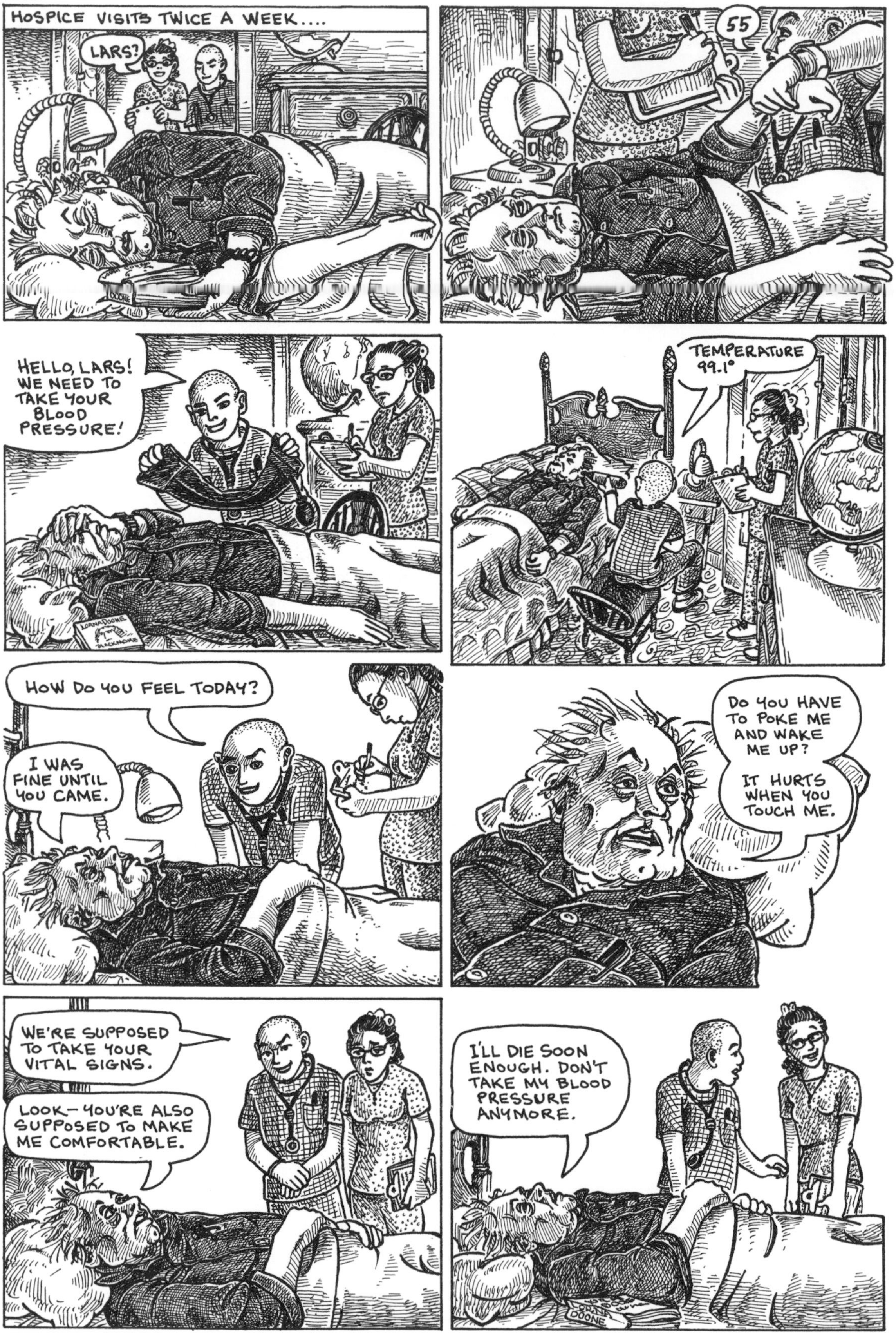
HOSPICE VISITS TWICE A WEEK....
LARS?
55
HELLO, LARS! WE NEED TO TAKE YOUR BLOOD PRESSURE!
TEMPERATURE 99.1°
HOW DO YOU FEEL TODAY?
I WAS FINE UNTIL YOU CAME.
DO YOU HAVE TO POKE ME AND WAKE ME UP?
IT HURTS WHEN YOU TOUCH ME.
WE'RE SUPPOSED TO TAKE YOUR VITAL SIGNS.
LOOK– YOU'RE ALSO SUPPOSED TO MAKE ME COMFORTABLE.
I'LL DIE SOON ENOUGH. DON'T TAKE MY BLOOD PRESSURE ANYMORE.

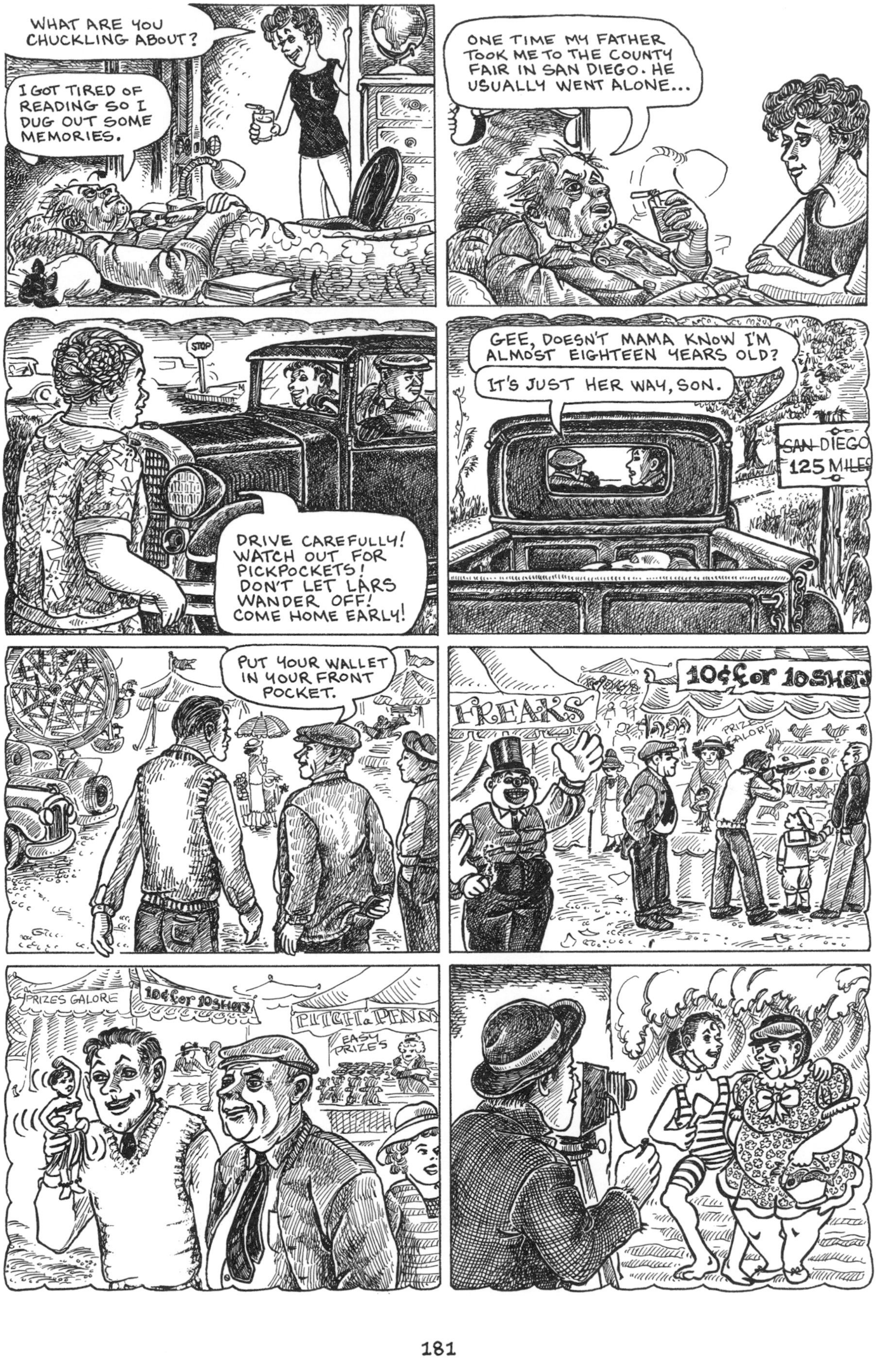
WHAT ARE YOU CHUCKLING ABOUT?
I GOT TIRED OF READING SO I DUG OUT SOME MEMORIES.
ONE TIME MY FATHER TOOK ME TO THE COUNTY FAIR IN SAN DIEGO. HE USUALLY WENT ALONE...
STOP
DRIVE CAREFULLY! WATCH OUT FOR PICKPOCKETS! DON'T LET LARS WANDER OFF! COME HOME EARLY!
GEE, DOESN'T MAMA KNOW I'M ALMOST EIGHTEEN YEARS OLD?
IT'S JUST HER WAY, SON.
SAN DIEGO 125 MILES
PUT YOUR WALLET IN YOUR FRONT POCKET.
10¢ for 10 SHOTS
FREAKS
PRIZES GALORE
PRIZES GALORE
10¢ for 10 SHOTS
PITCH a PENNY
EASY PRIZE'S

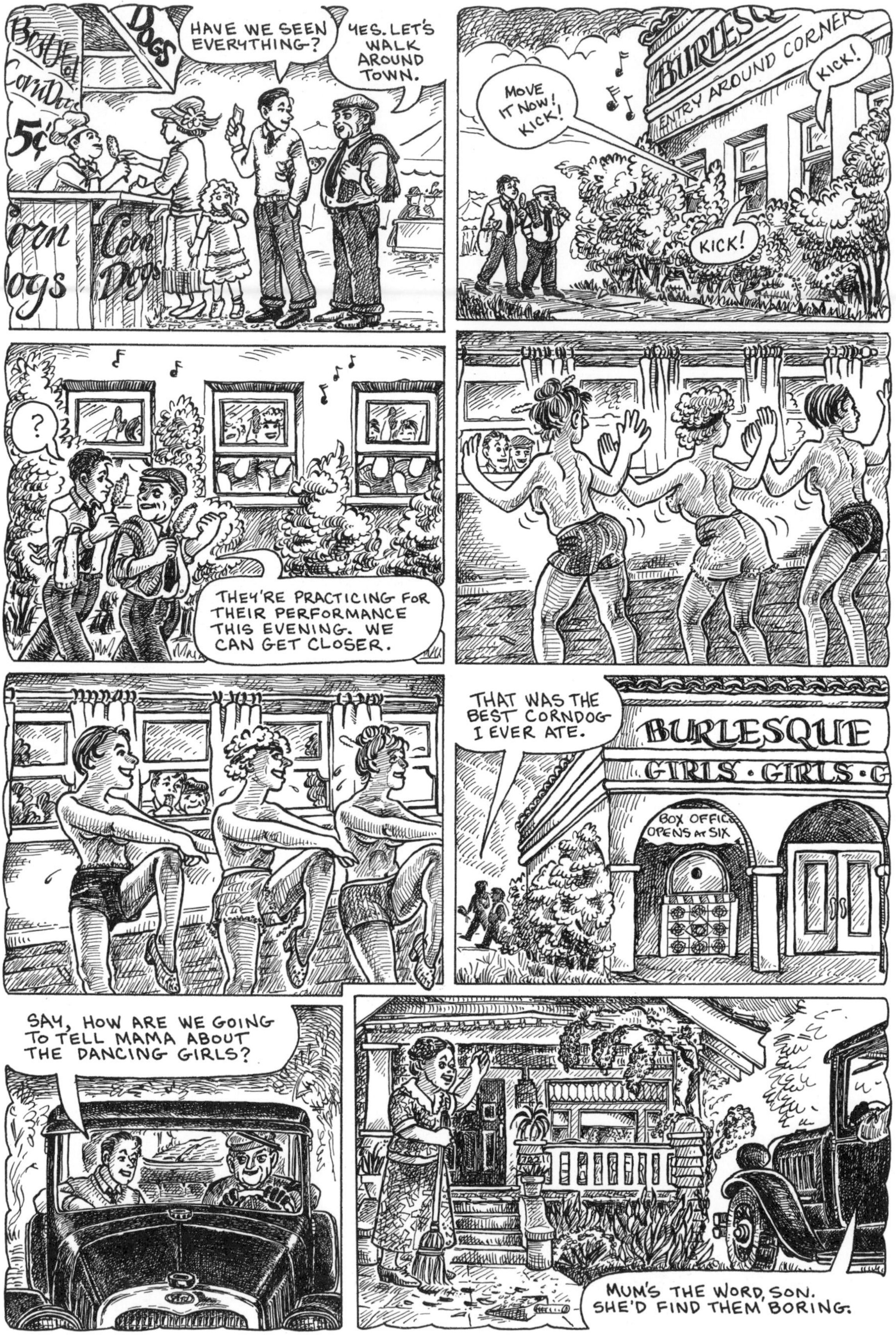
DOGS
5¢
HAVE WE SEEN EVERYTHING?
YES. LET'S WALK AROUND TOWN.
BURLESQ
ENTRY AROUND CORNER
MOVE IT NOW! KICK!
KICK!
KICK!
?
THEY'RE PRACTICING FOR THEIR PERFORMANCE THIS EVENING. WE CAN GET CLOSER.
THAT WAS THE BEST CORNDOG I EVER ATE.
BURLESQUE
GIRLS · GIRLS · G
BOX OFFIC OPENS AT SIX
SAY, HOW ARE WE GOING TO TELL MAMA ABOUT THE DANCING GIRLS?
MUM'S THE WORD, SON. SHE'D FIND THEM BORING.

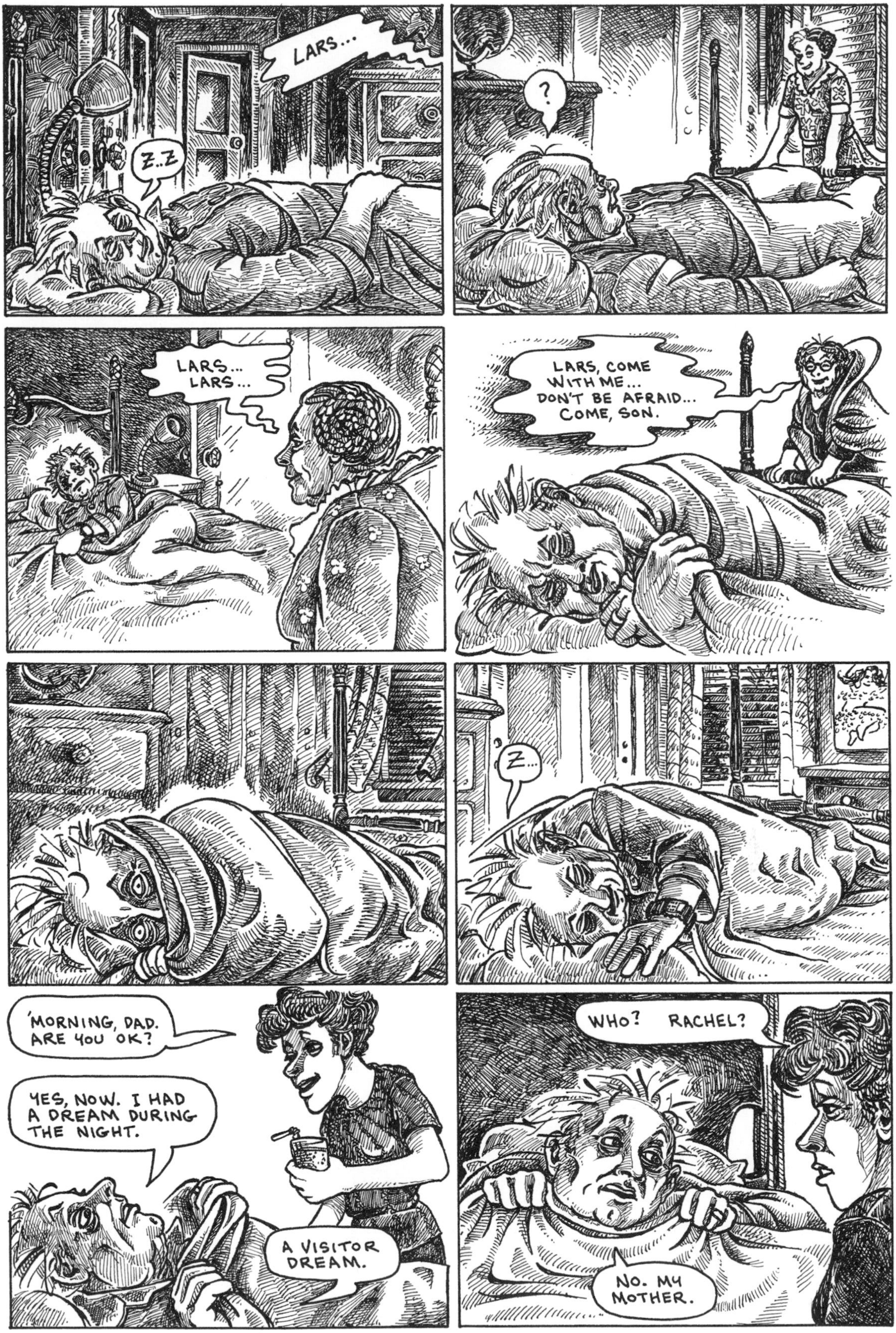
LARS...
Z..Z
?
LARS...
LARS...
LARS, COME WITH ME... DON'T BE AFRAID... COME, SON.
Z...
'MORNING, DAD. ARE YOU OK?
YES, NOW. I HAD A DREAM DURING THE NIGHT.
A VISITOR DREAM.
WHO? RACHEL?
NO. MY MOTHER.

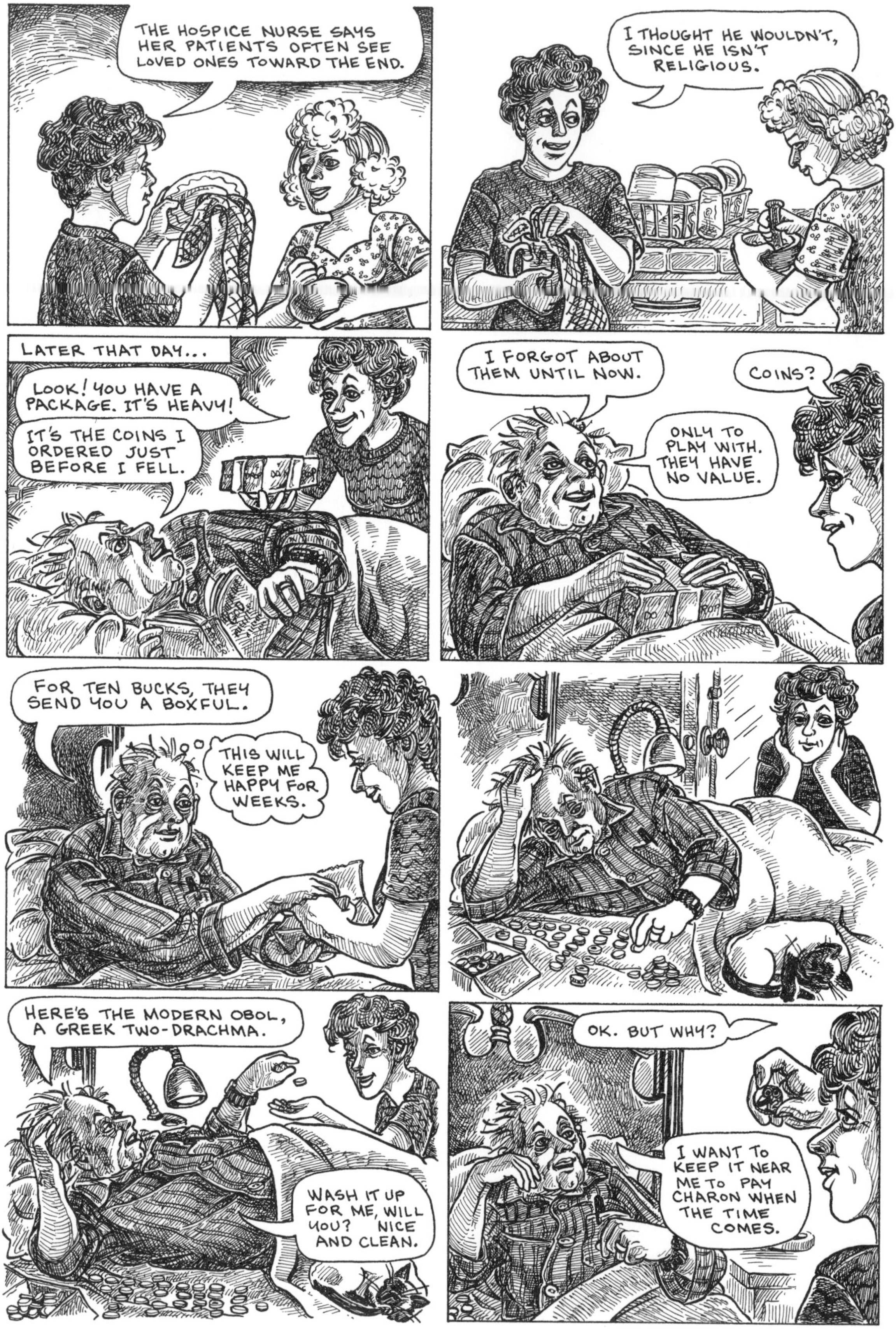
THE HOSPICE NURSE SAYS HER PATIENTS OFTEN SEE LOVED ONES TOWARD THE END.
I THOUGHT HE WOULDN'T, SINCE HE ISN'T RELIGIOUS.
LATER THAT DAY...
LOOK! YOU HAVE A PACKAGE. IT'S HEAVY!
IT'S THE COINS I ORDERED JUST BEFORE I FELL.
I FORGOT ABOUT THEM UNTIL NOW.
COINS?
ONLY TO PLAY WITH. THEY HAVE NO VALUE.
FOR TEN BUCKS, THEY SEND YOU A BOXFUL.
THIS WILL KEEP ME HAPPY FOR WEEKS.
HERE'S THE MODERN OBOL, A GREEK TWO-DRACHMA.
WASH IT UP FOR ME, WILL YOU? NICE AND CLEAN.
OK. BUT WHY?
I WANT TO KEEP IT NEAR ME TO PAY CHARON WHEN THE TIME COMES.

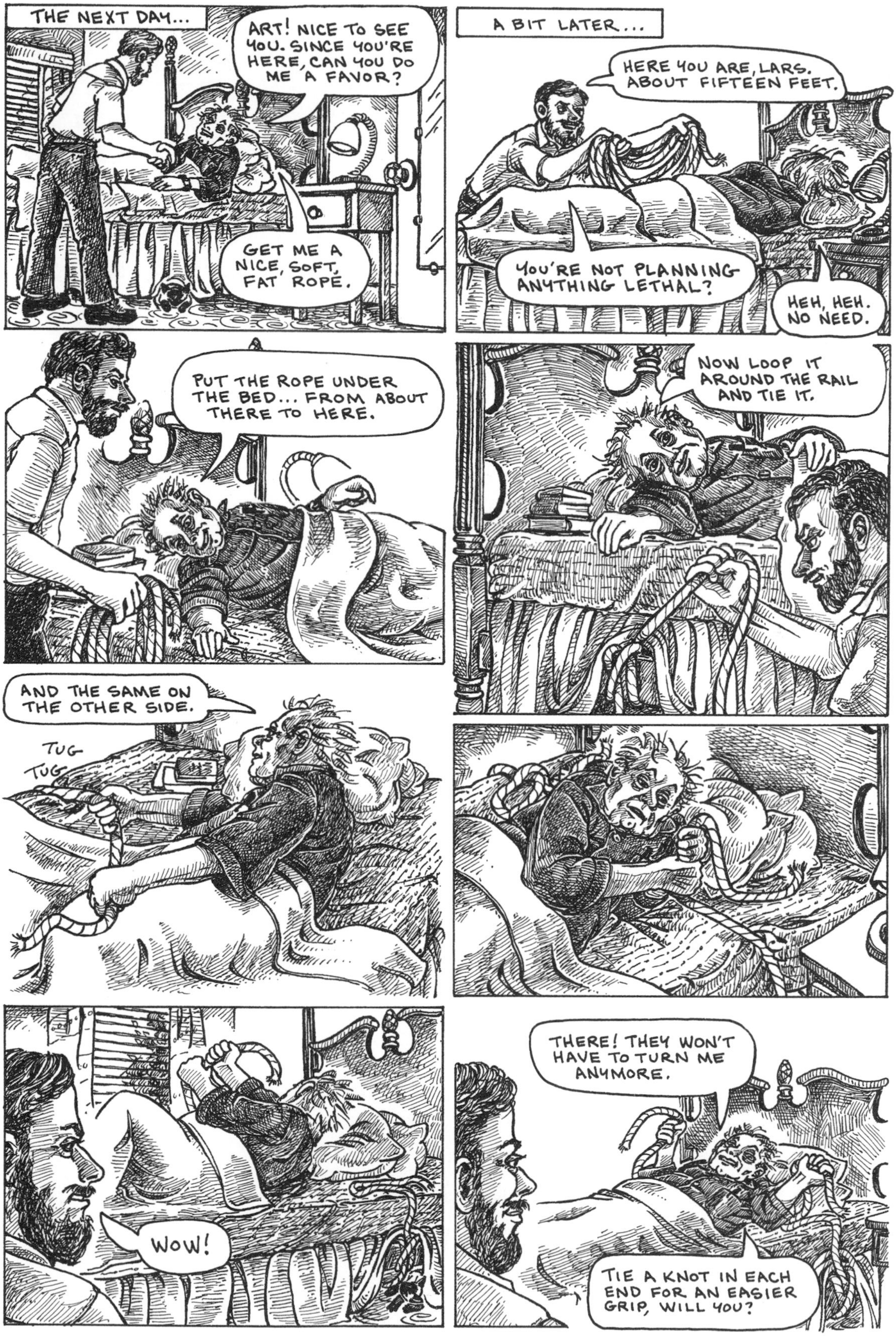
THE NEXT DAY...
ART! NICE TO SEE YOU. SINCE YOU'RE HERE, CAN YOU DO ME A FAVOR?
GET ME A NICE, SOFT, FAT ROPE.
A BIT LATER...
HERE YOU ARE, LARS. ABOUT FIFTEEN FEET.
YOU'RE NOT PLANNING ANYTHING LETHAL?
HEH, HEH. NO NEED.
PUT THE ROPE UNDER THE BED... FROM ABOUT THERE TO HERE.
NOW LOOP IT AROUND THE RAIL AND TIE IT.
AND THE SAME ON THE OTHER SIDE.
TUG TUG
WOW!
THERE! THEY WON'T HAVE TO TURN ME ANYMORE.
TIE A KNOT IN EACH END FOR AN EASIER GRIP, WILL YOU?

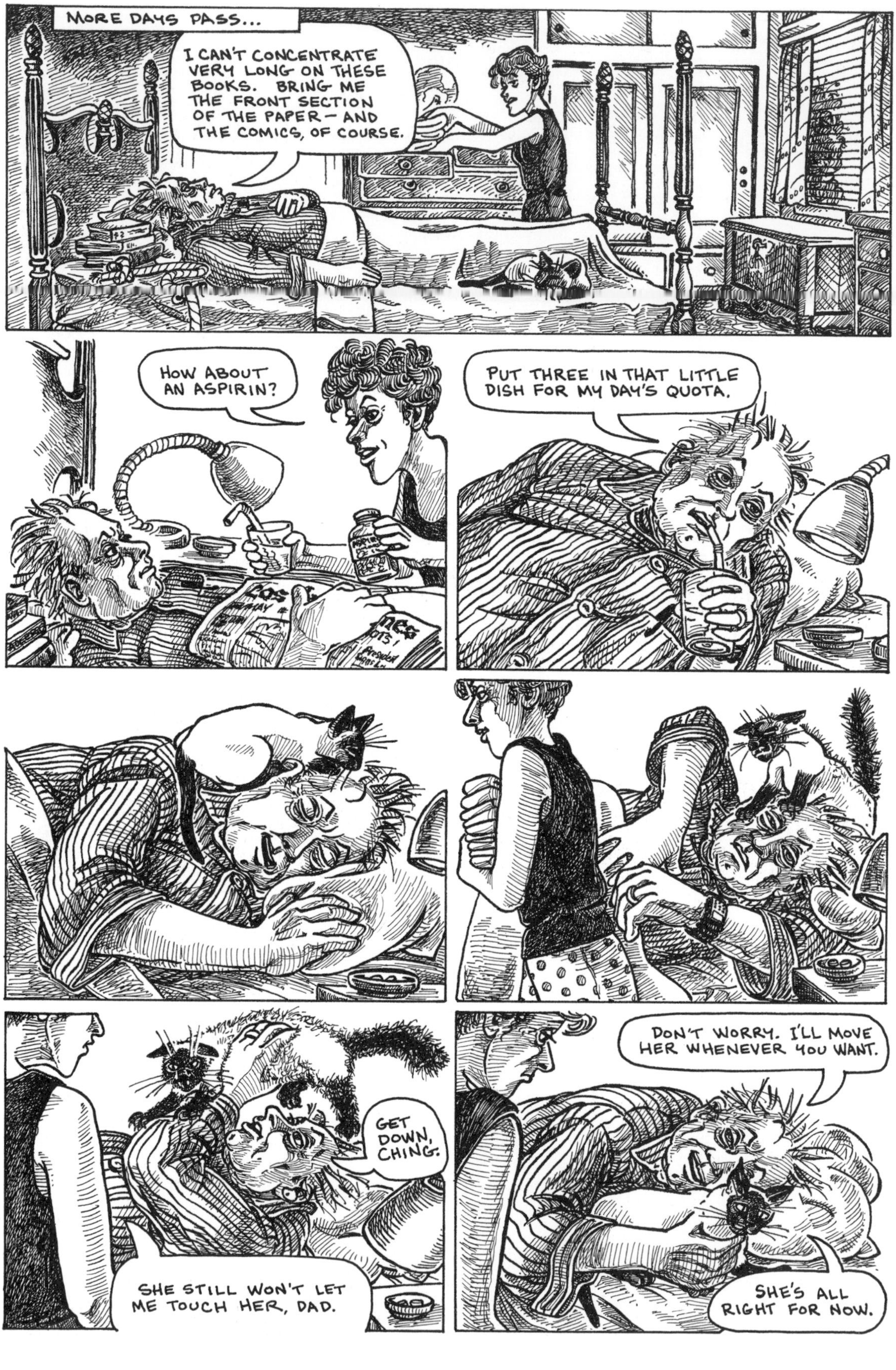
MORE DAYS PASS...
I CAN'T CONCENTRATE VERY LONG ON THESE BOOKS. BRING ME THE FRONT SECTION OF THE PAPER—AND THE COMICS, OF COURSE.
HOW ABOUT AN ASPIRIN?
PUT THREE IN THAT LITTLE DISH FOR MY DAY'S QUOTA.
GET DOWN, CHING.
SHE STILL WON'T LET ME TOUCH HER, DAD.
DON'T WORRY. I'LL MOVE HER WHENEVER YOU WANT.
SHE'S ALL RIGHT FOR NOW.

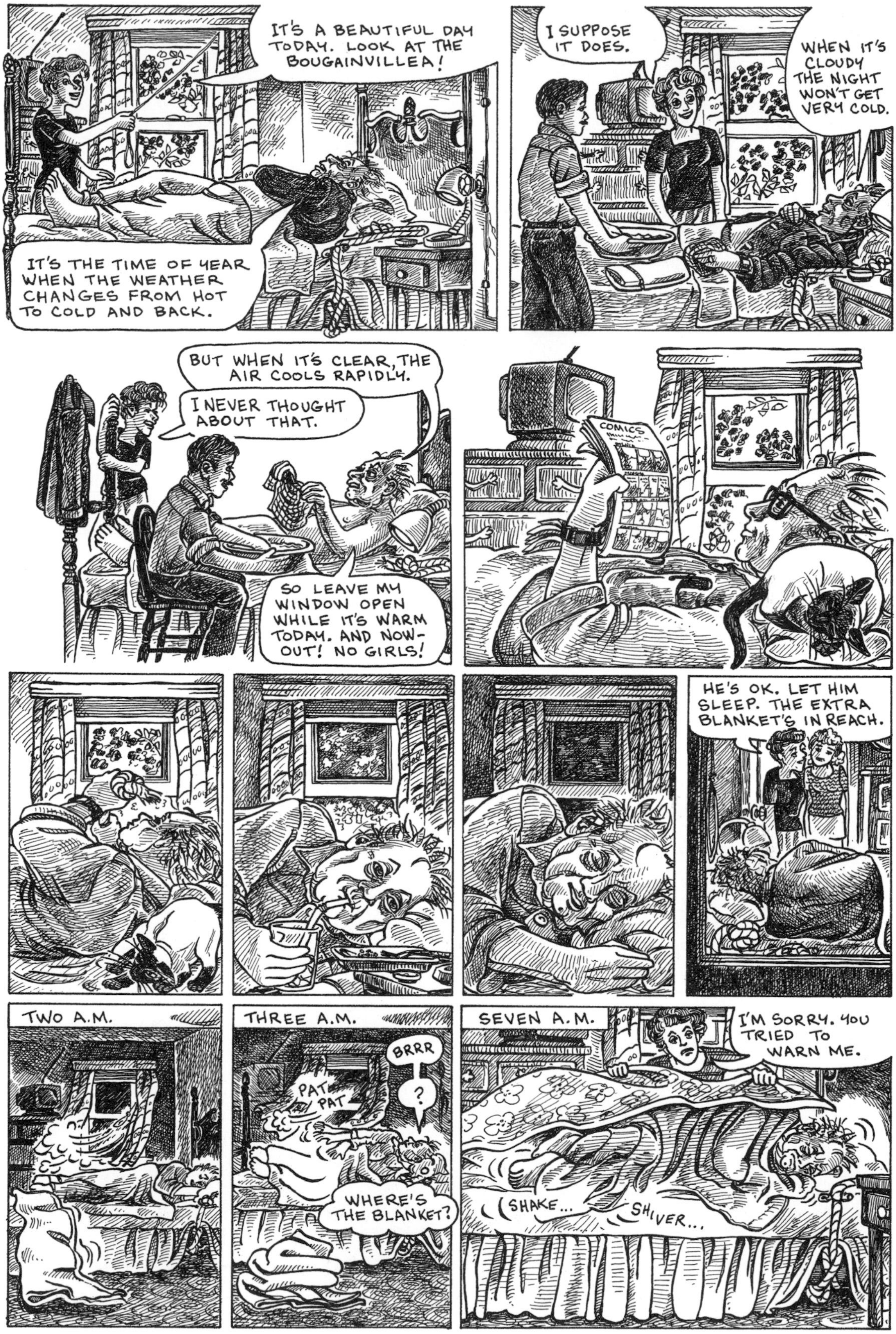
IT'S A BEAUTIFUL DAY TODAY. LOOK AT THE BOUGAINVILLEA!
IT'S THE TIME OF YEAR WHEN THE WEATHER CHANGES FROM HOT TO COLD AND BACK.
I SUPPOSE IT DOES.
WHEN IT'S CLOUDY THE NIGHT WON'T GET VERY COLD.
BUT WHEN IT'S CLEAR, THE AIR COOLS RAPIDLY.
I NEVER THOUGHT ABOUT THAT.
SO LEAVE MY WINDOW OPEN WHILE IT'S WARM TODAY. AND NOW- OUT! NO GIRLS!
COMICS
HE'S OK. LET HIM SLEEP. THE EXTRA BLANKET'S IN REACH.
TWO A.M.
THREE A.M.
BRRR
PAT PAT
?
WHERE'S THE BLANKET?
SEVEN A.M.
I'M SORRY. YOU TRIED TO WARN ME.
SHAKE...
SHIVER...

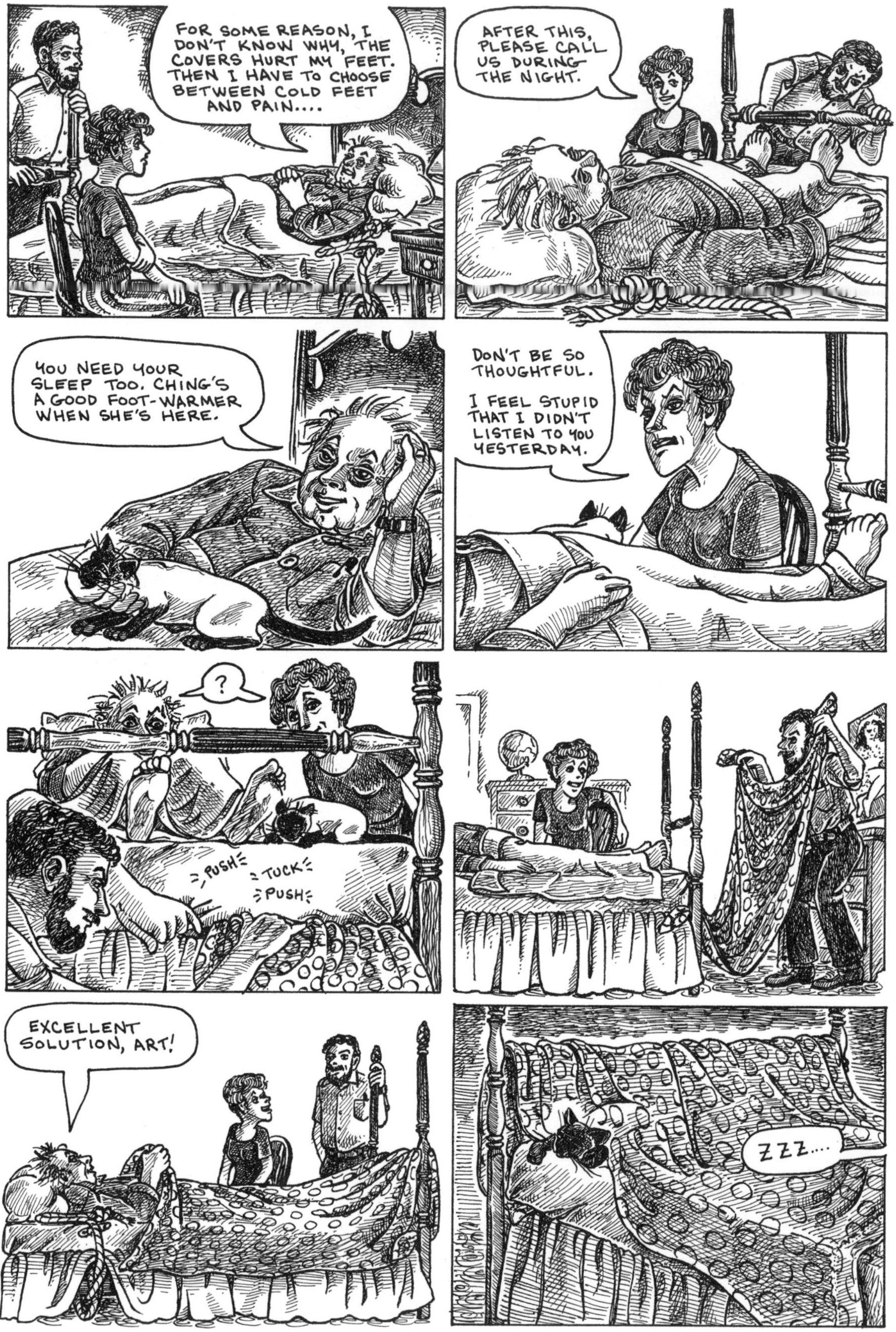
FOR SOME REASON, I DON'T KNOW WHY, THE COVERS HURT MY FEET. THEN I HAVE TO CHOOSE BETWEEN COLD FEET AND PAIN....
AFTER THIS, PLEASE CALL US DURING THE NIGHT.
YOU NEED YOUR SLEEP TOO. CHING'S A GOOD FOOT-WARMER WHEN SHE'S HERE.
DON'T BE SO THOUGHTFUL.
I FEEL STUPID THAT I DIDN'T LISTEN TO YOU YESTERDAY.
?
PUSH
TUCK
PUSH
EXCELLENT SOLUTION, ART!
ZZZ....

I'VE BEEN DAYDREAMING. THINKING OLD THOUGHTS.

WHAT ABOUT?

I USED TO HIKE IN THE SAN GABRIEL MOUNTAINS WITH FRIENDS EVERY WEEKEND. WE WERE ABOUT NINETEEN OR TWENTY YEARS OLD.

ON FRIDAYS, AFTER WORK, WE'D DRIVE TO ALTADENA AND START WALKING.

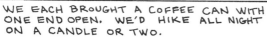

LATER, WHEN IT GOT DARK, WE'D MAKE "BUG" LAMPS.

YOU DIDN'T USE FLASHLIGHTS?

NO, WE COULDN'T AFFORD THE BATTERIES.

WE EACH BROUGHT A COFFEE CAN WITH ONE END OPEN. WE'D HIKE ALL NIGHT ON A CANDLE OR TWO.

YES! THAT'S IT! HANG IT THERE SO I'LL BE REMINDED OF THOSE STAR-FILLED TREKS.

LAURA?

YES, DAD?

YOU'RE INVENTIVE, LIKE YOUR MOTHER.

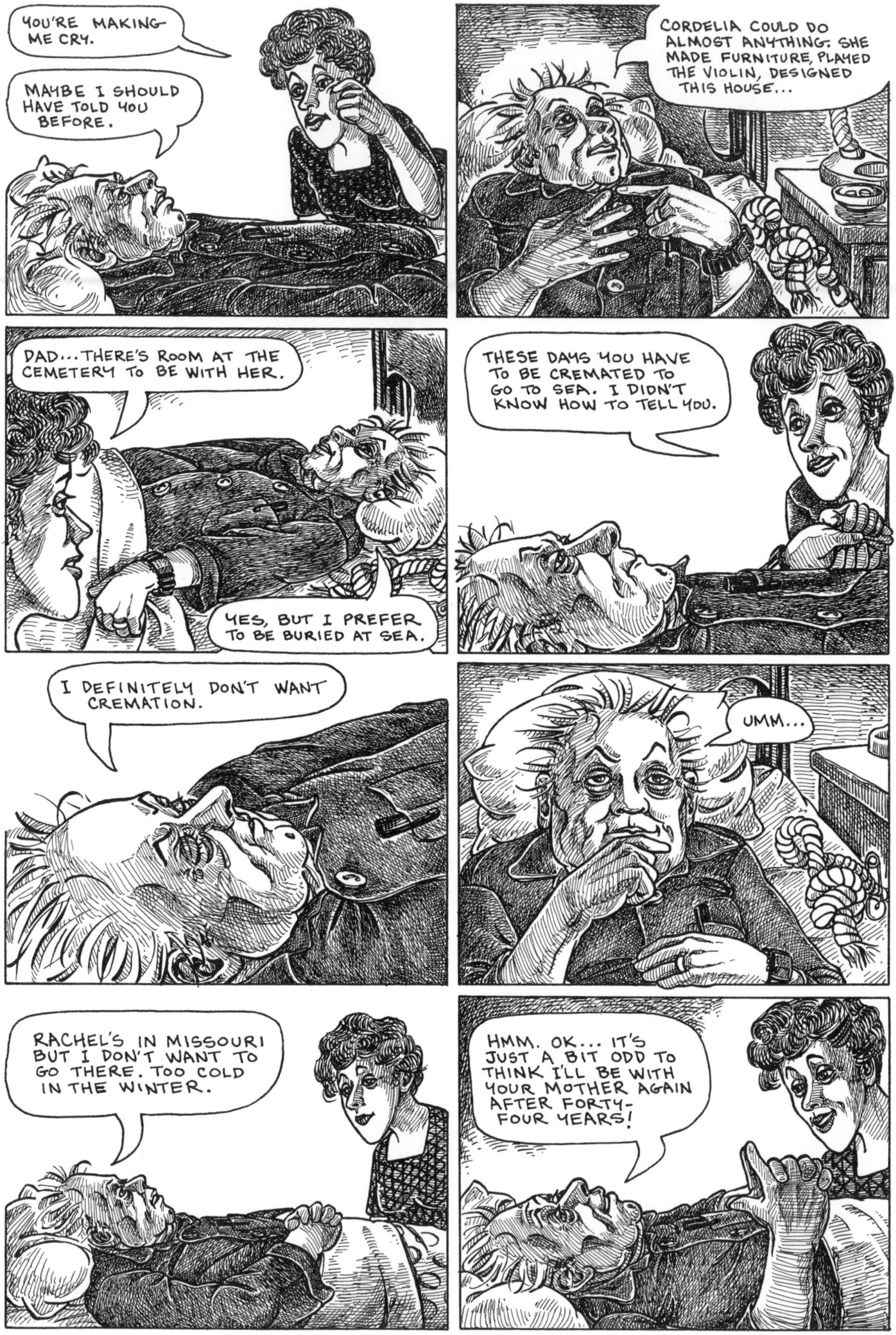
YOU'RE MAKING ME CRY.
MAYBE I SHOULD HAVE TOLD YOU BEFORE.
CORDELIA COULD DO ALMOST ANYTHING. SHE MADE FURNITURE, PLAYED THE VIOLIN, DESIGNED THIS HOUSE...
DAD... THERE'S ROOM AT THE CEMETERY TO BE WITH HER.
YES, BUT I PREFER TO BE BURIED AT SEA.
THESE DAYS YOU HAVE TO BE CREMATED TO GO TO SEA. I DIDN'T KNOW HOW TO TELL YOU.
I DEFINITELY DON'T WANT CREMATION.
UMM...
RACHEL'S IN MISSOURI BUT I DON'T WANT TO GO THERE. TOO COLD IN THE WINTER.
HMM. OK... IT'S JUST A BIT ODD TO THINK I'LL BE WITH YOUR MOTHER AGAIN AFTER FORTY-FOUR YEARS!

14

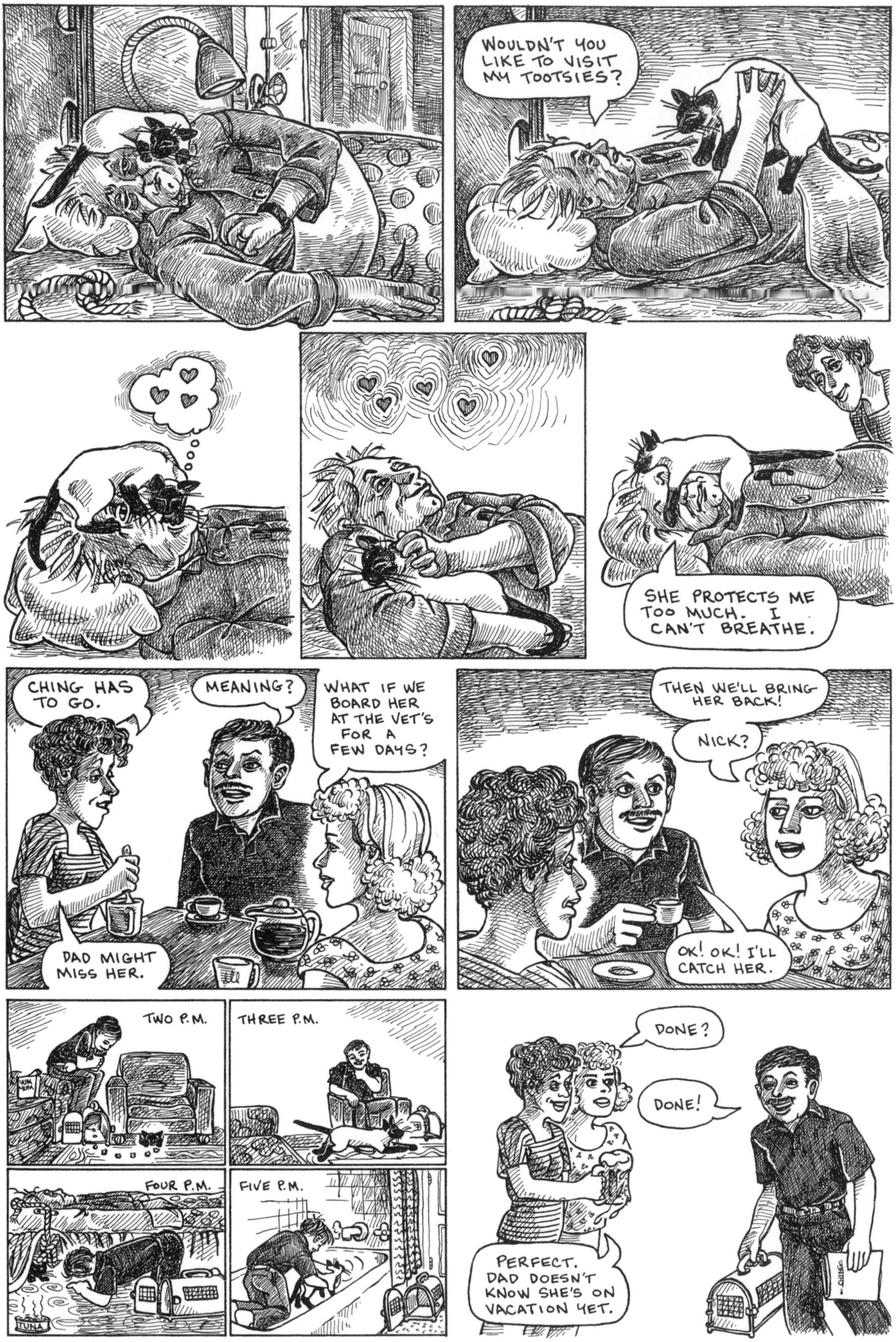
WOULDN'T YOU LIKE TO VISIT MY TOOTSIES?
SHE PROTECTS ME TOO MUCH. I CAN'T BREATHE.
CHING HAS TO GO.
MEANING?
WHAT IF WE BOARD HER AT THE VET'S FOR A FEW DAYS?
DAD MIGHT MISS HER.
THEN WE'LL BRING HER BACK!
NICK?
OK! OK! I'LL CATCH HER.
TWO P.M.
THREE P.M.
FOUR P.M.
TUNA
FIVE P.M.
DONE?
DONE!
PERFECT. DAD DOESN'T KNOW SHE'S ON VACATION YET.

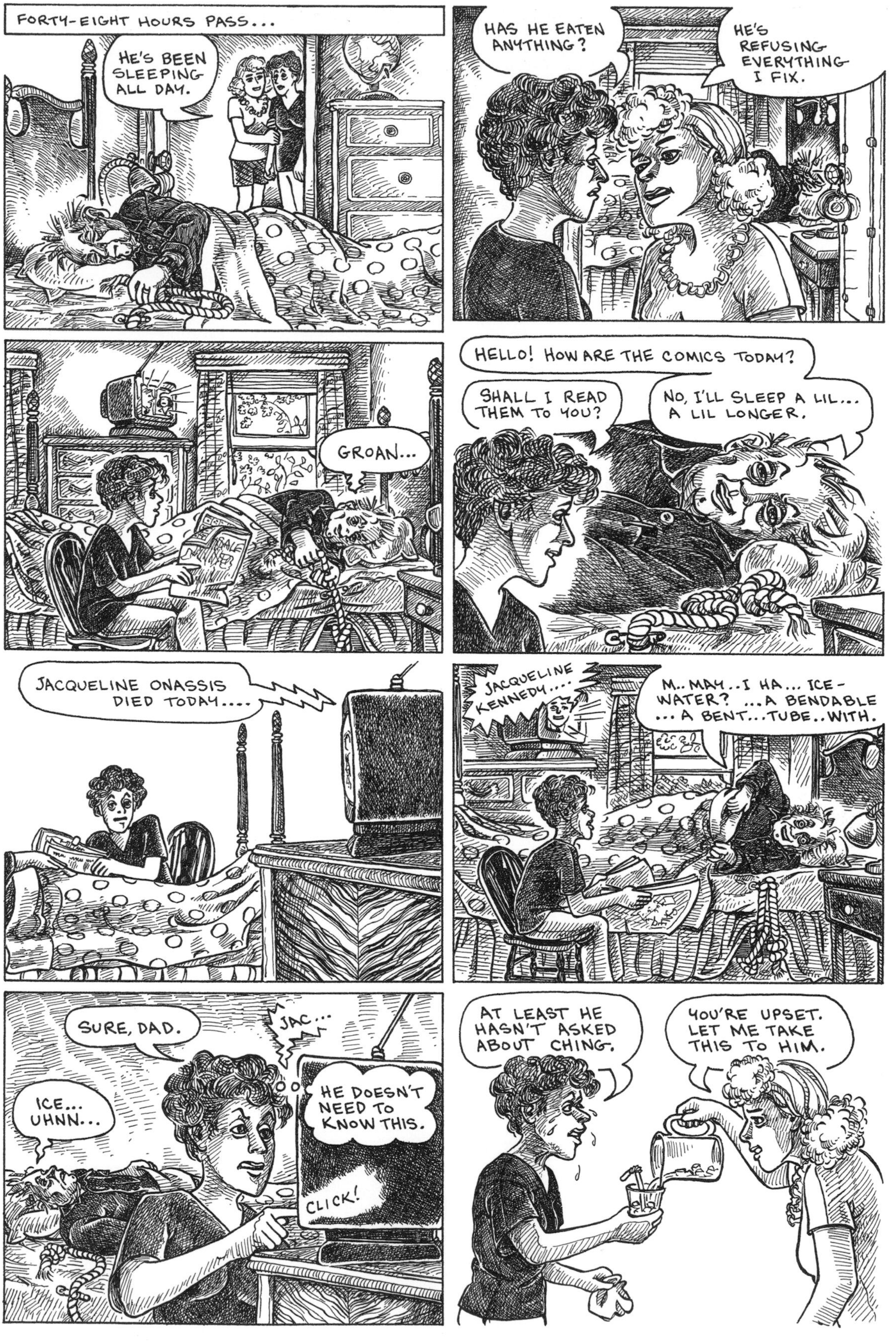
FORTY-EIGHT HOURS PASS...
HE'S BEEN SLEEPING ALL DAY.
HAS HE EATEN ANYTHING?
HE'S REFUSING EVERYTHING I FIX.
GROAN...
HELLO! HOW ARE THE COMICS TODAY?
SHALL I READ THEM TO YOU?
NO, I'LL SLEEP A LIL... A LIL LONGER.
JACQUELINE ONASSIS DIED TODAY....
JACQUELINE KENNEDY....
M.. MAY.. I HA... ICE-WATER? ...A BENDABLE ... A BENT... TUBE.. WITH.
SURE, DAD.
JAC...
ICE... UHNN...
HE DOESN'T NEED TO KNOW THIS.
CLICK!
AT LEAST HE HASN'T ASKED ABOUT CHING.
YOU'RE UPSET. LET ME TAKE THIS TO HIM.

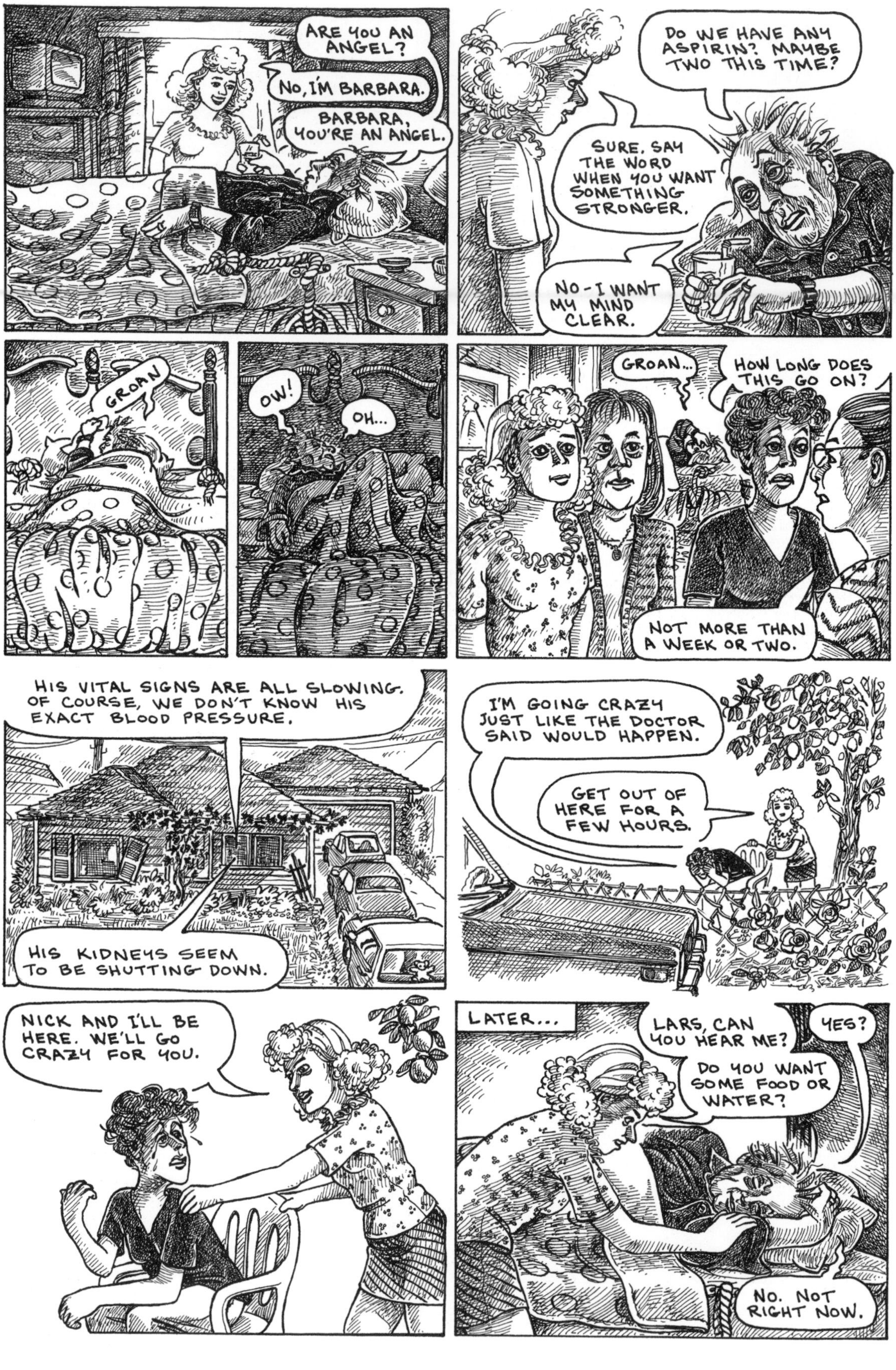
ARE YOU AN ANGEL?
NO, I'M BARBARA.
BARBARA, YOU'RE AN ANGEL.
DO WE HAVE ANY ASPIRIN? MAYBE TWO THIS TIME?
SURE. SAY THE WORD WHEN YOU WANT SOMETHING STRONGER.
NO - I WANT MY MIND CLEAR.
GROAN
OW!
OH...
GROAN...
HOW LONG DOES THIS GO ON?
NOT MORE THAN A WEEK OR TWO.
HIS VITAL SIGNS ARE ALL SLOWING. OF COURSE, WE DON'T KNOW HIS EXACT BLOOD PRESSURE.
HIS KIDNEYS SEEM TO BE SHUTTING DOWN.
I'M GOING CRAZY JUST LIKE THE DOCTOR SAID WOULD HAPPEN.
GET OUT OF HERE FOR A FEW HOURS.
NICK AND I'LL BE HERE. WE'LL GO CRAZY FOR YOU.
LATER...
LARS, CAN YOU HEAR ME?
YES?
DO YOU WANT SOME FOOD OR WATER?
NO. NOT RIGHT NOW.

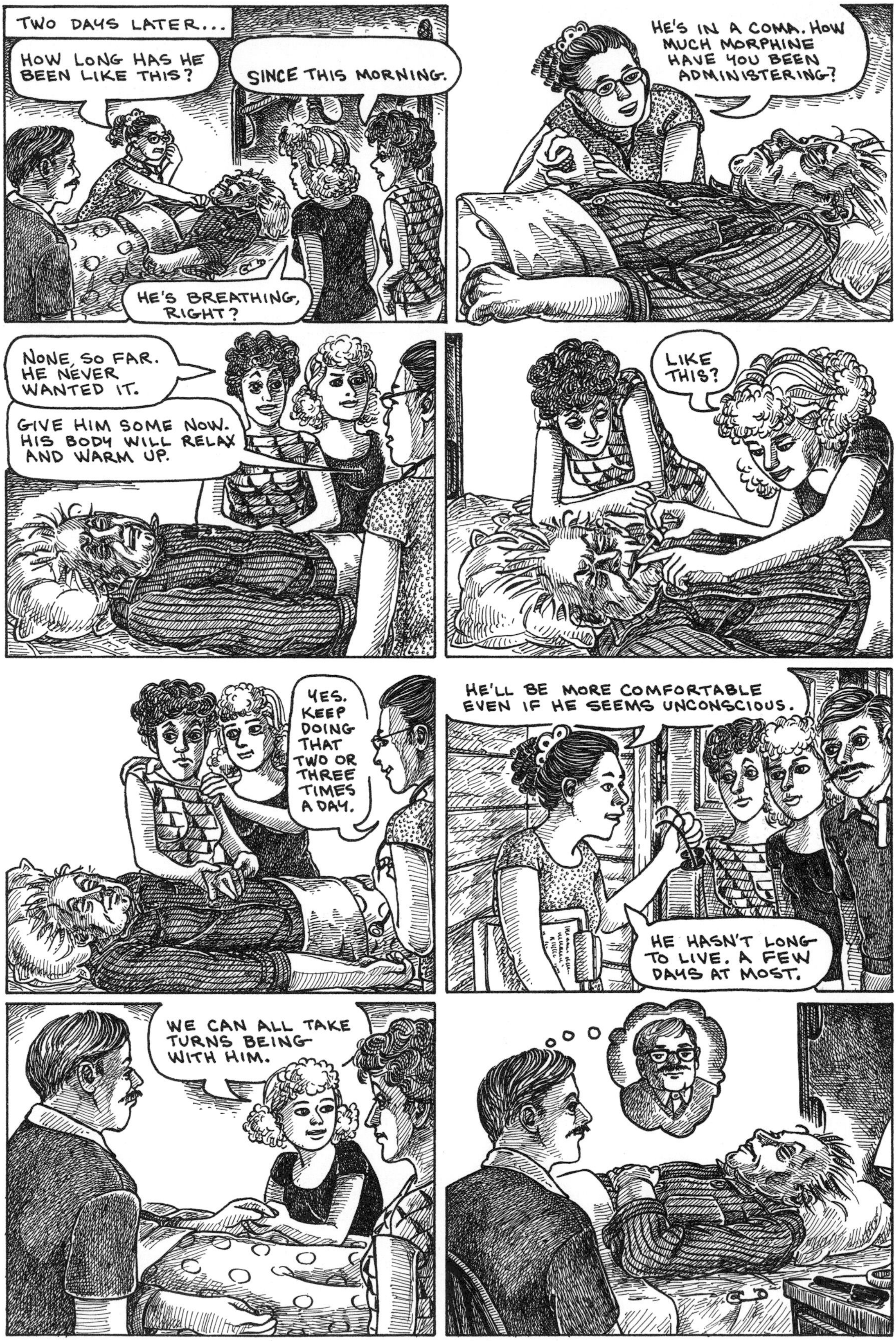
TWO DAYS LATER...
HOW LONG HAS HE BEEN LIKE THIS?
SINCE THIS MORNING.
HE'S BREATHING, RIGHT?
HE'S IN A COMA. HOW MUCH MORPHINE HAVE YOU BEEN ADMINISTERING?
NONE, SO FAR. HE NEVER WANTED IT.
GIVE HIM SOME NOW. HIS BODY WILL RELAX AND WARM UP.
LIKE THIS?
YES. KEEP DOING THAT TWO OR THREE TIMES A DAY.
HE'LL BE MORE COMFORTABLE EVEN IF HE SEEMS UNCONSCIOUS.
HE HASN'T LONG TO LIVE. A FEW DAYS AT MOST.
WE CAN ALL TAKE TURNS BEING WITH HIM.

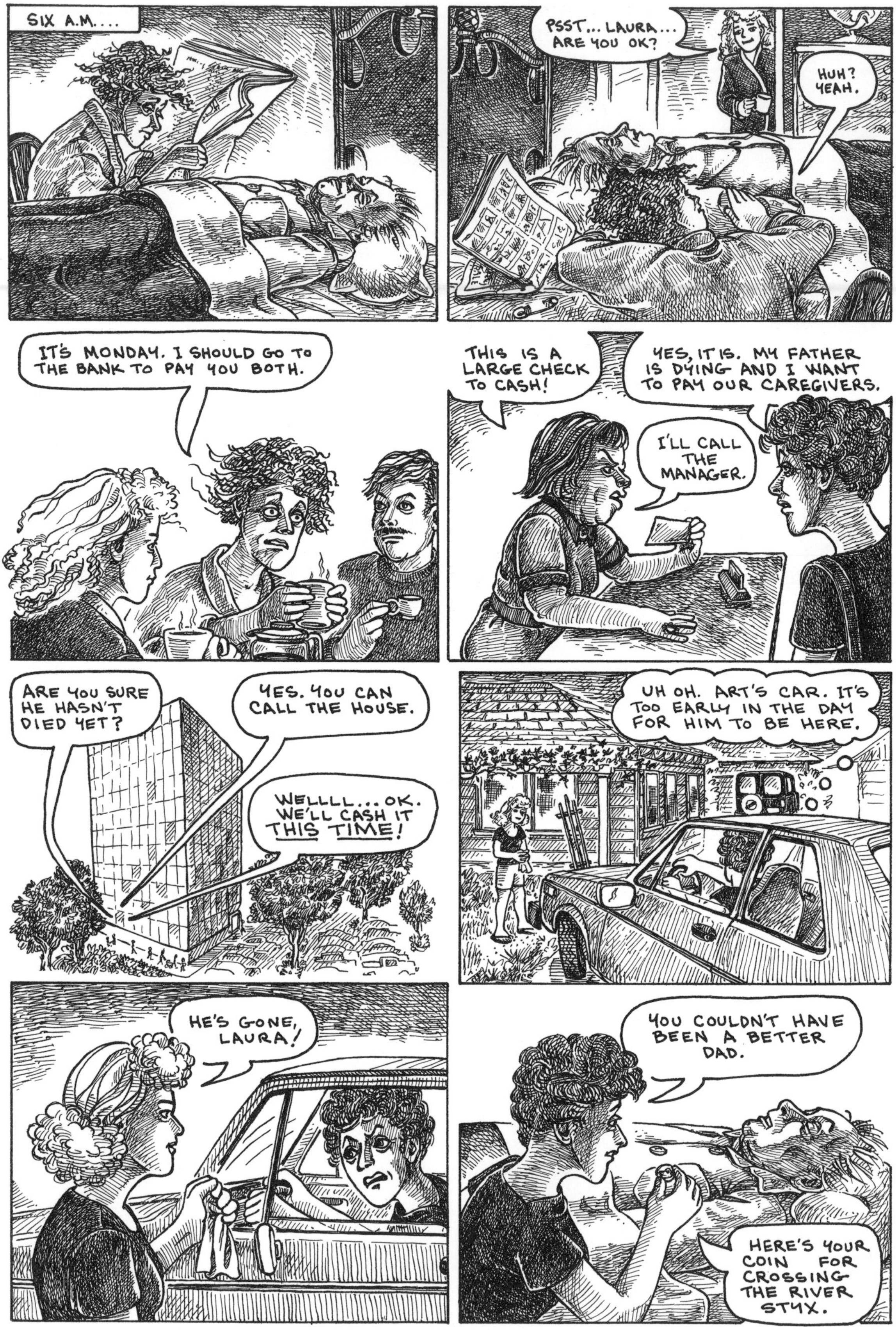
SIX A.M....
PSST... LAURA... ARE YOU OK?
HUH? YEAH.
IT'S MONDAY. I SHOULD GO TO THE BANK TO PAY YOU BOTH.
THIS IS A LARGE CHECK TO CASH!
YES, IT IS. MY FATHER IS DYING AND I WANT TO PAY OUR CAREGIVERS.
I'LL CALL THE MANAGER.
ARE YOU SURE HE HASN'T DIED YET?
YES. YOU CAN CALL THE HOUSE.
WELLLL... OK. WE'LL CASH IT THIS TIME!
UH OH. ART'S CAR. IT'S TOO EARLY IN THE DAY FOR HIM TO BE HERE.
HE'S GONE, LAURA!
YOU COULDN'T HAVE BEEN A BETTER DAD.
HERE'S YOUR COIN FOR CROSSING THE RIVER STYX.

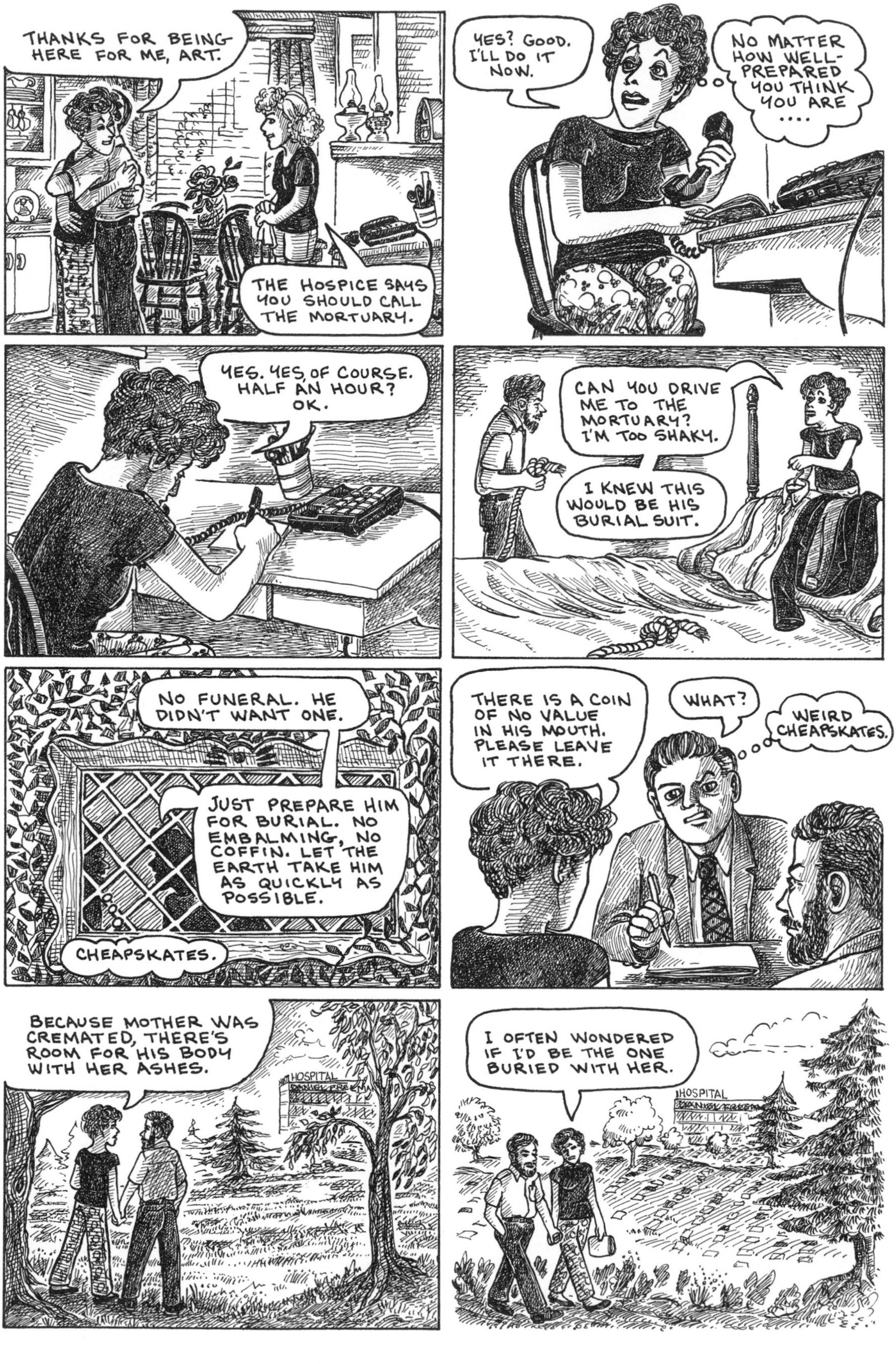
THANKS FOR BEING HERE FOR ME, ART.
THE HOSPICE SAYS YOU SHOULD CALL THE MORTUARY.
YES? GOOD. I'LL DO IT NOW.
NO MATTER HOW WELL-PREPARED YOU THINK YOU ARE ....
YES. YES, OF COURSE. HALF AN HOUR? OK.
CAN YOU DRIVE ME TO THE MORTUARY? I'M TOO SHAKY.
I KNEW THIS WOULD BE HIS BURIAL SUIT.
NO FUNERAL. HE DIDN'T WANT ONE.
JUST PREPARE HIM FOR BURIAL. NO EMBALMING, NO COFFIN. LET THE EARTH TAKE HIM AS QUICKLY AS POSSIBLE.
CHEAPSKATES.
THERE IS A COIN OF NO VALUE IN HIS MOUTH. PLEASE LEAVE IT THERE.
WHAT?
WEIRD CHEAPSKATES.
BECAUSE MOTHER WAS CREMATED, THERE'S ROOM FOR HIS BODY WITH HER ASHES.
HOSPITAL
I OFTEN WONDERED IF I'D BE THE ONE BURIED WITH HER.
HOSPITAL

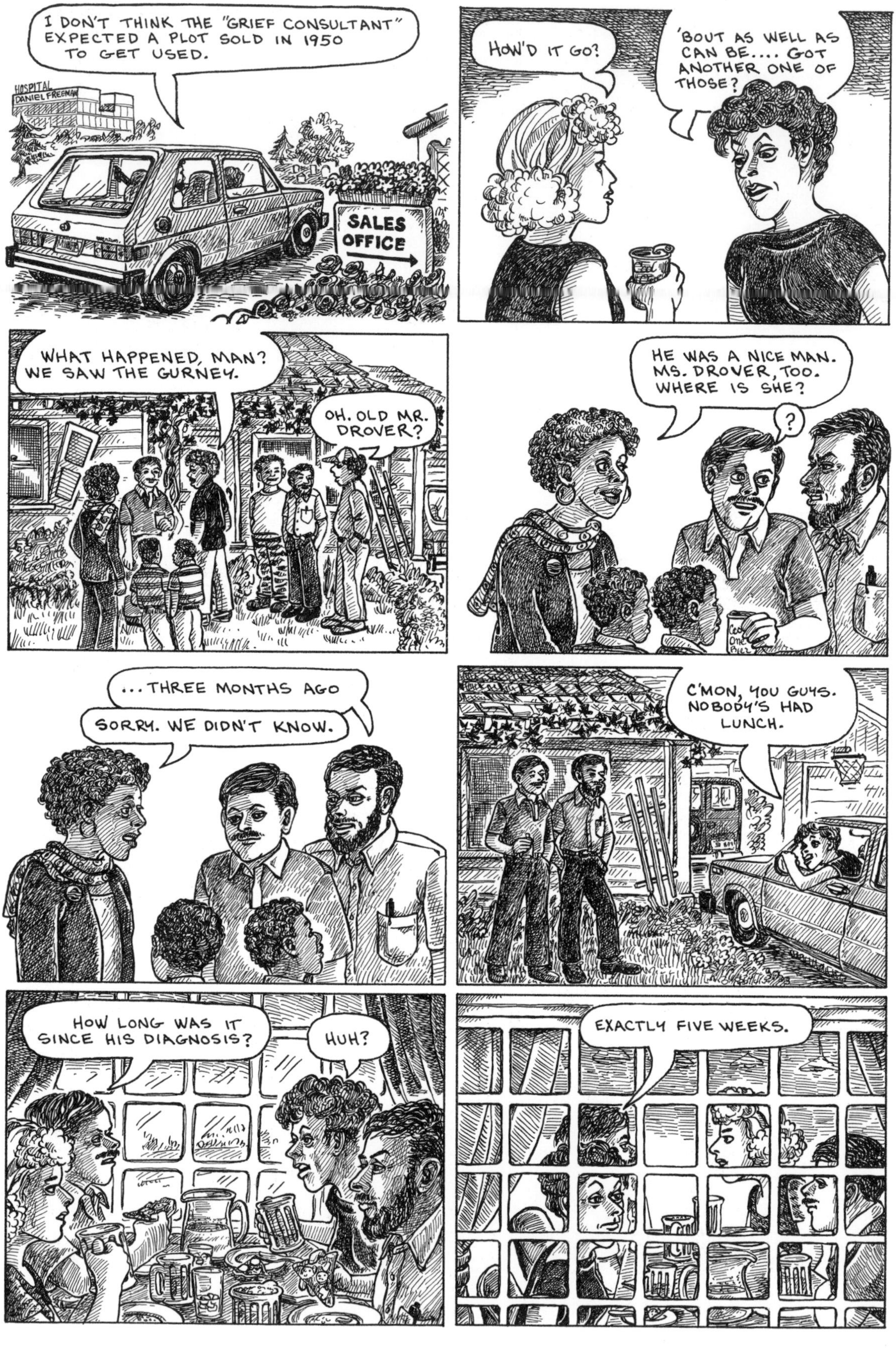
I DON'T THINK THE "GRIEF CONSULTANT" EXPECTED A PLOT SOLD IN 1950 TO GET USED.
HOSPITAL
DANIEL FREEMAN
SALES OFFICE
HOW'D IT GO?
'BOUT AS WELL AS CAN BE.... GOT ANOTHER ONE OF THOSE?
WHAT HAPPENED, MAN? WE SAW THE GURNEY.
OH. OLD MR. DROVER?
HE WAS A NICE MAN. MS. DROVER, TOO. WHERE IS SHE?
?
...THREE MONTHS AGO
SORRY. WE DIDN'T KNOW.
C'MON, YOU GUYS. NOBODY'S HAD LUNCH.
HOW LONG WAS IT SINCE HIS DIAGNOSIS?
HUH?
EXACTLY FIVE WEEKS.

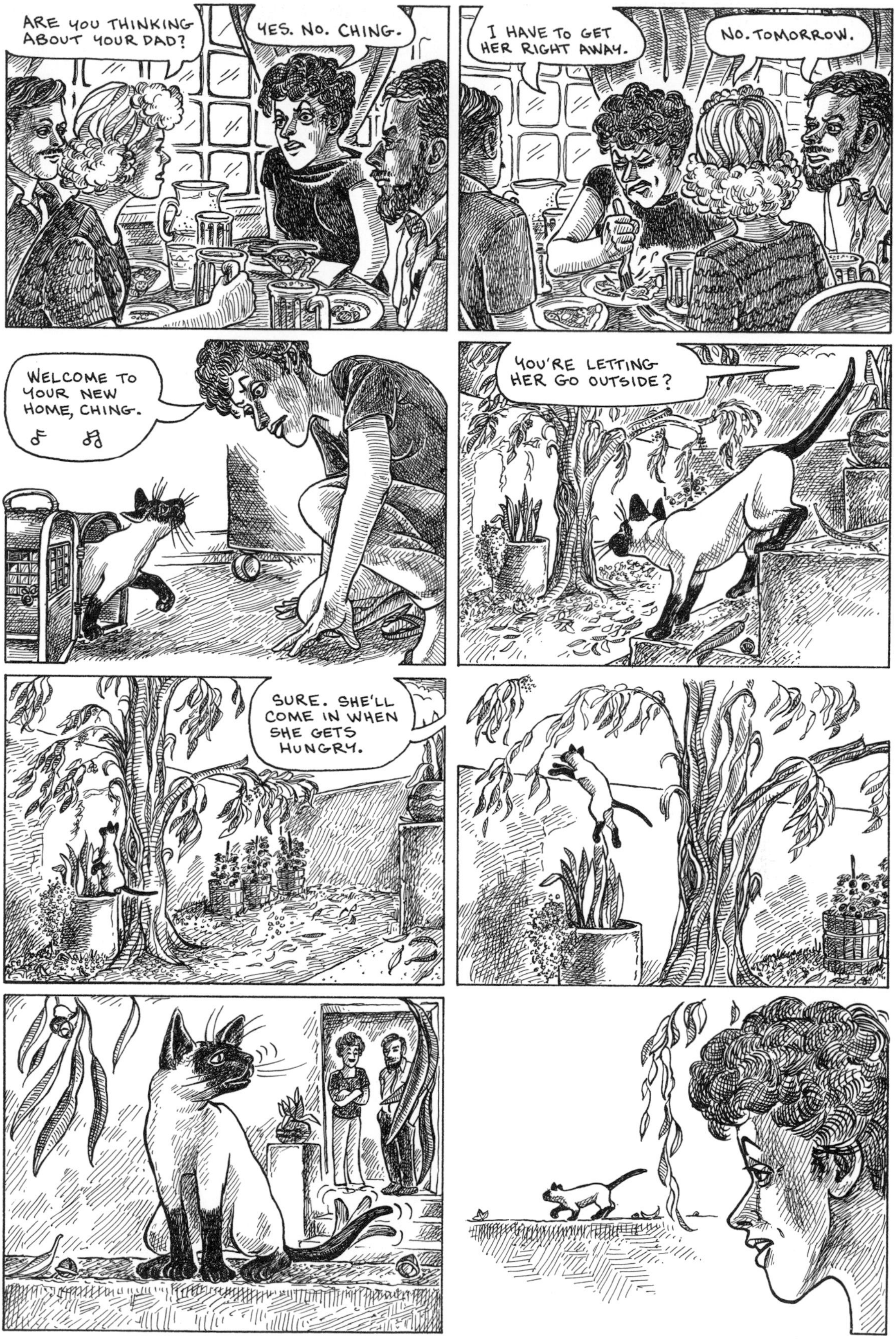
ARE YOU THINKING ABOUT YOUR DAD?
YES. NO. CHING.
I HAVE TO GET HER RIGHT AWAY.
NO. TOMORROW.
WELCOME TO YOUR NEW HOME, CHING.
YOU'RE LETTING HER GO OUTSIDE?
SURE. SHE'LL COME IN WHEN SHE GETS HUNGRY.

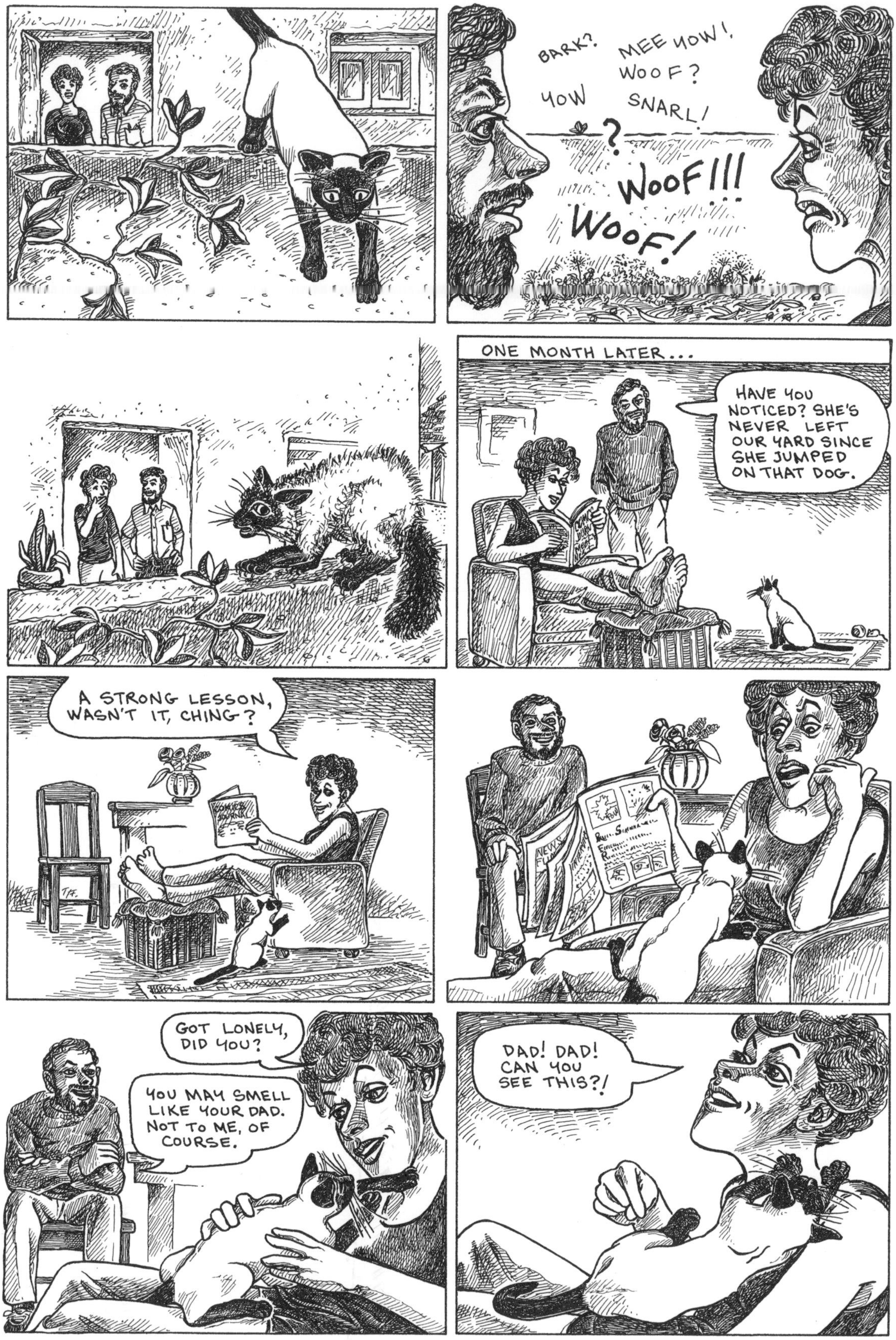
BARK?
MEE YOW!
WOOF?
YOW
SNARL!
?
WOOF!!!
WOOF!
ONE MONTH LATER...
HAVE YOU NOTICED? SHE'S NEVER LEFT OUR YARD SINCE SHE JUMPED ON THAT DOG.
A STRONG LESSON, WASN'T IT, CHING?
GOT LONELY, DID YOU?
YOU MAY SMELL LIKE YOUR DAD. NOT TO ME, OF COURSE.
DAD! DAD! CAN YOU SEE THIS?!

Further Information

You may wish to learn more about the topics touched upon in this book, such as eldercare, legal issues of ageing, health and safety issues for seniors, hospice care or Alzheimer's disease, to name a few.

Rather than suggest specific topics, we encourage readers to consult websites, using a few words or phrases indicating the area of interest. Keep in mind that websites with .gov, .org and .edu in the address are not commercial sites, and they tend to offer the most comprehensive and often best-researched information.

If no computer is available, consult your local reference librarian or city, county or state social services agencies.

About the Author

Joyce Farmer, born 1938 in Los Angeles, California, is a pioneering underground comics cartoonist. She and Lyn Chevli wrote and drew controversial feminist humor, starting in 1972, publishing the titles *Pandora's Box*, *Abortion Eve*, and *Tits and Clits Comix*. Farmer has also been published in *Wimmen's Comix, Mama! Dramas, Itchy Planet, Energy Comics, Zero Zero*, and the notorious women's sex comic *Wet Satin*. Her work has been exhibited internationally, including Austria and Italy. *Special Exits* is her first full-length graphic narrative.